CHANGING

WOMAN

CHANGING

WOMAN

A History of Racial Ethnic Women
in Modern America

Karen Anderson

OXFORD UNIVERSITY PRESS

New York   Oxford

Oxford University Press

Oxford   New York
Athens   Auckland   Bangkok   Bombay
Calcutta   Cape Town   Dar es Salaam   Delhi
Florence   Hong Kong   Istanbul   Karachi
Kuala Lumpur   Madras   Madrid   Melbourne
Mexico City   Nairobi   Paris   Singapore
Taipei   Tokyo   Toronto

and associated companies in
Berlin   Ibadan

Copyright © 1996 by Karen Anderson

Published by Oxford University Press, Inc.,
198 Madison Avenue, New York, New York 10016

First issued as an Oxford University Press paperback, 1997

Oxford is a registered trademark of Oxford University Press

Library of Congress Cataloging-in-Publication Data
Anderson, Karen, 1947–
Changing woman : a history of racial ethnic women
in modern America / Karen Anderson.
p. cm.   Includes bibliographical references (p.   ) and index.
ISBN 0-19-505462-8;   0-19-511788-3 (pbk.)
1. Minority women—United States.   2. Afro-American women.
3. Mexican American women.   4. Indian women—United States.
I. Title.   E184.A1A673   1996
305.42'0973—dc20   95-21250

Portions of this manuscript were previously published as
"African American Families," in Joseph M. Hawes and Elizabeth
I. Nybakken, eds., *American Families: A Research Guide and
Historical Handbook* (Westport, Conn.: Greenwood Press, 1991): 259–90.

1 3 5 7 9 8 6 4 2

Printed in the United States of America
on acid-free paper

Acknowledgments

WHEN I STARTED this book in 1980, I hoped to demonstrate that it was possible and desirable to do scholarship on women who had been largely absent from the developing canon in U.S. women's history. At the outset, I underestimated the difficulties presented by a project that required a kind of gleaning work as historical methodology and a new way of thinking about gender, history, and politics. Along the way, I was sometimes daunted at the enormity of the endeavor. Now that it is over, I am grateful that I rather naively committed to a work whose intellectual benefits far outweighed its considerable challenges.

I am keenly aware that white feminists undertaking the study of racial ethnic women risk projecting onto those women their own perceptions, their own political and intellectual concerns. Such projections distort the experiences, values, and contributions of women who live at the margins of political and cultural power. Moreover, the costs of such misrepresentations are paid primarily by the groups who have come under the gaze of white scholars.

Unfortunately, an awareness of these dilemmas of representation and experience, power and accountability does not provide a ready solution to them. My conviction is that historicizing the experiences of working-class and racial ethnic women offers some proof against objectification. In this work I have tried simply to bear in mind that people are best understood in the context of time, place, and social location—that if we know about their circumstances, we may be better placed to understand their efforts to build families and communities, sustain themselves economically, and create meanings in their lives. I have also focused particularly on the dynamism and internal diversities of racial ethnic communities and cultures, jettisoning the consensus model long since abandoned in the study of white elites and communities.

This study is a preliminary effort at synthesis and interpretation in the histories of Mexican American, African American, and American Indian women in the last century. Although the scholarship on racial ethnic women has become rich and exciting in recent years, the work that remains to be done means that any general conclusions must be advanced tentatively. If nothing else, I hope that this book contributes to these fields by heightening interest in them and by underscoring the critical importance of such scholarship to our understandings of women's history and U.S. history.

Over the years, my work on this book has been sustained by numerous individuals, communities, and institutions. I have benefited enormously from the expertise and willing assistance of archivists at the National Archives, the Arizona State Archives, and the Southern History Collection at the University of North Carolina. In particular, Jerry Hess and Aloha South at the National Archives helped me to identify materials germane to the project.

The University of Arizona has provided support for this book at critical stages. A small grant enabled me to spend a summer doing research at the National Archives in the early stages of the project. A sabbatical leave gave me time off to begin the writing and continue the research. The Social and Behavioral Sciences Research Institute provided a mini-grant for research as well as a semester off to focus on writing.

Many overlapping intellectual communities have sustained my scholarly development over the years. The Teaching Workshop on U.S. Women's History, which meets annually at UCLA, has contributed enormously to my understanding of gender and other inequalities in the lives of diverse women and to my ability to think historically about them. It has also provided a model of feminist community—unfailingly interesting and supportive, occasionally and constructively contentious. We all owe a special thanks to Kathryn Kish Sklar, whose vision and efforts initiated the group.

The Southwest Women's History group (a "daughter" of the UCLA meeting) has offered similar personal and intellectual sustenance. Moreover, because it includes graduate students, it has kept me in touch with the

ideas and concerns of the next generation of women's historians—to my
great benefit. I owe a special thanks to Virginia Scharff, Jane Slaughter,
Mary Rothschild, and Joan Jensen, who have kept me grateful that fate
brought me to the Southwest. Their friendship, advice, and keen intellects
have enriched me personally and professionally.

In the history department at the University of Arizona, Juan Garcia,
Roger Nichols, and others helped me identify scholarship and sources im-
portant to this book. In addition, a large number of graduate students have
contributed to my intellectual development. Penny Waterstone, Renee
Obrecht-Como, Leigh Pruneau, Fran Buss, Erin Rooney, Jan Faust, Kim
Grant, Sherri Goldstein, Vicki Weinberg, Melissa MacKinnon, Bob Dean,
Heather Tillman, and others have taught me a great deal about history and
much more. My research assistants, who included Virginia Scharff, Laura
Cummings, Fran Buss, Erin Rooney, Heather Tillman, and others, made the
completion of this manuscript possible while I balanced research with
heavy service and administrative responsibilities. Moreover, they were always patient with my requests for information, esoteric and otherwise.

The Women's Studies community at U.A. has offered support, humor,
and intellectual guidance in my efforts to develop interdisciplinary perspectives on women. Susan Aiken, Myra Dinnerstein, Judy Temple, Janet
Jakobsen, Ana Alonso, Barbara Babcock, Sallie Marston, and many others
have discussed feminist scholarship and enabled me to extend and complicate my analysis of gender.

Sheldon Meyer of Oxford University Press continued to support this
project despite the very lengthy delay in its completion. Stephanie Sakson
has provided careful copyediting while facilitating the editorial process for
the author.

I am particularly indebted to those people who read lengthy sections of
the manuscript: Tsianina Lomawaima, Vicki Ruiz, Maureen Fitzgerald,
John Wunder, Myra Dinnerstein, Janet Jakobsen, and Laura Tabili. They
helped me to rethink important conclusions, incorporate new evidence and
scholarship, clarify my meanings, and, in a few instances, to avoid serious
errors. I did not always take their advice, but I greatly appreciated it.

Finally, I want to thank Kent Anderson, whose love, support, and companionship enable all that I do.

Tucson, Arizona   K. A.
August 1995

Contents

CHANGING

WOMAN

"Changing Woman"
and the Politics of
Difference

THIS WORK SEEKS to provide historical perspectives on the lives of American Indian, African American, and Mexican American women in the United States over the course of the last century. It places racial ethnic women at the center of its inquiry in order to illuminate the historical processes revealed and shaped through their lives and actions. It also does so in the hope that Cornel West is right that

> Empathy is precisely an attempt to identify with the other fellow citizen's frustration, anxieties—what it's like to walk a mile in their shoes, to get inside their skin. One can do that most easily when one has a sense of history that keeps track of what they are up against, their conditions and circumstances.

In focusing in part on the ways in which exclusionary definitions of "fellow citizens" have inflicted harm on women of color (and others), this book also calls into question the emancipatory possibilities of identities based in national "citizenship."[1]

In recent years, feminist theorists have noted the importance of analyzing the ways in which women of color have experienced and shaped the intersections of systems of domination in the United States. Their works have revealed many of the connections between gender and race as socially constructed categories and have provided suggestive frameworks for analyzing those connections. In particular, they have called for a respect for the specificities of racial ethnic women's experiences and have noted the ways in which they have been, as Kimberle Crenshaw suggests, "unassimilable into the discursive paradigms of gender and race domination." An exploration of their experiences, therefore, provides an opportunity to reconceptualize those paradigms while developing a fuller understanding of the lives of women of color.[2]

Only by analyzing the specificities of women's lives—their class, race, time, place, and so on—can we make sense of their attempts to create meaning, claim resources and power, and reconstitute social relations. As scholars, we must attend to the understandings our subjects articulate—through their actions as well as their words. To do so will not only elucidate the historical and contemporary lives of women of color, but enable a much fuller understanding of the history, politics, and culture of the United States.

Because of the breadth entailed in this study, I have chosen to focus on certain topics and relations: the lives of women in rural economies and in urban working classes, the connections between economies and family systems, and gender as it is constructed in interaction with race, class, and other social relations. Among American Indians, I emphasize those nations that experienced the clash between government authorities and "traditional" cultures most severely in the twentieth century, many of them located in the Plains states or the West. For Mexican Americans, I stress experiences related to immigration in the twentieth century, acknowledging that the United States "came to" many Mexican Americans when it annexed parts of Mexico with the Treaty of Guadalupe Hidalgo in 1848 and the Gadsden Purchase in 1853.[3]

Processes of race, gender, and class formation are intimately linked. Vron Ware has noted, "Gender played a crucial role in organizing ideas of 'race' and 'civilization.' . . ." Gender relations and roles were endowed with moral meanings that contained material and political consequences and enabled racial categorizations. Indeed, the ability of those who were white and middle-class to claim a normative gender system conferred respectability and privilege on them, while "deviations" in gender relations marked others for derogation and were used to justify various forms of exploitation and discrimination.[4]

Moreover, race has had, in the words of Evelyn Brooks Higginbotham, "a powerful, all-encompassing effect on the construction and representation of other social and power relations, namely, gender, class and sexuality." Historically, women of color have frequently been perceived and treated quite differently from white, middle-class women. They have been expected, for example, to make their bodies available for labor and sex on very different terms from those offered to white women.[5]

The meanings that people of color assign to race create "a double-voiced discourse—serving the voice of black oppression and the voice of black liberation." Race also signified resistance to oppression and the construction of a community linked by powerful emotional and political ties. In the lives of people of color racial identities and experiences are a source of joy and pride, contain positive as well as negative meanings.[6]

The complex interconnections between race and gender have operated historically to divide women along the lines of race and people of color along the lines of gender. Moreover, differences in class status, sexualities, age, marital status, and so on have also divided all social groups. The mobilization of identities for political ends and the definition of "interests" based in those identities, therefore, are the results of political struggles and compromises within racial ethnic groups. As the histories of women of color reveal, those compromises often result from coercions and silencings, yielding ambiguous legacies, as the confirmation hearings for Clarence Thomas revealed.[7]

Internal conflicts among people of color have been heightened by the fact that masculinity has been defined as a source and form of political entitlement in the United States. As a result, race and class oppressions have often been represented and understood as a loss of masculinity and its privileges by men of color. "The discourse of black resistance has almost always equated freedom with manhood," bell hooks observed, "the economic and material domination of black men with castration, emasculation." Within this masculinist context, definitions of cultural imposition and resistance have usually been understood in terms of relations among men.[8]

When women of color challenged the androcentrism of this form of racial politics, many men of color denounced their actions as a betrayal of the race. Ramon Gutierrez concluded that Chicanos constructed a social movement in the 1960s grounded in gendered historical representations: "The Aztec past they chose emphasized the virility of warriors and the exercise of brute force." Moreover, its unfolding historical narrative focused on relations between American colonialist men and resisting Chicanos. When Chicanas challenged sexist treatment of women in the movement and offered competing historical narratives and political agendas, Chicanos "regarded their feminist critique as an assault on their Mexican cultural past, on their power, and by implication, on their virility." They called the women man-haters and lesbians, accusing them of betraying their culture by allying with white bourgeois feminists.[9]

The idea of woman as traitor, as old as the legends of Eve and Malinche, signifies women's anomalous position within cultures—responsible for their maintenance and reproduction, but expected to acquiesce in men's control over their definitions, and thus, over their political relations. As Micaela di Leonardo has observed, "ethnicity itself is seen to belong to men: they arrogate to themselves (and identify with) those ethnic characteristics maintained by women to whom they are connected." That ownership has meant that men from all social groups attempt to control the meanings of politicized identities and the social relations necessary to enact and support those identities.[10]

In order to preserve their form of male dominance and its legitimacy, white men often used racial difference to discipline women of their class and race (as well as poor and racial ethnic women) and to undermine the legitimacy of their claims to empowerment. The most telling example of this was the 1965 publication of the Moynihan Report, a government-sponsored attack on black families whose hostility to women's employment and autonomy from men served also to caution white women against such stigmatized behaviors at a time when they were entering the labor force in large numbers. The construction of racialized sexual identities in which white women represent chastity while women of color are associated with sexual immorality has operated to require the sexual control of white women as well as to justify the sexual exploitation of women of color by white men.[11]

Yet racial ethnic women have found white feminism a less than ideal means to a political remedy for these problems. White women contesting for power from white men have often been blind to the ways in which their "womanhood" has been defined by these and other racialized dichotomies and to the ways that their economic opportunities and standards of living (including their access to leisure time) have been particularly predicated on the racial oppression of other women. The availability of women of color for low-wage work in service and other fields has enabled many white, middle-class women to enact the domesticity expected of them, to become politically active, and to experience employment mobility. White women, however, have defined their gender politics within the limitations imposed by their blindness to these relationships. Their definitions of womanhood and the political claims they have made from them have sometimes made them hostile, or indifferent, to the interests and goals of women of color.[12]

At the same time, racial privilege has had contradictory implications for white women, who have been expected to exchange gender subordination for the protections and material advantages provided to them by the oppression of others. As a result, the agency of white women constitutes a potential threat to various systems of inequality. Their resistances to gender inequality have often motivated other whites, particularly men, to defend normative gender formations more strenuously in all social contexts. White insistence on "traditional" gender roles for people of color have heightened as conflicts among whites have jeopardized the control of men and middle-class whites over gendered definitions of "whiteness."[13]

For racial ethnic women, their positions as actors and objects in several systems of contested relations means that positioning themselves in relation to one struggle also situates them in relation to others. The "intersectionality" of their position, to borrow Kimberle Crenshaw's analytic frame, has made the definition of a politics of resistance especially difficult for them. They have had to engage in multiple, interrelated struggles for empowerment. These struggles are "internal" to particular families and communities; they are also engaged in relation to dominant institutions and ideologies. In this context, power is always relative.[14]

Women of color in the United States have, therefore, found themselves caught between competing and unstable systems of male domination. Dominant groups have sought to regulate the roles and activities of racial ethnic women in order to reproduce or reconstruct unequal race, class, and gender relations in a changing context. Men of color have often assumed that the oppression of women was necessary to the maintenance of families and communities and to the construction of a politics of resistance as they defined it.

Women of color have not simply constructed their lives in reaction to pressure from others, however. They actively shaped family relations, sexualities, work roles, and cultural activities reflecting their own visions and definitions of empowerment. The historical experiences of women of color suggest that cultural and political creativity has been and remains critical to resistances of all kinds.

Although the powers wielded by all social actors, including white men, are contingent and contested, they are not equal. As Aida Hurtado reminds us, divisions among women and within racial ethnic communities derive in important ways from the relationships of those groups to the white men who exercise much of the legitimated power in American society. The perception that these divisions derive solely from relationships within and between oppressed groups operates to sustain the legitimacy of white men's power in the American political order and to preclude an analysis that takes into account the complex social roots and consequences of inequality and political discord.[15]

Moreover, the divisions that are constructed also occur among women in communities of color. These can be based on age, generation, sexuality, class, and political disagreements over relationships to the dominant culture. They often derive from interrelated conflicts over acculturation and sexuality. Among Chicanas, for example, mother-daughter disputes over issues of accommodation or resistance to the dominant culture were often stimulated by daughters' selective adoption of Anglo practices in order to define alternative sexualities. Some American Indian girls and women have resisted marriages arranged by their parents, in part because Anglo American culture has offered support for their rebellion.[16]

Binary models of culture or race that assume clashes between social groups that are internally homogeneous and unified and diametrically opposed to each other preclude an adequate understanding of the actions or values of racial ethnic women. As Belinda Bozzoli has recognized, the meanings of various cultural encounters will differ depending on the circumstances and resources available to particular actors within the system with ". . . those in subordinate or oppressed positions . . . [responding] differently to external forces, perhaps seeing their encroachment as a potential benefit to them in their [domestic] struggle." The complexity of these dynamics is suggested by Cherrie Moraga's observations regarding her negotiations between competing patriarchies:

> I gradually became anglocized because I thought it was the only option available to me toward gaining autonomy as a person without being sexually stigmatized. I can't say that I was conscious of all this at the time, only that at each juncture in my development, I instinctively made choices which I thought would allow me greater freedom of movement in the future. This primarily meant resisting sex roles as much as I could safely manage and this was far easier in an anglo context than in a Chicano one. This is not to say that anglo culture does not stigmatize its women for "gender-transgressions"—only that its stigmatizing did not hold the personal power over me which Chicano culture did.[17]

My analysis of the ways in which women of color negotiated the politics of inequality differs somewhat from that offered in an influential article by Nancy Hewitt. Hewitt concluded that women of color have historically allied with their communities in their struggles against race and class inequalities and have concluded that alliances with white, middle-class women offer little of benefit for their empowerment. Hewitt's work offered an important corrective to the misconception that womanhood was monolithic and that shared gender oppression could provide the basis for an all-inclusive sisterhood. Her important observation that "both history and politics affirm that a strong sense of community can also be a source of exclusion, prejudices, and prohibitions" should be extended to working-class and racial ethnic communities and to an analysis of the ways in which gender and other differences divide those communities.[18]

Racial ethnic women's commitments to their communities derive from their understanding of the onerous centrality of race in their lives, the relations of intimacy they have constructed in their communities, and the importance of those relations in resisting oppression. As Kimberle Crenshaw concludes, in some situations where women have privileged race as a political concern, they have done so in a context that involved internal coercion and the silencing of feminist dissent. The result has been androcentric definitions of racial interests that exclude the gendered concerns of women of color.[19]

In fact, there is no one pattern in the ways women of color have struggled for equality. Some have, as Hewitt notes, subordinated gender issues to those of race. Audre Lorde's insistence that "Black feminism is not white feminism in blackface" enabled her and others to define feminisms specific to their complex circumstances. Because they experience multiple oppressions simultaneously, women of color have not separated their struggles for empowerment into discrete categories. Instead, they have embraced a situated politics based on a multiplicity of identities. Paula Gunn Allen, for example, defined her politics in context:

> . . . if I am dealing with feminism, I approach it from a strongly tribal posture, and when I am dealing with American Indian literature, history, culture, or philosophy I approach it from a strongly feminist one.[20]

The importance racial ethnic women invested in their empowerment as women is often fully revealed by an analysis of the domestic domain, as it is often the site of critical resistances to subordination. Racial ethnic women have found all aspects of their "private" lives regulated by the state and other institutions as well as by their families and communities. Their sexuality, family relations, political associations and activities, and paid and unpaid work have been domains of struggle as policy-makers, employers, and others have attempted to reproduce or reconstruct race, class, or gender relations in a changing context. Aida Hurtado has rightly concluded that "there is no such thing as a private sphere for people of Color except that which they manage to create and protect in an otherwise hostile environment."[21]

In the twentieth century, politicians, bureaucrats, educators, missionaries, and other agents of white culture focused particular attention on the power of women as mothers and made the regulation of maternity a critical component of the construction of race, class, and gender relations in the United States. Many feared mothers' power to shape the values and behaviors of their children and affect whether those children would support or subvert existing relations of power in American society. As mothers, women of color have been expected to convey to their children an ideology of opportunity while preparing them for lives of limitation. Specifically, whites expect that children of color will internalize the idea of the superiority of white culture and its "democratic" institutions without expecting the performance of those institutions to match their rhetoric.

As Ann Stoler has noted regarding imperial relations in Sumatra, officials feared that children would remain "affectively bound to the sentiments and cultural affiliations of their native mothers" and that those ties would ground an oppositional politics. The recognition that women were critical to the assimilationist agenda contributed to whites' anxiety and vigilance regarding women's relationships to "civilization." Under these circumstances, women became the object and vehicle for change—changing "woman," thus, became a concern of various agents of white, middle-class culture. The centrality of racial ethnic women in shaping the loyalties and competencies of their children was a source of power and danger for them—it positioned them to resist some whites' impositions while making them vulnerable to drastic intervention in their families. Moreover, it meant that protecting, socializing, and empowering children was an ambiguous and risky business.[22]

According to Aida Hurtado, "the loss of children is one of the main reasons for the anger felt by many women of Color." That loss has taken many forms, from the removal of children so that others might socialize them to state-sponsored sterilization to various societal practices that erode the ability of women of color to nurture and protect their children. Despite apparent similarities in the motives of those who would reshape motherhood to white, middle-class specifications, the importance and form of maternalist interventions varied from group to group and over time. As Audre Lorde noted, the stakes are high:

> Some problems we share as women, some we do not. You fear your children will grow up to join the patriarchy and testify against you, we fear our children will be dragged from a car and shot down in the street, and you will turn your backs upon the reasons they are dying.[23]

Women of color experienced regulation in other areas of their lives as well. Women's labor was and is contested terrain, sought and deployed by all interests as a resource in the formation and contestation of gender, race, and class relations. Racial ethnic women's paid labor has been critical to profits in various sectors of the economy, most notably those of service, agriculture, and manufacturing. Employers benefit from and foster the racism and sexism that justifies the concentration of women and people of color in work that is poorly paid, often seasonal or part-time, arduous, and unpleasant. Moreover, many people of color have been driven by poverty to become what Fran Buss calls "stigmatized service workers." Their dangerous labor is constructed by "a voracious and insatiable demand for such services as prostitution and the smuggling of drugs, goods, and people" in the dominant society.[24]

As Jacqueline Jones and others have observed, the centrality of the labor of women of color to American economic development has at times made their engagement in domestic labor for their families a subject of political dispute as whites attempted to coerce their paid employment. At the same time, white authorities have viewed that domestic work and its support for the construction of the nuclear family under male provision as antidotes to the deprivations and temptations created by poverty. Enjoined to a frugal domesticity and the construction of stable, harmonious families through their emotion and kin work, racial ethnic women have been expected to cushion the effects of economic oppression in the lives of their husbands and children. By this logic, if only women canned enough food, clipped enough coupons, and provided a happy, warm home life, all members of the family would receive adequate sustenance, men of color would be motivated to work under the conditions offered to them by capitalism, and the children would grow up well behaved and happy to reproduce this pattern in their adult lives.[25]

The romantic view of normative gender and family relations belies the realities confronted by most racial ethnic women, who have had to rely on paid work, welfare, and extended families and communities just to get by. Whether they are confronting poverty or managing to stave it off, racial ethnic women have worked actively to construct emotional connections in which sacrifices of time and money for the sake of others are routinely expected. This work has often put relationships to the test. In the words of Rayna Rapp, "Women must constantly test, strain, and repair the fibers of their kinship networks" in order to secure support for themselves and others. As Micaela di Leonardo concludes, separating the elements of altruism from those of self-interest in this kin work is impossible.[26]

As is true of other women, women of color also engage in a great deal of "the work of brokering between the family, on the one hand, and the market and public bureaucracies, on the other." This "servicing work," as Laura Balbo has termed it, includes everything from interpreting the specific needs of family members to dealing with the schools, waiting in the welfare office, shopping, and getting appliances repaired. According to Paula Gunn Allen, Native American women's powers include "locating and/or allocating virtually every resource used by the people."[27]

Because there is often an inadequate fit between the needs of families and the resources and services provided by welfare capitalism, this work is intensive and, as Fran Buss has concluded, often requires that women "make triagelike moral decisions" about "how scarce family resources will be used and how more resources will be acquired." Deciding entails profound moral dilemmas. If welfare payments cannot meet the family's needs, should a mother deny her children a basic subsistence or "cheat" on the system? Should a mother use another child's immigration papers if her child who is an "illegal alien" needs medical attention? As Maureen Fitzgerald has cogently noted, public officials have constructed a system for poor women that places good citizenship and good mothering in conflict.[28]

Those who have touted the benefits of the normative nuclear family have often been the ones who ensured that the material base required for its construction was denied to peoples of color. From the theft of Indian lands so that they might be sold cheaply to whites to the denial of land to freed blacks after the Civil War, the ownership of the means of production in this country has been racialized. As David Mura observed with regard to the dispossession of his Japanese American grandparents' property during World War II on racial grounds, "the laws of property in our society have served to make permanent what was stolen in the past." Indeed, the centrality of property rights in American law and politics has close historical links to the construction of white privilege.[29]

The fact that the normative gender relations of middle-class, white Americans were structurally unavailable to most racial ethnic women and men did not reduce the power of ideologies that assumed that all had equal access to property in American society. Belief in a masculine economy of opportunity was a necessary prop for the construction of the meanings of the gendered categories of class and race in the American experience. Specifically, the dominant society's stories of opportunity and success implicitly associated "the American dream" with whiteness and an androcentric individualism. As Toni Morrison has noted, ". . . individualism is foregrounded (and believed in) when its background is stereotypified, enforced dependency."[30]

Public authorities believed that relationships to property and work defined one's moral capacities for political participation. Gwendolyn Mink has noted that the idealized citizen was decidedly masculine; he was economically self-supporting and, thus, assumed to be invulnerable to political corruptions. The conflation of racial differences and impoverishment in the minds of middle-class, white Americans heightened their "concerns about the compatibility of democracy and diversity." The economic dependence of men of color and new immigrant men "unmanned" them and threatened the operations of democracy.[31]

According to Mink, "Dependent manhood did mischief to motherhood and through motherhood to republican order" by forcing women to work outside the household and to neglect their critical domestic and maternal responsibilities. In order to remedy this, state policies were devised to attempt to construct nuclear families supported by men and to make men accountable to the state for members of their families. To do so, women's roles and status had to be altered, their subordination fixed politically, economically, and culturally in order to fit racial ethnic and immigrant men for participation in the political economy. In short, the state saw the patriarchal family as an extension of its needs.[32]

Moreover, this project of "racial rehabilitation" required a politics of assimilation linked to the surveillance and regulation of working-class motherhood. Middle-class women were to model good motherhood and monitor the conditions and practices of motherhood among immigrants, racial minorities, and the poor in order to ensure the reproduction of capitalist workers and democratic citizens. This vigilance was especially pronounced in relation to female-headed families. According to Mink, mothers' pensions (and, subsequently, the federally sponsored Aid to Families with Dependent Children) in particular "more directly and more rigidly policed and prescribed the moral qualities of motherhood." The gendered politics of race and citizenship, however, included various forms of exclusion and maternal dispossession as well as maternal regulation.[33]

Differences of view about family life and its connections to a market economy and a republican polity mean that the domestic economy was and is a site of conflict between public authorities and communities of color. Struggles over women's reproductive and productive labor reveal women's culturally constructed roles in linking the public to the private—men to children, political economy to family—and in mediating the contradictions between them. Moreover, political constructions of race and class depend on the cultural meanings and economic practices associated with masculinity and femininity.

As Chandra Mohanty has noted:

> Feminist struggles are waged on at least two simultaneous, interconnected levels: an ideological, discursive level which addresses questions of representation (womanhood/femininity), and a material, experiential, daily-life level which focuses on the micropolitics of work, home, family, sexuality, etc.[34]

This study focuses particularly on everyday life as a site of oppression and resistance in order to reveal more fully the connections between the social relations of everyday life and the construction of important areas of the public world in the United States. Struggles over the politics of gender and race motivated and structured policies ranging from immigration and American Indian policies to those involving welfare and economic development.

What the histories of racial ethnic women reveal is that imposed subordination was often difficult to achieve, in part because women themselves are agents as well as objects of change. They constructed oppositional family systems, defined alternative sexualities, and enabled the material and psychological survival of their families. They did so by negotiating the contradictions and faultlines in systems of domination. They used welfare, work, and extended kin networks to challenge men's authority in their lives. They resisted pressures from various cultures and some members of their families to enact a domestic and subordinated womanhood, fostering changes in the gender division of labor in their households. Women of color have created, maintained, and used support systems in the family and community in order to resist the powers deployed by employers, bureaucrats, missionaries, and other agents of white culture.[35]

Racial ethnic and working-class women find that their ability to challenge oppressive practices and discourses derives from a complex constellation of conditions. Their status and roles in families interact with their employment and labor force status in sometimes contradictory ways. Some experience family and workplace oppression as mutually reinforcing. For others, employment outside the home and participation in workplace organizing promote shifts in consciousness that alter gender relations in the family and at work. When the woman worker is a contradiction in terms, a woman speaking as a worker can revise the meaning of both categories.[36]

Racial ethnic women have organized politically to resist segregation, employment discrimination, political exclusion, cultural impositions, sterilization abuse, and other oppressions in their lives. Although these struggles receive brief attention in this work, they are related to the daily lives of racial ethnic women in important ways. Karen Sacks, for example, has noted that women use the workplace, religious, and community networks that they construct through their emotion and other work to build political coalitions. Moreover, women's political activisms are particularly motivated by their desire to remedy the difficulties they encounter in their daily lives. In short, resistance is gendered.[37]

It would be possible, however, to read that history of resistance more optimistically than is warranted. Interpreting the connections between structure and agency, opposition and collusion is a difficult enterprise, particularly when examining the actions of those who occupy the borders of systems of inequality. For feminist scholars, distinctions between accommodations to power and quests for power are not as clear as was once assumed. Laura Balbo has concluded:

> In fact, one has to look at women in these institutions and processes as continuously caught between complying and resisting. They add an inventive-adaptive component through their work and experience, but also a measure of resistance and opposition.[38]

The context in which actions occur is critical to understanding their meanings. What appears as complicity may result from constraints and possibilities not readily accessible to the scholar and/or may signify other than conformity to dominant group values. Those who "accommodate" to systems of power may find themselves in a different structural position, with fewer resources to resist or greater rewards for compliance, than those who do not. Moreover, what appears to be accommodation viewed from the perspective of one power relationship might entail an effort to resist a different oppression.[39]

As Patricia Hill Collins cogently notes in her work on black feminist theory, in a political context that concedes the women's agency only in order to blame them for the oppressions in their lives, representations of power dynamics contain critical pitfalls:

African-American women have been victimized by race, gender, and class oppression. But portraying Black women solely as passive, unfortunate recipients of racial and sexual abuse stifles notions that Black women can actively work to change our circumstances and bring about changes in our lives. Similarly, presenting African-American women solely as heroic figures who easily engaged in resisting oppression on all fronts minimizes the very real costs of oppression and can foster the perception that Black women need no help because we can "take it."[40]

Dominant institutions and discourses incorporate and accede to women's continuing resistances. There is, thus, a dialectical relationship between structure and agency. The outcomes of women's struggles reveal, in the words of Linda Gordon, that "to be less powerful is not to be powerless, or even to lose all the time." Structures of control are, thus, not unilateral impositions, but the results of conflict. Some scholarship in women's history illustrates how we might move beyond the conflict between models stressing oppression and those accounting for women's agency. This study seeks to illuminate the complex and contradictory meanings of racial ethnic women's actions in a system in which power is unequally organized.[41]

Those who occupy the "borders" of social relations have become analytic and political icons in postmodern theories. The lives of the women presented in this study, however, call into question such an optimistic reading. The creation of oppositional discourses, communities, and practices is very difficult in the face of pressures to keep fixed the boundaries sustaining various forms of privilege in American society. Gloria Anzaldua has called for the development of a *mestiza* consciousness that contains and synthesizes the contradictions and ambiguities of multiple identities. At the same time, she recognizes that this process entails anguish as well as possibilities: ". . . though it is a source of intense pain, its energy comes from a continual creative motion that keeps breaking down the unitary aspect of each new paradigm."[42]

The idea of the unity of cultures and identities is not easily undermined, in part because it serves existing power arrangements well and in part because it has been used as a form of strategic opposition to oppressive practices. As Joan Scott has astutely concluded, however, when "identity is taken as the referential sign of a fixed set of customs, practices and meanings, an enduring heritage, a readily identifiable sociological category, a set of shared traits and/or experiences," it assumes the quality of the given and obscures the ways in which "practices of discrimination and exclusion [make] differences meaningful." The absence of an analysis of power relations in the construction of difference, then, will enable powerful groups and institutions to decide, as in the past, which differences to empower and which to marginalize, all in the name of a pluralist consensus.[43]

This study is based on the premise that historical perspectives can illuminate some of the ways in which discourses of difference have received public substantiation and structural support, while others have operated on the margins. Central to this work is an examination of the ways in which powerful institutions—economic, political, religious, and educational—have exerted their authority in order to construct unequal relations based on race, class, and gender. They have done so by wielding the power to hire and fire, educate and alienate, reward and penalize, confer prestige and dishonor. Their practices have been critical to the construction of the social categories of race, gender, and class with profound consequences for the lives of all Americans.

The founding feminist insight that the omission of women's perspectives on social relations distorts our understandings of women and of human societies remains critical to good scholarship today. In addition, it is important to acknowledge that women experience different forms of oppression and create various kinds of oppositional politics. In examining the ways in which women of color experience and shape history, it is important to understand the specificities and commonalities of different groups of women under study. Although racial ethnic groups have experienced similar pressures—discrimination, impoverishment, and cultural stigma—they have varied in their political, economic, and cultural relations to dominant social groups and in their constructions of relations of gender and generation within families and communities. For all the pressures to conformity, then, gender relations and dynamics have been highly variable in the United States.

As those familiar with Navajo culture realize, Changing Woman was its most revered deity, a figure whose beneficence and wisdom left an enduring cultural heritage. A symbol of cyclical change and continuity, for Navajos she represented a maternal power of great benefit to family and community. For whites, however, she and other American Indian spiritual figures represented a subversive "superstition" that sustained a dangerous communalism and a disorderly system of gender relations. For Navajo women, she could support a variety of sometimes contradictory ideas.[44]

For racial ethnic women generally, the meanings of "Changing Woman" have been mobile, contested, and contradictory. This study seeks to offer some partial insights into the ways in which those meanings were enacted in the lives of American Indian, Mexican American, and African American women in the modern United States. It is an effort to meet the challenge of Jacqueline Dowd Hall that we "think simultaneously about the construct 'woman' and about concrete, class- and race-specific historical women."[45]

American Indian Women
and Cultural Conflict

UNDERSTANDING THE HISTORICAL EXPERIENCES of American Indian women means taking into account the diversity of traditional Indian societies, especially with regard to economic systems and kinship structures, and the varieties of their experiences since their first contact with Europeans. Women's status and roles within tribal cultures varied, depending on whether the tribe was matrilineal or patrilineal, primarily dependent on agriculture or on hunting and gathering for its subsistence, and on the meanings attached to masculinity and femininity and to women's and men's activities.

Although they varied in linguistic, cultural, and other ways, traditional cultures were similar in their general economic systems. All relied on agriculture, hunting and gathering, or a combination of the two for their subsistence. Although not as nomadic as many whites assumed, many Indian groups did move occasionally, allowing the land and its resources a periodic rest while moving on to more fertile grounds. In many areas, hunting and gathering alone provided an adequate subsistence. In some cases, the shifting agriculture practiced by Woodland and Prairie Indians required less labor than the intensive agriculture employed by whites. In addition, whites often associated hunting with leisure, rather than with subsistence work. These differences from white practices drew the condemnation of many whites, who assumed that Native Americans, particularly the men, were lazy and hedonistic.[1]

Land was communally held and non-alienable because it was believed to belong to future generations as well as to those currently utilizing it. In some nations, land was distributed to specific families, who traditionally kept the same plot. In many nations, including the Senecas and the Hopis, the people believed that the land had been given originally to the women of the nation for their use on behalf of all. Within all nations, women had central economic roles and contributed a substantial share of the food supply through their labor.[2]

In general, Native American cultures were not premised on the mind/body split so central to Western ways of knowing and acting and so critical to women's oppression in European cultures. Moreover, American Indians were, in the words of Calvin Martin, "participant-observer[s] of Nature," not the nature "voyeurs" of Western tradition. Indians saw themselves as part of the relational world of nature—a world peopled with spirits who offered guidance and meaning to humans. Their philosophies stressed that the sustenance that humans derived from the earth was a gift that entailed reciprocal obligations to the natural world.[3]

Most women's studies scholars today hold to the view that Native American cultures were more egalitarian than white societies at the time of first contact, arguing that Indian women exercised power and performed culturally valued work. They locate the wellsprings of gender equality in matrilineal kinship systems wherein male authority was divided and thus ambiguous, promoting female autonomy; in symbol systems which revered fertility and acknowledged female contributions to reproduction and production; in a family system that allowed divorce at will and gave women reproductive autonomy and domestic authority; and/or in women's central economic roles in communal land systems and their control over the products of their labor.[4]

Many societies manifested only some of these attributes, suggesting that Indian gender systems contained contradictory implications for women's empowerment. In some societies, special prestige was associated with hunting and warfare, men's activities. Many nations had patrilineal descent systems and many had economies based primarily in hunting. In such societies, women also exercised power and performed culturally valued work. Patterns of domestic authority in Indian societies have not been systematically explored by historians, although restrictions on women's sexuality and on their political participation were pronounced in many cultures.[5]

Placing Native American women in history entails an understanding of the relationships among cultural symbols, economic and social structures, and gender as a system of power. This task is rendered enormously more difficult when historians lack the range of personal narratives from Indian women that would reveal more about the meanings women from different nations, classes, and time periods attached to symbols and practices. When the cultural systems under investigation differ significantly from those of feminist scholars, it heightens the risk of misrepresentation. Paula Gunn Allen has concluded that the historic tendency for Euro-Americans to perceive Indian cultures as brutal to women operates as a rationale for genocide and that "this unstated but compelling rationale for genocide is at the bottom of the academic, political, and popular attempts to paint Native American cultures as patriarchal when they are not." According to Allen, this ethnocentrism operates systematically:

> Western studies of American Indian tribal systems are erroneous at base because they view tribalism from the cultural bias of patriarchy and thus either discount, degrade, or conceal gynocratic features or recontextualize those features so that they will appear patriarchal.[6]

Aihwa Ong has cautioned feminists against using the benchmarks for women's power and dignity derived from the experiences of white women in modern Western cultures. Instead, she has suggested that they explore the social meanings of change as other women have experienced and shaped it.[7]

The sources available to historians for understanding Native American women's power and status present important methodological and interpretive challenges to this endeavor. Most historical documents were written by whites, usually men who were attempting to exploit or "reform" Indians. They expected the forms of masculine authority within the family and society with which they were familiar and tended to view the lack of a tradition of "gentility" toward women as evidence of women's degraded status. Many white feminists, other the other hand, view that tradition as oppressive and interpret Indian cultures as empowering to women.[8]

When Indian women engaged in tasks considered to be men's work in white society—like agriculture and home-building—whites tended to conclude that Indian men were lazy and Indian women were exploited drudges. As Christine Bolt has noted, this was particularly the case in the nineteenth century, when middle-class women's leisure became more socially visible than their work. Interpreting different cultural systems on their own terms means reading through the ethnocentrism and sexism of these accounts.[9]

At the same time, one cannot begin with the a priori assumption that all Native American societies were egalitarian. The presence of certain cultural practices, such as double standards in sexual mores or violence against women or the exclusion of women from domains of power reserved to men, may not have meant precisely what they did in Western societies, but they suggest that certain forms of male dominance predated contact with European cultures and deserve scholarly analysis. At the same time, evidence from this study and others documents that gender inequality was also occasioned or exacerbated by enforced assimilation at the hands of whites.[10]

As Theda Perdue and Devon Mihesuah have noted, most of the Indian women who left personal narrative accounts of their experiences were those who adapted most systematically to white cultural practices. As a result, they view the cultures within which they were raised through the lens of their subsequent acculturation. Evidence of the values and interests that motivated many Indian women to resist white power sometimes have to be inferred from white accounts, the record of the women's actions, and our understandings of the historical context within which they acted.[11]

Moreover, most anthropologists who studied American Indian cultures were white men who relied on male informants to provide information on women's activities and status. Often they ignored or misunderstood women's contributions to Indian cultures and societies. In addition, scholars studying Native American cultures in earlier time periods have used ethnological studies ahistorically, projecting conclusions drawn about women's cultural and social positions from later studies back in time.[12]

Locating gender change in historical context is rendered more difficult by the ahistorical, static view of Indian cultures implicit in such scholarship on Native American societies. Sherry Ortner has attributed this to a "capitalism-centered world view" that treats history "as something that arrives, like a ship, from outside the society in question. Thus we do not get the history *of* that society, but the impact of (our) history *on* that society." This framework obscures the fact that culture is always contested terrain, that Indian societies experienced the internal conflicts, cross-cultural interactions, and environmental changes that cause cultural dynamism before as well as after the arrival of whites in North America. Indeed, Native American societies had institutional structures and cultural practices that revealed patterns of conflict and exchanges with other nations and a record of cultural syncretism prior to contact with Europeans.[13]

Because Indians had oral traditions, rather than written ones, recovering much of their past through traditional historical methods is difficult or impossible. This book, however, does not attempt to do so. Instead it examines Indian women's experiences with and contributions to historical changes since the arrival of Europeans in North America, focusing especially on the last century when white bureaucratic and political control culminated centuries of aggression against Indian peoples. Many elements of white policies persisted over time—especially the dispossession of Indians from their land and attempts to enforce acculturation to white values and institutions—while some new policies in the twentieth century deepened the oppression of Native Americans and presented women with profound dilemmas. Even those policies designed to empower Indians had contradictory implications for women's status and well-being.[14]

This account seeks to contextualize American Indian women's lives by exploring their multiple struggles for empowerment and the shifting historical contexts for those struggles. Wherever possible, it relies on women's personal narratives to elucidate the ways in which they experienced and constructed cultural changes. It explores the ways in which meaning and experience, politics and culture, material relations and symbol systems were mutually constituted.

Women and Native American Societies

In general the economies of American Indians were based on a fit between their economic practices and the land and natural resources available to them. They believed that the land was there for the use of the community and its descendants, not for the establishment of individual titles in the form of private property. Native Americans practiced extensive cultivation or hunting and gathering, occasionally moving to contiguous areas to allow depleted lands to restore themselves. Except in the arid lands of the Southwest, where droughts posed an almost constant threat to their subsistence, they were able to provide adequate food, clothing, tools, and shelter for themselves.

Native American women had a central role in the economies of all nations. They had to be resourceful in utilizing every aspect of the environment to sustain life and engaging in cultural exchanges to incorporate new productive techniques. They gathered wild plants for food, herbs for medicines and dyes, clay for pottery, bark and reeds for weaving cloth. In many nations, they also tilled the soil and sowed the seeds, cultivated and harvested, made cloth and clothing, dried vegetables, and ground grains for breads. In hunting societies, they cured the meats and dried the skins. They also assisted in the hunt in some cultures. Among the Paiutes, the whole tribe participated in the mudhen hunts that supplied much of their meat.[15]

Although the gender division of labor sometimes entailed mixed-sex activities, American Indian societies generally were highly sex-segregated. Women spent most of their lives and performed most of their work in the company of other women and children. Although work was assigned on the basis of gender, the allocation of specific jobs varied from nation to nation. In all groups, however, women were delegated the primary responsibility for child care, home maintenance, and food preparation, while men were expected to engage in hunting, fishing, and warfare. In some societies, women assisted in hunting and, in exceptional cases, participated as warriors. Religious and political activities were generally the preserve of men, although the exclusion of women from public power was not as systematic as it was in Western societies prior to the twentieth century.[16]

The work of Native American women (and men) was very labor-intensive. Women's daily tasks—gathering and processing foods, preparing clothing, hauling wood and water—made strength, stamina, and industry important attributes for women. From the time their daughters were very young, mothers instructed them in the work they would assume as adults. Indian cultural values reinforced this training, signifying the centrality of work to female (and male) identity.[17]

Native American cultures often attributed significant cultural meanings to sex differences. Many Indian cultures required physical and task segregation by gender because of taboos associated with menstruation and pregnancy. Indian belief systems varied, but many forbade menstruating or pregnant women to touch food that others would eat, to come in contact with hunter/warriors or their weapons, or to walk through fields of crops lest they jeopardize the food supply or safety of the nation. Some societies required that menstruating women spend their periods in segregation huts. The idea that women's bodies contained strong and potentially dangerous powers also justified their exclusion from certain sacred places and roles, at least until menopause. As Annie Lowry, a Paiute, concluded: "men were afraid of women's blood."[18]

In most nations, the onset of menstruation signified a young woman's eligibility for marriage. Some Native American cultures marked this with a puberty ceremony which celebrated the strengths and responsibilities of adult women in the nation. Soon thereafter, parents, brothers, or other relatives arranged a marriage for the young woman. Although women were usually given a voice in the matter, some remembered the cultural pressures and apprehension they experienced at that time. When Mountain Wolf Woman, a Winnebago, expressed her reluctance to marry the man chosen by her brothers, her mother advised her:

> I prize you highly but nothing can be done about this matter. It is your brothers' doing. You must do whatever your brothers say. If you do not do so, you are going to embarrass them. They have been drinking again, but if you do not do this they will be disgraced. They might even experience something unfortunate. . . . When you are older and know better, you can marry whomever you yourself think that you want to marry.[19]

In many nations, divorce offered a means to escape a particularly unhappy union. The woman could return to her parents, order her husband to leave, or leave his possessions outside their dwelling as a sign of her wishes. Securing a divorce was made more complicated in some cases by the need to return property given by parents at the time of the wedding. Some cultures, including the Paiutes and the Plains nations, stigmatized women for their decisions to divorce. In general, however, women and men had the power to terminate their marriages.[20]

The ability to divorce at will was especially important to women who experienced violence in their marriages. Culturally sanctioned violence against women often occurred as a means to enforce the regulation of women's sexuality. Many Indian nations prized marital fidelity in women and punished adultery severely. Winnebago and Apache husbands, for example, could punish their wives' infidelity by cutting off their noses. Among the Blackfeet, such punishments were meted out by the men's warrior societies, explicitly revealing their basis in men's political organization and power.[21]

Indian values regarding premarital sexual activity by women varied greatly. In some Indian nations, virginity was valued and the conduct of single women was closely controlled. In order to enforce chastity, some nations secluded young girls in their tents and arranged their marriages very soon after puberty. Other cultures, by contrast, encouraged sexual experimentation by young women. Navajo women socialized girls who had entered puberty regarding sexuality and did not supervise their conduct closely. For virtually all Indian women, however, heterosexuality was compulsory for most or all of their lives. In many Native American cultures parents arranged the marriages of their daughters, often when they were very young. According to Clara Sue Kidwell, women who did not marry were regarded as excessively proud in some cultures.[22]

Permission for alternative sexualities for women was not as common in Indian cultures as that for men. In a few nations, women could adopt a male cultural identity and marry other women. Some other nations permitted the expression of lesbian sexualities before marriage. Many Native American societies included men who had assumed the cultural identity of women, doing women's work, wearing some women's clothing, and often engaging in sexual relations with men. Scholars disagree regarding the connections between gender and sexual identity entailed in these practices, most concluding that the respect accorded to "two-spirit" individuals attests to flexible and egalitarian norms regarding sexualities in Indian cultures. Ramon Gutierrez, by contrast, sees the berdache role as imposed by some men on others, often enemies defeated in war, in order to demean and control them by associating them with women and the feminine. Over time, according to Gutierrez, "they gradually came to be regarded as temple experts or as shamans who fulfilled magical and cosmological functions."[23]

The power to make decisions binding on the group and to handle relations with outsiders generally rested with men, although women in some nations exerted substantial influence in these domains. Women in the nations that constituted the Iroquois Confederation organized as a Women's Council and selected a leader, the Beloved Woman of the nation. Through their clan-based political structures, they could control the public treasury of the nation, nominate men for chief, and initiate the removal of a chief. Among the Cherokees, Senecas, and others, women could also speak in men's councils or send a man to represent their views.[24]

Such indirect political power was usually found in matrilineal societies where women had an active role in agriculture. Because authority in Indian cultures derived primarily from custom and face-to-face interactions, women's absence from formal politics was less of a disadvantage than was the exclusion of women from the hierarchical and powerful governments of European nations. As pressures from whites increased, however, internal conflicts intensified and took new forms in Native American cultures. As a result, women's political weakness became a more serious liability for them.[25]

The rest of this chapter describes the major Indian policies imposed by whites in the last century and suggests some ways in which the politics of gender, race, and class shaped and derived from these policies. The following chapter will examine more closely the ways that Native American women experienced and shaped intercultural and gender relations in this period.

American Indians and Historical Change

After the Europeans arrived in the New World, they tried not only to drive the Indians off their land or appropriate their labor, but also to destroy native institutions and values and replace them with those of whites. From the beginning Native American cultural differences served as a pretext for whites to murder Indians, steal their lands, destroy their possessions, and undermine their social systems. Native Americans simultaneously experienced epidemiological, military, environmental, and cultural assaults that jeopardized not only their subsistence economies, but their systems of meaning and social relationships.

White power made it impossible for Native Americans to retain their cultures intact, as Indians experienced economic crisis, many deaths from white violence and diseases, and, in some instances, a perceived loss of efficacy in their traditional belief systems. The threat entailed in enforced acculturation was profound—to identity, esteem, and a sense of moral order. External pressures necessitated cultural innovations, but effective resistance entailed the construction of shared symbol systems within and sometimes among nations. Creating a culture of resistance within a context of crisis proved to be extremely difficult for many nations.[26]

This problem was exacerbated by the fact that individuals and social groups within nations were often positioned differently with regard to issues of resistance and accommodation. As a result, many nations experienced deep and complex divisions over who was to define the terms of their relationships to whites and, therefore, to each other. These divisions took many forms—some were based on age, gender, economic status, or position in political hierarchies; others on politically freighted religious differences that developed a life of their own in succeeding generations as nations experienced schisms between converts ("praying Indians") and traditionalists. By the twentieth century, divisions between full-bloods and mixed-bloods became pronounced, exacerbated by the differential treatment they received under certain white policies and differences of view regarding tribal policies.[27]

Most scholars tend to equate resistance to white authority with the preservation of culture. Although this is often the case, culture is always contested terrain and selective adaptation may have benefited some tribal members. Moreover, the need for innovation in a new context meant that the preservation of traditions may not always have served the purposes of resistance to white authority.[28]

Most Indian women and men, however, felt compelled to appeal to the idea of tradition in support of contemporary goals. Given that women's relationship to cultures was often contradictory, they faced special difficulties in establishing the legitimacy of their needs and perspectives. Because Indian men often faced particularly severe acculturative pressures, their desire to control definitions of culture and resistance received substantial reinforcement. The attempt to construct a usable past, then, sometimes reflected and constructed gender and other conflicts.[29]

Even those labeled traditionalists endowed elements of pre-contact culture—often those associated with gender roles and relations—with new meanings in the politics of resistance to external authorities. Those who refused those meanings risked being labeled as traitors. In some cases, colonized men have experienced colonization as a masculine dispossession and have tried to reclaim or reconstitute the powers and prerogatives they associated with the definitions of masculinity conventional in their cultures.

Joan Jensen's study of the Senecas' interactions with whites in the 1830s to 1850s provides a valuable perspective on these processes in one nation. When their military activities were ended by defeat at the hands of whites and their hunting limited by the encroachments of white settlers and the constraints of their small reservation, Seneca men faced the need to adopt new economic activities and to redefine their place in the social structure of the nation. Under coercion from Quaker missionaries and other whites, the men took over the women's customary agricultural work and advocated the establishment of a nuclear family system with the husband-wife relationship at the center of kinship relations.[30]

According to Jensen, some Seneca women resisted the changes because they robbed them of economically productive roles and diminished their control over economic resources; eroded their domestic power and political influence; and fragmented women's clan organizations. These women urged others to refuse to bear children for such a political order and denounced the idea that wives were to be subordinated to husbands. The men discredited the rebellious women as witches and used their control of politics to have some of them (mostly older women) executed. Seneca men's cultural power required and enabled their control over women's sexuality and reproductivity.[31]

As Jensen demonstrates, the politics of gender and race took complex forms as Seneca men and women clashed over the meanings of economic, familial, and cultural change in gender roles. Confronted with the material and political constraints imposed by the U.S. government and possibilities offered by missionary-sponsored gender role change, the men sought to control the processes of adaptation at the expense of women. For whites, the domestication of women and the "civilization" of Indians were assumed to be mutually dependent.[32]

The Federal Government and the Politics of Race: From Removal to Assimilation

The attempt to reconstruct gender and other social relations among Indians did not become systematic until the late nineteenth century. By that time, the federal government had begun intervening in the economic structures, kinship organizations, and religious belief systems of all Native Americans. Although most white policy-makers and reformers intended the rapid destruction of Native American communities, they relied on the maintenance of reservations for their acculturative work and the political control of Indian lives.

Until the 1840s the federal government used a policy of removing Indians from their traditional lands in order to facilitate white exploitation of these areas, while keeping Indians distant from major areas of white settlement. Ironically, white policy-makers justified this practice by claiming that it was necessary in order to protect Indians from white exploitation. Although federal policies in this period also included efforts to acculturate Indians, they did not involve the direct supervision of economic and cultural activities that developed in the reservation period.[33]

With the addition of vast new territories taken from Mexico in 1848 and the continuing movement of white settlers into areas of the West, the policy of containment broke down. Indian resistance to white theft of their lands led to wars between the federal government and several nations. The political pressures of whites, who wanted to take Indian lands peacefully, led to the forced imposition of a very restrictive reservation policy on most Indians.[34]

The reservation system was predicated on the use of military force to remove Indians to distant land or to contain them on smaller areas that the government assigned to them and to end the Indians' considerable resistance to this assault on their land, livelihood, and cultures. Once they had contained Native Americans within reservation boundaries, federal officials began a systematic effort to destroy their cultures and replace them with the values and practices of middle-class whites. In the words of Carl Schurz, Indians faced a "stern alternative: extermination or civilization."[35]

The assault on Indian customs was complete: the agents of white culture sought the destruction of their religious beliefs and rites, family relations, economic systems, and recreational practices. Religious instruction and formal education were to serve as pillars for assimilation. In the decades after the Civil War, the federal government relied heavily on religious institutions to supply Indian agents and commissioners. In addition, to further its civilizing mission, the government subsidized religious schools on the reservations.[36]

In this same period, public officials instituted publicly supported schools for Indians in order to destroy their tribal values and loyalties. Whites especially promoted off-reservation boarding schools because they enabled them to remove Indian children from their families and communities for extended periods of time. In 1892, the platform of the Lake Mohonk Conference of Friends of the Indian expressed a common contempt for Indian parents: it advocated compelling them to send their children to school on the grounds that "we do not think it desirable to rear another generation of savages."[37]

On the reservations, Native American families could no longer rely on traditional work activities to produce a subsistence. The government had restricted them to "agricultural" lands, reserving the timber and mineral areas that might produce wealth to whites and locating many Indians in arid areas without the irrigation systems essential to successful farming. The destruction of the buffalo had left Plains nations without a major source of food and livelihood.[38]

Moreover, the government failed to provide the education, capital, and training necessary to enable Indians to make the transition to a farm economy. As a result, starvation haunted the reservations and many Indians suffered from exposure to the elements because they lacked adequate clothing. Despite the hardships experienced by Indians, most whites opposed the provision of rations to them on the grounds that the practice would erode the work ethic. An 1874 appropriations bill, for example, required that all male able-bodied adults had to work for their rations.[39]

The passage of the Dawes Severalty Act of 1887 extended and consolidated the federal government's earlier efforts to enforce family farming and construct a nuclear family system. Under the bill's provisions, each "head of household" was to receive 160 acres of allotted land, each single adult 80 acres, and each minor child 40 acres. For the first twenty-five years, the government would hold the allotments in trust for the allottees or their heirs. "Surplus" Indian lands were to be sold by the government. The power to decide which lands would be allotted and which declared surplus rested, of course, with the federal government. Supporters of the Dawes Act claimed that without its protections for Indian land, greedy whites would take all that they wanted. In fact, the bill accomplished two desired goals: it enabled whites to secure Indian lands at little cost and it promoted the "civilizing" mission of white reformers.[40]

Scholars have drawn contradictory conclusions regarding the effects of allotment on women. According to Dolores Janiewski, Nez Perce women lost their individual holdings more rapidly than men and continued their traditional gathering activities in order to contribute to family support. Patricia Albers notes an ironic outcome: men lost the ability to contribute substantially to family support and women became central in a family economy organized around distributing limited resources.[41]

The process of allotment often created or deepened divisions among Indians. Acculturated and traditional Indians sometimes disagreed about allotment policies. As it was implemented, allotment deepened these divisions by promoting the assimilation of some Indians to white values regarding property and family and constructing a highly stratified class system within some Indian nations. The rights of absentee Indians to reservation allotments were unclear and sometime contested. Some tribal leaders feared that allotment would reduce their access to land and, thus, their authority. In some areas, intertribal disputes over land occurred.[42]

On balance, the Dawes Act failed to turn Indian men into farmers. Because they lacked the skill, capital, and quality and quantity of land possessed by whites in this period, Indian farmers received a lower return for their labor than white farmers. As Leonard Carlson has pointed out, this made leasing a more attractive economic option for Indians and promoted their resistance to farming. Moreover, the rural economy was declining rapidly as a source of livelihood for whites in this period.[43]

In those Native American cultures where women were the farmers, men were often reluctant to take on women's customary labor. Nez Perce men believed that "the white man was asking us to become like women when they wanted us to garden." In many cases, men had to redefine their gender identity and learn farming techniques in order to enact the changes being required by whites. In the nineteenth century, for example, reconstructions of the Navajo origin myth enabled men to achieve "an honorable transfer from hunting to doing agriculture" by endowing such work with ceremonial significance and defining it as a source of social authority.[44]

Even when they chose to try, most Indians could not secure a livelihood from leasing or farming. Their continued economic dependence fueled a strong backlash against all forms of government assistance to Indians and led to efforts to force them to farm or give up their land to whites. In 1906 Congress passed the Burke Act, amending the Dawes Act so that allotted Indians would retain their land tax free under federal supervision and without receiving a fee patent for twenty-five years. The protective intentions of this policy, however, were undermined by the provision that allowed the Secretary of the Interior to declare an Indian competent to run his or her affairs. Once declared competent, the Indian would receive the patent fee with all limits on the sale, incumbrance, or taxation of the land removed. As a result of this process, many Indians lost their land in this period, the victims of bureaucrats intent on making Indians "free" and unscrupulous whites who used deception to acquire their lands.[45]

As Frederick Hoxie has persuasively argued, liberal optimism regarding the prospects for full Indian assimilation was relatively short-lived. Because it was predicated on the idea of Indians as passive objects on whom whites might unilaterally impose their wills and ways, it was doomed from the start. By the 1910s, politicians, scholars, and others advanced ideas and policies based on the assumption that Indians—like blacks, Hispanics, and other racialized groups—"could most easily and efficiently be incorporated into society's bottom ranks." Moreover, the goal of Indian assimilation was always subordinated to white economic interests, especially in the West.[46]

As early as 1903, Commissioner William Jones articulated very limited aspirations for the Indians under the tutelage of the federal government, stating that the goal of education should be to equip the Indian man to "wring an existence from the too-frequently ungenerous soils the white man has allowed him to retain." Reflecting the contradictory mix of cultural, racial, and political assumptions that grounded discussions of the future of Indians, he noted that "nature, environment, and necessity will and should make at least nine-tenths of the Indian youth tillers of the soil and breeders of stock."[47]

Whether they were deemed competent or not, whether their lands were allotted or not, Indians lost most of the lands that they had held in 1880. Through a combination of fraud and coercion, some at the hands of the federal government and the rest by private interests, approximately 90 million acres were taken from Indian nations and individuals between 1887 and 1934. Whites were especially successful at securing valuable agricultural, mining, and timber lands, leaving poor quality, arid lands for the Indians.[48]

Many reformers argued that the Indians' increasing vulnerability to exploitation by whites made it necessary for the government to hold them in wardship status. They pointed to the poverty of Indians and concluded that

government guidance and assistance were essential to ameliorate their extreme hardships and enable economic development. Others claimed that
such protection impeded Native American assimilation to white ways.
Only by enforcing complete "self-reliance," they argued, could Indian
poverty and dependency be eliminated. Not surprisingly, Indians often
found it hard to choose between their white friends and their white enemies.[49]

By the 1910s, family farming had failed as a panacea for Indian poverty, and, in the words of Frederick Hoxie, "a campaign for equality and total assimilation had become a campaign to integrate native resources into
the American economy." The long-held white conviction that resources
should belong to those who can develop them justified their takeover by
agribusiness, as well as the mining, timber, and other industries.[50]

Indian women and men confronted a system that increasingly emphasized the necessity of their incorporation into white farming systems or a
landless proletarian class. White officials justified the extreme impoverishment of Indians as an incentive for wage work and, thus, an essential pre-
requisite to "civilization." Edgar B. Meritt, Assistant Commissioner of Indian Affairs, testified before Congress: "We refuse to issue rations to
able-bodied Indians. We let them go hungry rather than to feed them when
they are able-bodied and capable of earning their own living. We think it
is a means of promoting civilization and industry." In fact, Indian agents
promoted Indian labor in agriculture even when it had been demonstrated
that their land would not even yield a subsistence for them. Thomas Biolsi noted "the remarkable ability of the agencies to compel Indians to labor,
even when that labor was irrational and nonproductive" in order that the
Indians learn the value of industry to "civilization."[51]

Not surprisingly, the character-building effects of poverty were also
invoked when policy-makers wanted to justify cutting appropriations for
services to Indians. At the same time, the poverty that the destruction of
Indian subsistence systems had created also necessitated continuing government services and assistance for Indians. As Francis Paul Prucha concluded, the allotment "policy that had sought to promote individualism,
self-support, independence, and hope for the Indians had instead increased
government paternalism and Indian dependency and despair."[52]

White policy-makers not only controlled access to land and resources,
they also retained the right to define difference and establish its meanings
for others. The equality they envisioned and offered to Indians was predicated on an economic and legal individualism that received little cultural
sanction from Native American traditions and that American society denied to virtually all Indians. It was hardly surprising, then, when officials
construed Indian resistance as incompetence or immorality, thus justifying

their decisions to impose further controls on Indian life. Those controls embodied the contradictions of a system designed to coerce Indians into embracing "freedom."[53]

A series of policy and court decisions that employed race as a significant, albeit elusive, legal construct undermined the system's professed goal of legal individualism. In its 1913 decision in the case of *United States v. Sandoval*, the Supreme Court made the Pueblo Indians subject to the regulatory authority of the federal government for the first time, asserting that the Pueblos, "although sedentary rather than nomadic . . . and disposed to peace and industry, are nevertheless Indians in race, customs and domestic government. . . . they are essentially a simple, uninformed, inferior people." The authority of the United States over their affairs came from its status as "a superior and civilized nation." In 1916 Commissioner of Indians Cato Sells declared that all persons with less than one-half Indian blood would be assumed competent to manage their own affairs and receive the fee patents for their land, whereas the others would be subjected to government review for competency.[54]

The conflation of racial difference and culture "competency" in these official statements revealed the contours and contradictions of Progressive era racial thinking. The perpetual tutelage and wardship to which Native Americans were consigned reflected the tensions toward and against assimilation in American policies. Moreover, as the Supreme Court decision underscored, whites would retain the power to invoke "civilization" as support for their goals and power.

Gerald Sider has concluded that domination in Indian-white relations was characterized by "domination as a form of incorporation" and "domination as a form of creating distance, difference, and otherness." This entailed a basic contradiction: "domination cannot both create and incorporate the other as an other—thus opening a space for continuing resistance and distancing." Formal political authority was critical to these processes:

> . . . state power must not only destroy but also generate cultural differentiation—and do so not only between different nation states, and between states and their political and economic colonies, but in the center of its grasp as well. The historical career of ethnic peoples can thus best be understood in the contest of forces that both give a people birth and simultaneously seek to take their lives.[55]

For Indians, the political and ideological power of whites had critical material and cultural consequences. By the early twentieth century, the level of change experienced by American Indians varied substantially. Enforced acculturation had accelerated as had economic dislocation. Most Indians remained rural, earning a livelihood as farmers, ranchers, farm laborers, or craftsworkers. The vast majority of those who entered wage work did so on the margins of the urban economy, finding jobs in service and in various forms of unskilled labor.[56]

In the East, where reservations were smaller and less common, and in Oklahoma, the destination of many dispossessed eastern Indians, many had settled into individual family farming and/or wage work, and tribal structures and values had weakened considerably. In the Midwest and Southwest, reservation life meant an eroding economic base for tribal groups (especially once populations began to increase after 1920) and diminishing political control over their own lives. At the same time, however, the reservation provided a basis for cultural and political struggle against whites.[57]

The Federal Government and the Politics of Race: From White Reform to Red Power

For some Indian reformers in the 1920s and 1930s, the reservation also symbolized a communitarian alternative to the alienation, competition, and materialism characteristic of the rest of American society. John Collier, the reformer who became director of the Bureau of Indian Affairs during the New Deal, exemplified and promoted this view of Indian cultures. Under his leadership, Congress passed the Indian Reorganization Act (IRA) in 1934. The goals of the IRA included maintaining traditional Indian cultures, creating tribal governments to promote Indian self-determination, and promoting economic development for Indians.[58]

These goals were often contradictory. Given that the environmental base for traditional economies had already been destroyed by white policies, it became impossible to end Indian poverty while fully protecting cultural traditions. Because Indian societies were not homogeneous, the process of creating tribal governments often revealed and exacerbated internal political conflicts. Moreover, political structures in many traditional Indian societies had been local, informal, and fluid. Some groups did not usually cooperate beyond the level of the extended family or band; most others united politically only for the purposes of warfare. Each tribal government created after 1934 was, as Graham Taylor concluded, "an essentially artificial institution in Indian life," not an expression of Indian tradition. Despite these problems, the Indian New Deal marked the first attempt in American Indian policy to safeguard Indian traditions and to involve Indians in decisions regarding their futures.[59]

Even during the reform years, advocates of Indian assimilation opposed efforts to safeguard Indian cultural autonomy and condemned tribal governments as "communistic." They continued to insist that Indians be forced to accept individualism as it was understood in white culture. As before, they intended the elimination of government support for impoverished Indians but not an end to government regulation of Indian life.[60]

These attacks intensified during World War II, focusing on the Indian New Deal and the BIA. Conservatives charged that Collier and his supporters were fostering "tribalism" and segregation for Indians. As large numbers of Indians served in the military or migrated to take defense jobs, reservation and Indian community-based programs appeared anachronistic to supporters of assimilation. Many Indians resented the impositions of the BIA and sought access to the material benefits and political prerogatives offered by mainstream institutions. Congressional opponents of the Indian New Deal succeeded in reducing BIA budgets and those for other programs that supported economic development on the reservations and secured the transfer of BIA headquarters to Chicago.[61]

By the end of the war, it became apparent that the wartime experiences of Native Americans had increased their participation in the institutions of the dominant society, especially the military; improved their standard of living; and heightened their expectations for the postwar period. William Brophy, who was appointed Commissioner of Indian Affairs in 1945, wrote that the Indians' "acquaintance with a wider world and a higher standard of living" might "prove a powerful stimulus to Indian progress."[62]

As a result of the war experience and the persistence of discrimination and poverty in the postwar period, increasing numbers of Indians began to advocate for selective participation in white institutions and to demand more access to the jobs and goods of the society at large. At the same time, they struggled for the right to determine the terms of that access and used white political structures to defend Indian cultural autonomy. Throughout the period, they confronted continuing assaults on their traditional and revised economies, increasing impoverishment, and intensified pressures to join the urban wage economy.

By the early 1950s political enthusiasm for the maintenance of tribal institutions and cultures had waned, undermined by the conservatism and nationalism of the postwar era and by the failure of the Indian New Deal to reverse the damage done by centuries of dispossession and enforced acculturation. As Larry Burt noted, policy-makers "envisioned a narrowly defined American culture and saw liberty and freedom as simply the opportunity to compete individually within the nation's dominant economic institutions in the absence of any government involvement."[63]

Under the termination policy, designated nations were required to eliminate their communal properties through sale, allotment into individual holdings, or conversion into private corporations. Despite their continuing poverty, Indians were to be "freed" from special government services and assistance in managing their properties. With the passage of Public Law 280 in 1953, the federal government also required six states with large Indian populations and enabled the others to take over areas of law enforcement previously exercised by the BIA or by the tribes. They could, thus, make and enforce state laws inimical to Indians without securing the consent of the affected Indian nations.[64]

Because of their relatively strong economic base, the Menominee Indians of northeastern Wisconsin were among the first nations mandated for termination. Ironically, Menominee economic viability had developed as a consequence of their ability to resist allotment, protect their forest lands from white expropriation, and maintain a communal economy. By the 1940s Menominee timber enterprise was an important source of employment for the Menominee people. It also yielded profits to the nation so that it could operate utilities and support a school, hospital, and other services while providing small annual payments to members of the nation.[65]

Their fate exemplified the liabilities of Eisenhower-era policies for the Indians they were supposed to benefit. Under the Menominee termination plan, the reservation was organized into a county of the state of Wisconsin and its economic resources incorporated as MEI. Thereafter, its economic operations were subject to state regulation and taxation and economic decision-making powers shifted to state politicians, bankers, and expensive corporate experts hired by MEI. Within a few years, whites began developing and buying Menominee lands, Indian unemployment and impoverishment increased, the utilities were sold and the hospital closed. Many Menominees were forced to migrate to cities in search of work.[66]

The economic development strategies attempted with the Menominees reflected a strong postwar consensus among whites that wage work provided by the private sector represented the only hope to end Indian poverty and reliance on federal programs. Large numbers of Indians shared this desire for improved economic circumstances. Many had enlisted in the military or taken jobs in war industries during World War II, promoting selective assimilation. The federal government, however, was not able to implement a systematic development policy for Indian communities. The best it could accomplish was to persuade a few companies to locate plants near reservations and provide federal aid for some irrigation and other development projects.[67]

Federal officials signified their pessimism about the possibilities for economic development on Indian lands, whether the nation had been "freed" through termination or not, by supporting a program of Indian relocation to cities. Over 35,000 Indians received travel money to seek wage work in urban areas. Most found that discrimination, isolation, and cultural differences made a satisfactory adjustment to the city difficult.[68]

While promoting the termination and relocation policies as the favored solution, officials confronted an ongoing economic crisis on many reservations. The Navajos and Hopis, for example, faced extreme deprivation in the late 1940s caused by bad weather conditions and the lack of a viable subsistence base. Throughout the 1940s and 1950s, the federal government passed "rehabilitation" acts to assist Indians in desperate need. As indigenous economic practices disappeared, wage work and welfare became the main sources of support for most American Indians, whose poverty deepened while many Americans experienced unprecedented prosperity.[69]

The 1960s witnessed two interrelated developments: the rise of Red Power, a militant Pan-Indian movement, and a heightened government commitment to Indian self-determination and services that drew upon the historical legacy of the Indian New Deal. The tactics and goals of the American Indian Movement epitomized the new politics of Red Power. It relied on dramatic confrontations with local and federal authorities in order to secure an end to government-sponsored and other racial oppression and a return of control to Indians over their lands and lives.[70]

Although the new Indian leaders did not secure all their goals, they drew sympathetic attention to the problems of Indians. In the 1960s, economic development policies for Indians provided much needed money and permitted a new local voice in their design and implementation. Although the relocation program was continued, these policies particularly targeted the reservations for training, placement, and development programs. Along with other racial ethnic groups, Indians benefited from the civil rights laws and anti-poverty programs of the 1960s and 1970s.[71]

By the early 1970s, federal officials had given up on their relocation plan, announcing their intention to focus almost solely on economic development on the reservations. Whether this was motivated more by economics or politics was not completely clear. Federal officials noted that the urbanization policy had not succeeded in promoting social mobility or assimilation, its primary goals, but had instead created urban Indian ghettoes that had become an important basis for the development of Indian militancy. Moreover, at least 40 percent of the urban migrants had returned to reservations, some moving back and forth between reservations and cities.[72]

Conclusions

The meanings of Indian policies cannot be adequately understood unless their interactions with Indian cultures and their connections to gender politics are investigated. Otherwise, we write Indian history without Indians and without women. In addition, the values and actions of whites and Native Americans, women and men lack a full explanatory framework.

Native American women shaped and experienced the dynamics of Indian-white politics and policies from the beginning. Throughout their historic confrontation with white officials, settlers, missionaries, traders, and others, they sought dignity, security, and well-being for themselves and their communities. The next chapter examines the diverse and contradictory meanings of acculturative politics and economic changes in the lives of Indian women in the allotment era.

3

An Expensive Luxury

WOMEN, CIVILIZATION, AND RESISTANCE,

1887–1934

> Civilization has been built up largely upon the altruism of the woman, at the cost of her independence and is still an expensive luxury to her.
>
> —Jane Gay[1]

BEGINNING WITH THE DAWES ACT, Native Americans faced intensified efforts by whites to "civilize" them through a process of gender-specific acculturation. White acculturative goals for Indian women included the abandonment of their traditional cultural values and activities, subordination to and economic dependence on husbands, and the loss of meaningful authority over their children. For men, whites urged the assumption of a power over women and children that was ostensibly to be secured by masculine privilege in a capitalist economy and in political life. The degree of Indian conformity to the normative gender division of labor and authority became the measure of Indian "civilization."[2]

The acculturative policies of white officials embodied the paradoxes of coerced change: in order to impose the benefits of the normative Western family system, policy-makers were compelled to contradict many of its central values; in order to "emancipate" Indian women, they often had to cur-

tail women's traditional powers. In order that Indian men might claim patriarchal powers as they were constructed in white society, officials undermined much of the cultural and political authority traditionally exercised
by Indian men and ended up partially replacing it with that of a state controlled by white men.[3]

The proponents of assimilation, however, believed that these contradictions posed no difficulties for their goals. They assumed that they spoke
from and for a stable, coherent culture whose superiority to other human
societies was transparent to all who had had sufficient exposure to its values and benefits. Most whites were convinced that once Indians had acquired the cultural values of civilization through education, they would
adopt its economic, political, and family relations enthusiastically.

"Civilized womanhood," they believed, would hold special attractions
for Indian women, promising to relieve them of the drudgery and degra-
dation whites associated with Native American gender systems. Because
they believed that the white, middle-class system of gender relations offered
dignity, protection, and meaningful work to women, they hoped that Indian women would embrace monogamy, domesticity, and dependence on
men eagerly. Moreover, they saw a revision of gender roles as essential to
the elimination of poverty among Indians. Indian women's failure to support change, however, would jeopardize the whole project, undermining
men's motivations and abilities to participate as responsible citizens,
providers, and protectors and jeopardizing their children's progression
from wards of the United States to citizens.[4]

Gender-based acculturation necessitated a high level of intervention in
intimate relations and in the conduct of daily life. Those experiences long
deemed "private" in middle-class ideology—sexuality, marriage, parenthood—came within the purview of government and other authorities intent on enforcing their particular moral views. These interventions were
supported by the forced education of increasing numbers of Indian children
in institutions run by whites and by the growing presence of missionaries,
field matrons, BIA officials, traders, and other agents of white culture on
or near the reservations.[5]

Native American women's resistances often confounded the middle-
class white women and men who proselytized on behalf of white institutions and values. These officials decried the "conservatism" of Native
American women, attributing it to a stubborn irrationality, and worried
about its effects on men and children. Flora Warren Seymour, a member of
the Board of Indian Commissioners, concluded in 1923 that Apache
women were "a mountain of rock across the trail of advancement." In its
annual report in 1921, the Indian Rights Association bemoaned women's
power in Pueblo cultures, concluding that "their present attitude is one of
the greatest obstacles to progress."[6]

Those who represented white culture to Native Americans were not all of one opinion on these matters, however. Jane Gay's observations of the Nez Perce allotment process prompted her to conclude that "civilization has been built up largely upon the altruism of the woman, at the cost of her independence and is still an expensive luxury to her." Gay's feminism reveals that the politics of the dominant society were neither monolithic nor static. Among whites themselves, the meanings of "civilization" and its gender relations were also subject to dispute.[7]

In the Meriam Report, a 1928 study commissioned by the Secretary of the Interior that was critical of some BIA policies and their consequences, officials concluded that the gender divisions of labor derived from Indian traditions were "ill suited to the conditions that now confront" them and that "when the women lag behind the men, as is more often the case, the home does not fulfill its function of renewal of energy as it should." At the same time, it stated that to blame "the unprogressive character of [Indian] women" for "the backwardness of the Indian race" was to "over-simplify" a complicated problem. Despite its bow to the complexity of the issue, its recommendations stressed the importance of ensuring that women enacted a chaste womanhood and a frugal domesticity in order that men would be motivated to assume the breadwinner role and that women's labor would cushion the effects of economic oppression in the lives of their husbands and children.[8]

Transformations in the American economy and in social relations had made the problem of poverty more visible and salient and had intensified various power conflicts in the late nineteenth and early twentieth century. The growth and increasing militance of the working class posed challenges to capitalist dominance. Ethnic and religious heterogeneity threatened white, Protestant control over politics, the economy, and culture. Women's increasing participation in education, employment, politics, and the "cheap amusements" of city life challenged men's authority at home and in public life.[9]

The instability and heterogeneity of cultural values among whites of all classes threatened the identification of "whiteness" with a particular package of beliefs and practices. This posed serious dilemmas for white officials promoting Indian assimilation. If Indians were to become like whites, precisely which whites should they be emulating? How should cross-cultural contacts between whites and Indians be institutionalized and regulated?

The gender, class, and racial politics of the dominant society provided an important context within which Native American women's struggles for survival and empowerment were enacted. They were, however, not the only context. The different histories of cultural formation, institutional arrangements, and Indian-white contact created great diversity in Native American women's experiences with acculturation.

Many found that they were positioned differently from men with regard to the politics of culture. As noted above, the meanings of Native American values and practices for women's empowerment were varied and contradictory. Moreover, the structural supports for traditional gender roles eroded as traditional economies were undermined. Women's economic activities in indigenous economies and in the wage economy differed from those of men, as did their access to resources. As in other social groups, women's responsibility for child nurture and domestic work affected their participation in productive tasks and public life.[10]

In such a dynamic situation, the relationships among assimilation, resistance, and women's empowerment were complex. Native American women found themselves engaged in multiple struggles for economic survival, health, dignity, and a measure of cultural and political power to exercise on behalf of themselves, their families, and their communities. When necessary, they invoked tradition to justify change and appealed to Western values in order to secure support for indigenous traditions. Their active constructions of cultural and social relations defied the categories that the "civilizers" sought to impose.

Gender, the State, and the Politics of Family Life

The centerpiece of the American government's assimilation policies was the Dawes Act. It attempted to construct an Indian citizenship premised on private property, gender hierarchy, and a masculinist individualism. Sherry Ortner has noted that citizenship in a hierarchical political system entails the construction of a gender system in which men are accountable to the state for the maintenance of orderly family relations. As she explained it:

> The family became in a sense an administrative unit, the base unit in the political-economic structure of the state. The husband/father was no longer simply responsible *to* his family, but also *for* his family vis-à-vis the larger system. It became the base, and often the only base, of his jural status.[11]

Of necessity, masculine accountability to the state requires the construction of "stable" families under men's control. The restriction of women's sexual activity and economic support to monogamous marriage was a critical component of such control. American Indian cultural values and economic traditions made the imposition of this state-defined family system difficult. As a result, Native American family structures became a locus for struggle between government authorities and Native Americans.[12]

Because of their different economic and social roles, Indian women and men were differently positioned with regard to policy-makers' attempts to coerce the formation of nuclear families under male control. Most men lacked the economic and political basis for assuming the breadwinner and protector roles advocated by whites. Under these circumstances, adopting white gender values entailed risks of failure and censure. At the same time, Native American men found their traditional economic, cultural, familial, and political roles under sustained attack and often had to revise or recontextualize customary definitions of masculinity. Those women whose material well-being and autonomy from men were tied to the communal relations of Native American societies experienced economic and cultural changes as threats to their power and security.

The gender and class goals of white "friends of the Indian" were closely linked. Most officials viewed Native American communal cultures as alien and threatening. They found the idea of legal and social relations defined in terms of group membership profoundly unsettling. Indeed, they equated communalism with license and immorality. In 1877 the agent for the Yankton Sioux condemned the customs permitted by village ties:

> As long as Indians live in villages they will retain many of their old and injurious habits. Frequent feasts, community in food, heathen ceremonies, and dances, constant visiting—these will continue as long as the people live together in close neighborhoods and villages. . . .[13]

Reformers therefore tried to reconstruct the Indian as an individual— separated from the kin and tribal loyalties, responsibilities, and identities he (or she) had developed. They believed that the construction of the "civilized" individual required the adoption of private property, Christianity, American systems of law, and the nuclear family. The assimilated Indian of white imaginings was paradigmatically male—self-reliant, independent, and able to construct an unmediated relationship to property, God, law, and the family. Time and again, reformers invoked the autonomous, sovereign self as the necessary source and repository of culture and progress. Within the Victorian system of gender relations, such a construction of self was conceivable only for men.[14]

Henry Pancoast in 1882 advocated extending the privileges of masculinity to Indian men: "Acknowledge that the Indian is a man and as such give him that standing in our courts which is freely given as a right and a necessity to every other man." In an 1885 report, reformer Merrill Gates articulated the masculine anxiety that subtended the discourse on self, society, and civilization: "The highest right of man is the right to be a man, with all that this involves. The tendency of the tribal organization is constantly to interfere with and frustrate the attainment of his highest manhood." In 1884, the Indian Rights Association linked a secure and civilized manhood with the right to individual property holding:

> No man in these United States to-day can be rightly termed civilized, nor can his position be considered a safe one, who is removed from both the

protection and the punishment of law, who is denied a protected title to land
and the right of holding it as an individual . . . .[15]

Married women at this time were denied that right in many states, signifying their formal exclusion from the economic self-reliance thought to
undergird civilization and from the personal autonomy believed to be its
reward. Under federal law, the Indian male head of household became a
citizen of the United States when he received the title to his land. For reformers, this was a critical step, signifying his independence from a coercive communal culture that had "unmanned" him and his entry into civilized masculinity. His wife, however, remained an "alien," excluded from
a polity based on property ownership.[16]

Not surprisingly, women were also excluded from decision-making regarding allotment and other issues. Jane Gay, who worked on the Nez Perce
reservation during the 1880s, provided cogent commentary on the social
relations of allotment in her journal. She reacted as follows when federal
agent Alice Fletcher convened a tribal meeting to explain allotment: "They
are all men, the women staying at home in an exemplary manner, just like
civilized white women when any matter particularly affecting their interests is being discussed by the men."[17]

Moreover, as Gay noted, identifying men as heads of household entailed
recording and classifying families according to the dictates of patrilineality, regardless of the kinship system used by the Indians. She described
Fletcher's difficulties in "tracing relationships through labyrinthian channels, searching after the suppositious head of the family who is to have 160
acres thrust upon him *nolens volens* when found." The very process of allotment entailed the attempt to construct patriarchal families.[18]

Official efforts to domesticate and restrict Native American women
were closely linked to the goals of establishing patrilineality, feminine
chastity, and monogamous marriage. Susan Aiken has observed, "In a system that equates female propriety with male appropriation, any woman
who refuses to relinquish her parental priority—refuses, as they say, *to
name the father*—risks being read and written as an *improper figure,* an illicit sign of the ultimate capriciousness."[19]

The need to name the father, to locate and register the "suppositious
head of the family," to use Gay's terms, informed the movement to legalize
Native American marriages and linked it to the need to ascertain property
descent lines for a capitalist order. In addition, white authorities sought to
repress all non-marital sexual relations. They used their police powers, religious and moral authority, and control of resources to replace courtship,
marriage, and divorce by tribal customs with white practices. The multiple
and changing strategies used by policymakers reveal the experimental and
incremental nature of federal policies.[20]

Those strategies met with considerable resistance from Indian women

and men, many of whom continued to work and form families in customary ways and to protest the government's interventions in their personal
lives. In 1894, Hopi women and men successfully petitioned the government to stop the allotment process. They explained the land allocation traditions that enabled them to cultivate corn in the arid climate of northern
Arizona and emphasized the importance of their matrilineal social order to
the support and cohesion of their families:

> The family, the dwelling house and the field are inseparable, because the
> woman is the heart of these, and they rest with her. Among us the family
> traces its kin from the mother, hence all its possessions are hers. The man
> builds the house but the woman is the owner, because she repairs and pre-
> serves it; the man cultivates the field, but he renders its harvests into the
> woman's keeping, because upon her it rests to prepare the food, and the sur-
> plus of stores for barter depends upon her thrift.[21]

Although officials attempted to impose white family and property systems all at once, the selective successes of Native American resistances
posed strategic difficulties for the government. The continuation of Indian
custom marriages and divorces threatened to undermine the goals of allotment by constructing a class of propertyless (and potentially indigent)
women outside the state-endorsed system of monogamous marriage. In response, officials attempted to modify the law in order to secure support for
unmarried women without undermining incentives for permanent marriages. By contrast, many Indians suggested that the solution was to allot
land to all persons equally, regardless of sex, age, or marital status.[22]

Congress failed to enact such a proposal in 1890, despite a favorable
report from the House Committee on Indian Affairs. Instead it concluded
that allotment policies harmed some Native American women because
women could not farm and because Indian men tended to desert their
wives. Not only did this disregard the traditional agricultural work of
women in many Native American societies, it also assumed that the women
did not choose divorces and that they desired and would benefit from life-
long marriage and economic dependence on men.[23]

Therefore, in 1891 Congress amended the Dawes Act so that those who
could not work their land "by reason of age or other disability" could rent
it to others. The lawmakers assumed that men would earn a livelihood on
their land by farming, "deserted" women by leasing. Surprisingly, the new
law also changed the allotment rules so that each Indian was to receive 80
acres. In the face of men's inability or unwillingness to function as
providers, white officials were forced to provide property to women. In a
further concession to Indian family values, the law also classified as "legitimate" the children of those who cohabited (married) according to Indian
custom. This law reflected the success of Native Americans' resistance to
the coercive family policies of federal officials at this time.[24]

White authorities, however, did not abandon their attempts to force Indians to marry and divorce according to white laws and customs. As they imposed allotments on increasing numbers of Indians, public officials became even more committed to imposing legal marriage as a mechanism for identifying legal heirs and defining Indians' relationship to the state. As early as 1900, a bill was introduced into the U.S. Senate legalizing existing Indian custom marriages and mandating marriage and divorce according to state or territorial laws for the future. It also required that all Indian marriages be recorded with the Indian agency and stipulated that all Native Americans who refused to provide the information required by the bill could be denied their rations, annuities, or per capita tribal payments.[25]

Despite the failure of this bill, the Office of Indian Affairs issued instructions to its agents and superintendents to record all the marriages and family relationships in their jurisdictions, to issue marriage licenses to Indians, and to insist that state laws on marriage be observed. Any Native Americans who refused to secure a marriage license or to provide family information could be refused rations—for many, a marry-or-starve order. The memorandum also stated that the Indian Office would continue to try to get legislation passed mandating Indian marriage under the laws of states or territories.[26]

A few states and territories did consider marriage laws for Indians. The legislatures of the state of Nebraska and Oklahoma territory introduced similar laws, legalizing customary unions, requiring marriage according to law after the passage of the bill, and outlawing polygamous marriages. On the latter issue, they were more punitive than the federal government. Each bill required that the husband choose one wife and abandon the others or be vulnerable to prosecution. The Oklahoma law, which applied only to allotted Indians, passed, while the Nebraska bill apparently failed.[27]

Such efforts proved inadequate in the face of Native American preference for traditional family systems. Indians told white bureaucrats that they were reluctant to get married "too tight," fearing the expense and difficulty of divorce under white laws. Significantly, the women were as reluctant as the men to abandon their family customs, including especially the freedom to divorce, for white visions of proper family life.[28]

Moreover, neither the federal nor local governments had a clear authority over family law among Indians. Federal officials often complained that state and local governments were unwilling to enforce state laws on marriage and family, when, in fact, it is not clear that they had any jurisdiction. For their part, the states generally regarded reservation Indians as a federal responsibility. As a result, BIA officials had to rely on the Indian courts and the various powers of other reservation authorities, including missionaries, to coerce the creation of nuclear families. On the Pine Ridge Reservation, the federally appointed court of Indian offenses prosecuted a large number of cases involving "illicit sexual relations," adultery, and other offenses related to sexuality and family formation.[29]

White authorities devised ad hoc and punitive strategies to exert authority in these areas. In 1926, the government transferred a Navajo girl from a mission school to a government boarding school in order to prevent her entering into a marriage that her parents had arranged according to tribal custom. When the parents demanded the return of their daughter, the father was sentenced to 30 days in jail by the Indian Court. In 1918, the Commissioner of Indian Affairs ordered the superintendent of the Osage agency to withhold revenue payments from those married by Indian custom until they married under state law. Most did so, probably because their revenues from oil made nonconformity too costly.[30]

On occasion, federal authorities went to tribal elders to try and secure their cooperation. In 1909 the Navajo agency superintendent had planned to persuade a Council of Headmen that fathers who tried to arrange marriages for daughters who were too young by white standards should serve six months at hard labor. The superintendent tried to construct paternal responsibility to the state for the conduct of family members, revealing the patriarchal assumptions grounding white policies.[31]

By the mid-1920s, an irregular and often contradictory pattern of compliance and resistance characterized Native American family patterns. The degree of conformity to sexual and family mores enforced by whites reflected the congruity of those values with tribal customs, the effects of religious proselytizing among Indians, and the success of white coercive strategies. The Pima Indians of Arizona, for example, experienced high rates of conversion to Christianity by the 1910s and organized their family lives according to the legal requirements of white society.[32]

By contrast, the Apaches resisted conversion to Christianity and maintained many aspects of their traditional culture. At the same time, they conformed very closely to white mores and laws regarding marriage and sexuality. Doing so, however, did not represent a substantial break with tradition. Apaches had customarily supervised young girls closely and severely punished women who failed to exemplify premarital chastity and marital fidelity. Interestingly, white officials did not notice that these same "sexually civilized" women were ones they routinely denounced as impediments to civilization because of their refusal to adopt white mores in other areas of family and social life.[33]

Education, Gender, and Acculturation

No area of policy in the early twentieth century pitted Indian women's (and men's) interests against the U.S. government more systematically than the effort to promote education for "civilization." Native American resistance grew as more schools were opened and white officials made more systematic efforts to enforce mandatory school attendance policies. Indian parents routinely hid their children from reservation officials, and federal agents responded with "roundups" of truant children and attempts to coerce parents into turning over their children.[34]

Public officials viewed the erosion of Indian parental authority as essential to acculturation. For women, that meant an attack on their most important social role and identity. Government-mandated boarding school policies removed their daughters and sons from them, sometimes for years at a time. Moreover, acculturative pressures were designed to create a cultural divide between mothers and children. Not surprisingly, many women resisted these assaults on their most cherished roles, values, and relationships.[35]

Cynthia Dakota (a pseudonym), a Winnebago, remembered her mother's account of the time when federal officials came to take her brother to boarding school. She put Cynthia (then only one or two years old) in the car also, telling the superintendent: "As long as you want them, you might as well take her too. Take all I've got." Not surprisingly, he had no interest in assuming responsibility for a baby. Later he returned her son because he could not adjust to school life. Eventually, however, all four of the children attended government boarding schools.[36]

In November 1931, Navajo tribal authorities went to As-ton-pia looking for her oldest daughter. According to As-ton-pia, they sought to prevent the daughter's marriage and to send her to boarding school. Reservation officials later stated that they had been seeking her two youngest children to send to boarding school. As As-ton-pia related the incident (through a translator), she refused a policeman's order to get into his car because she did not want to leave her children in charge of a large herd of sheep. The policeman then "hit me twice on the back of the head with the stock of [his] gun." She was jailed as a result of her resistance.[37]

In a letter of complaint to the Commissioner of Indian Affairs in July 1932, As-ton-pia stated that this was "the third case where women have been mistreated and I am of the opinion that something should be done." Although it is not possible to document the truth of her charge, the social relations of Navajo culture at this time suggest its plausibility. For Navajo mothers, the forced removal of their children, especially their daughters, constituted a threat to maternal authority and the complex system of economic and emotional interdependence between mothers and daughters in their society. It is no wonder that As-ton-pia and others fought back.[38]

In September 1932, she went to the Franciscan mission on the reservation to lodge another complaint against reservation officials for assaulting her and for costing her hundreds of sheep lost in a blizzard during her jail stay. She succeeded in getting the Board of Catholic Missions to seek compensation for her from the BIA. The Rev. Msgr. William Hughes, director of the board, however, objected only to the means employed by reservation officials, not their goals, concluding that "While the woman was probably an old offender in keeping her children out of school, there are other ways of prevailing on parents to send their children to school."[39]

As As-ton-pia's case reveals, official intervention in family relations to support white educational goals had multiple meanings in the lives of women. Mothers lost the right to train and socialize their children according to their values and needs and to compel their labor for the family economy. Daughters were removed from their families and from family traditions regarding marriage and work. According to As-ton-pia, her oldest daughter's marriage was prevented twice by white authorities, once when she was 15 and again when she was 19.[40]

Tensions between Native Americans and white officials over the socialization of Native American children took many forms. Cecelia Sneezy, an Apache, described her grandparents' opposition to secular schooling for her in terms of their desire to ensure strict supervision of her activities:

> When I was seven years [old the authorities] wanted me to go to public boarding school. [They] forced [students] to go over there, but grandma and grandfather said we don't want you to go there, cause lots of kids go and play outside, you know, dancing. They said, "I don't want you to do 'that.'"

Instead, they had her sent to a mission school.[41]

Their discomfort at the sexual mores of some whites was shared by some Native American students. In 1899 students at the Phoenix Indian School complained to the Indian Commissioner about conditions in the school, including the practice of forcing girls to dance with strangers in a dance class. Using the language of Victorian gender relations, they stated that this situation had caused girls to weep "at the outrage imposed on their maidenly modesty." The abusive treatment and cultural assaults children experienced in boarding schools and other white-run schools reinforced parental resistance and caused some children to run away.[42]

Upon arrival at school, most children went through an almost ritualistic "purification" designed to remove their Indianness. They were bathed, had their hair cut, were forced to wear Anglo clothes, and were renamed by whites. Many were punished for speaking their native language. Educators' attention to the bodies of girls was particularly pronounced, extending even to the monitoring of their menstrual periods. According to K. Tsianina Lomawaima:

> [T]he acute, piercing focus on Indian girls' attire, comportment, posture and hairstyles betrays a deep-seated, racially defined perception of Indian peoples' bodies as "uncivilized."

Poor conditions, homesickness, strict discipline and regimentation, and the derogation of many aspects of Indian culture were common school experiences. Polingaysi Qoyawayma, a Hopi, recalled her first months at the Sherman Institute as a "time of torture."[43]

Because Indian education was inadequately funded, federal officials forced students in boarding schools to work in order to cut costs. Children raised gardens, cattle, and poultry and did much of the domestic and repair work of the schools. In addition, most schools implemented the "outing system" whereby the students were placed in jobs in the local economy, usually in agriculture or household labor. Accord to Harwood Hall, superintendent of the Phoenix Indian School, their wages were "not equal to those paid to white people but . . . quite satisfactory to the Indians." In short, students' unwaged labor subsidized the taxpayers and their wage work underwrote profits in the local economy and subsidized middle-class families' lifestyles.[44]

Educators regarded it as especially important to train Indian girls in the homemaking skills and values of white society. Such instruction, they reasoned, would equip the girls to engage in the labor-intensive domestic work and frugal consumer practices essential for the wives of workers and farmers. Moreover, it would enable them to provide the encouragement, incentive, and support for men's wage work. K. Tsianina Lomawaima has concluded that it was also designed to train Indian girls in submission to authority.[45]

In many Indian schools, the line between domestic science training for girls and their economic exploitation was not clear. Many girls spent long hours at arduous labor, doing laundry, cleaning, cooking, dishwashing, sewing, and other work on behalf of the school. Their work load left the girls little time for study or play and sometimes interfered with their attendance in classes.[46]

For girls, the outing system usually meant employment as domestic workers in the homes of local whites. Officials justified the practice as an extension of the vocational training mission of the schools, claiming that it was designed more to train girls in white standards of home care and to expose them to white cultural values than to provide a cheap labor supply for white employers. Whatever the intentions of its officials, the system probably achieved more of the latter goal.[47]

As was the case with other household workers, especially those from impoverished social groups, Indian girls often faced an abusive work situation. They were expected to shoulder a heavy workload for low wages and faced a paradoxical combination of strict surveillance and vulnerability to sexual harassment on the job. Irene Mack Pyawasit described her resistance to harassment at the hands of her employer as follows:

He tried to push me into a corner between the door and the refrigerator, but I gave him a good example of what a knee was built for. I had him walking like a camel.

They took his word against mine and figured I was disobedient and unruly. Of course, I was punished, but I never went back to that house to do any more work.[48]

Frances Page, a teacher for the BIA, related the story of a very young Native American girl who was sent from the Sherman Institute to Salt Lake City to work as a domestic for the summer. She came back pregnant and refused to reveal the name of the father. She vowed that she would not keep the child or live after its birth. Despite the efforts of white medical officials, she died after a routine delivery. Her family, who raised the daughter she bore, believed the child (who appeared white) to be that of the male head of household in the home where she had been employed.[49]

White officials were very aware of the hazards of the outing system for Indian girls, although they often defined them as problems in regulating the morality of the girls rather than as abuses deriving from gender, race, and class inequality. Regulations for outing students at the Sherman Institute in Riverside, California, included the restriction of girls to homes that did not have sons over the age of 12. Employers had to agree to supervise the girls carefully, ensuring that they did not stay out after 6 p.m. and were not left alone overnight. In addition, the BIA established outing centers in Los Angeles, Oakland, and elsewhere to provide employment, welfare, and housing assistance to Indian girls and women who worked in domestic service.[50]

Whatever the protective intentions of those who monitored the outing system, they could not prevent the abuses that often accompany employment in domestic service. William Ketcham described the outing system as "unAmerican and repellant," stating euphemistically that the contact with whites it provided had serious "disadvantages," especially for girls.[51]

Intent on enforcing women's chastity and on protecting the legitimacy of their schools, BIA educators went to great lengths to control the heterosexual relations of Indian girls. Fueled by fears that their students came from homes where "the most deplorable promiscuity exists," school officials limited and closely surveilled the interactions of girls and boys in school. Girls were especially encouraged to participate in temperance activities and religious services. Officials supervised student activities in town and sought to prevent students from dating. Not surprisingly, girls and boys responded with ingenuity to these restrictions, often subverting the intentions of those in charge.[52]

At the Chilocco Indian Agricultural School in Oklahoma, girls were allowed to wear their "home clothes" to the biweekly dances that were held, but were also required to wear their daily government-issue bloomers underneath them. One student remembered the policy as follows:

> And I remember this old matron, one time, said something about us arousing the boys' passions, that's the reason we had to wear these bloomers . . . and I didn't know, I hardly knew what that meant, you know. Really, it seems strange to this day and age, but the farthest thing from our minds was sex, I guess. And yet, the matrons seemed to be concerned.

The girls devised various strategies to avoid the requirement, from hiding the hated bloomers after they had left the school to wearing only the bottoms (which could easily be pulled up or hidden later) to fool the school officials. Whatever their strategies, they were eventually caught.[53]

For those girls who had internalized white sexual and familial mores in the schools, the failure to conform to them could be painful, even tragic. One such girl, who had married according to Navajo custom, returned to the Phoenix Indian School pregnant. She was able to hide her condition and delivered her baby at the school. Convinced by the teachings of the matron that a child born of a customary marriage was illegitimate in the eyes of God and that "God will burn me forever if he finds out," she killed her infant.[54]

As her case reveals, the borders between cultures contained great dangers for Indian girls and women. The partial success of the schools in inculcating Native American students with contempt for traditional beliefs and practices introduced profound tensions into many families and communities. As the Meriam Report noted in 1928, the home had become "the place of conflict between the old and the new." Polingaysi Qoyawayma's return to the Hopi mesas in the 1910s after an extended boarding school stay illustrates the painful struggles that sometimes ensued when daughters' internalization of different values undermined maternal authority and roles.[55]

Polingaysi returned to the Hopi mesas disturbed by the difficulty and privations of Hopi life: "The poverty of the scene made her heartsick. This life was not for her." She demanded that her father make a bed and table for her and insisted on demonstrating the cooking skills she had learned at Riverside, however inappropriate they were for Hopi resources and traditions. Sevenka, her mother, wondered: "What shall I do with my daughter, who is now my mother?"[56]

At the same time, Polingaysi would not grind corn with her mother, insisting that Sevenka use a grinding mill. More significant, she refused to marry as custom dictated, rejecting the Hopi womanhood her mother symbolized and valued. Instead Polingaysi vowed that "for no man . . . would she grind corn on her knees." Such labor for her mother, however, carried deep moral significance. She lectured her daughter:

Mother Corn has fed you, as she has fed all Hopi people since the long, long ago when she was no larger than my thumb. Mother Corn is a promise of food and life. I grind with gratitude for the richness of our harvest, not with cross feelings of working too hard. As I kneel at my grinding stone, I bow my head in prayer, thanking the great forces for provision. I have received much. I am willing to give much in return. . . . It is sad that the white man's way has caused you to forget the Hopi way.[57]

Polingaysi Qoyawayma's wholesale adoption of white culture did not typify the response of most Native American girls to the Indian education program in this period. Most former students returned to the reservations or their communities and resumed many of their traditional activities and roles, whether out of choice or necessity or both. The lack of fit between their training and the conditions at home made it virtually impossible for most young Native American women to enact the domestic roles their education had encouraged. This "return to the blanket" occasioned much white criticism of educational policies and of Indian cultures.[58]

At the same time, the conspicuous hypocrisy of white officials who kidnapped women's children in the name of civilized motherhood provoked heated debate. Critics of boarding schools invoked ideologies of motherhood from white culture, noting the extent to which federal officials violated the family values they claimed to be fostering among Indians. In testimony before the Indian Investigation Committee of the U.S. Senate, Dane Coolidge questioned "whether the benefits of this compulsory education justify the separation of little children from their mothers at the tender age of six or seven."[59]

He related the story of a family that had sent eight of its ten children to boarding schools, only to lose seven to disease and one whose whereabouts could not be determined. The government then wanted the other two. Their mother "cried all the time." Coolidge reported to Congress: "I told [the father] and I tell the world that a mother has a right to her children." For Coolidge and other reformers, day schools constituted the best compromise between Indian parents and white officials. Even day schools, however, replaced maternal expertise and care with the authority of white educators.[60]

In the final analysis, white educational policies were predicated on a fear of Native American women's maternal authority. Intent on providing the cultural competence to fit Native Americans into their place in a stratified economy and polity, public officials made maternal dispossession a central component of their civilizing mission. For their part, Native American mothers fought to retain the emotional and cultural loyalties of their children. Their daughters—caught between cultures—invested those cultures with new meanings as they assimilated and resisted selectively.

Sexual Order and Social Order in the Jazz Age

By the 1920s, the failure of the property and gender revolution white officials had sponsored had become apparent, a product of white greed and
complex patterns of resistance and accommodation by the women and men
of America's native peoples. As the extent of Indian land loss became clear
so did the resultant failure of the Dawes Act to establish the nuclear family under male provision. Moreover, a growing ambiguity and heterogeneity in mores, particularly those pertaining to family life and sexual practices, characterized Native American cultures.

The causes and meanings of those heterogeneous practices are difficult
to sort out, particularly when examined from the point of view of women.
Some represented the persistence of customary practices which took on new
meanings as cultural and economic contexts changed. Others were bor-
rowings from an equally diverse white culture, itself in the throes of a considerable dispute regarding gender, sexuality, and family relations. Many
were the unintended consequences of economic and political changes sponsored by the federal government—the fuller integration of Native Americans into the wage labor system, education under white auspices, and the
success of acculturation in reducing the authority of tribal elders and traditional mores.[61]

Native American parents found that their authority to supervise their
daughters' sexual conduct and arrange their marriages had diminished, undermined not only by white-sponsored changes but by the rebellion of some
of their children. Some young women found the idea of marrying a man
chosen by their parents unappealing, particularly if they had been exposed
to white marital mores. In this context, it is not surprising that some sought
autonomy from their parents in their sexual and marital decisions. In traditional cultures, the responses of girls who opposed their parents' choice
of husbands for them ranged from reluctant obedience to resistance.[62]

As Polingaysa's conflict with her mother over marriage suggests,
women's reactions to marriage arranged by their elders revealed the ways
in which family relations and cultural affiliations were mutually constituted in Native American societies. Cecelia Sneezy remembered her decision
to marry a stranger chosen by her grandmother:

> I just don't want to get married, but I would do it. Because I do according
> to the traditional way. I didn't way to disappoint [my grandmother] because
> she raised me and I obey her.[63]

Annie Lowry, a Paiute born in the 1870s, was pressured by her family
into marriage to a man she did not like. At a time when destitution shaped
their lives, they were convinced that he would be a good provider and husband. He followed custom and slept in her tent for five nights, signifying

their marriage. When he touched her, she "started fighting him and . . . fought like a cat." She contemplated running away, but was certain that her community would hunt her down and kill her if she tried to leave. Her fear attested much more to her sense of powerlessness in the face of customary practices enacted by her family than to the likelihood that this would happen. After several years of marriage, she came to love her husband, but she remained angry that she had been "given to Sanny against my will."[64]

In many cultures, girls traditionally married at a young age, reducing the risk of premarital childbearing. By the 1920s, a rising age of marriage in these cultures and patterns of sexual experimentation, some sanctioned by Native American traditions and others by elements of white culture, heightened official concerns regarding the moral regulation of young Native Americans. In the cities, the participation of young Native American women in an urban working-class leisure economy heightened anxieties regarding the sexual meanings of acculturation.[65]

As Melissa MacKinnon's work demonstrates, assimilationists had intended that Native American women become urban wage workers (especially as domestic servants), but sought to quarantine them from the challenges to the sex/gender system fostered in the cities of the 1910s and 1920s. Many American Indian women, however, joined other working-class women (and men) at the "cheap amusements" afforded by dances, movies, and other urban attractions. Moreover, they sometimes dated and married men from other racial groups.[66]

In Tucson, Arizona, their actions prompted white officials to attempt a stricter regulation of Native American women in order to restrict their spatial and sexual freedoms. Declaiming against what they called "Red Slavery," white authorities constructed a rhetoric of sexual victimization that construed Native American women as the innocent prey of men from other racial categories. As MacKinnon cogently concluded, this rhetoric justified the appointment of an outing matron to supervise American Indian women working as domestic servants in Tucson and "removed the discussion of sexual exploitation of domestic workers from the middle-class home, the site where such exploitation in fact occurred, and placed the threat instead in the public spaces of the city occupied by working-class and racial-ethnic people."[67]

The goal of Indian assimilation required a faith in the possibility that Native Americans could be "redeemed" culturally, a faith that officials were unwilling to extend to women who willfully constructed nonconformist sexual lives. For many white officials the rhetoric of sexual victimization employed in the discussions of "Red Slavery" offered the only way to explain changes in Native American women's sexual mores while retaining their belief in the possibility of acculturation. In 1918, William

Ketcham, a member of the Board of Indian Commissioners, reported that there was extensive evidence that white men saw Indian women, especially young ones, "as their rightful prey" and concluded that these women needed protection from the "beastly passions of white men." Commissioner Malcolm McDowell reported in 1917 that Indian women and girls around the mining camps of Nevada were "regarded as common property by the low class of men . . . ."[68]

Other authorities saw Native American women as vulnerable to victimization at the hands of Native American men. In a letter endorsing a 1926 bill to mandate marriages under white laws, Secretary of the Interior Hubert Work claimed that "the loose relationship between the sexes and the resultant difficulty in maintaining law and order and determining when Indian couples actually intend to enter into the permanent relationship of husband and wife" had occasioned many difficulties. He especially blamed acculturated young men for taking advantage of the lack of penalty for "various acts of immorality, seduction of innocent girls, etc."[69]

The vulnerability of Native American women to sexual exploitation at the hands of white men took many forms and was well known to public officials, especially those on the Board of Indian Commissioners. The problem, however, was not restricted to one group of white men or to obvious forms of sexual victimization. Some opportunistic white men saw marriage to Indian women as a mechanism for dispossessing them from their land. Others defined their marital commitments to Native American women more narrowly than they did those to white women, as Annie Lowry's mother found when her white common-law husband left her and their children, sold their house and property, and married a white woman.[70]

The rhetoric of victimization simultaneously obscured and revealed the sexual politics of acculturation. By construing women's sexuality as passive, it denied women's culturally constructed needs and agency in sexual matters. That denial itself constituted a form of sexual exploitation—one that alienated women from their bodies by placing them in the service of a male-dominated political and cultural order. The fear that women might be exercising sexual volition, whether they married according to custom, married white men, or chose sexual relationships outside marriage, revealed one dimension of the sexual politics of Indian-hating.

Native American women's resistance to this system revealed its contradictions. When confronted with women who refused to confine their sexuality to legal marriages, some white officials harassed and derogated them. Abandoning the discourse of victimization, they acknowledged women's sexual agency while labeling it immoral. This reinforced the stereotype of Indian women as sexually loose and, therefore, outside the system of "protections" promised to conforming white women.[71]

These conflicts intensified federal officials' concerns regarding the relationship of Indian families to the state. White officials sought explanations and solutions for the failures of acculturative strategies. The discussions of "immorality" among Indians and its implications for "law and order" in Indian communities in the 1920s revealed the ideological connections between notions of social order and sexual order in the construction of Indian policy. They also revealed the intense preoccupation with the regulation of women's sexuality at the heart of the civilizing enterprise.[72]

The resistance of many Indians to the coercive strategies used to force them to marry according to white custom and law prompted federal officials to attempt to secure a federal law requiring them to do so. In 1926 Secretary of the Interior Hubert Work sent a bill to the House Committee on Indian Affairs that included a provision to abolish Indian custom marriage and divorce. The bill, which was introduced into the House of Representatives shortly thereafter, recognized the validity of existing marriages by custom and further declared that the children of customary unions were to be considered legitimate. It also stipulated that the Secretary of the Interior could provide for the mother of such children by selling, leasing, or otherwise using the trust property of the father.[73]

The 1926 law included "law and order" provisions requiring state jurisdiction over Indians in certain areas of the law. Federal officials wanted to bring Indians under the authority of state laws in order to regulate family and sexuality, traditional domains of state and local authority. Indeed, many agency superintendents and others viewed the regulation of marriage as essential to the construction of the rule of law among Native Americans.[74]

Within this context, opponents of the "law and order" bill had to wrest the moral high ground from those who would place the regulation of Indian morality in the hands of the white-controlled state. In their testimony on the bill before the House Committee on Indian Affairs, white reformers often justified Indian autonomy in marriage on the grounds that customary practices served to regulate women's sexuality and construct monogamous unions at least as effectively as white laws. Congressman Edgar Howard of Nebraska, for example, stated that the Omahas regarded their customary marriages "more sacredly" than the average white man did his marriage vows. John Collier stated that the Pueblos were "strictly monogamists," and much more restrictive regarding divorce than whites.[75]

Their enthusiasm for the maintenance of Native American traditions regulating the sexuality of women had limits, however. C. Hart Meriam, a research associate at the Smithsonian Institution, cited a case, perhaps apocryphal, where traditional practices enforced women's marital fidelity: "I know of a case, but not of my own personal knowledge, where a Blackfoot married woman committed adultery, and it was decreed that she should be killed in the way in which the tribal law specified, so her nearest of kin, her two brothers, stoned her to death." When questioned by the committee, he stated that he certainly did not believe that the government should tolerate such practices. He further assured them that the custom he was describing had been abandoned.[76]

Only by projecting certain Anglo-American values onto Native American cultures and collapsing distinctions among those various societies could reformers muster a defense of Native American "autonomy" in their sex-gender systems. Although this appropriative move enabled reformers to defeat the 1926 bill, it did not enable them to articulate a coherent critique of assimilation. Indeed, despite their professions of regard for Native American traditions, important reformers shared with conservatives the assumption that Native American cultures should practice monogamous marriage and enforce women's chastity.

In fact, the Native American practices that constructed sexual meanings in this period were much more complex than those described in the 1926 hearings. Moreover, Indian women played a critical part in these processes. Because sexuality constructs economic, emotional, and political relationships, their actions and values reflected their particular locations in shifting contexts and were a constituent element in the sexual politics of Indian-white relations.

Work and Employment

For many centuries, environmental changes and contact with other nations, Native American and white, fostered or necessitated change in Native American economies. Of course, nothing had greater or more devastating effects on Indian life than the destruction of their subsistence base caused by the theft of their lands by whites. In the period under study, 1887 to 1934, deprivation and starvation haunted many Indian communities. Securing a livelihood was a central preoccupation of women, men, and children in these societies.

Most supported themselves with a combination of economic activities and resources: commercial farming and ranching, subsistence work, wage labor, arts and crafts production, rations and welfare, and income from leasing or selling their land. The federal government promoted economic development in a very limited fashion, offering some assistance with training, credit, and materials. Most of this was designed to turn Indian men into farmers, so that women landowners were excluded from these minimal benefits.[77]

The effects of economic transitions on women's work roles and status have not been systematically explored. Some scholars have concluded that Indian men were more damaged by externally imposed changes than women because they lost the structural supports for their most important roles—warrior and hunter—while women experienced continuity in their roles in families. Most studies, however, stress women's loss of traditional productive roles and the erosion of their customary sources of power. As Joan Jensen, Patricia Albers, and others suggest, the changes experienced and shaped by Indian women were complex, variable, and sometimes contradictory.[78]

Most scholars conclude that changes in Indian women's work and gender relations were caused by the unilateral imposition of white economic systems and gender values on resisting Native American women. By examining domestic, subsistence, and waged labor, this work seeks to complicate that framework by suggesting that Indian women selectively (and sometimes successfully) resisted and appropriated white economic practices and technologies. In a context of cultural imposition and economic crisis, Native American women worked to construct viable economic and cultural practices. Their efforts reveal the ways in which cultural resistance necessitated cultural innovation.[79]

Scholars have drawn contradictory conclusions regarding the effects of allotment policies on women. According to Dolores Janiewski, Nez Perce women lost their individual holdings more rapidly than men and continued their traditional gathering activities in order to contribute to family support. Patricia Albers notes an ironic outcome: in the long run, "federal policy governing Indian land and its use had undermined the influence of [Dakota] men in domestic settings." Women's unpaid work and access to welfare made them central in a family economy organized around distributing limited resources. At the same time, however, "attitudes of male supremacy began to emerge" as a consequence of the influence of whites.[80]

As Albers's study suggests, the meanings of shifts in the family economy for women's empowerment were complex and culturally mediated. Native American cultural practices inimical to women's autonomy and empowerment predated the Dawes Act, although they received increasing institutional and ideological support after it was implemented. In most Indian nations, the interdependence between women and men that developed after their dispossession from their lands was not predicated on women's superior economic prerogatives. The loss of a subsistence base, the increasing authority of men over certain economic decisions (including the disposition of allotted lands), women's meager opportunities in the wage economy, and women's continuing responsibility for children and other kin meant that their dependence on others for economic assistance of all kinds had increased.

Much acculturative work among Indians after the Dawes Act was designed to erode their customary obligations to extended kin and community so that all men would feel compelled to adopt farming or wage work.

For women, however, the maintenance of their traditional patterns of mutual assistance provided a means of security in an increasingly uncertain economic situation. As Rayna Rapp has noted, people who cannot provide their reproduction costs within nuclear families must rely on extended kinship networks to "[spread] out the aid and the risks involved in daily life." Women's labor, including their emotion work, is critical to the maintenance of these networks.[81]

White officials regarded the redefinition of women's work, paid and unpaid, as critical to the economic well-being of Indian families and essential for enabling Indians to take their place in the capitalist order. Home extension agents, field matrons, and others charged with inculcating domesticity in Native American women stressed several forms of labor: frugal housewifery, which included the need to produce goods and services for the family; child socialization compatible with acculturation; home-based production for the market (usually of native craft items); and the necessity of encouraging wage work and the work ethic for men in the household. Because of the lack of technology and capital, much of this work was to be labor-intensive.[82]

This cultural package, encompassing production, reproduction, and socialization, derived from several understandings held by whites: that Indian men's wages would remain low and uncertain; that wage work outside the household was inappropriate for married women; and that poverty made the nuclear family under male provision simultaneously precarious and desirable. White reformers also assumed that traditional economic practices of Native Americans were either inefficient, socially damaging, or obsolete and that acculturation would end poverty. Although many who worked with Native American women noted their "industry" and observed the range of labor-intensive tasks they performed, they assumed that a gender-based integration into the wage economy would lighten women's load and be easily achieved.[83]

In fact, poverty and discrimination made that transition difficult and rendered the work of most Native American women more onerous and even more central to their families' well-being than it had been in the past. Interactions between white officials and Native American women afforded opportunities for cooperation or conflict over the organization of domestic labor. Beginning in the 1890s, the BIA assigned field matrons to reservations in order to train Native American women in the domestic skills and values deemed critical to the civilizing enterprise. By the 1920s, the field matrons had been joined (or replaced) by field nurses, teachers, and home extension agents charged with similar or related missions.[84]

The relationships between Native American women and these agents of white culture were complex. Indian women often refused the field matrons' teachings on domesticity because to conform meant increasing their labor or violating cultural beliefs, while they sought out white agents when such contact enabled them to meet their family responsibilities more easily or effectively. Minnie Randolph, for example, noted the resistance of California Native American women to the use of cook stoves because they could use nearby sagebrush in camp fires but had to go to the mountains to gather pine wood for the stoves. On the other hand, Indian women would frequently come to field matrons when they needed cultural mediation, goods, or services, including food, clothing, medicine, and treatment for the sick.[85]

While field matrons and teachers saw most such requests as an opportunity for instruction and practice in the domestic arts, Indian women would sometimes try to avoid coming under their tutelage while securing assistance in their work. Mary Ramsey, field matron for the Shoshoni, reported that when she participated in their labor "in some unaccounted way I soon have their confidence—partially, not entirely. . . ." In addition, some Native American women sought to obtain finished goods, particularly clothing, from white officials while avoiding the addition of sewing to their already arduous daily labor.[86]

Women's desire for assistance derived from the many hours of labor necessitated by their traditional work and the needs of their families. Native American women often spent their days hauling water and wood, making pottery and other goods, weaving cloth, gathering food, cooking, caring for kin and for the ill. Women living in arid environments often had to travel long distances to bring water to their families, engage in especially labor-intensive gathering or agricultural work, and spend many hours grinding corn and wheat into flour on stone mills. Anna Moore Shaw, a member of the Pima nation in Arizona who became an acculturated working-class homemaker in Phoenix, reflected on her cultural journey:

> Our ancestors' lots were tough. The men raised their crops with one hand and stopped enemy raids with the other, while the women worked day and night gathering wild foods, carrying wood and water, and weaving. Although I have long strived to preserve our old Pima ways, the poverty, grueling work, and bloody battles are things I do not miss![87]

Field matrons and other agents of white culture constantly lamented the difficulties of training Native American women in middle-class domesticity when they lacked its material base. They particularly complained that traditional Indian homes were not conducive to the maintenance of cleanliness or the successful accomplishment of other domestic tasks. Minnie Randolph, field matron in Bishop, California, claimed that getting Indians "out of their dirty wickiups into houses" helped more than anything else in promoting domesticity.[88]

Whites had a deep faith in the cultural and practical benefits deriving from the acquisition of material goods from the dominant society. Indeed, the addition of new household furnishings was metaphorically understood as uplift. The 1931 report of the Commissioner of Indian Affairs lauded the effects of home extension work, claiming that "in some homes, the Indians have literally been raised from the ground to chairs and beds and their food has actually been taken off of the earth and placed on tables."[89]

White officials particularly emphasized the delivery of Western medical practices to the Native Americans, many of whom were understandably reluctant to abandon traditional practices for remedies whose efficacy had not been demonstrated to them. Moreover, the adoption of Western medicine entailed many changes in their cultures. Native American healing practices enacted their belief in the connections between body and spirit, individual and social health. In American Indian cultures, disease symbolized and embodied a relational world in disequilibrium. Through curative rituals, spiritual leaders sought to return individuals to harmony with their world while restoring their health. In a real sense, the patient was the community, not the individual.[90]

Western medicine, by contrast, attempted to isolate diseases and apply technologies to remedy them. White doctors and nurses encountered resistances to their efforts when they undermined the communal and relational basis for Native American healing. The efforts of field matron Jolie Palin to use a quarantine to stop an outbreak of diphtheria among the Zunis illustrated these cultural differences. Palin found that they were unwilling to abandon their customary visits to the sick. Medical efforts to get Indians to go to hospitals for treatment often met with opposition because they separated the sick from the nexus of family and community relations deemed essential to their recovery.[91]

This does not mean, however, that Native Americans resisted all elements of Western medical practice. As Clara Sue Kidwell has pointed out, American Indian healing practices were adaptive and incorporative, taking in those elements of Western practices that seemed useful while benefiting "from a sense of community and balance that Native American ceremonies bring about." Women had a critical role in mediating between traditional healing practices and the services offered by whites, adding white medicines to their healing practices and using government officials as labor resources in the face of the chronic and contagious diseases that plagued Indian peoples. Although men were more likely to engage in ceremonial curative activities, women had a critical, although informal, role in treating and caring for the sick. The frequency with which they requested help from field matrons and nurses revealed their need for assistance in meeting their extensive caretaking responsibilities as well as their cultural adaptivity.[92]

In other areas also, new technologies enabled Indian women to reduce their work, to do it more effectively, or to produce goods for sale. For Zuni women, the construction of a new flour mill in 1919 meant a decrease in the number of hours they would spend grinding flour. On occasion, Native American women adapted white goods to traditional activities. Hopi women, for example, took the bedsprings they had been urged to acquire and used them as a place to dry peaches. For those who could afford them, sewing machines were very popular. Women could use them to make clothing for their families or to sell on the market.[93]

By the early twentieth century, Native American women were producing many goods to sell outside their communities. The products they made were a combination of traditional items and those introduced by whites: moccasins, quilts, clothing, pottery, baskets, beadwork, and produce. For many Native American families, women's home-based production constituted one of the main sources of cash or of goods acquired in trades. Among the Kiowas, for example, women's egg money purchased many of the groceries. Traditional craft items became an increasingly important consumer good among whites.[94]

White business leaders and BIA officials worked to "sell" Native American cultures and the products that symbolized them in order to enhance the tourist industry in certain regions of the country and to promote economic development and "self-reliance" among Indians. Although many whites believed that support for Indian arts and crafts would simultaneously preserve Indian traditions and provide adequate incomes to Native Americans, the requirements of the market tended to undermine both goals.[95]

What was being marketed was the idea of a static, homogeneous "tradition" embodied in products to be displayed in cultural contexts radically different from those in which they were produced. Those "traditions" and the demand for their products were constructed as they were marketed. In some societies, traditional crafts had fallen into disuse and had to be re-invented, using archaeologist's findings and the resources of the federal government to provide instruction in pottery-making, weaving, and the like. Moreover, the desire for the maintenance of "quality" and uniformity in production led to efforts by public officials, traders, and others to supervise the selection and production of raw materials and finished products and to certify the authenticity of Indian arts and crafts. The latter strategy was prompted by contradictory fears: that imitations mass-produced by whites would undercut the market for Indian-produced goods and that consumer demand was predicated on a desire for hand-made goods that reflected traditional Indian cultures.[96]

Field matrons, educators, traders, and others encouraged this home production for the market by women and attempted to mediate between traditional practices, the demands of customers, and the desire of Indian women to control the conditions of their labor and the meanings of its products. In the process, the economic and cultural relations of "marketing tradition" were defined. The commodification of products traditionally made to serve the daily needs of Native Americans and as an expression of their cultural values entailed conflicts between agents of white culture and Native American workers. Those conflicts were complicated by the desire of women to maximize the economic benefits of their labor.[97]

Among the Navajos, for example, women weavers were encouraged to introduce new dyes and spinning techniques in order to meet the demands for "quality" of white consumers. The market, however, could sustain different definitions of quality. White officials tried to encourage labor-intensive basketry techniques by Havasupai women in order to maintain a particular standard of quality, while the women wanted to market the cheaper baskets that sold readily among white tourists. Their position is hardly surprising, given that a small basket made to exacting standards could take one woman two weeks to produce. The low return for their labor in craft work often made other sources of income more appealing to Native American women. The increasing availability of wage work during World War II prompted Tohono O'Odham (Papago) women to abandon the production of pottery and baskets.[98]

Many Indian women engaged in wage work outside their households. As was true for the other groups of racial ethnic women in this study, they often ended up employed as domestic servants, laundresses, or agricultural laborers. Indeed, the assumption that Native American women should work as domestic servants was so deeply institutionalized that field matrons and other officials routinely assisted in placing them in white households.[99]

There they encountered low wages, arduous work, cultural condescension, and maternalist surveillance. Their wages were often supplemented with food and clothing "left over" by the white families for whom they worked. Some Native American household workers also found advantages in their work. Annie Lowry noted that Paiute women were often able to bring their children with them, enabling them to combine their caretaking and support responsibilities to their families. Polingaysi Qoyawayma learned English and white domestic skills, concluding that her experiences had improved her self-confidence as she entered the white world.[100]

Throughout this period, whites expected that most American Indians would earn their livelihood from farming and ranching. They assumed that rural work would be characterized by a division of labor in which men made the economic decisions, did most of the field work, and raised the livestock. Women were expected to raise gardens and poultry, process products for family consumption, and maintain the household. As a result, only men were given training in white farm technologies and practices or access to the credit essential to farming in a capitalist economy. Women were provided assistance in domestic work, particularly growing and processing foods, and on home health issues.[101]

In fact, the inadequacy of the land and capital available to Native Americans meant that women's work diverged substantially from white expectations. Many Indian women continued to fish, gather fruits, berries, and other products for their families' use, and engage directly in customary and new agricultural work, including gardening. Navajo women, for example, persisted in sheepherding, despite government restrictions on the size of herds that substantially reduced their incomes in the 1930s.[102]

Home extension agents tried to increase the production, canning, and drying of food by Native American women. The effects of these efforts are hard to assess. In many cases, the diets of American Indians were enlarged as a result of the thousands of cans of fruits and vegetables that resulted from women's labor. Such strategies could easily be undermined by the forces of nature, however. On the Cheyenne River Reservation in South Dakota, 495 gardens were planted and cultivated in 1933. Drought and grasshoppers destroyed all of them. To make matters worse, whites gathered the wild fruit in the area, preventing the Indians from using it as a source of food.[103]

Although white officials often trained Native American women to become "farm wives," many of them worked as seasonal farm laborers instead. Mountain Wolf Woman, a Winnebago who preferred rural wage labor to farming, concluded that as farmers "we make money for the white people and we never see any money." Indeed, she and her husband spent all their income from farming to pay the debts they incurred for farm animals and equipment. As rural wage workers, they claimed their own earnings and were free to quit if they objected to working conditions. Moreover, farm labor was often collective, engaging whole families and communities.[104]

In other cases, seasonal workers consisted primarily of either men or women. The availability of other employment for either women or men often influenced their participation as farm laborers. Navajo men, for example, did rural wage work in part because the women were generally too busy with sheepherding and blanket weaving to do other labor.[105]

White policies and attitudes toward Native American family economies remained contradictory throughout this period. Policy-makers intensified their efforts to construct a family system in which men supported their wives and children. At the same time, they recognized that men's incomes were not adequate to achieve this and so they encouraged income-producing activities on the part of women, including those who were wives and mothers. In addition, they provided minimal rations (welfare) to some families in need.

Their inability to impose the system they espoused frustrated white officials, who heightened their criticisms of Native Americans in the 1910s and 1920s. Whites blamed Indians for their own impoverishment, attributing it to indolence, immorality, and the persistence of "socialistic" traditions. In fact, customary values that supported generosity to those in need and stigmatized individualistic economic effort as selfish became particularly important to women's survival in this period.[106]

Women in nations that had experienced a partial transition to white economic practices were particularly vulnerable to economic deprivation. The basis for traditional subsistence work had eroded; wage work and other productive activities yielded very low returns; and they could not easily combine wage labor with family responsibilities. At the same time, as Patricia Albers has shown with regard to the Dakotas, women's gathering, gardening, and other labor provided their families with some protection from the vicissitudes of the market and of federal support programs. Albers also argues that that protection had contradictory implications for the Dakotas as it also

> contributed, albeit indirectly, to promoting grossly unequal exchanges in the selling of cash-crops, and to low wages (in cash or kind) for male employment in the federal sector and in seasonal agricultural work on neighboring white farms.[107]

Many widowed and elderly women faced dire destitution. In Nevada, the disabled and the old, who received rations only three times a year, relied on begging to survive. Similarly, among the Walapai, some elderly women were reduced to begging.[108]

Unmarried older women often relied heavily on extended kin and the community for support. Their economic well-being depended in part on their economic roles over the life course and the degree of autonomy deemed appropriate to women in their culture. Warren Moorehead, a member of the Board of Indian Commissioners, reported that older Choctaw women who had been swindled out of their allotments were supported by other Choctaws, who took turns bringing supplies to them. The Jicarilla Apaches organized an Old People's herd, tended by all members of the nation, in order to provide support for the elderly.[109]

Among the Havasupais of Arizona, customary patrilineal inheritance practices increasingly disadvantaged women as gathering and gardening became less important to their sustenance while agriculture and wage work became more central. As a result, women's inability to inherit land became an important source of their discontent, heightened by their understanding that white women had more property rights than they did. In the 1920s, one widow appealed to the federal agent for the right to inherit her husband's land. He approved her request, but the members of her community ostracized her and the men refused to do their customary cooperative work of repairing the irrigation ditches critical to agriculture in the desert. She did it on her own.[110]

The economic changes experienced by American Indian women in this period were highly variable. Some had already entered the capitalist system of property and labor before allotment. Others retained many customary work roles—gathering food, fuel, and water; cooking traditional foods; and caring for children. Most, however, witnessed the erosion of the material base for traditional economic practices and relations and had to find new ways to sustain their families. In general, they supplemented customary work with wage work, crafts production for the market, government support, and intensified domestic labor as means to provide goods and services to their families. Many added some elements of white technologies, goods, and services to their daily lives.

Their work was central to diminishing the gap between the needs of their families and the resources available to them. Neither the frugal housewifery enjoined by whites nor the various productive roles they assumed in their societies could fully meet those needs, however. For many, impoverishment deepened as the Great Depression undermined the capitalist economy they were expected to enter.

Indian Women and the Politics of Acculturation

In order to enable the construction of the "free" Indian male citizen, white policy-makers insisted on the simultaneous creation of a dependent and subordinated Indian woman. His "independence" required her labor—domestic, reproductive, emotional, and productive. White insistence on rigid gender roles for Native Americans heightened as conflicts among whites jeopardized the conflation of race and culture at the heart of the assimilationist enterprise. Couched in the language of property and propriety, the colonialist discourse employed by reformers and conservatives alike revealed the connections between the politics of class, race, and gender in official attempts to define an Indian citizenship.

There was no consistent pattern among Indians in their reactions to the pressures exerted by whites on their gender relationships, economic systems, and cultural values. In some nations men and women found a common ground for handling attempts at enforced acculturation, while other Native Americans experienced pronounced gender and generational conflicts. In most cases, evidence on this issue has not been adequately developed. Whatever the case, officials increasingly blamed Native American women for the failure of previous policies and focused much of their "rehabilitative" crusade on efforts to reconstruct womanhood.

At the same time, a simple social control model that assumes a monolithic and homogeneous white culture and state imposing an always damaging program of economic and social change on equally homogeneous Indian cultures distorts our understandings of the history of Native American women. Some of the competencies and technologies offered to them by whites provided a means to improve their circumstances in a changing cultural and economic context. Moreover, Native American women's selective and situated appropriations and transformations of white cultural practices in the areas of family, sexuality, and economy reveal their cultural agency in historical processes.

As the next chapter reveals, the official demise of the allotment policy in 1934 did not fundamentally alter the dilemmas and possibilities confronting Native American women. Acculturative pressures intensified in their lives, reflecting the persistence of racism and discrimination. The complex connections between racial and gender oppressions often created profound political dilemmas for them.

From the Indian
New Deal to Red Power

WOMEN, "SELF-DETERMINATION," AND POWER

THE DISCONTINUATION OF federal allotment policies in 1934 marked the end of one phase in white assimilationist strategies, but not the end of official paternalism and regulation in the lives of American Indian women. Official efforts to impose patriarchal families changed as economic trends, assimilative successes, and public policies motivated many Native Americans to form nuclear families. By the 1950s, the formal agencies of the welfare state replaced and supplemented the Bureau of Indian Affairs as the mechanism for regulating women's sexuality, maternity, and family relations. Whether the government focused on reservation-based economic development or on assisting Indian movement to urban economies, Native American women found that the heightened importance of a market economy in their lives often meant increasing economic dependence on men and held contradictory implications for their autonomy.

During the post-allotment period, the participation of Indian women and men in the institutions of the dominant culture increased dramatically. Growing numbers of Native Americans received their education in public schools and colleges, migrated to cities, entered the wage economy, served in the military, and came into contact with social welfare and other white agencies unconnected to the BIA. These changes derived from and supported Indian desires to partake in the possibilities offered by white society as nearly as possible on their own terms. This did not represent an abandonment of their cultures by Native Americans, but rather an effort to recreate them in a new context.[1]

As active participants in the cultural struggles of the period, Native American women sometimes found that balancing their needs for empowerment with their goals for Indian peoples had become more difficult. Indian men's control over the tribal governments created in this period enabled some to assert that male dominance in tribal relations was customary, making it difficult for women to claim an indigenous sanction for gender equality. Many women experienced pressures from within their cultures to eschew some of their civil and political rights in order to secure tribal claims to land or legal sovereignty, restore some customary practices, or to safeguard the health and well-being of others in their families and communities.[2]

At the same time, agents of white culture and politics worked to impose their systems of male dominance in Indian societies. As before, public officials sought to construct nuclear families under male provision among Native Americans. This priority affected all Indian policies, from economic development to relocation. Indian women's increased participation in white-controlled institutions simultaneously made them vulnerable to the race and gender discriminations enacted by those institutions and provided them with some opportunities to claim resources and challenge the oppressions in their lives.

Indian Women in the Age of Reform

In 1934 power in the Bureau of Indian Affairs was transferred to John Collier and other critics of many historic Indian policies. These reformers set out to end allotment, support Native American autonomy in some areas of cultural life, establish tribal governments, and promote economic development for Native Americans. As difficult and contradictory as those goals were, they were made more difficult by the fact that they had to be successfully implemented during the worst depression in American history. Moreover, the androcentrism with which reformers defined policies made Indian women particularly vulnerable to further economic and political marginalization.

Under the Indian New Deal, economic development programs and relief policies together shaped the economic circumstances of American Indians. Work relief programs were particularly important in accelerating the integration of Indians into the wage labor system, while the government attempted to develop an economic base that would provide jobs for the long term through its loan and technical assistance programs. These programs failed to achieve their goal, creating permanent jobs for a small number of men and even fewer women. As a result, Indian poverty persisted and women's subsistence labor remained critical to the survival of Indian communities.[3]

A 1934 study by the Civil Works Administration revealed the extraordinary economic difficulties facing American Indians. It found that about 40 percent of Indian income came from annuities and leases on their land; 41 percent from wages, including jobs on relief; and the rest from farming, ranching, crafts, and garden produce. That one-third of the wages came from government relief programs attests to the extreme poverty of Native Americans, whose earnings were far below those of white farmers, themselves in the throes of a long and devastating depression. Despite their needs, Indians received much lower amounts of direct relief than whites under the New Deal.[4]

It is highly probable that the CWA study undercounted the economic contributions of women because it included only production for the market and omitted Southwestern tribes, where women's arts and crafts production contributed substantially to family incomes. Gardens and other forms of production for subsistence were deducted from the totals for agricultural income, although they also contributed to the economic well-being of Native Americans. Other aspects of women's domestic labor received no analysis.[5]

The androcentrism that shaped this study also affected the economic and political policies of the Collier administration. As a result, the Indian New Deal had mixed effects on Native American women. Given that the premises of its political reforms and development policies were defined by white men and drawn from white models, it is not surprising that their vision for women's empowerment did not extend beyond the right to vote (only recently secured by white women). Noting the contradictory intentions and effects of the Indian New Deal, Alison Bernstein concluded that it offered some increased possibilities for women within their indigenous cultures, but "it proved a double-edged sword for Indian women living among whites."[6]

The reformers did abandon the historic concern with imposing marriage and divorce under white laws on Indians. In 1935 the Indian Service issued a regulation recognizing the authority of tribal governments to define family relations as they saw fit and requiring that all tribally sanctioned marriages and divorces be recorded. A few tribes required conformity to state laws; others created mechanisms for defining and recording tribal custom unions and divorces.[7]

The gender inequalities sanctioned by Indian traditions, especially in the realm of politics, posed a dilemma for white reformers intent on sponsoring Indian "self-determination." Federal officials sought to construct an Indian political identity congruent with Anglo gender ideologies. By 1934, this meant the extension of the right to vote and hold office to women. At the same time, the "democratic" model on which the Indian New Deal was based had already managed to confine white women to auxiliary and subordinate roles in politics.

Many tribal cultures had not traditionally allowed women's formal participation in politics. John Collier and other federal officials successfully insisted that woman suffrage be included in all tribal constitutions drafted under the Indian Reorganization Act (IRA) and that women must be allowed to vote in referenda on those constitutions, regardless of traditional practices. In a meeting with Collier and others in 1934, a member of the All-Pueblo Council asked whether the two-thirds vote required to pass a tribal constitution included women. Collier responded that it did and that even "a crazy man" could cast the deciding vote.[8]

Neither Native American women nor men served as insiders during Collier's Indian New Deal. Some Indian women, however, did serve in leadership roles during these years. They included Ella Deloria, Sioux; Ruth Muskrat Bronson, Cherokee; and Helen L. Peterson, Sioux. Bronson and Muskrat each served as executive director of the National Congress of American Indians, and Deloria was an educator, folklorist, and novelist. According to Alison Bernstein, their success in securing leadership positions derived in part from the critical assistance and sponsorship they received from white women's organizations, particularly the General Federation of Women's Clubs and the Young Women's Christian Association.[9]

In general, Native American women had very limited roles in the formal political structures created by the new tribal constitutions, in those tribal governments organized outside the Indian New Deal, and in the increasingly important negotiations between Indian nations and the federal government. Because they did not rely on decision-making by consensus and on flexible and informal processes, the new tribal governments represented an important break from traditions that had deleterious effects on women. A few women served on elected tribal councils. Most others continued to exercise an informal influence over politics, while some participated in public organizing and lobbying efforts on behalf of Native Americans.[10]

Because they could define tribal membership and legitimize particular interpretations of "tradition," male-dominated tribal governments could exercise great power in determining tribal interests and constructing gender politics. In some cases, the exercise of that power could have detrimental effects on women and their families. In 1939, for example, the Santa Clara Pueblo (a matrilineal culture before the Spanish conquest) decided to legalize patrilineal descent under its constitution, creating a policy that discriminated against women who married outside the group and their children in matters of tribal property and participation in tribal affairs.[11]

Similarly, economic development and relief policies on the reservations reflected the allotment era assumption that jobs should be created for men as breadwinners, while women should be trained as frugal housewives. At the same time, the educational programs of the Indian New Deal and Collier's decision to give preference to Indians in Indian Service jobs improved women's access to clerical and professional jobs on the reservations. These jobs, however, were in fields traditionally assigned to women—teaching, nursing, and secretarial work—and benefited only a small number of Native American women.[12]

Among the Navajos, federal policies begun in the 1930s to halt the serious overgrazing of the land by reducing the number of sheep raised on the reservation cut sharply into a traditional income source for women. Sheep-grazing permits were provided by BIA agents to regulate the number of sheep, but they were issued in the name of the husbands, thus removing control from the hands of the women whose livelihood depended on sheep-herding.[13]

Navajo women and men united to resist the threat to their livelihood posed by the herd reductions. They opposed Collier's Indian New Deal, refusing to approve a Navajo constitution. They also harassed white officials seeking to implement herd reduction and other soil erosion policies and withheld their children from school to protest federally imposed economic changes. At the same time, Navajo women and men successfully resisted official attempts to introduce white livestock management methods in part because those techniques were incompatible with the Navajo family system of labor and land use.[14]

Efforts by New Deal officials to encourage and regulate Indian participation in the market economy had contradictory effects on Indian women and men. The arts projects of the Indian New Deal were designed to achieve the goals of economic development and cultural renewal simultaneously. The Seneca Arts Project, for example, trained Indian women and men in traditional crafts in order to provide them with cultural pride and a livelihood. Sarah Hill, an elderly Seneca, trained others in the art of weaving baskets, burden straps, and sashes.[15]

The economic benefits expected from crafts programs did not always materialize. Senecas were paid less than whites working on relief projects. Once the Seneca Arts Project ended, they found that the tourist demand for these crafts was not strong enough to provide them a living. Navajo women received a lower return for their blankets than they had before the Depression.[16]

Federal officials and Indians often cooperated in experiments to diminish the power of traders over prices for Indians' crafts and over the costs of raw materials. In the early 1930s, the Cherokee Indian Agency in North Carolina created the Cherokee Handicraft Guild to operate its own store. This enabled Indians to avoid the trader, who paid them only in goods, and to receive cash for their products. In the late 1930s, officials increased their support for arts and crafts programs among the Navajos and assisted in the organization of a guild to market them. The Jicarilla Apaches bought a reservation store with a federal loan and turned it into a cooperative that lowered prices for its goods.[17]

These policies revealed the advantages to Indians of taking control of economic institutions on their land. Although it is difficult to assess directly their benefits to women, lower prices for consumer products, more access to cash, and the potential for better return on their crafts work would ease somewhat the labor attendant to providing a subsistence for their families and give them more flexibility in managing resources and allocating their own labor.

The intensified subsistence crisis of the 1930s increased the economic importance of federal home extension work with Native American women. In all racial ethnic groups, training and assistance in gardening, food preservation, sewing, and home maintenance enabled women and girls to use their labor to better their families' circumstances. As in other poor communities, Indian women's labor was supposed to bridge the gap between their families' needs and the sparse resources made available by the economy and the state. For Indians and others, domesticity could not and did not eliminate poverty.[18]

The extension of Anglo practices and institutions increased as a result of the Indian New Deal, most notably in the areas of education and health. The BIA built more day schools and hospitals on reservations. The former often served as centers for community activities and work. Women would bring their laundry, sometimes from great distances, to use the schools' machines. By 1941, 80 percent of Indian women were giving birth in hospitals, compared with 50 percent of all women in the United States.[19]

The effects of the Depression and New Deal on Native American women resembled those for Anglo women in certain ways. In both groups women's waged and unwaged labor became increasingly important to the survival of their families and communities at the same time that their relationship to the state shifted. In both groups, federal officials paid much more attention to assisting women in their domestic labor than they did to addressing their need for employment. Among whites, the stigma on women's paid employment restricted women's opportunities in certain professional categories and justified gender discrimination in all public policies related to relief and employment. At the same time, economic need drove white women to take jobs in service and other work usually occupied by racial ethnic women.[20]

War, Termination, and Urbanization

The period beginning with World War II witnessed the increasing importance of the institutions of the dominant society in the daily lives of American Indian women and men. Their integration into Anglo-dominated systems had contradictory consequences for Native American women. It made them vulnerable to the regulatory practices of those systems—practices that focused on poor women's sexuality, reproductivity, and family relations—and to the politics of backlash against women generally and against poor women particularly that have characterized the last half of the twentieth century in the United States. At the same time, some were able to use the resources and expertise obtained within dominant systems to seek empowerment for themselves and their communities.

Moreover, many Native American women found that their increasing participation in a capitalist economy meant entering a labor force stratified by race and gender and constructed in part by the developmental priorities of the federal government. Whether the BIA was controlled by reformers or conservatives, its policies were generally based on the assumption that married women and mothers should not work outside of the home. Their ability to secure an independent livelihood restricted by the possibilities offered in the larger economy, American Indian women also found that their economic dependence on and subordination to Indian men had intensified.

The pace of Indian integration into white institutions increased with changes that began during World War II. For Indian women, as for other women in American society, the war meant changes in the gender division of labor, family relations, and community roles. Many Native American men were drafted or enlisted in the armed services, leaving women to support and nurture families and sustain community life. Moreover, they had to do so while traditional economies continued to erode and acculturative pressures increased.[21]

Changes in the work roles of Native American women involved taking on wage work in the war economy and assuming previously male work in reservation economies. Approximately 20 percent of the women left the reservations, some to take production jobs in munitions, aircraft, and other war industries. More commonly, Indian women worked in service jobs in cafeterias, restaurants, and other establishments. Some enlisted in the armed forces. On the reservations, women took over work in agriculture, equipment repair, and forestry. Among the Zunis and Navajos, women even broke into silversmithing, a traditionally male craft. At the same time, many women abandoned their traditional crafts work for better-paying jobs or because allotments for servicemen's wives offered a source of support.[22]

These dramatic improvements in employment opportunities were not sufficient to eliminate poverty among Native Americans. Moreover, the benefits provided to servicemen's families were at least partly offset by the decline in the relief programs of the past. As a result, the unwaged domestic labor of Native American women remained critical to their families' survival. By 1944, the government reported that American Indian women had canned 3,600,000 quarts of food and dried 1,590,000 pounds of food for their families' use. These figures do not take into account other forms of domestic provision undertaken by Native American women.[23]

Because the war necessitated the evacuation of many Christian missionaries from foreign fields, the numbers assigned to proselytize on Indian reservations grew. Cultural pressure on Indian women (and men) to adopt white family practices, including legalized marriages, buttressed political and economic compulsion.[24]

Indeed, during the war years the federal government finally secured its goal of requiring marriage according to state laws among most Indians. The provision of government payments for servicemen's wives created the mechanism for the government to enforce its wishes. In order to qualify for dependent benefits, Indian wives of servicemen had to be legally married or obtain documentation of their customary marriages from the tribal council. Because the former was easier and because some tribal councils abolished Indian custom marriages and divorces, the incidence of customary marriages declined. At the same time, many Native American women in the postwar period found it much more difficult to secure a divorce because of the costs and inconvenience of using white legal systems. Indian men's integration into the state as soldiers, therefore, meant that Indian men and women were incorporated more fully into the state's gender system.[25]

The regulatory power of the state expressed in the operations of the allotment system for dependents of servicemen was extended into other domains of Indian life in the decades after World War II as conservatives regained power over Indian policies. Termination, relocation, and Public Law 280 represented interrelated attempts to incorporate Indians into white modes of citizenship and into the wage economy. In addition, Indians were made eligible for public assistance programs, including Aid to Families with Dependent Children (AFDC), and were more frequently educated in local public schools.

AFDC in particular enabled the survival of many Indian families while exposing them to criticism for public dependence on a program that signified the inadequacies of the nuclear family for the support of women and children. At the same time that AFDC offered women an alternative to marriage that would ensure their continued impoverishment, other public policies were designed to limit their employment options to a few poorly paid fields deemed appropriate for single women.

At this time, American Indians experienced the virtual elimination of traditional communal economies, substantial population growth, and an increasing dependence on a market economy unable and unwilling to provide enough jobs for the men or women. The postwar economic policies of the Indian Service mirrored those the developed nations imposed in the third world in the same period. Officials and private interests concluded that population growth on the reservations had outstripped the economic resources of reservations and that Indians would have to move to cities, abandon traditional cultures, and adopt the development strategies of the first world in order to survive. They also assumed that the gender divisions of work accepted in the dominant economy would also prevail among Indians. They continued to advocate the provider role for men as necessary for their dignity and well-being and as critical to social order among Indians.[26]

As before, most of the federal policies to provide jobs, loans, and training (whether on or off the reservations) assumed that only men were breadwinners. When they were available at all, vocational training and placement services for women were limited to certain "women's" occupations. Although most of the jobs created on or near reservations went to men, especially those that paid adequate wages, federal officials and private developers did not provide enough of them to enable American Indian men to provide for families.[27]

In fact, the postwar years witnessed continuing rural poverty and increasing unemployment among Native Americans accompanied by the entry of more women into the labor force. In 1949, the average income of Indian farm families was about $500, compared with a national average income in the rural sector of about $2500. By the mid-1970s, Indian incomes remained the lowest in the nation.[28]

Their poverty persisted despite efforts to improve their education through integration into the public school systems of the United States. During the 1940s and 1950s, a growing number of Indian children received their education in local public schools. Policy-makers decided that federal boarding schools were to be operated only for those children for whom other kinds of schools were unavailable and for children from "broken homes" or homes deemed "unsuited for raising children."[29]

The postwar Indian migration to the cities included many women, some of them formally assisted by the relocation program, most moving on their own. If the Navajos are representative, discrimination against women in the relocation program was pronounced. Of the 232 Navajos given financial and other assistance to relocate in 1953 and 1954, 142 were in families, 57 were single men, and 10 were single women.[30]

When they arrived in the cities, Indian women found the same patterns of gender and race discrimination encountered by other women of color. Job opportunities for them were largely confined to certain kinds of low-wage service and factory work. Vocational training programs reinforced these patterns of occupational segregation, although some Native American women received instruction in clerical skills. Most Indian women who stayed in the cities received substantially higher wages than they had on the reservations, although the higher cost of living in the cities meant that their standard of living was, at best, only marginally improved.[31]

The assumptions regarding proper gender roles that had informed BIA policies in the allotment era persisted in the new setting, structuring the services made available to Indian women in towns and cities. Federal officials, sometimes in conjunction with corporate employers, offered courses for women on money management, shopping, frugal homemaking, childrearing, and hygiene. The Choctaw Family Training Project in Mississippi, a joint project by the BIA and RCA developed in the late 1960s, trained men for urban jobs, women in home economics, and children in remedial education. The assumption that married women and children would be supported with men's wages was not borne out among the Mississippi Choctaw, however. By 1971 at least half of the Choctaw mothers of young children were working for pay.[32]

The meanings of the urban experience for women varied, depending on their prior experience with towns and cities, their education and work histories, marital status, and cultural and familial ties. Joan Weibel's study of Indian migrants to Los Angeles revealed that most Navajo women moved to the city as single women and entered training programs or took jobs. Most Oklahoma Indian women, by contrast, migrated as married women with children, ending up as homemakers. Moreover, single women apparently had much greater access to training programs than married women, reinforcing the employment differences among women based on marital status.[33]

In 1970–71, women comprised 24 percent of the Indians placed in jobs under the relocation program and 42 percent of those enrolled in adult vocational training. Whether this represented an increase from the 1950s is not clear. By this period, some policy-makers and scholars were suggesting that offering relocation assistance or training to women undermined the goals of the programs because women might leave the labor force or leave the cities in order to marry or for other family-related reasons. Men's labor force attachments, they believed, would be reinforced by their family roles.[34]

Native American women who moved to cities were less likely than the men from their home communities to have gained exposure to white culture through military service and often experienced urban institutions, including the urban economy, differently than men. Much of women's work, whether paid or unpaid, was organized through individual households and was, therefore, isolating for them. Many worked in domestic service or in putting out work for factories, especially in the garment industry. Married women often did not work outside the household. Their urban experiences centered around family, Indian community institutions, social welfare agencies, and the public schools attended by their children. Indeed, Shirley Fiske concluded that "for [Navajo] women, it seems that the organizational cement to the urban world is provided largely through their children."[35]

Indian women and men worked to create Indian communities, activities, and services in the cities, enabling many to adapt to urban life while constructing cultural identities and practices compatible with those they had left behind. Although the failure to acculturate contradicted the expectations of white officials, cultural continuity often made the transition to urban living possible.[36]

For most women and men the transition to urban life was difficult and painful. Racism and poverty haunted daily life. A Creek woman who had moved to Los Angeles from Oklahoma avoided contact with whites: "I don't go to the store often. Everybody laughs at me." She wanted to go back home, but found that her husband's wages did not enable them to save enough to do so. Even those who received training for white-collar jobs could find urban life unrewarding. Virginia Cloud, for example, learned clerical work at a Job Corps Center in Los Angeles, but sought employment on her Navajo Reservation so that she could return home. Many urban migrants stayed in the cities primarily because of continuing poverty on the reservations, the federal government's unwillingness to finance their return, and because jobs requiring their new skills had not been created on the reservations.[37]

The poverty of Indians, wherever they lived, posed a challenge to the state policies that had excluded Indians from eligibility for benefits under the AFDC program since its inception in the 1930s. The passage of Public Law 280 in 1953 transferred the civil and criminal jurisdiction over reservation Indians to five state governments and offered other states the opportunity to claim the same jurisdiction. In addition, the principles of termination necessarily implied the assumption of legal authority over Indians by state and local governments.[38]

Among other things, this meant that conservative and liberal advocates of termination supported the extension of AFDC benefits to Native Americans. The Report of the Hoover Commission in 1949 explicitly recommended this change, primarily because the drafters of the report anticipat-

ed that many Indian women and children in the cities would not have a
male provider, revealing the profound contradictions at the heart of assimilationist policies in the postwar period. A 1954 decision by the U.S. Court
of Appeals in *State of Arizona v. Hobby* upheld an earlier ruling by the So-
licitor of the Interior Department mandating Indian eligibility for AFDC.[39]

By the mid-1950s, the extreme impoverishment of Native Americans,
both in the cities and on the reservations, forced growing numbers of Native American women and children to rely on AFDC for support. Their
public dependence—a visible manifestation of the failure of the newest policy panaceas to construct "stable" nuclear families supported by men—
generated a backlash against Indians and the AFDC program. Authorities
complained about the rising costs to state government, claiming that AFDC
families promoted immorality, child neglect, and juvenile delinquency.[40]

Welfare officials in North Dakota, for example, compiled case studies
of "delinquency breeders" among Indians in Rolette County for a 1956
Senate Judiciary Committee investigation of juvenile delinquency among
Indians. The following case typifies the discourse of reproductive derelic-
tion employed by authorities:

> This woman received ADC. She has had three illegitimate children since the
> death of her husband. There are different fathers named for the three chil-
> dren. She has many parties, brews her own liquor, has many minor children
> frequently coming to her home for these parties.[41]

The charge that women's profligate "breeding" represented and engendered antisocial conduct, including alcohol abuse, hedonism, and crime,
exposed the concern with cultural transmission at the heart of the anti-
ADC rhetoric. The subversion of masculine authority occasioned by
women's failure to legitimize their maternity (and sexuality) with marriage
threatened to reproduce social disorder in future generations. In order to
preclude such possibilities, BIA and other authorities sought to enforce legal marriage on Indian women and to compel paternal support for children.[42]

The detailed records kept by various officials revealed the ways in which
"political voyeurism" characterized these efforts. At the Turtle Mountain
Indian Agency in North Dakota, welfare and law enforcement officials
monitored and kept records of non-marital heterosexual unions in order to
"persuade" cohabiting Indian couples to marry. Their surveillance yielded
only limited compliance from Native Americans. The Advisory Council of
the Menominees used records from welfare, law enforcement, and other
agencies to supervise recipients of AFDC and others declared "non com-
pos mentis" in their use of the payments each Menominee received as a result of the termination program.[43]

Although the federal courts still allowed tribes to regulate their own domestic relations in the absence of federal statutes to the contrary, in the 1950s Congress passed a series of laws, including Public Law 280, transferring authority over such matters from specified tribes to white-controlled state governments. Moreover, the centrality of the wage economy in American Indian lives by this time prompted some tribal councils to assume an active role in constructing paternal responsibility for the support of children in cooperation with federal and local authorities.[44]

As they became increasingly dependent on a discriminatory wage economy, American Indian women turned to public authorities to mandate the support of children by their fathers, to obtain property rights conferred in divorce decrees, or to attempt to hold on to their troubled marriages. Haudenosaunee (Iroquois) women, for example, used the white legal system to secure child support and to protect them from domestic violence. In 1953 a Navajo woman went to the legal counsel, a white, to complain that her husband was cohabiting with a reservation teacher. The attorney sought to have the teacher transferred and to get support for the children. In other cases, women turned to him to get grazing permits for sheep transferred from their ex-husbands so that they could support themselves and their families with work traditionally assigned to women. Other women used his services to seek child support payments. Like white women, however, Indian women found that the legal system provided inadequate assistance in enforcing child support or providing protection against domestic violence.[45]

The increasing economic dependence of Indian women in less acculturated tribes contributed substantially to their declining divorce rates. As a result of economic development policies, Navajo income came increasingly to depend on wage work, usually done by men. During the war years, Navajos, mostly male, began taking work on the railroads, in ordnance depots, and as seasonal agricultural workers. In 1940, Navajos earned 58 percent of their income from stockraising and agriculture, 25 percent from federal reservation jobs, and none from off-reservation work. By 1958, the latter accounted for 38 percent of income, while stockraising and agriculture contributed only 10 percent of income. By the early 1950s, 98 percent of off-reservation workers were men.[46]

The increasing dependence of women on male wages altered all of their family relations, increased their subordination within marriage, undermined traditional residence patterns in matrilocal tribes, and changed childrearing practices. Navajo women increasingly praised and valued men for their abilities as breadwinners, their willingness to share money with their families and to accommodate women's wishes with regard to their work decisions and family residence choices. The necessity to accommodate the needs of male wage workers sometimes meant living at a distance from female kin and thus relinquishing traditional cooperative childrearing patterns. According to Laila Shukry, younger Navajo women complained that raising children in individual homes imposed economic burdens on women and circumscribed their personal autonomy.[47]

Among the Havasupai, also, women's increasing inability to support themselves and others with traditional communal work or with the limited opportunities provided by the wage economy heightened their economic dependence on men. Some came to resent the property rights of men in their traditionally patrilineal culture and looked favorably on the inheritance rights of white women. In her 1959 study of Havasupai women, anthropologist Carma Lee Smithson observed a competition among women for the support and attention of men as well as a culturally supported subordination of women to their husbands.[48]

By the 1960s, policy-makers abandoned the idea that urbanization would be a panacea for Indian poverty and extended their development efforts to the reservations in order to create new jobs for men. In some cases, however, they succeeded also in providing employment to women. White officials construed this success as failure, worrying that "matriarchal" family relations would ensue from women's employment.[49]

Indian "Self-Determination" and Gender Politics

Women leaders contributed in significant ways to the emergence of the movement for Indian self-determination in the postwar decades. Some, like Irene Stewart, entered politics from traditional women's organizations, like the Parent-Teacher Association, and from tribal social welfare positions. She attempted to join Annie Wauneka, the only woman on the Navajo Tribal Council in the mid-1950s, but she lost the election, hampered in part by men's prejudice against women holding political office. Although disappointing to Stewart, the loss did not interrupt her career of service to her people. Her varied public activities ranged from the distribution of surplus grain to the mediation of various disputes in her role as a local chapter secretary.[50]

Other women leaders emerged from the college campuses and from the politicized urban milieu of the late 1960s and 1970s. The ten Indian college students who formed the National Indian Youth Council in the early 1960s included five women. Urban activists quickly formed links with rural and reservation Indians, links that were critical to the formation of the American Indian Movement (AIM) and other protest organizations.[51]

In the 1960s, the women and men of the National Indian Youth Council helped to organize the "fish-ins" in the state of Washington devised to mobilize and enact Indian resistance to white laws restricting their fishing rights. Janet McCloud, a Nisqually, was an outspoken advocate for the rights of Indians to fish in the rivers they had been forced to give up to whites long before. Her activism meant that she faced arrest and harassment along with other demonstrators.[52]

Women made critical contributions to the movement to end termination and restore federal tribal status to the Menominees. As family and community members, Menominee women picketed corporate and public officials, marched to protest the plans of Menominee Enterprises, Inc., to sell Menominee lands to whites, and gave countless hours to mobilize Menominee and non-Menominee opinion in support of restoration. Ada Deer, in particular, assumed a critical role in the organization of Determination of Rights and Unity for Menominee Shareholders (DRUMS), the successful take-over of the corporate-controlled MEI, and lobbying for an end to termination. Once restoration was achieved in 1973, Deer and other women continued their active involvement in community politics. By 1975, they held a majority of seats on the tribe's governing board.[53]

Their political successes and policies did not compel the support of all Menominees, however. On January 1, 1975, members of a group that called itself the Menominee Warrior Society seized an abandoned novitiate owned by the Alexian Brothers Order of the Catholic Church. They demanded that the order give them the property to be used as a hospital or an educational facility, claiming that it was on Menominee land and, thus, should revert to the Menominees under federal law.[54]

The Warrior Society sought more than the 225-acre novitiate. The dissident group, two of whom had waged losing campaigns for the Menominee Reservation Committee in the last elections, also wanted to undermine the legitimacy of the governing committee. At one point, the leaders of the revolt claimed the Menominees were suffering from a "dictatorship of women." They demanded the resignation of three women from the governing board and the "restoration" of patriarchal control of Menominee politics. Ada Deer stated that sexism was one of the motivations for the takeover of the novitiate, but that a desire for a "dramatic, easy" remedy for the real problems of poverty and prejudice also accounted for the actions of the dissidents.[55]

The gender politics of the dispute were complex. Some Menominee women participated in and others supported the takeover of the church facility. When Ada Deer appeared in Shawano, Wisconsin, to deplore the racism encountered by Indians, a group of Menominee women supporting the dissidents jeered her. The politics of race and gender operating in the lives of the women on both sides of the dispute left no clear path to "self-determination" for either group. The women protestors were asked to cede formal political power to men in order to embrace a specific form of militant activism, while women who formed part of the governing group had their authority to speak for their community questioned. Invoking "tradi-

tion," some Menominee men used a difference over how to handle relations with powerful whites to delegitimize women's right to represent
Menominee people and culture.[56]

Indian men's hostility to women's cultural and political authority was
not limited to the Menominee Warrior Society. Within the Red Power
movement, subtle and overt sexism affected the gender division of labor
and authority. The takeover of Wounded Knee on the Pine Ridge Reservation by Oglala Sioux and AIM activists exemplified these dynamics. During the lengthy siege, women cooked, cared for children, and sewed shirts
and sleeping bags. The men assumed primary responsibility for political decision-making and military defense, although women also took up arms in
defense of the AIM position.[57]

Indian men and women defended this arrangement on the grounds that
the disempowerment of Indian men as a result of centuries of white dominance had cost men their traditional powers. As Mary Crow Dog saw it,
"Once our men had gotten their rights and their balls back, we might start
arguing with them about who should do the dishes. But not before." At
least a few of the leaders repaid the women's support for men with open
contempt for women. According to John Koster and Robert Burnette,
chairman of the Rosebud Sioux and no supporter of AIM, AIM leader
"Russell Means's male chauvinism is blatantly obvious to anyone who has
spent ten minutes in his company."[58]

The overt sexism of some Red Power leaders did not preclude women's
participation as leaders and activists in the Indian movement of this period. For many Indian women, Red Power offered the first experience of
power against racial dominance in their lives. At the same time, it also subjected them to arrest, imprisonment, and harassment at the hands of white
authorities.[59]

Anna Mae Aquash, a Micmac, gave her life in the struggle for Indian
empowerment. She participated in the Indian takeovers at BIA headquarters, Wounded Knee, and at the Alexian Brothers novitiate. She was ar-
rested and questioned by the FBI in 1975 and, she stated, threatened for
her lack of cooperation. When her body was discovered on the Pine Ridge
Reservation in 1976, authorities declared that she had died of exposure.
When her family insisted on their own autopsy, it was revealed that she had
been shot in the head. Her murder has never been solved.[60]

In at least one instance, masculine opposition to women's office-hold-
ing was translated into official tribal policy. The Forest County Potawatomi Community of Wisconsin formally barred women from holding offices
in tribal government. When the women appealed the exclusion in federal
court under the Indian Civil Rights Act of 1968, the court turned them
down on the grounds that internal differences should be settled within the
tribe. This decision, however, ignored the fact that those differences were

constructed and maintained by gender inequality. The only appeal the women had was to the governing body that had excluded them in the first place.[61]

As the struggles over women's political roles suggest, the question of women and Indian self-determination was a complex one. No case illustrates the contradictions women faced more fully than the case of *Martinez v. Santa Clara Pueblo*. In 1972, Julia Martinez and her daughter, Audrey Martinez, sued the Pueblo so the children of women who married outside the tribe could retain full rights as members of the Pueblo. Julia Martinez, who married a Navajo in 1941 and raised her children as Pueblos in the Santa Clara village, took her case to tribal authorities before deciding to sue in U.S. courts. The case pitted the right of Indian tribal governments to define their own members against the right of Indian women to seek redress against sex discrimination under the Indian Civil Rights Act of 1968.[62]

That law embodied all the contradictions in American Indian policy and law that preceded its passage. It stated that individual Indians were to be granted most of the legal protections accorded to U.S. citizens by the Bill of Rights, except those pertaining to the separation of church and state and the Fifteenth Amendment's prohibition against the use of racial categorization in determining voting eligibility. At the same time, it sought to protect the political sovereignty of Indian nations. Some proponents expected little conflict between Indian practices and the protected rights enumerated under the act. The volume of litigation that ensued proved them wrong. Advocates of Indian sovereignty particularly feared federal intrusion into the prerogatives and autonomy of Indian nations under the provisions of the act. Given the federal government's history of pernicious intervention, such fears were well placed.[63]

The Martinez case, however, called into question the assumption that the maintenance of legal sovereignty by established Indian governments offered empowerment to Indian women. It also raised complex issues regarding the connections between legal sovereignty and Indian cultural autonomy in a context where culture is contested and its construction cannot be conflated with the actions of government. It revealed the dilemma encountered by women who are charged with reproducing culture by raising children within that culture while being excluded from participating as equals in the tribal government officially recognized as the authorized voice of that culture.

In 1939, the Santa Clara Pueblo Tribal Council amended its constitution so that women who married outside of the tribe would not be able to convey tribal membership or property rights to their children. The children of Santa Clara men who married outside retained their rights to land use and tribal participation. Proponents of the amendment, then and later, claimed that it was necessary because tribal lands were being lost to "outsiders"—that is, the husbands and children of those Santa Clara women who married outside the Santa Clara community—and those lands were essential for the cultural and economic viability of the Pueblo. Ethnographic accounts, however, reveal that although marriage outside the Pueblo was increasing for both women and men, the numbers of Santa Clara women who remained in the Pueblo after marrying outsiders was quite small.[64]

Because the Santa Clara Pueblos had become patrilineal and patrilocal under Spanish rule, many women lacked the property base to remain in their village unless they married within the group. As a result, estimates of the number of women marrying other Indians who stayed at Santa Clara varied from two to four in the late 1920s to four in the early 1940s. The case for the tribal government, however, hinged on its assertion that a patrilineal property system was necessary to preserve its cultural identity and economic well-being.[65]

Basing its decision on respect for tribal sovereignty and custom and on the law's failure to specify forms of relief in such a case, the Supreme Court upheld the right of the Santa Clara Pueblo to discriminate against women in defining tribal membership. The strength of official Indian opinion was reflected in the decision by the National Tribal Chairmen's Association, the All Pueblo Council, and various other Indian governments to submit *amicus curiae* briefs in support of the Santa Clara Pueblo. Yet many of the tribal councils authorized to speak for Indian cultures (not including that of the Santa Clara Pueblo) had been based on Western models and created under the auspices of the federally sponsored Indian New Deal. The men who controlled these governing bodies balked at supporting gender equality in politics and culture, deeming it an alien imposition, while using Western "democratic" institutions to authorize their definitions of tradition.[66]

Moreover, the Supreme Court reversed a federal appellate court decision in favor of Julia and Audrey Martinez that had taken seriously the importance of changes in the meanings of "tradition" in a new context, concluding that the 1939 amendment was passed "to deal with an unprecedented phenomenon, namely mixed marriages on a relatively wide scale" and that it was "a product of economics and pragmatics" rather than tradition. The court also noted that the Martinez children had been raised as Santa Claras, spoke the native Tewa language, and functioned on a daily basis as members of the culture. Under the ordinance, the children of Santa Clara men who were raised outside the culture could claim the identity and prerogatives of tribal members without participating in or understanding Santa Clara culture. In finding for the Martinez family, the court stated that "The Tribe has not shown how such an incongruous and unreasonable result fosters and promotes cultural survival."[67]

The Martinez case revealed the ways in which Indian men could selectively appropriate and resist the politics of the dominant society, without having their legitimacy as Indians brought into question while Indian women's right to assert their values and interests as Indians and as women remained suspect. By the 1970s, the defense of tradition and the defense of the prerogatives of male-dominated tribal political bodies had become conflated, leaving some women with an impossible choice between deferring to Indian male authority or appealing to a white power structure historically hostile to Indian interests.[68]

That white power structure contained its own contradictions. As Catherine MacKinnon noted, federal respect for Indian sovereignty was more pronounced when that sovereignty protected property in women than in other instances: "Perhaps the control of Indian women matters less to the United States than does the control of land, fish, minerals, and foreign relations, as to which tribes are not as sovereign."[69]

Nothing revealed the hypocrisy of the government's profession of respect for cultural autonomy more than its practice of sterilizing Indian women and other poor women and women of color without their knowledge or informed consent, a practice that reached its height in the 1970s. Doctors, welfare officials, and other government agents engaged in a variety of practices to coerce such women into tubal ligations and hysterectomies for contraceptive purposes. In order to secure women's permission to be sterilized, officials withheld information that sterilization was irreversible or that other contraceptive means were available, sought consent during or after labor, and threatened to withhold welfare, Medicaid, or other benefits or to take their children. The fact that only women were forced to undergo the regulation of their bodies, reproductivity, and sexuality entailed in forced sterilization reveals the sexism that pervaded these policies.[70]

Native American women experienced such abuses in especially large numbers, the victims of racist assumptions about Indian cultures, the power of the Indian Health Service in their lives, and of prejudice against the poor, especially those receiving welfare payments. It is impossible to ascertain how many Indian women were victimized in this way. One study estimated that one-fourth of all Indian women of childbearing age had been sterilized.[71]

Dr. Connie Uri, who was Choctaw and Cherokee, reported one of the many cases that came to her attention. A Native American woman was given a complete hysterectomy for contraceptive purposes at the age of 20 because she was an alcoholic who could not care for the two children she already had. At the age of 26, she was sober and engaged to be married. She sought medical assistance, but found that there was nothing that could be done to reverse the surgery or the physical, emotional, and social damage it caused.[72]

In response, American Indians, African Americans, Mexican Americans, feminists, socialists, and others organized to demand an end to sterilization abuse. In 1978, the federal government issued new regulations requiring written, informed consent for sterilizations and barring past abuses, including the practice of securing "consent" during or after childbirth or abortion. This change did not occur because policy-makers suddenly decided to respect the cultural autonomy or bodily integrity of women of color. An effective coalition, including women from AIM and from the Native American Women's Caucus, forced the government to monitor medical authorities closely with regard to sterilization procedures.[73]

The increasing power of the welfare state in the regulation of American Indian women's maternity took another form in this period. Many lost custody of their children when white officials decided to place them in foster homes, institutions, or in adoptive homes. In South Dakota, for example, Indian children were 20 times more likely to be placed in foster care than white children. The vast majority of Indian children removed from their families found themselves placed in white households, primarily because whites had more of the economic resources authorities deemed critical to good parenting. Mary Crow Dog, a Lakota Sioux, concluded, "A flush toilet to a white social worker is more important than a good grandmother."[74]

The extreme poverty of Indians, cultural differences over parenting practices, and the superior political power of whites resulted in the removal of from one-fourth to one-third of Indian children from their families for at least part of their lives in this period. The childrearing responsibilities assumed by extended families in Indian cultures, for example, sometimes caused white officials to conclude that children living apart from their parents were neglected or abandoned. In other cases, cultural differences over appropriate means of punishment and supervision prompted authorities to conclude that Indian children were not being adequately disciplined. Some Indian women were deceived into signing documents that turned out to be adoption papers for their children.[75]

As early as 1970 Indian activists began documenting the crisis in cultural reproduction caused by the loss of so many children to their families and communities. Years of organizing, lobbying, and lawsuits followed, culminating in the passage of the Indian Child Welfare Act of 1978. The law mandates informed consent for parents giving up custody of their children, gives tribes sole jurisdiction over custody of reservation children, requires that families and tribes be notified of proceedings affecting off-reservation children, enables tribes to intervene in state actions, and gives Indians preference for custody of Indian children.[76]

Although most activists understandably pointed to the ramifications of child removal for the survival of Indian cultures, the loss of children clearly had special implications for women. In a context where women still assumed primary responsibility for childrearing, state removal of children was an especially painful and disempowering experience. Moreover, the erosion of maternal authority diminished women's power in shaping the values of their communities.

Not all Indian child removals were occasioned by racism and class bias in social welfare policy. Some Indians were poorly equipped to handle their family responsibilities, disabled by poverty, ignorance, and illness, including alcoholism. Acknowledging the problems in these families confounds a simple social control explanation for the child placement decisions of state officials. At the same time, the failure of policy-makers to provide adequate family services to Indian communities points to their complicity in the weakening of Indian families.[77]

Nothing reveals more clearly the complexity of gender and reproductive issues in Native American communities than the crisis occasioned by rising rates of fetal alcohol syndrome (FAS). Persons born with FAS, which is most commonly and directly associated with the consumption of alcohol by pregnant women, exhibit a variety of mental and physical defects. The most important of these derive from damage to the central nervous system resulting in seriously impaired intellectual functioning.[78]

Those children and adults who are seriously impaired by FAS cannot function independently. The incidence of FAS varies widely among Indian groups, but in some reservations it may involve up to 25 percent of children. Their needs for constant supervision and assistance and for special educational programs have created a crisis of dependency in many Indian communities. At the same time, those communities lack the resources to handle the other problems they face.[79]

Women's unpaid labor in families and paid work in the caring professions has been critical in meeting the needs of FAS victims. The toll taken on them and others affected by the crisis has been extraordinary. Many who are laboring in the front lines to cope with the effects of FAS advocate the incarceration of pregnant women who drink; some support their forced sterilization as well. A few tribes have begun to imprison alcoholic women who are pregnant.[80]

Some Indian women and men express great hostility to mothers who drink, especially those who bear FAS children, accusing them of selfishness and hedonism. Jeaneen Grey Eagle, director of a drug and alcohol rehabilitation program on the Pine Ridge reservation, echoed the social welfare officials who linked welfare dependency, irresponsible behavior, and drinking. Noting that some Indian adults have a live-for-today attitude, she concluded that there was "A whole generation of irresponsibility, and I think a lot of it is mothers drinking and neglecting their children."[81]

This mother-blaming derives from deeply felt needs: a need for women who can be counted on to put their children's well-being above their own rights; a need for a simple solution to the FAS crisis and an eventual respite from the labor and frustration of caring for FAS victims; and a desire on the part of some caretakers to place great social distance between themselves and Indians who drink irresponsibly. It also receives enormous support and sanction from the mother-blaming ideologies of the dominant culture. As in the debate over abortion rights, discussions of FAS often tend to assume that the women's needs and those of their fetuses are at odds and to view women almost solely in terms of biological reproduction.[82]

The language of self-indulgence often used to describe the behaviors and choices of FAS mothers obscures their circumstances and needs. Most suffer from severe alcoholism; many succumb to it. In one study of FAS children, 69 percent of the birth mothers were known to be deceased. Mother-blaming also leads to the emphasis on coercive rather than rehabilitative strategies to deal with pregnancy and alcoholism. The focus on the importance of healthy pregnancies and deliveries to Indian societies as the rationale for treatment programs for women who abuse alcohol tends to obscure women's roles as adult members of the community whose worth and potential inhere in their humanity, not only in their maternity.[83]

Alcoholism, which has replaced tuberculosis as the major health problem of American Indians, affects women in many ways. Whether they drink or not, they are more vulnerable to domestic violence at the hands of men who have been drinking. Women who abuse alcohol are likely targets for sexual assault and have little credibility in court if they bring charges against their assailants. Alcoholism leads to the loss of spouses, children, jobs, and lives.[84]

The attention paid to women's maternal roles by whites and Indians signifies their centrality in the daily life of Indians and in cultural reproduction. Even more so than was true in earlier periods, white officials feared the maternal power of Indian women. Ironically, the more fully Native American women participated in the institutions of the dominant society, the more their continued poverty and cultural difference provoked contempt and efforts at regulation from policy-makers.

White-dominated federal and state government exercised great control in the family, sexual, and reproductive lives of Indian women, while the national government refused to intervene in order to protect their political rights and cultural claims against tribal governments. Those tribal governments, modeled in part on liberal democratic institutions, were sometimes as male-dominated and androcentric as their white counterparts. Moreover, Indian women increasingly faced sexual abuse, domestic violence, and other problems deriving from gender subordination within their communities.[85]

Through their activism and their cultural roles in Native American communities, Indian women contested these inequalities, sometimes successfully. Their greatest victories occurred when they fought racial injustice in collaboration with Native American men. Their efforts to define a politics to challenge the sexism of the dominant society and that within Indian communities, however, entangled them in complex cultural conflicts.

"Recovering the Feminine" and the Politics of Gender

Most Native American women have regarded the feminist movement as something deriving from and serving the interests and concerns of white women. Some feared that organizational and political separatism focusing on women's issues might be divisive and detract from the struggle against racial oppression. Many stated that they did not need feminism because traditional beliefs and practices offered a culturally appropriate form of empowerment to women.[86]

Paula Gunn Allen, a writer of Pueblo and Sioux heritage, finds common ground and historic connections between traditional American Indian views of womanhood and those offered by radical feminism. According to Allen:

> Traditional American Indian systems depended on basic concepts that are at present being reformulated and to some extent practiced by western feminists, including cooperation . . . , harmony . . . , balance, kinship, and respect.

For her, both traditions value egalitarianism, pacifism, and the natural world.[87]

Allen believes that "recovering the feminine" in Indian traditions is essential if women and Native Americans are to fight oppression in their lives. According to Allen, the "sacred way of the women" has been lost in the face of the patriarchal values and practices imposed by whites in the process of acculturation. By defining male dominance as a white imposition on previously egalitarian Indian societies, Allen is able to claim the imprimatur of tradition in her effort to sanction her feminist politics among American Indians. Her analysis simultaneously exposes the deleterious effects of white and Indian patriarchal power on Native American women while denying that gender inequalities received cultural sanctions in traditional Indian societies.[88]

For Allen and for the Native American men whose sexism she critiques, tradition operates as a political claim. The question of who would be able to invoke tradition in support of a particular gender politics remains open, revealing the centrality of conflicts over gender relations to contestations over the meanings of culture. All parties invoke custom to give sanction to contemporary cultural transformations. For them, the invention of a tradition free of white coercion is necessary for the construction of a usable past and present.

For some Indian women "recovering the feminine" contains substantially different implications than it does for Paula Gunn Allen. Ruth Roessel, a Christian Navajo, claims that Navajo traditions offer equality to women while linking those traditions with conservative white teachings on gender. Citing Helen Andelin's *Fascinating Womanhood,* an antifeminist book of the early 1970s, Roessel urges Navajo women to put their husbands first, to make each "the kingpin around which all other activities of her life revolve." Women's failure to do this, according to Roessel, has driven "husbands either out of the home or to the bottle."[89]

Mary Crow Dog experienced not continuity but contradiction between Lakota men's professions that their tribal tradition conferred gender equality and their behavior, observing as follows:

> The men pay great lip service to the status women hold in the tribe. Their rhetoric on the subject is beautiful. They speak of Grandmother Earth and how they honor her. Our greatest culture hero—or rather heroine—is the White Buffalo Woman . . . who brought us the sacred pipe and taught us how to use it.[90]

She also questioned whether the gender division of labor, in which men specialized as hunters and warriors and women in primarily domestic pursuits, was sufficient to empower women:

> The men kept telling us, "See how we are honoring you . . . ?" Honoring us for what? For being good beaders, quillers, tanners, moccasin makers, and child-bearers. That is fine, but. . . .[91]

She concluded that the men "always stood up for our rights—against outsiders!" The internal battle for empowerment as women, however, continued. Crow Dog found inspiration among the Pueblos, whose ability to fend off white culture "without bragging about what great warriors they were or had been" seemed to offer more to women. Their matrilineality and "strength without macho" appealed to her.[92]

The different readings of Indian traditions offered by Allen, Roessel, Crow Dog, and some Native American men demonstrate the protean and contested nature of culture in a context of social conflict and institutional change. They also reveal the ways in which shifts in social relations within Indian cultures and in interactions with white culture have increased the heterogeneity of Native American women's experiences and the meanings they attach to them.

Conclusions

In the post-allotment era, policy-makers have remained intensely preoccupied with Indian women's maternity, attempting to regulate it as a critical site of cultural reproduction and of socially necessary labor. Their efforts often resulted in various forms of maternal dispossession, including forced sterilizations of Indian women and the removal of Indian children from their homes. More subtly, the decline of extended families, dispersion of Indian peoples to towns and cities outside the reservations, and increasing economic dependence of Indian women on men, wage work, and welfare have changed the material conditions of motherhood and of other roles and relationships in women's lives. As their participation in the institutions of the dominant society increased, Native American women's need to confront the oppressions engendered by those institutions also heightened. Finding a common ground with Indian men in that struggle was complicated by the increasing prevalence of patriarchal values and behaviors in Native American communities.

As in the past, civilization remained an "expensive luxury" for Indian women. At the same time, many were able to use resources provided by the dominant society to challenge its racial and gender politics and to nurture and support their families and communities. Others acted to alter Native American cultural values and practices in order to enhance women's power in community life. The transformative powers of Indian women remained a vital part of Indian traditions.[93]

5

Mexicanas

THE IMMIGRANT EXPERIENCE, 1900–1950

Beginning around 1910 Mexican migration into the United States increased substantially as many people fled the violence and social dislocation of the Mexican Revolution and others sought improved economic opportunities in the American economy. Once they arrived in the U.S., Mexican women and men alike faced discrimination, prejudice, poverty, and insecurity as they confronted a hostile Anglo world and an exploitative market economy. Mexican women, however, found that the processes of migration, settlement, and cultural adaptation affected them in unique ways as a consequence of their complicated position as working-class, minority women within the dominant Anglo culture and their problematical gender status within their own and the larger culture.[1]

Their situation was further complicated by the fact that their migration coincided with a period of dramatic change in the United States. The rise of a consumer economy, the imperatives of war and depression, and the dynamics of gender politics altered women's lives in complex ways. Women's political rights and roles were expanding, their labor force rates increasing, and their family roles shifting. Husband/wife relations received increasing emphasis in prescriptive literature and companionate marriage became the ideal. As a consequence of this, women's sexuality was redefined, birth control became increasingly acceptable, and women's claims to power on the basis of maternity came under attack.[2]

For Mexican-origin women, their place between and within two changing cultures caused ambiguity, conflict, and difficulty. Their different traditions regarding gender and their unique place in the American political economy placed them in an ambivalent position relative to the dominant culture. Equally important, their gender status and the roles it mandated for them placed them in a different relationship to that culture than Mexican-origin men. Although the structural and ideological constraints which they encountered systematically limited their power and narrowed their possibilities, Mexicanas' location on the fault line between two gender systems also created the opportunity for selective transformations in all areas of their lives—from the family to the workplace. Although they were expected to be culture bearers and they fulfilled this expectation in many ways, Mexicanas also used their roles as mothers, homemakers, consumers, and workers to transform Mexican American culture. More so than was true of the men of their group, they promoted changes in gender norms and roles and, thus, in all aspects of Mexican American politics and life. Their actions and experiences as "border-crossers," then, would both reinforce and subvert traditional cultural patterns and expectations, creating the "dynamic hybrid" of Mexican American culture.[3]

As George Sanchez has noted, its analysis entails the examination of the diversities and contradictions engendered by the "complex interactions between variant cultures" that occurred primarily in the American Southwest. Viewed from this perspective, Mexican American culture is neither monolithic nor static, nor is it defined and organized solely by men or by the political, economic, and social institutions created by the dominant culture. Instead, it reflects and affects the processes of change in all social relations which have occurred in the last century, especially in the border region of the Southwest.[4]

The Mexican Heritage

Within the Mexican family system, authority and prestige were allocated on the basis of an ascribed age/gender status with male authority over women receiving a strong ideological sanction. The lynchpin of the gender ideology was a belief in the dangerous potential of an unregulated female sexuality whose power had to be contained through the religious training and social restriction of women. Men's reputations were directly tied to the sexual control of women within their families ("good women") and the sexual exploitation of others ("bad women"). All recognized that women as well as men had agency in sexual situations, making the regulation of women's conduct a pervasive concern of men. To an important extent, then, definitions of morality and social order centered on the sexual control of women.[5]

Ideally, a young girl was to be pious, obedient, and virginal until marriage, chaste after marriage. To accomplish this, her family kept her close to home whenever possible and male relatives supervised her when she was outside the household. The ideal of premarital virginity received conspicuous attention, although it was often met only in a technical fashion. For the married woman, the situation was, if anything, more ambiguous and difficult—after all, virginity was no longer possible or desirable. An absence of sexual enthusiasm, a general obedience to her husband, and a visible observance of cultural requirements regarding reproduction, maternal sacrifice, and domestic dutifulness provided some security regarding a wife's worthiness. The most effective proof of conformity, however, was pregnancy, which validated her husband's interrelated claims to virility and dominance.[6]

Maternity provided the main source of dignity and self-respect available to Mexican women in a system otherwise predicated on a radical distrust and devaluation of women. Motherhood formed the core of a women's identity, the source of her self-worth, and a central focus for her work. Mexican maternal ideology required that a woman have as many children as nature provided and make whatever sacrifices were necessary to ensure the well-being of those children. Although this system of sacrificial and subordinated motherhood enabled the mother to create some moral claims on her husband and children, it did not confer legitimate authority or give women any means to subvert or overthrow the system of male dominance. As Jane Jacquette notes, this respectable womanhood was predicated on the presence (and threat) of the "bad" woman and on women's conformity to the gender scripts authorized by this duality. Motherhood dignified women, then, because it was radically separated from sexuality in the Mexican tradition.[7]

The powerful legend of Malinche—who is assumed to have used her sexuality to seek personal gain at the expense of her people—exemplifies the ways in which women's sexual transgression became encoded as historical explanation and gender script. A woman who was sold into slavery by her family, Malinche served as the interpreter and mistress for Cortez and was labeled a traitor for her "complicity" in the conquest. The legend thus enabled men to deny their own powerlessness in the face of colonizing European powers, while defining women as subversives whose threat to cultural identity and autonomy must be signified and contained.[8]

Compensation for the treason of Malinche came in the figure of the Virgin of Guadalupe, who reportedly appeared to Juan Diego, a poor Christian Indian, on the hill at Tepeyac. Her miraculous transformation of the commoner's cloak so that it bore the image of the Virgin persuaded the local bishop to build a shrine to her. Not coincidentally, the hill had been the site of a pre-Conquest temple to the fertility goddess, Tonantzin (Our Lady Mother), who had symbolized a maternal gift of abundance, harmony, and sensuality. Her appearance as direct revelation enabled Indians to claim a syncretic Christianity as their own and served as a symbol for political resistance to oppression for centuries. As often happens, however, recourse to a feminine symbol of liberation did not entail the empowerment of women. Indeed, it may have operated to preclude that possibility. According to Eric Wolf, the development of the cult of the Virgin of Guadalupe coincided with the evolution of machismo as the dominant ideology and attempted practice in Mexican society.[9]

An examination of the institutional sources of Mexican gender ideology and analysis of its implications for women's power and status reveal the complexities which always characterize gender systems. In all groups, the actual experiences and behaviors of women will diverge in some ways from expressed ideals and the assessment of women's informal powers within households will modify conclusions regarding women's subordination. The same mythic traditions which defined womanhood in limiting ways could also be used by women to assert maternal authority and worth and to enforce men's allegiance and responsibility to family in particular ways. Folk tales, for example, served to buttress women's authority over children by providing "instructive" examples of the consequences of disobeying their mothers. Stories which emphasized the dangers of leaving women alone reinforced fears of women's sexuality but they also functioned to compel men's time and attention at home and, indirectly, to secure the wages of migrant male workers for women and children.[10]

Moreover, the incidents of family violence documented by William Taylor and the divorce cases examined by Silvia Arrom indicate that women challenged men's right to extreme forms of domination. Although male dominance persisted as ideology and practice, women frequently sought to limit men's authority and, thus, to redefine the normative system itself. As Taylor observed, the fact that women are less likely to turn to the authorities in societies where wife abuse is condoned make the numbers who did so in Mexico even more striking. Whether the importance of violence in women's divorce petitions in nineteenth-century Mexico affected public attitudes is not clear, but it is interesting that Arrom found more public concern about wife abuse and a slight willingness to liberalize the laws at a time when women's legal actions gave women a forum for shaping discourse on the issue.[11]

Neither were women systematically excluded from community politics. In the colonial period, native men often took up young girls' claims regarding visions of the Virgin Mary as the basis for profound revolutionary challenges to Spanish rule. The girls' reversal of cultural norms regarding women in public life appropriated religious symbolism from European culture to bestow political legitimacy on those seeking its overthrow. Similarly, William Taylor found that spontaneous village rebellions typically included men, women, and children in violent confrontation with local officials. According to John Tutino, women's very exclusion from formal politics and the wage labor system enabled them to occupy the forefront of community riots and other forms of protest in the eighteenth century. Because the state had made men responsible to the political economy (and vulnerable to its sanctions), women could confront authorities with greater impunity than men. They could do so, however, only on behalf of the community and within its normative confines, not as a means to legitimate political authority for women.[12]

It is, thus, not possible to conclude that women had equal voice over Mexican gender ideology or that these arrangements advantaged women. Even the social visibility and centrality of women's work, exemplified in the metate as a symbol of female industry and virtue, did not enable women to claim greater personal autonomy or dignity. In Mexico women had to marry in order to have access to the land and its products. As wage labor became more important, women's unequal opportunity in that domain reinforced, rather than undermined, their material and marital subordination.[13]

By the late nineteenth century, outside pressures on Mexican village society had reached crisis proportions. American capitalists had extended their investments into the entire Borderlands region, dramatically altering social and economic structures in Mexico and the U.S. Southwest. Within Mexico the introduction of commercial agriculture focused on the export market, and the promotion of industrial development in certain sectors of the economy led to the displacement of many rural workers. These changes received assistance from the government of Porfirio Diaz, which deprived the peasants of their rights to the land and encouraged the use of debt peonage and other controls on Mexican workers.[14]

The shift from a subsistence to a market economy meant that Mexican peasants were often unable to feed themselves and their children through the cultivation and crafts production that had characterized the traditional economy. They were then faced with the problem of increasing income or decreasing consumption in order to meet the crisis. According to Eric Wolf, peasants in this situation have more flexibility in disposing of surplus labor time than in changing subsistence techniques, so they seek wage labor in order to support their families. Some scholars have assumed that the appropriation of the productive tasks done in the household by the commercial sector enabled women to join the ranks of waged labor as easily as men.[15]

Such flexibility, however, was much more evident for men than for women in Mexico. Because they continued to assume responsibility for the necessary labor-intensive work in the household—including childrearing, crafts production, and the processing of food and other items for family use—women (especially wives) could not be spared for wage labor. Modern technology changed the work of the household later than other areas of village life. Moreover, such innovations sometimes involved political challenge within the household as men resisted changes which would lessen women's labor or transform their status. In the village of Tepoztlan, for example, the initial attempt to introduce a mill to grind corn failed as a consequence of men's insistence that the tortillas made from such corn were inferior in taste and that a woman's reputation would be diminished if she was seen taking her corn to the mill too regularly. A second mill, established in 1927, prospered as a result of the successful "revolution of the women against the authority of the men." Its availability saved women from four to six hours of labor daily and enabled them to begin raising fruit and animals for the market.[16]

For many decades, however, it was predominantly the men who sought work on nearby estates or at distant centers of industrial employment in order to support their families. In 1895, women constituted only 0.4 percent of agricultural laborers and 26 percent of industrial workers. In those areas of northern Mexico where opportunities for men were greater than elsewhere in Mexico, some women shifted from domestic to subsistence production on lands rented with men's earnings. As was true of the women of Tepoztlan, the non-traditional work of women in the north was still subordinated to the requirements of the household. For these women, as for most others, the structure of the Mexican rural economy in transition meant a heightened dependence on male earners.[17]

The gender attributes of the developing capitalist economy were becoming clear as Mexico replicated some patterns already evidenced in the more developed economies. The structure of demand encouraged a preference for male labor in most sectors of the economy as railroad construction, mining, and farm labor called for skills generally associated with male workers. In the industrial sector, the number of jobs created for women was smaller than the numbers displaced from cottage industries. Those women who went to the cities in the face of economic decline and population growth in the rural areas found jobs in such conventionally female categories as domestic service, prostitution, and textile work. In 1905 Mexico City had at least 16,000 prostitutes out of a female population of 72,000 aged 15 to 30. Moreover, women's precarious foothold in the new industrial order meant that they would lose ground in times of economic depression, as occurred in the period after 1890. In the words of Silvia Arrom, "employment may have permitted some women and their families to survive, but it did not normally make them prosperous and emancipated, nor was it an avenue for upward mobility."[18]

When revolution erupted in 1910 in response to the oppressive conditions in Mexico, women and men confronted violence, poverty, severe food shortages, disease, homelessness, and general social disruption. Women, particularly, faced sexual and other forms of violence. Despite the formal resolution of the internal conflict in 1917, violence, economic distress, and political disorder continued into the 1920s, encouraging continued migration. According to Lawrence Cardoso, per capita agricultural production declined 18 percent in Mexico between 1907 and 1929. The problem of prostitution, already quite serious, became the measure of women's oppression in war-torn Mexico. According to Anna Macias, "it is possible that during the revolution more than half the female population turned to prostitution to stay alive." That most commentators and officials blamed the women for their plight indicates the extent to which gender assumptions remained intact in revolutionary Mexico, despite efforts to envision a reconstructed society. Not surprisingly, women made up a large proportion of the many refugees who fled north to avoid the dislocations of war.[19]

Al Norte

Once they arrived in the southwestern United States, Mexican women and men found that that region also was experiencing important demographic and economic changes. Anglos were consolidating political and economic control in the area with the result that Hispanics were being displaced from their lands and, in many cases, being forced into wage labor. In New Mexico, for example, many Hispanic farmers lost their land after the development of irrigation systems prompted a rise in water costs which they could not meet. Throughout the Southwest, "factories in the fields" were beginning to replace the family farm or ranch. Encouraged by the tariff, irrigation projects, and the Newlands Reclamation Act of 1902, corporate growers placed large tracts into cultivation. These large-scale enterprises sought to dominate all aspects of their sector of the economy, from the fields to the market. Many of the crops they planted—including citrus fruits, cotton, beets and other vegetables—required large amounts of labor on a seasonal basis. Because they needed workers willing to accept low wages and to be available at precisely the right time in the crop cycle, the growers tended to define anything less than a sizable surplus of workers as a labor shortage. Through various growers' associations, they secured this labor supply and control over labor relations.[20]

For a variety of reasons, the growers became convinced that the Mexican immigrant met their labor needs. The native-born southwestern Hispanics displaced by economic changes were not numerous enough to meet the demand. In order to secure their profits, growers needed a large labor force sufficiently desperate and powerless that it would accept the conditions they were imposing. The use of aliens who could not readily influence the politics of the host country and who would not demand an "American" standard of living seemed an ideal solution. Moreover, their status as noncitizen migrants made them useful as a buffer for native-born Anglos against the vicissitudes of the American economy. Welcomed in times of prosperity as a cheap and tractable labor force for agricultural wage labor and some blue-collar and service work, and then "repatriated" during the Depression of the 1930s, Mexicans found their economic and political status within the U.S. to be dependent on the requirements of structures they could not control.[21]

For women as for men, the circumstances of their arrival were a cause and consequence of larger historical processes. From the beginning, however, Mexican women's migration experiences have differed in some important ways from those of men. Immigration policies, cultural norms, and the structure of the U.S economy operated together to ensure that Mexican women who migrated were much more likely to be married than Mexican men, that the distances involved would be shorter than for men, and that the jobs which women found frequently involved work in a familial context. That single women did not often migrate alone is indicated by a sample of 50 Mexican families in the Pima County, Arizona, census of 1910, which revealed that the vast majority of migrant women had come north either as minors or as wives. The dynamics of migration are also indicated by urban sex ratios, which were lowest in the border towns and highest in the Midwest. Moreover, those women who went to the Midwest were more likely to be married than those who found their way to border communities, indicating that single women were unlikely to migrate long distances.[22]

For a very long time, however, the United States has also served as a refuge for women leaving difficult marital and familial situations, seeking an independent livelihood, or looking for other new possibilities in their lives. Elisa Silva, who married at 17, later divorced her husband and came north with her mother and sisters. She took a job in a dance hall—a choice which she admitted would have been disreputable in Mexico, but acceptable in her new environment. Her rebellion was selective, however. She was not willing to marry an American because "they let the women boss them." Señora Ceballos married someone chosen by her mother when she was fifteen, but then resisted having intercourse with him despite the insistence of her mother and her priest that it was her duty. After he raped and beat her, she fled to Los Angeles where she received assistance from the YMCA. Elena Torres de Acosta divorced her husband for infidelity and headed north, observing later, "I like this country a lot because a woman has many opportunities which she needs." For such women, clearly, migration became the means to escape some of the restrictions of the Mexican gender system.[23]

It is difficult to document the motivations of the many married Mexican women who chose to come to the United States rather than stay behind in Mexico, but they included a desire to maintain family life, increase family income, and insure their own economic security. In many cases, husbands preceded their families to the United States, found work, and, if circumstances permitted, sent for their wives and children. Whether they were able to do so depended to a great extent on the nature of their work. Men employed in agriculture, where family members could be contributing earners, could easily reunite their families. Those working on the railroads were better able to send for their families if employed as shop workers than if working as mobile section hands. Married women, however, did not generally migrate as independent wage earners. To the extent that women were being recruited as workers for the American economy, they were perceived as secondary earners, as adjuncts to the men in their families. The recruitment of a specifically female Mexican labor force was not important at this time, either in northern Mexico or in the southwestern United States.[24]

As the large numbers of solos (single men) in the Mexican migration corroborates, migration was more an act of individual autonomy for men than it was for women. For those men who were married, however, the effort to bring their wives and children with them whenever circumstances permitted attests to the importance of families to them. For all involved, however, economic needs eclipsed all other concerns. The structure of economic opportunity in the United States probably accounted for the predominance of family or individual migration in a particular time and place.[25]

Mexicanas in American Society

For Mexican migrant women and their daughters, the American experience has meant an extraordinary tension between the role expectations derived from Mexican society and the economic and social circumstances in which they found themselves in the capitalist colossus to the north. The low wages of Mexican men and the insecurity of life in the north meant that women had to assume some responsibility for family support, yet cultural norms prescribed a protected domestic and familial role for women. Moreover, visible differences in gender expectations from those of Anglo culture led to ambiguity, discrimination, and exploitation for migrant women. The contradictions between ideology and material reality also, however, offered the long-term possibility for a revision in the circumstances of women's lives, especially in the second generation.[26]

Because immigrant cultural identity has frequently been defined in terms of traditional family organization and associated with activities often carried out by women, including food preparation, child socialization, and religious observance, the problem of adapting to the dominant culture and its institutions has automatically involved a challenge to gender roles and relationships. As such, it has promoted gender and intergenerational conflict as women and men define their roles in the process of adaptation and/or resistance to the dominant culture.[27]

The acculturative pressures of the dominant society had contradictory effects on women's family roles and power. They diminished women's maternal power by socializing their children to new values and promoting changes which made maternal experience an inadequate guide to effective behavior in a new cultural setting. At the same time, however, they sometimes prompted women to revise the gender basis for parental authority in their families. Because they experienced the liabilities of patriarchal family structures along with their children and because they often identified with the concerns and goals of their second-generation children, Mexican women often subverted the traditional family order. They, thus, found themselves experiencing conflicts with their husbands over parental decisions and roles and over the implications of cultural adaptation for the interrelated politics of gender and ethnic identity.[28]

At the same time, however, the circumstances of the American immigrant experience necessitated a strong familial orientation, especially for women. The social isolation of some Mexican farm households in the Southwest and the migratory nature of much Mexican work enhanced the importance of kin networks. Poverty and prejudice increased the need to maintain family ties in order to ensure economic security and provide emotional support in the face of an often hostile Anglo society. For Mexican women, the family often served as a buffer against the vicissitudes of American life. The complicated interconnections of emotional and practical dependency, however, created particular difficulties for women as they sought a measure of self-definition and autonomy in their lives.[29]

Continuity in family roles and power relations was strengthened by migration dynamics. For Mexican immigrants the continuous nature of the movement north, which was interrupted only by the repatriation of the 1930s, meant that traditional values and institutions were continuously reintroduced and reinforced within the Mexican community. More so than was true for other immigrant groups, Mexicans in this period viewed their stay in the United States as temporary and thus did not seek American citizenship in significant numbers, resisted assimilation, and did not establish stable communities primarily because of the mobility required by their work. Unlike European immigrants, Mexicans lived close enough to their home country to make return trips to visit families, select spouses, and maintain close ties with the traditional culture.

Moreover, the Mexican government encouraged family migration, beginning in 1920. It published a model employment contract and attempted to require that emigrants take their families with them when they went north. They did so in order to prevent the abandonment of women and children in Mexico and to prevent Americanization of the migrants. The latter motive indicates the centrality of women in the maintenance of culture and in securing kin networks extending back to Mexico. Whether government policies or economic dynamics were the cause, the numbers and proportion of adult women migrating from Mexico after 1920 increased dramatically.[30]

Given these contradictory meanings of family life for Mexicanas, one would expect, then, that the family would be the domain in which Mexicanas would experience the greatest strains. It was to be the place where the tensions between compliance and resistance would be most felt and, given the structural and ideological impediments to effective revision of power relations, the locus for informal and indirect attempts to enhance their security and dignity. Because of this, historical assessments will inevitably be rendered difficult. These women often hid from themselves and others (most notably, their husbands) the extent of their dissent, relying instead on covert and ambiguous mechanisms to effect their goals. Thus, some wives in Richard Thurston's study of a Los Angeles-area working-class Mexican community disguised their familial power with claims that their husbands made the decisions or shared in them.[31]

Mexicanas and Material Resources

Mexicanas' family roles, status, and power were shaped in important ways by their material circumstances in the wage economy of the United States. They found that they could secure a livelihood for themselves and their children through paid labor, gaining access to the wages of others (usually men), and, beginning in the 1930s, through various transfer payments provided by the welfare state. The poverty of Mexican men and the consequent fragility of the Mexicano family meant that the earnings of relatives were not always reliably available to women or adequate to their needs. Mexicanas' utility as a very low-wage labor force and racial discrimination in public assistance policies meant that neither wages nor welfare compensated sufficiently for the inability of family to serve as a source of support.[32]

Once they had arrived in the United States, Mexican women found that their place in the American economy was at the bottom of the ladder. In the first few decades of this century, employers encouraged Mexican migration into the Southwest in order to secure low-wage laborers in agriculture, mining, construction, and on the railroads. Given that the primary goal was the recruitment of adult male workers, especially for non-agricultural work, Mexican women had to find work in the fields or at the bottom of an underdeveloped urban female labor force. Within the urban sector, Mexican women could be found primarily in service work (especially domestic service), garment-making, food processing, and other such low-paid work.[33]

In the 1910s and 1920s, intensive agriculture in the Southwest expanded rapidly, with the result that the number of jobs available in field work and food processing increased substantially. In order to secure a more stable male labor force, agricultural employers encouraged the migration and employment of families. The family system also provided them with a labor force which was—at least initially—large, relatively tractable, and willing to accept low wages, even for adult males, because the family wage economy would allow its members a subsistence living. Such practices also ensured an available labor force of women and children for the most labor intensive work in the fields, jobs which male workers often refused to do because of the incredibly low return on their labor. Men mediated this system of farm labor, serving as labor recruiters and crew leaders for the growers and representing the family wage group to the employer. In agricultural wage work, women were hired as members of a family group and pay was collected by male family heads. Many female heads of household from migrant families found it difficult to secure needed work in the fields without the presence of an adult male.[34]

Because of the assumption that women were less productive, hourly wages and acreage allotments were often lower for women than for men in field work. Growers in Dimmit County, Texas, paid women and children 10 cents an hour for non-contract work, while paying men 13 to 14 cents per hour. In the beet industry, where workers were paid on the basis of acreage tended and the annual wages were especially low, growers assumed that women could tend only 75 percent of the acreage assigned to a man, thus effectively reducing the amount available for any family to work. Whether women actually were less productive in the fields is not clear— Paul Taylor reported that some women were faster workers in the onion fields of Texas than men. For obvious reasons, the growers never tested their assumptions regarding women's efficiency. Workers on strike in the cantaloupe fields of Arizona, however, included in their demands the goal of equal hourly wages for women and men.[35]

Whether women worked in the fields depended less on the level of return for their labor, which was inevitably low, than on their age and family situation. In Ruth Allen's study of Mexican rural women in Texas, she found that mothers who worked in agriculture had fewer children than those who did not. The critical variable was clearly the presence of older children, who could substitute for their mother as earners, rather than the numbers of younger children who might need their mother's care. Women field workers had 2.6 children under the age of 15, while homemakers averaged 2.4. In the rural economy, a high fertility strategy was clearly economically reasonable as well as culturally congenial.[36]

The demand for Mexicanas in manufacturing categories resulted from the growth of industries which had traditionally employed women. In California, especially, the food processing industry grew in conjunction with the rise of agribusiness. When labor unrest in eastern cities sent employers in search of a more tractable labor force, garment-making began to expand in the Southwest. That these employers were seeking out a specifically Hispanic labor force is indicated by the fact that garment factories were often located in Mexican neighborhoods in southwestern cities. During World War II, one San Antonio garment employer was investigated for discrimination against Anglo women because a complainant had charged that he hired only Hispanics.[37]

Another important source of employment for Mexicanas was domestic service, although such work was often regarded with suspicion because it removed women workers from family supervision. Whether such cultural preferences could be enforced depended in part on the structure of local economies. In places like San Antonio, where the presence of black women created an alternative source of domestic servants and Mexicanas had access to work in manufacturing, the number of Hispanic women in service was relatively small. In the rural areas, however, and in some urban centers, Mexicanas, especially those who were unmarried or foreign-born, took jobs as domestics. Not surprisingly, the wages were low—$3.50 to 4.50 for a seven-day week in South Texas.[38]

The difficulties created by an exploitative economy were exacerbated by further limitations on women's work choices deriving from strongly held cultural values. Despite the very low wages received by Mexican men and the large number of dependents in Mexican families, the men often believed that women's employment constituted a direct threat to their familial authority. A Mexican printer in Chicago asserted that "if our wives went to work, they would meet some other men and would go away with them; I would not blame my wife, I would blame myself, because I have control of her." As a result, most married Mexican women took work outside the home only as a last, desperate necessity. A Children's Bureau study of sugar beet laborers in Colorado in 1939, for example, found that 33 percent of the Spanish-speaking mothers in migrant families worked in the fields, while 83 percent of the Russian-German mothers were engaged in agricultural wage work. These dramatic differences held even when taking into account the numbers and ages of minor children.[39]

Those urban wives who had to supplement meager family incomes frequently did so by doing home work, which included laundry, sewing, and other forms of home industries; cooking foods to sell on the streets; or taking in boarders and lodgers. Such activities yielded very low earnings. A Bureau of Labor Statistics study of 90 Mexican families in Los Angeles in the 1930s found that wives worked in only 28 of the households and that 10 of them were engaged in home-based work. One-half of the working wives contributed less than 20 percent of family incomes. According to George Sanchez, working children in Mexican American households were often able to contribute much more substantially to family incomes.[40]

Despite the fact that 21 of the households included a grandmother, only two wives in these families sought employment outside of the home. Obviously, some of these grandmothers were not able to take on the responsibilities of homemaking and child care, but that so few wives in this situation were employed indicates that neither husbands' earnings nor wives' domestic work loads are sufficient to explain employment patterns. Only those few wives who worked regularly in factories contributed a substantial proportion of their families' income. Within these families, adult male incomes tended to be especially low and irregular.[41]

Mexican immigrant women found, then, that southwestern economic structures, migration dynamics, and Mexican family structures and values reinforced each other through the 1930s. The presence of large numbers of minority group women available on employers' terms for secondary sector work—especially in culturally congenial home work—attracted capital in the food processing and garment industries. Whether employed in the rural or urban sector, Mexicanas found themselves limited to jobs which were labor-intensive, seasonal, insecure, and low-paid. As a result, they were especially vulnerable to structural unemployment caused by economic crisis, technological change, or changes in public policy. As is always the case with workers in secondary sector jobs, they faced a situation in which collective efforts to improve their conditions prompted determined employer resistance. Because their desperate plight necessitated action, Chicanas often assumed a prominent role in the bitter labor politics of the Southwest in this period.[42]

Nothing better illustrates the dynamics of labor market segmentation and the economic marginality of Mexicanas than their experiences during

the Great Depression of the 1930s. A 1936 study by the U.S. Women's Bureau of working women in Texas revealed that most Mexican women found
work only within a narrow range of occupations in the female labor force
and were more likely than Anglo or black women to be employed in industrial home work. Moreover, their pay levels were significantly below
those of Anglo women, "even when working side by side in the same occupation and establishment." Mexican women reported a median weekly
salary of $5.85, while Anglo women received $8.75. More than one-half
of the Mexican industrial home workers earned less than 5 cents an hour
for their labors. One 19-year-old woman was the sole support of her unemployed sister and her mother, who was confined to her bed with tuberculosis. She told the investigators, "[I] can't live on what I make; the prices
are lower each time I get a bundle. What can I do?"[43]

Although the rigidity of the historic division of paid work between
women and men did reserve female-dominated work categories for women
during the Depression years, the role of minority workers as buffers for Anglos meant that Mexicanas shared with the men of their group the vulnerability created by racial discrimination. Encouraged to migrate during periods of prosperity as a convenient labor supply for low-wage work,
especially in southwestern agriculture, Mexicans found themselves regarded as unwanted competitors in this country when large-scale unemployment made Anglo workers available for their jobs. When Mexicans' high
unemployment rates threatened to make them a relief burden, local and
federal officials decided to resort to "repatriation" to Mexico as a means
of averting responsibility for their support.[44]

Many Mexicans had already decided independently that the American
promise had been withdrawn and had returned to their home land voluntarily. Others were coerced by welfare and immigration officials to leave
rather than starve here. By the end of the 1930s, over 400,000 Mexicans
and their children, many of whom were American citizens, had left the
United States. Families were separated and placed under enormous
strains.[45]

Anglo enthusiasm for "repatriation" varied, however. In San Antonio,
where Mexicanas constituted an important source of workers for certain
labor-intensive industries, they were not displaced by Anglo women and
the rate of deportation was low. The threat of expulsion, however, kept des-
titute Mexicanas from applying for welfare benefits. High unemployment
rates, low wages, and welfare discrimination probably accounted for the
large number of Hispanic women who lodged non-support complaints
against their husbands and former husbands during the Depression.[46]

Hispanic workers in both the rural and urban sectors faced the loss of
jobs and the lowering of wage levels. In the Southwest, tenants and croppers faced displacement as a result of Agricultural Adjustment Act crop al-

lotments; in New Mexico, land owners lost their property when they could not pay their taxes. Those who no longer had access to the land sought wage labor in the cities or in the fields. At the same time, displaced Anglos swelled the migrant worker stream, increasing competition for the available jobs. In the urban sector, cutbacks in manufacturing, construction, and service work swelled the ranks of the Mexican unemployed. According to Julia Kirk Blackwelder, many women-employing industries in San Antonio closed as a result of the minimum-wage requirements of the Fair Labor Standards Act of 1937, costing many Chicanas their jobs.[47]

The structural barriers faced by Latinas who sought to use legislative strategies or unionization as a means to improve the conditions of their labor are illustrated by the problems encountered by Mexicanas employed in pecan shelling in San Antonio in the 1930s. The pecan-shelling companies reversed the trend toward mechanization in their industry and reverted to hand-shelling processes in order to take advantage of large numbers of Mexican workers displaced from agricultural and other work by the Depression. As a result, wages in this work averaged 3 to 8 cents an hour. Through various stratagems, employers evaded minimum wage regulations by the National Recovery Administration and the Fair Labor Standards Act, claiming that they could not stay in business if forced to pay their workers 25 cents an hour. They also evaded a state law banning home work by selling whole pecans to workers and then later buying back the shelled pecans with only a small return to those doing the work. According to the owners, the pecan shellers had become independent entrepreneurs, not home workers flouting Texas law.[48]

Wages for pecan shellers, many of whom were women, were so low that supplemental income had to be obtained in order to ensure survival. Some workers alternated pecan shelling with seasonal farm labor. Others relied on relief and charity in various forms. When the companies reduced the piece work rates by a penny per pound in 1938, thousands of workers went out on strike. Despite police harassment and judicial complicity with the companies, the workers, who were led by activist Emma Tenayuca, won a settlement which provided a small raise. In response, the companies decided once again to mechanize. The number of employees declined from 12,000 in 1938 to about 800 in June 1939. Because of their structural location within the southwestern economy, the Hispanic men and women found themselves facing either very low wage work in labor-intensive jobs or the possibility of technological displacement as changes in the legal context and productive techniques encouraged mechanization.[49]

Although all Mexicans were oppressed by these conditions, those women who did not have access to adult male wages faced special difficulties. Despite the values of Mexican familism, many women could not rely entirely on family strategies for support. From the mid-nineteenth century on, Mexican women experienced high rates of desertion (sometimes temporary) and widowhood. Those Hispanics who had established stable communities in the Southwest found that economic changes in the late nineteenth century forced alterations in family structures and work roles for men and women. In Los Angeles, the proportion of Hispanic families headed by women increased from 15 percent in 1844 to 30 percent in 1880. According to Albert Camarillo, this was caused by premature male deaths, abandonment of families by men, and/or the seasonal migrations of men seeking employment.[50]

Some women had found that traditional family structures and expectations had already been destroyed by conditions within Mexico. During the Mexican Revolution, many women lost their husbands, while others found that social dislocation in that period disrupted families and made marriage difficult. In 1920, 49 percent of the Mexicanas in El Paso aged 15 and over were unmarried; 20 percent of all adult women were widows. Moreover, the number of women counted as married exceeded substantially the number of married men in the population, indicating that large numbers of men left their families while they sought work elsewhere in the Southwest and Midwest.[51]

Border towns in fact acted as magnets for unmarried Mexican women. As early as 1900, 19 percent of El Paso Mexican families were female-headed. A study of the San Antonio Mexican population done in the 1920s revealed that fathers were missing in 17 percent of the families surveyed, with four-fifths of these female-headed households accounted for by widows. Given that the average weekly earnings for foreign-born women in this sample were $6.70, compared with $15.71 for foreign-born males, it is clear that these women had to rely on other earners in order to secure a livelihood for their families. In San Antonio, for example, the majority of child workers aged 14 to 17 came from female-headed households. Donna Guy's study of widows in Arizona revealed that some Hispanic widows turned to prostitution if they did not have relatives to aid in their support.[52]

As a result, widowed Mexican women had to rely on a fragile system of family, community, and paid work as sources of support. Older widows with adult children could often move in with them or live on adjacent property. Of the 90 Mexican families studied by the Bureau of Labor Statistics in Los Angeles in 1935, 32 included relatives outside the nuclear family. Eighteen included the mother of one of the adult householders; fourteen of those mothers were widowed. In Arizona, some widows formed collective households with other widows and their children in order to share earnings and to organize child care and housekeeping cooperatively. Many had to seek paid employment in whatever work they could find. Although it was easier to secure field work if attached to an adult male, many widowed women, assisted by their children, made a living as best they could in rural work. Others took jobs in the urban sector, as laundresses, factory workers, or in home industries. In El Paso in 1930, some 44 percent of widowed and divorced Latinas worked for pay. Church groups, local charities, and mutual aid societies provided some assistance as well, although for a widowed woman living on her own it was not sufficient.[53]

In this period, discrimination against Hispanics in public welfare laws reinforced women's dependence on their families for support in the absence of a male breadwinner. Under state and federal laws, various provisions and practices operated to exclude Hispanics from eligibility or to discriminate in the level of support provided. In Arizona, for example, the mother's pension law made assistance available only to citizen widows whose husbands had been citizens, thus excluding most Mexican women from coverage. The exclusion of agricultural workers and the imposition of residency and citizenship requirements under Social Security disqualified many Hispanics from Aid to Dependent Children and other programs. In Graham County, Arizona, the relief administrator reported the case of a woman (who was an American citizen married to a Mexican national) who had applied for welfare after her husband had been "repatriated" to Mexico. She, along with many others in similar circumstances, was refused assistance.[54]

At the local level, employers' determination to keep Hispanics available at low wages affected relief decisions. In Bisbee, Arizona, a manager for the Phelps Dodge Company served as a member of the local relief committee. Despite protests from local Hispanic groups, the committee set relief standards of $24 a month for Mexican-origin families of eight or more and $32 a month for "American" families of six or more. In Cochise County, Arizona, an Anglo family of five received 56 hours of relief work a week, while a similar family of Mexican descent got only 36 hours. Mexicanos in the community complained to Governor B. B. Moeur that the amount provided for Hispanic families was "lower than the minimum required to sustain life." The governor, however, was advised that ending the discrimination would cost him more politically than it would benefit him, given Anglo sentiment and political clout in the state.[55]

In many cases, a federal relief fund was used to coerce workers into service as strike breakers. When the Agricultural Workers Industrial Union struck the Arizona cantaloupe harvest, demanding union recognition, the abolition of the piece work system, higher wages, and equal pay for women and men in the fields, the Reconstruction Finance Corporation relief service ordered workers applying for assistance to take the jobs vacated by the strikers. Although New Deal officials in California had initially made relief assistance available to rural workers, in order to support a more equitable wage structure, by 1935 WPA administrators in the state had capitulated to grower pressure and refused work relief to rural workers "regardless of the probable lower wage scale on the farm."[56]

In communities where migrant farm workers constituted a large proportion of the Hispanic population, the correspondence between the requirements of a segmented labor market and local welfare decisions reflected growers' influence. A federal study of 342 families in Hidalgo County, Texas, in 1941 found that the median annual earnings per family were $340. Despite their obvious need, only 45 families had been aided by any relief or work program in the previous years. In the Colorado beet fields, where Mexican families also faced discrimination in access to non-agricultural work in the community and where they were supporting larger numbers of dependents on lower earnings than the Anglos employed in the beet fields, a lower proportion received government assistance payments.[57]

In New Deal jobs programs also assumptions regarding "appropriate work" based on ethnicity and gender affected access to such programs and the kinds of work and compensation provided. An administrator for the WPA in Colorado concluded that Hispanics in the program "will be happier and more useful to society when pursuing the trades to which they are accustomed." Young Mexicanas were thus taught spinning and weaving, "for which they have a natural aptitude."[58]

The federal structure under which New Deal welfare laws were enforced enabled local officials to provide only a minimal subsistence to the unemployed without altering economic structures or practices in any fundamental way. Poverty may have been alleviated to some extent, but its roots remained intact, especially for minorities. Discrimination against minorities and women, thus, was an inherent attribute of the New Deal programs, which served to maintain existing gender, race, and class relationships.

Welfare policy was thus predicated on the assumption that the Mexican family and community would manage somehow to take care of its own. Despite the widespread perception that they constituted a heavy burden to the Anglo community, Mexicans and Mexican Americans clearly contributed disproportionately to regional economies while making few claims on their resources. Their ability to survive through mutual support, however, was held against them, as it became one justification for lower funding. A relief official in the mining community of Superior, Arizona, rationalized discrimination there as follows:

> A Mexican family of the low class always do [sic] in any event live on about half what would an American family. They demand and get too free rent and ofttimes "free" water from neighborhood hydrants and pick up in the Mexican colonies private donations that a white family cannot and should not.[59]

For Mexicanas, the reliability of family support systems was variable. Many who were recent migrants, part of the large numbers of agricultural workers displaced during the Depression who had moved to border cities, or members of families separated by repatriation had limited access to support networks. Moreover, those areas with large numbers of Mexicanas inevitably had large numbers of dependents with very few adult male earners. Their desperation accelerated the downward spiral of wages in those jobs available to them.[60]

For women of color especially the Depression exposed the fragility of their economic status. Victimized by an economy that was both inefficient and discriminatory, they suffered from the inability of the New Deal to bring about recovery and its unwillingness to challenge the assumptions and practices of a historically segmented labor market. The Mexican community particularly remained outside the New Deal coalition forged by President Franklin Roosevelt. Because most were not citizens and many regarded their stay in the United States as a temporary one, they lacked the organization and political base to influence the political process. Instead, they became scapegoats for the inability of the American political economy to solve its problems as federal and local officials collaborated on the so-called repatriation of tens of thousands of Mexicans and Mexican Americans to an even more depressed Mexican economy.[61]

The aging of the Mexican migrant population, the high rate of widowhood, and other trends meant that young adult Mexican American women experienced increasing pressure to secure paid work in the 1930s and 1940s. By 1950, 37 percent of Mexican-born women over 45 were widowed. Depression unemployment and child labor legislation increased the pressure on older children to contribute to family support. In addition, the Mexican-origin population also experienced important demographic disruptions in this period. The repatriation of the 1930s removed a disproportionate number of men in the prime breadwinning ages from the Mexican population, with the result that the number of men per 100 women in the 30 to 39 age group was only 82.7 in 1940. Those family members who remained in the United States thus had a smaller number of young adult males to depend on financially.[62]

Many Mexican American women grew up in households with a working mother who required their assistance, either in housework or in paid work. Ruth Allen's 1930 study of rural Hispanic women in Texas found that unmarried older daughters who made essential contributions to family income were much more common than unmarried older sons. In San Antonio, Mexican American girls left school and entered paid employment at a younger age than either Anglo or black girls and married later than black women. In some cases, parents refused permission for their daughters' marriages because they wanted to retain them as part of the family wage economy. The large proportion of Mexican American women reported as unmarried in the 1950 census (38 percent of those over 14) suggests that many were deferring marriage while they contributed to the support of themselves and others. Even in comparison with other immigrants, these rates were high. For all native-born women of foreign or mixed parentage, the proportion over 14 who were single was only 22 percent.[63]

These patterns intensified as a result of social and economic conditions during World War II. Wartime labor demand promoted some improvements in the labor force opportunities of Latinas, especially those who lived in the urban areas of southern California where the burgeoning aircraft and shipbuilding industries grudgingly made a place for some Chicanas in production work. Young Mexican American women often found that their ability to take advantage of wartime opportunities exceeded that of other members of their families. Discrimination against aliens in defense jobs impeded the ability of Mexican citizens to secure employment in such industries. Thus, their American-born children were in a better position to take advantage of new opportunities. In addition, the large number of young Hispanic men in the military meant that family support responsibilities were in some instances shifted to young women.[64]

Some areas were slower to open doors to Latinas than others in this period. Discrimination against Hispanics in general and women in particular persisted in many mining communities and in those areas where large numbers of migrant workers were located. The San Antonio office of the U.S. Employment Service had to be ordered in April 1945 to issue releases for Hispanic women employed in the garment industry in order that they could secure higher-paying defense work. In Morenci, Arizona, Phelps Dodge refused to hire Mexican American women for the company mill, where it had added large numbers of Anglo women, but told federal officials that it did employ Latinas in the company store, hotel, and hospital. This suggests that in many places the wartime experiences of Chicanas mirrored those of black women. They were hired later in the war and in smaller numbers than Anglos and experienced most of their gains in service and unskilled manufacturing work.[65]

The war years also witnessed the creation of the Bracero program, a cooperative arrangement whereby Mexico facilitated the recruitment of migrant workers (predominantly male) for specified agricultural and railroad employers in the Southwest. This program offered several advantages to those employers—it gave them more political control over a labor force which had been troublesome in the 1930s and enabled them to keep farm wages down in a period when competitive pressures operated to raise them. Because the Braceros were generally unattached men, the program also reduced the importance of a family labor system in the fields. In addition, changes in the organization and technology of agriculture, shifting opportunities and expectations for women (especially in urban economies), and the reduction in child labor resulted in a rapid decline in the proportions of field workers who were women.[66]

Because of the costs and constraints entailed for all parties by the provisions of the Bracero agreements, the program also promoted a dramatic increase in the numbers of illegal migrants, both women and men. Many employers were willing to hire illegals in order to secure the workers they wanted and many workers found that they could secure better wages and conditions outside the legalities of the Bracero system. Whether legal or illegal, however, those women who remained in field work found little improvement in wages and conditions. Many employers set hourly wage levels lower for women than for men—even the Bracero program stipulated that women could legally receive less than the 30 cent per hour minimum prescribed for the braceros. The wage exemption did not have practical effect as no family members were imported under the agreement in effect from 1942 to 1947, but it did signify that both governments were concerned only with a minimal protection of adult male earnings.[67]

The loss of jobs for women in agriculture was balanced by gains in manufacturing, clerical, and sales work for Mexicanas. Many who were employed in clerical and sales worked in barrio businesses, but some were able to use this experience to move into such jobs in the dominant economy. Although the largest number of Mexicans were still found in the operatives and kindred category, 27 percent of second-generation Latinas found jobs in clerical and sales work. The reasons for these changes varied, but clearly the improved educational levels of the native-born, the growing numbers of Mexicanas migrating to states other than Texas, and the continuing expansion of the tertiary sector in the American economy provide partial explanations. At the same time, Chicanas' representation in professional and managerial categories remained quite low. As a result of improved opportunities in some occupations, the labor force rates of Latinas increased and paid work outside of a familial context became an important component of a Mexican American woman's life. By 1950, the labor force participation rate of the daughters of Mexican immigrants was 26 percent, compared with 20 percent for their Mexican-born mothers.[68]

These changes do not indicate, however, that Mexicanas' labor force experiences can be read as a simple mobility tale. Most who came to the United States found that inadequate wages for men dictated a reliance on a family wage economy, but that discrimination, poverty, and other social conditions often led to high male mortality rates, the dissolution of marriages, a small range of low-paying, insecure jobs for women, and a lack of access to relief benefits. The moderate mobility experienced by the second generation does not signify a change in Mexicanas' economic status relative to other social groups. It does, however, confirm Mario Barrera's observation that the movement into the urban setting by Hispanics in the Southwest reduced employer limitations over their lives and opportunities—especially for women. Moreover, these shifts in the location and organization of work meant that women would be working in greater numbers outside of the family and community structures.[69]

Gender, Family, Work, and Women's Status

As long as work was organized within a familial context, social control over women remained relatively effective. Within the household, women were delegated the responsibility for socializing and restraining young women, whereas fathers and brothers frequently supervised the activities of girls outside the household. Jessie Lopez de la Cruz has described how such monitoring occurred in the fields:

> When I was a girl, boys were allowed to go out and have friends and visit there in the camp, and even go to town. But the girls—the mothers was always watching them. We couldn't talk to nobody. We were allowed nowhere except out to the field, and then we always worked between my two older brothers. One brother was on one side, and me next, then my two sisters, and then my next oldest brother on the other end. And we were not allowed to talk.[70]

Such controls were much more difficult within an urban context, however. For many Mexican mothers, the "New Woman" symbolized social license and increased women's vulnerability to various forms of sexual exploitation. One such mother complained as follows:

> It is because they can run around so much and be so free, that our Mexican girls do not know how to act. So many girls run away and get married. This terrible freedom in this United States. The Mexican girls seeing American girls with freedom, they want it too, so they go where they like. They do not mind their parents; this terrible freedom. But what can the Mexican mothers do? It is the custom, and we cannot change it, but it is bad.[71]

The threat to motherhood as a central source of power and a mainstay of dignity posed by Anglo middle-class institutions and values made Mexican women wary of the dominant culture's influence in their lives and, especially, those of their children. Some tried to take their daughters to Mexico to secure husbands and avert American social patterns. Others sought to impose rules to diminish their daughters' contacts with American institutions, fearing that those contacts would pose a threat to religious values and maternal authority.[72]

The opposition of some Mexican mothers to the recreational institutions found in an urban, consumer economy was reflected in the popular southwestern folk tale about the "Devil at the Dance." According to this story, a young Hispanic girl decided to go to a dance hall or a skating rink despite her mother's refusal to give her permission. At the dance, she met a charming and handsome stranger who asked her to dance with him. Soon she noticed that he bore some sign of his true identity—long fingernails, hooves for feet, strange bumps, and so on. She read the situation accurately and drew the appropriate conclusions regarding her imperiled circumstances. The stranger then disappeared, and she vowed to obey her parents always and to avoid such sinful places in the future. In one version, the "girl who had been the Devil's partner became a nun not long afterwards." In many accounts, the site of the devil's appearance soon went out of business. The tale is important also for its exaggerated sense of the moral calamity— a partnership with the devil—entailed in her disobedience.[73]

The perception that the flapper represented a substantial challenge to Mexican values was quite accurate and was expressed in a large number of *corridos* (ballads) written about the threat she posed. In "El Enganchado," or "the hooked one," the singer laments that "the girls go about almost naked" and "even my old woman has changed on me—she wears a bob-tailed dress of silk, goes about painted like a *pinata* and goes at night to the dancing hall." He concludes that he is returning to Michoacan and "as a parting memory I leave the old woman to see if someone else wants to burden himself." These ballads consistently link Mexicanas' adoption of the fashionable femininity symbolized by the flapper with a neglect of domestic responsibilities and an abandonment of the language, food, and gender systems of Mexican culture. By virtue of her independent sexuality, the subversive *agringada* disrupted the entire moral order and threatened a political capitulation to the dominant class/ethnic order.[74]

The terms of assimilation of and resistance to the dominant culture frequently created significant divisions between Mexican men and women. Moreover, the fact that Mexican women could exercise power through their cultural roles in order to claim and sometimes establish new definitions of Mexican American culture indicates, as Maria Herrera Sobek concludes, the strength of their commitment to some forms of change.[75]

The complex dynamics of gender, class, and ethnicity are revealed in interviews conducted by Rene Cardenas in his 1970 study of acculturation. The family of Jacinto Lerma illustrates the diversity of Mexican American culture and indicates the importance of social and economic experiences in cultural definitions. Patriarch Lerma had been orphaned at a relatively young age and had, as the oldest son, kept his siblings together by eking out a precarious living in migrant farm work. Despite the difficulties, he looked back on his rural experiences with nostalgia and described his more recent attempts to secure a niche and a community in Los Angeles as demoralizing and unrewarding. Lerma prized familism—and the male authority on which he believed it to be predicated—because it offered dignity, identity, and security in the face of exploitation and denigration at the hands of grasping Anglos. In order that families maintain their integrity, he believed that sons had to be raised to assume difficult responsibilities for which they were rewarded with authority and sexual freedom. As he put it:

> Why should I not let my sons enjoy their youth? Their sun begins to set when they are born. And because they have to carry all the weight of the family, they should be treated very well because there will be moments when they no longer can enjoy life—only the obligation they have makes their life very sad and hard. . . . a Mexican son must be raised . . . [to] enjoy the little pleasures because a man's work and obligation is cruel.
>
> Women are like little flowers and the man is the bee. And every flower has honey and every bee knows that all honey tastes different, and so man has to drink from many cups—that is his only pleasure in life.[76]

His wife, however, was not so nostalgic for their rural past, commenting as follows:

> Jacinto always says that the old days were happy days. He did not have to bear seven children, often without a midwife, in unheated Labor Camps, get up from bed and do the family washing and cooking the next day. I remember the old days as abuse, poverty and suffering—not having money for food, for luxuries, for toys and presents. I once saved all year for Christmas toys and had to use those savings that winter for food.[77]

Her sense of improvement in her circumstances with urbanization developed despite the fact that she had suffered abuse at the hands of her husband after the move to the city, had to rely on welfare for support at times, and still faced insecure and impoverished circumstances. For her, however, the possibilities for her children to be educated and find greater freedom and opportunity for themselves secured her identification with the country of her birth. She defended her sons' more egalitarian relationships with their wives, claiming that "a macho is a man who helps his wife and family in an honorable way." She supported and identified with her daughters' desire for more autonomy, noting that "the Mexican wife and daughter are changing and look for more freedom."[78]

Thus, Mexican women's attitudes toward acculturation were ambivalent and diverse. Many Mexican mothers decided to encourage greater social latitude for their daughters than they had known in their youth. Some did so out of sympathy for their daughters' goals and others because they found the attempts to seclude and restrict their daughters ineffectual in the face of Anglo values and feared that their daughters' rebellion against strict rules would create even greater difficulties. For their part, the daughters had often made a successful transition from the external control used in traditional Mexican culture to the internalized restraints characteristic of industrial societies. Whereas the mothers often perceived the dangers in Mexican terms, the daughters were more aware of the practical limits of

Anglo norms and adamant that their parents were not going to turn them into "moscas muertas," or dead flies, as one young woman termed it.[79]

Some Mexican American girls found the task of meeting the requirements of two cultures very difficult. A Chicago social worker reported that one such girl was "so restricted by her father that she lowers the hem of her dress at home and raises it when she goes to school, in order not to be too far out of style at school and yet satisfy the demands of her father at home." Other girls complained that they were not allowed to talk with their friends after school, attend movies, or go out unchaperoned. Enforcing such rules became increasingly difficult as more Mexican American girls were being educated in Anglo schools, experiencing exposure to the mass media and culture in America's cities, and entering the labor force.[80]

Their mothers also found sanctions for new work and family patterns from American practices. Like Mrs. Lerma, many women found that advocating for their children's adaptation to the new culture necessitated revision of power relations within marriage. Some Mexican women expressed a preference for American-born husbands, who were accustomed to greater social freedoms for women, over more traditional Mexican men. For their part, the men frequently preferred to return to Mexico in order to secure a wife more amenable to conventional role relations. Other Mexicanas sought paid work. One such woman, who began selling lunches to factory workers after her husband lost his job during the Depression, explained that working was common and acceptable for women in America and Mexican women were coming to accept similar values.[81]

For those women who migrated to U.S. cities, access to and acceptance of birth control became more possible as well. Some refused to use contraception, citing religious values or their husbands' opposition. One social worker observed that "the Mexican man does not like the idea of preventing conception. He feels that if his wife is not bearing children she will have relations with other men. Also he may think it immoral. The Mexican women would like to know but they are afraid of their husbands." Some Mexican women and men, however, were glad for the opportunity to control the frequency and timing of pregnancy. One woman reported that her husband was glad that she could get birth control devices because "he is getting very weary and worn out with such hard work as is necessary to keep food for so many mouths. He is a good man and works regularly whenever there is work to do." On the whole, however, Mexican-born women tended to hold to traditional beliefs regarding contraception, while their daughters increasingly found birth control to be a necessary adjunct to the new role definitions they were gradually adopting.[82]

The new circumstances of life in the wage economy of the United States also prompted gender conflict over material resources. In Jerome, Arizona, for example, salesmen reported that they had to make sure the husband was present when they negotiated a sale or the husband would later tear up the contract. In this instance, husbandly control over family expenditures was not the operative concern—moral vigilance over their wives' contacts with men from outside the family took precedence. In other cases, husbands refused to turn over money from their paychecks and handled most or all of the shopping themselves. By the 1940s, disputes over economic control in the household, as well as other areas of disagreement over authority, were causing some women to seek divorces.[83]

For most Mexicanas, however, claiming consumer authority was not the main problem in their family lives. Poverty, family mobility and separations, and strained relations with the dominant Anglo community made the maintenance of family harmony and integrity and the provision of everyday material needs difficult. In a variety of ways, Anglo political and economic dominance eroded women's power to improve living conditions or to claim maternal power within their families.

Most Mexican families lived in substandard, overcrowded, makeshift housing. While Anglo, middle-class women were experiencing a reduction in arduous work as a result of technological change, Mexicanas found that drudgery still characterized their household labor. An absence of electricity, indoor plumbing, and labor-saving devices made cleaning, laundry, and cooking needlessly difficult. A study of 297 New Mexico households in the 1930s found that only one-eighth had electric lights, while 95 percent used outdoor toilets. Over half of the sample got water from hand pumps, while the rest relied on wells, springs, and their neighbors for water in that arid environment. In Los Angeles, Mexican women often did their laundry by building a fire in the yard to heat water and then using a scrubboard. On occasion, families would pool their resources in order to purchase a washing machine. For those who attempted to make a home while a part of the migrant labor pool, the situation was especially difficult. Workers' families were housed in abandoned farm buildings, shacks, tents, or wagons. Not surprisingly, sanitation was poor and other facilities were primitive.[84]

Poor living conditions caused extremely high infant and child mortality rates in Mexicano neighborhoods. A study of Texas Hispanic migrant households found that 23 percent of the children born in these families had died before reaching the age of 18, with two-thirds of the child mortality occurring before the end of the first year of life. In San Antonio, malnutrition and enteritis claimed the lives of large numbers of Mexican children. Public health clinics there reported that 90 percent of the Mexican children they served suffered from malnutrition. Los Angeles, by contrast, witnessed a decline in Mexican American infant mortality rates beginning around 1930, although tuberculosis and other diseases remained quite serious in the Mexicano community.[85]

For those children in migrant worker families, opportunities for education were seriously curtailed. In a study of Texas Hispanics in migrant labor, only 58 percent of the children aged 6 to 15 had been enrolled at all in the 1940–41 school year, and less than 8 percent had attended as many as 32 out of 35 school weeks. A variety of circumstances explain these low figures—the mobile nature of farm labor, lack of money and the consequent need for the labor of children, and discriminatory policies on the part of local school districts. Whether girls were more likely than boys to miss school is not clear, although the literacy gap between Mexican men and women in California in 1930 was greater in the rural areas.[86]

Even in more settled areas, discrimination by politically dominant Anglos made equal education inaccessible for most Hispanic children. In New Mexico, for example, mandatory English-language instruction placed Spanish-speaking students at a considerable disadvantage. Even though all teachers were required to be fluent in Spanish, most were not and the ban on the use of Spanish at school made the ability virtually useless anyway. Those students who did not learn English readily were often labeled retarded, their chances for a quality education reduced very early. As Joan Jensen observed, the insistence on the use of English devalued the Spanish language taught Hispanic children by their mothers and cut off those mothers from effective contact with the schools. Even when they wanted to participate in such organizations as PTA, Hispanic women faced subtle and overt forms of discouragement.[87]

For some Mexicanas and their daughters the schools were but another place where their culture was demeaned and they were forced to change without any acknowledgment of the real circumstances of their lives or the effects of enforced acculturation on themselves or their families. Despite their inequitable treatment, Mexicanas experienced greater opportunities to become literate and to develop intellectually than had been the case in Mexican village society. Moreover, the exposure to alternative normative systems enabled some to redefine their place within their culture. In another generation, some would use education as a tool to challenge their places within the dominant society as well.[88]

In this period, however, most Mexicanas found that private, individual challenges to their status within the family were the only ones available to them. Even in this domain, their resources for empowerment were limited. Within most Mexican American families, women found that men's authority was reinforced and legitimated in terms of their breadwinner role, their control over economic resources, and their function as mediators with the Anglo world. For a variety of reasons, rural women experienced greater social isolation than the men. Lack of transportation, cultural limitations on movement, responsibility for children, poor English-language skills, and a lack of appropriate clothing kept rural Mexican American women away from towns and diminished their access to outside resources and their power over family purchases. Even in an urban setting, Mexicanas experienced a level of workplace discrimination and material deprivation that precluded radical revisions in gender roles or authority patterns. Even as they appropriated some aspects of Anglo gender ideology, they lacked the institutional and material base to take advantage of the benefits or to avoid the pitfalls of the modern revision of gender norms in the United States.[89]

Conclusions

By the late 1940s changes in Mexico and the United States were dramatically altering the processes of migration and adaptation, portending the patterns of the future. In Mexico, dramatic population increases, accelerated industrial development processes, and concomitant changes in social relations prompted widespread migration to the north—often outside the channels specified by international agreements. Because the labor program of the time was almost wholly concerned with the recruitment of male workers, women constituted a growing component of the "illegals" entering the United States, whether they migrated to join husbands already here or to seek work on their own. The increasingly political character of their work and residency status placed them in an especially vulnerable position.

By 1950, Mexican-origin women had become a more heterogeneous group within the American population than they had been a few decades earlier, their lives shaped by age, marital status, class, region, and the length of time they had spent in the United States. Their place between two cultures had had contradictory effects, depending on these and other circumstances. For some married migrant women, especially those in the rural economy, their insecurity and marital dependence had been increased by the circumstances of their northern sojourn. Reliant on their husbands for economic support and cultural mediation, they had experienced many of the disadvantages of migration, but had not been able to explore the possibilities. In many cases, their lives were marked by arduous work, cultural alienation, and powerlessness, tempered only by the solace, reward, and occasional hope deriving from their family roles and relationships. Even the latter, however, exacted a price in sacrifice, stress, and subordination that signified the female debt in a society where women's bodies and emotions had too often become mere commodities in an exchange system they did not control.[90]

The second generation, who experienced both cultures at one remove, received a complicated and variable legacy from their Mexican mothers. Most learned that hard work was a woman's lot and that paid employment would be an inevitable component of a woman's life, although domestic responsibilities and familial values would still take precedence. Many were forced to secure employment at an early age, cutting short their education and their youth in service to families in desperate need of extra earners. For some, this meant deferred marriage (in a culture in which this signified adult status) and an apprenticeship in sacrificial womanhood. For others, it became the means to greater economic and social independence and spurred their workplace activism. That that activism did not usually secure immediate and substantial gains should not lead to the conclusion that their lives remained unaltered by the shift in consciousness it required.[91]

Intergenerational conflict and support inevitably accompanied these changes. The emotional ties between daughters and mothers were obviously very strong, so that daughters' efforts to modify the gender scripts by which they lived often involved a painful re-examination of the terms of their relationship to their mothers. At the same time, their immigrant mothers often chose to learn from their children and simultaneously reconstitute maternal and marital roles.[92]

However diverse their circumstances or values, in Anglo eyes Mexicanas remained marked by racial, economic, and/or cultural differences still regarded as an appropriate basis for determining their political and social status. Although their movement to the cities, improvements in education, and a broadening economic base had enabled some Mexicanas to redefine their place in American society, the successful resistance of the American political economy to their challenges in the workplace and in politics had placed limits on their ability to translate education, experience, and talent into social power and economic equality.

If such shifts have occurred as a response to natal family obligations and the deferral of marriage in order to meet those duties, they constitute at best an imperfect form of liberation. Although ethnic and gender prejudice dramatically affected the lives of Chicanas, some economic and cultural constraints were diminishing for them. These changes were caused by shifts in economic structures, immigration policies, the cumulative effects of depression and war, and a gradual and incremental process of intergenerational change. Initially economic structures and patterns of segmentation in southwestern economies facilitated a compromise between the requirements of Mexican gender ideology and those of the family wage economy.[93]

As time passed, however, second-generation Mexicanas found that their life-cycle patterns had diverged dramatically from those experienced by their mothers. Mexican migrant women had married early, had large families, spent most of their years in the United States as wives or widows, had worked for pay largely within a familial context, and had relied on familial and maternal strategies as a means of coping with economic insecurity and social dislocation within the United States. Their daughters married later and thus had somewhat smaller families, spent their young adult lives as single and employed women, and experienced a somewhat wider range of social and economic opportunities than their mothers had. At the same time, they located themselves, as their mothers had done, within a nexus of family relationships and responsibilities.[94]

Border Women

GENDER, CULTURE, AND POWER IN MEXICAN

AMERICAN COMMUNITIES FROM 1950 TO THE

PRESENT

IN RECENT DECADES, Chicanas have challenged and redefined their labor force and family status, entering wage work, improving their educational levels, and shifting their roles and responsibilities within families. Inevitably, their challenges have been selective—contingent on the centrality, visibility, and tractability of the problems confronted; the resources available (on an individual and social level) to resolve them; and the costs of change. As a result, the process of transformation has been gradual, uneven, and sometimes contradictory. As occupants of various borderlands—between nations and cultures as well as between past and future—they have shaped and experienced changes in a global context.

Shifts in the Mexican American gender system have been part of a larger transformation in gender relations as changes in basic institutions and in the circumstances of women's lives in postwar America have placed conventional assumptions regarding women's roles and rights under great strain. In the last few decades, women have entered the labor force in increasing numbers, have organized to improve the circumstances of their lives in all areas, and have substantially revised their values with regard to family, reproduction, sexuality, work, and their place in public life. They

123

have done so in part as a response to the increasing demand for workers in tertiary sector jobs traditionally held by women, changes in family structures and functions, the values of a consumer society and the mass media, and the political movements of the late twentieth century.[1]

Within Mexico, also, dramatic changes in women's status and roles have revised familial power relations and altered women's relationship to the public sphere. Mexico's continuing developmental crisis has promoted women's entry into paid work and their participation in the migrant stream, while increasing their economic insecurity and impoverishment. Some middle-class women have benefited from improvements in educational and employment opportunities. Many women have begun openly to question male dominance in the family and in the public world. At the same time, however, conventional ideas about womanhood—especially as they relate to sexuality and maternity—continue to exert a profound influence on women's lives and status.[2]

Increasingly, Mexican women, like women in other underdeveloped countries, have entered wage work in the "formal" sector of the global economy. Third World workers, including growing numbers of women, now provide a critical component of the labor force for multinational corporations, sometimes in their home countries in the so-called runaway shops and sometimes as migrant workers in plants in the developed world. Because Mexico shares a long border with the United States, these developments reinforce one another. Mexican and Chicana women are, thus, part of a fragile, international border economy where the dominant sectors are service work and highly competitive old (apparels, food processing) and new industries (electronics and telecommunications).[3]

Moreover, Chicanas are the creatures and creators of a cross-national culture. Despite the incredible acceleration in the rates of Mexican migration to the United States, a growing proportion of the Mexican-origin population is American-born. Straddling two cultures, these "pochos" have created a third—a selective amalgam of elements of both which provides an alternative identity and means to cope with inconsistent expectations. The process, however, has often been painful and confusing, as Cecilia Preciado Burciaga has written:

> At the age of 17, I made my first trip to Guadalajara, Jalisco. My parents had been born there, and they wanted their daughters to understand their world. I, in my naivete, thought that because I spoke Spanish fluently, I would finally find total acceptance and be warmly received by relatives eager to welcome me "home." I found instead, a subtle form of rejection from uncles, aunts, and cousins who perceived me as "too independent," too modern, not the quiet and reserved young woman considered "proper" by Mexican standards.
>
> Ironically, I had just graduated from high school in southern California

and had been told by counselors that I seemed "too attached to my family and that I should not be so timid about expressing my own ideas." . . . It was a crushing blow to discover that I was treated as an "americana" in Mexico and a "Mexican" in the United States.

The rejection was difficult to overcome. I came back from Guadalajara a very angry, confused, and disillusioned "pocha." I then made a conscious effort to develop an identity with this country. . . . There was, however, a feeling of emptiness that prevailed during those four years of make-believe. I felt an underlying alienation that I couldn't define.[4]

As Burciaga's account indicates, American institutions exerted greater pressures on Mexicanas to acculturate than they had in the past. Chicanas were now living in cities in even greater numbers, spending more years in school and in the labor force in the United States than previously, learning and working with Anglos more, interacting more with an age-peer culture, experiencing greater exposure to the mass media, and even marrying Anglos in much larger numbers. With the growth of the social welfare state, their dependence on outside institutions for support and services had also increased substantially.[5]

Required by the dominant society to conform to Anglo norms and expectations, Chicanas also found that many Chicanos expected them to continue to represent and transmit Mexican-American culture only in conventional ways—through child socialization, food preparation, religious observance, the retention of the Spanish language, and, most important, by maintaining a primary orientation to family. As Gloria Anzaldua has observed, women's role in cultural reproduction meant that "[Mexican American] culture expect[ed] women to show greater acceptance of, and commitment to, the value system than men." Women's roles and status were an integral part of masculine cultural identity. Given the dynamism and diversity of Chicano family patterns and cultural life, such a charge created considerable ambiguity.[6]

Moreover, it overlooked, and sometimes condemned, the Chicana's active role in cultural change—a role enjoined at times by necessity and on other occasions by the benefits to be secured through new values and activities. Chicanas, thus, continued to find their place on the border between two cultures to be both dangerous and promising, a site of oppression, resistance, and creativity. As noted by Gloria Anzaldua, a woman situated on the borders of cultures "not only [sustains] contradictions, but turns the ambivalence into something else."[7]

In many regards, shifts in the roles and status of Chicanas were a reaction to changes in the institutional basis for gender relations affecting the whole society as well as a product of the specific circumstances of Mexican American life. The dramatic growth of the female labor force, the expansion of the welfare state, the successes of the modern feminist movement, and the power of mass culture have made it increasingly difficult to maintain values and practices derived from Mexican village society. In addition, the role of Mexicanas in the creation and development of civic, political, and cultural institutions within their community has provided an internal basis for a redefinition of their place in a multicultural society.[8]

That redefinition, however, has not occurred automatically or easily. Instead it has required political challenge by Chicanas within all institutions and social groups. In the larger society, they have had to struggle to secure access to the material and cultural resources which provide the basis for empowerment and well-being and, thus, to confront the class/race system which oppresses them. At the same time, their participation in public life and their efforts to adopt more egalitarian gender practices have sometimes prompted Chicanos to label them "vendidas," or sell-outs, who have sacrificed their people to selfish goals unwisely adopted from Anglo models. Thus, internal disputes over gender power relations have become inextricably linked to discussions of the definition of Chicano culture and its relationship to larger political questions. In response, some Chicanas have claimed feminism as an integral part of their Mexican and Chicano heritage, implicitly asserting their right to define the meaning of that heritage.[9]

Labor Markets, Work, and Resources

For a variety of reasons, many Mexican Americans found that the need to redefine their relationship to the dominant society had become more pressing by the 1950s. Most Mexicanos had become dropouts from the migrant labor stream, moving in large numbers to the cities in order to establish a permanent residence for their families. In fact, a 1971 study found that they were more likely than Anglo or black rural-to-urban migrants to indicate a desire to remain city-dwellers. Audie Blevins's study of poor rural-to-urban migrants revealed that Mexican Americans had lower return rates than Anglos and blacks. This tendency was reflected and reinforced in the greater proportion of Mexican Americans who migrated in family groups. Many Mexican migrants had realized that their stay in the United States was permanent and that their children's Americanization had become an established fact.[10]

The decision of Mexican Americans to leave migrant rural work reflected a constellation of factors: declining demand for migrant workers, the widening of the income gap between rural and urban workers, increasing opportunities for urban employment (especially for men), access to public assistance, and, to a lesser extent, the presence of kin who had already settled. According to Anne Brunton, men made the decision to establish a stable residence, probably because their work constituted the most important source of family income. It is unlikely, however, that such decisions were generally taken against the objections of their wives because women and children benefited in significant ways from the decision to settle.[11]

For those women who still worked in the fields, the oppressive working and living conditions constituted a continuing burden. The work was arduous, wages low, and housing conditions deplorable. A woman who had worked as a migrant from the age of 5 to 15 described conditions on the road: "We all came from Texas in a big truck, several families of us. There was no place to sleep, and some people had to stand up for the entire trip, we were so crowded." Maria Elena Lucas recalled, "Sometimes we used horse stables, old hay barns, and chicken coops with three walls and then an open place."[12]

Once established in towns and cities, however, Mexicanas would find many obstacles to their well-being. The limited opportunities and low incomes of Hispanic men and the large number of dependents in Hispanic families meant that women had to contribute whatever they could to aid in their family's struggle for survival. The continuing migration of large numbers of Mexicans to the United States, legal and illegal, contributed to a labor surplus in many southwestern cities, depressing wages and worsening working conditions in many secondary sector jobs. These dynamics were especially evident in female-employing factory and service work.[13]

As the experiences of Mexicanas reveal, both capital and workers have become mobile in the post-industrial world. The development of the Sunbelt economy has, in fact, been a movement of capital to low-wage, unorganized workers, especially women and minority workers. According to Susan Christopherson, those industries which have abandoned the Snowbelt the most rapidly, including apparel and electronics, employ a labor force which is 51 percent female, while those which are slow to relocate use a labor force which is 85 percent male. Moreover, within the fast-moving industries, the process of job allocation on the basis of ethnicity and gender has been transformed with minority women, especially Hispanics, taking over many of the production jobs previously held by Anglo males.[14]

The gender division of labor in "high tech" industries is very pronounced. In Santa Clara County, California, 95 percent of the assemblers in the electronics industry were women, while the vast majority of engineers, managers, craftsmen, and technicians were men. Wages in production jobs were very low, especially compared with those paid to the engineering and managerial jobs held by white males in the same industry. In the 1970s entry-level wages for assemblers—most of whom were Hispanic or Filipino—began at the minimum wage, $2.50 an hour. By comparison, engineers started between $12,000 and $35,000 a year.[15]

Often overlooked in discussions of women's labor force status is the rise of service work as the dominant growth sector in the late twentieth century. This trend has been especially pronounced in border communities, where the composition of the labor force and the growth of tourism and commerce have encouraged the transition. In northern Mexico the highest rates of population growth have occurred in cities dominated economically by the service sector. Between 1950 and 1970, the proportion of workers employed in service jobs increased from 15 to 27 percent. On the American side also, small towns and large cities have witnessed a disproportionate growth in the number of low-wage service jobs.[16]

For Mexicanas, the development of the Border Industrialization Program in 1966 reflected and influenced the changing character of the demand for Mexican workers. Because large numbers of workers had already migrated to northern Mexico in the previous decades, including many women, U.S.-based companies could take advantage of an often desperate low-wage labor force in those industries which required a small amount of start-up capital and a relatively unskilled labor force. Under the BIP agreement, U.S. companies send parts to assembly plants on the Mexican side of the border, which then return the assembled products to the United States for finishing. The companies do not pay Mexican import duties on the parts and pay only American duties on the value added to the products by the Mexican plants.[17]

Because most of the workers employed in the twin plants program have been located on the Mexican side of the border, employers have experienced several benefits. Mexican workers were available at about one-sixth the wages paid in the United States. Employers could evade American laws establishing a minimum wage and regulating factory conditions; minimize the costs of pension, health, and other benefits; reduce the possibility of unionization; shift most of the costs of the reproduction of the labor force to Mexico; and avoid the taxation required to support Social Security and other social benefits packages in the U.S.[18]

Because the production work relocating below the border has been labeled feminine in the U.S. economy and because so many Mexican women in the border area need work, the workers recruited in Mexico for the maquiladora program have been predominantly female. Moreover, employers' assumptions that women are superior at repetitive tasks and more tractable workers have reinforced this gender division of labor. By 1983, over 140,000 workers were employed in border plants in Mexico, most in the electrical and electronics products, most of them women. In Ciudad Juarez, they earned about $28 for a 45-hour week.[19]

Although some critics of the program have faulted it for creating a "matriarchy" in border families, it is clear that the wages of women employed in these industries constitute a critical component of family income in border households. This is the case in part because male earners are unemployed or have deserted their families, but even if work for men were more widely available and more secure, Mexican women would require wage work. Although some blame the maquiladora industries and the jobs they provide to women for the increasing numbers of female-headed households in the area, most women enter factory jobs only as daughters in impoverished families or after they have been deserted or widowed. As Susan Tiano has documented, women's unemployment rates in northern Mexico (as in the rest of the country) are about double those of men. Indeed, the border plants attract U.S. capital only to the extent that northern Mexico provides a labor surplus of women sufficiently large to keep wages depressed. Those women who cannot secure maquiladora employment often end up in very poorly paid service work on both sides of the border.[20]

Unlike the men, however, they are less likely to become illegal migrants. Those illegals who are best able to take advantage of the U.S. job market are experienced and sophisticated with regard to the system; they have the information and money to secure false papers and employment in interior cities at higher than minimum wage rates. Women are unlikely to have access to the resources essential to a successful negotiation of the system, even on a temporary basis. The kinds of jobs available to them in the United States do not offer the level of return provided to the men. Even in identical jobs, men are paid more. Moreover, women are deterred from crossing illegally by family responsibilities, especially those posed by their children, and by the problems of securing safe passage into the United States.[21]

When women have crossed to the other side of the border, they have often done so on a daily or weekly basis, commuting to work in domestic service and in similar kinds of jobs in border cities. Some enter illegally, while others secure "green cards" enabling them to work legally as commuters. These "greencarders" have ensured that wages in domestic service, hotels and restaurants, garment work, and other women's work categories remain at the level of the minimum wage and make unionization much more difficult. Their presence has also increased unemployment rates in border communities, especially in those economic sectors which employ commuters. Moreover, the use of commuters diminished the opportunities for Mexican American farm workers to find seasonal or permanent urban employment, especially in places like Texas where the technological displacement of rural workers was not accompanied by the creation of work in other sectors. Employers' use of commuters and illegal aliens has made the enforcement of minimum wage and homework laws much more difficult.[22]

El Paso typifies the new migration and employment patterns in border economies. By the late 1960s, commuters constituted 15 percent of the labor force, where they were concentrated in garment-making and domestic service work. In the former industry, for example, the level of production doubled between 1954 and 1969, accounting for 90 percent of the increase in El Paso manufacturing employment. Mexican-origin workers, many of them commuters, comprised about 85 percent of the apparel labor force.

Many of these workers—most of them women, many of them heads of households with young children—had moved out of domestic service work in order to receive the minimum wage.[23]

By the 1960s, commuters had become a larger component of the Mexican migration to the United States. Their wages often sustained families and communities in Mexico. The Mexican government, which was encouraging migration to northern Mexico, estimated that temporary migrants contributed up to 36 percent of the wages earned in some of its border towns. Because their families were dependent on their economic contributions, many commuters, women as well as men, used the situation to familiarize themselves with job opportunities across the border so that they might eventually move to the United States as permanent resident aliens.[24]

Among those migrants, legal and illegal, who come from the interior areas of Mexico to the border area and to the United States, men still constitute the majority. Mexican economic structures, family systems, and gender ideals make it more likely that men will be the ones sent north to supplement inadequate family incomes. When women can be spared from the household economy, they are more likely to earn by selling garden, crafts, and food products in local markets. Because migration requires a cash investment, the greater return available to men in the United States makes it more likely that they will leave. Moreover, the stigma attached to women who migrate, both in their local villages and in the Mexican migrant community in the United States, reduces the number of single women leaving Mexico's interior.[25]

As Barbara Macklin's study of Mexican Americans in Toledo demonstrates, single women migrants were especially vulnerable to gossip and community ostracism on both sides of the border. One woman who had come to Toledo with only a brother to function as chaperone and guardian of her reputation faced gossip regarding her morals and did not associate with the community much until after her marriage. Ten years and three children later she was still regarded as a moral pariah and ostracized by some members of her family. As a result, most *toledanas* had migrated with families.[26]

There is some evidence, however, that more single women are migrating illegally. Rosalia Solorzano-Torres interviewed women illegal aliens in San Diego County and found that single women had a distinctive migration experience. Most had come from cities in Mexico, had moved once prior to crossing the border, and overwhelmingly sought urban residence and jobs in the United States. Most had worked in factory jobs in Mexico, indicating that maquiladora employment was a transitional experience for many young women. They often received assistance from female kin in securing their first American job, which was usually in domestic service.[27]

Despite a structural position which places workers at an especially pronounced disadvantage relative to management, Chicana workers have launched organizing drives and strikes in the garment industry, in canneries, in agricultural field work, and in other industries. Those who are immigrant workers have been subject to deportation by the Immigration and Naturalization Service if they were not legally working in the United States and sometimes to harassment when they were. The INS cooperates with management by staging raids requested by owners in the midst of strikes or other labor activities. The threat of deportation makes unionization of the large number of illegals in garments and other industries especially difficult.[28]

For Mexicanas, employment status derives from the structure of local economies, their migration status, their educational level and English-language skills, and their class status. As is true of other women, they find jobs primarily in female-dominated industries and occupations. Compared with Anglo women, Mexicanas are employed in factory jobs in greater numbers and are underrepresented in white-collar categories. Like black women, occupational mobility for Mexicanas has occurred within the female labor force—a pattern which seriously limits their occupational choices and ensures that their income levels will remain low.[29]

Although most Mexicana workers remain segregated in a few low-wage occupations, the expansion of opportunities for them has been sufficient to encourage their entry into the labor force in increasing numbers in recent decades. This shift in work roles has been a cause and consequence of related changes in family relations.

Chicanas and Families

Given the variability in the circumstances of Mexicanas' lives, it is not surprising to find that their family lives have been characterized by a wide range of values and behaviors. Some women have expressed and generally lived according to very traditional ideas regarding women's roles and responsibilities. Others have made startling changes in their family politics and structures. All, however, have contested unequal power relationships to some extent in this period. It is impossible to determine the extent to which Mexicanas have adopted egalitarian expectations in recent decades, much less to specify precisely the degree to which they have equalized their marital power. It is possible, however, to analyze the causes of marital conflict and the direction and magnitude of change in marital relations. By placing such shifts in their historical context, one can identify the institutional and ideological bases for Mexicana family status.[30]

By the early postwar period, Chicanas had begun to acknowledge and challenge the constraints and liabilities imposed by traditional definitions of familism within their culture. These not only dictated that family relationships be affectively central in the lives of Chicanas, but also required women's total absorption with and within the family. The ideology of the homebound Mexicana was also closely tied to a culturally sanctioned ideal of sexual constraints on women. The traditional Mexican pattern had dictated men's control of public spaces and activities with women assuming a variable level of informal power within the household, dependent on the degree to which their husbands were able to translate control in the public realm into private power. For many Mexicanos, the maintenance of a public posture of male dominance and the retention of women's isolation from Anglo and other outsiders served to secure masculine identity, self-esteem, and power.

Because no family can expect to live consistently according to a set of norms which expects masculine power to be monolithic and unchallenged, some disparity between patriarchal profession and actual family practice always exists in such systems. As a result, many men subscribe strongly to an ideology of family privacy. In Carolyn Matthiason's interviews, for example, the men asserted the importance of family privacy more emphatically than the women, claiming that to reveal problems to others would open them up to ridicule and shame. As one put it, "I don't want others to know what happens in my house. It would be shameful to have others know my life."[31]

Men's desire to control the public representation of family life has created enormous difficulties and constraints for Mexicanas. Many found, moreover, that traditional ideals had become inconsistent with the institutional context within which they lived and with their shifting expectations for themselves. Their attempts to revise Chicano norms and practices regarding the nuclear family—especially those centering on marriage, sexuality, and childrearing—made the definition of familism a source of conflict and dynamism within Chicano culture.[32]

An examination of women's agency in these processes reveals what much of the scholarship on family life and women's power has missed—the understanding that women do not automatically translate resources into power. Their ability to do so is contested by the men in their families with the result that they have to struggle to secure access to outside resources and to claim the familial power which those resources facilitate. As Richard Thurston concluded from his 1951 study of a Los Angeles-area Mexican American community, Mexicanos have not given up power voluntarily, rather it has been wrested from them by women. Even more so than in the past, Mexican American women in the postwar period contested Chicano ideas about the proper roles and values of women.[33]

As Alfredo Mirande and Maxine Baca Zinn have observed, men's absence from the household sometimes contributed to women's informal power within it. According to Mirande, "The male may officially be the ultimate authority but he is frequently aloof or uninvolved in family matters." As a result, some women have substantial informal influence—an arrangement some prefer. Lidia Curiel, whose husband worked elsewhere and came home only on the weekends, expressed her satisfaction with that pattern, explaining, "I'm happier when I'm by myself. Here in the house nothing pleases him."[34]

Such women often exercised considerable authority in socializing and disciplining their children, sometimes in ways displeasing to their husbands. In a social context which virtually required intergenerational change, women's desire to maintain family harmony and secure the well-being of all members of the family sometimes proved impossible to achieve. One older-generation father in Thurston's study blamed his wife for his sons' rebellion, claiming that she was "with them."[35]

Women's attempts to use their informal powers to moderate patriarchal authority sometimes failed in the face of men's legitimated power and men's concern with controlling the external representation of the family. One of Winifred Murray's informants told her of paternal restrictions on her adolescent extracurricular activities, and especially her interactions with boys. She was allowed to join the Pep Club at school only because her mother pleaded for her and because it did not admit boys. She established a relationship with a boyfriend, which was hidden from her father, but which her mother must have tacitly condoned. She related to Murray that her father returned home early one evening to find that she was not there: ". . . I was so afraid to go into the house that I ran away and got married. I would never have done this if my father was less strict with me." Another woman in Murray's study reported, "I was married at fifteen to a man of twenty-nine whom I never loved. I did it one night because I was afraid to go home."[36]

Women's informal power was often predicated on men's absence from the household and on women's confinement to it. This arrangement created conflict because it circumscribed Mexicanas' autonomy and, especially, because it undermined their control over the material and other conditions for their domestic work, including childrearing. As a result, they wanted to redefine the terms of their family life in the areas of reproduction, family relations, and sexuality. In order to accomplish their goals, Chicanas required more control over their own time, access to resources, and spatial mobility.

By the late 1940s many Mexicanas, especially in the second generation, wanted to establish a more companionate form of marriage, based in a greater sharing of recreational and social activities with their husbands. Implicit in the revision of marital norms regarding sociability was a questioning of the sexual double standard as it was expressed and secured in men's freedom to claim the space outside the household as theirs alone. Although often unsuccessful, younger-generation women in Thurston's study attempted to curtail their husbands' philandering and to establish different mores for marital sexuality.[37]

In at least one instance, young Mexican American wives resorted to informal collective action to overthrow traditional social practices. Aware that their husbands were planning to attend a dance without them, the women went shopping in Los Angeles for new dresses, went to the dance on their own, and started dancing with men who were not their husbands (usually a strongly proscribed behavior). Having secured their husbands' attention, they also claimed more of their recreational time in the future.[38]

That the desire for more family togetherness derived from and reinforced a wish to avert men's outside relationships was also indirectly indicated by one of the informants interviewed by Winifred Murray in her 1954 study of poor Mexicano families in a San Antonio housing project. This young wife revealed the influence of Anglo middle-class gender ideology, describing the importance of women's domestic roles for family integrity as follows:

> I do my best to please my husband and keep him home at night. I try to get him interested in sports and other *American* [emphasis mine] amusements but he prefers pool rooms and beer parlors. You know most Mexican men do not take their wives out as the places they go are not decent. They just like to get drunk. . . . In the afternoon I clean the house, take a bath, give the children a bath and fix him a nice supper to try to keep him happy. I feel that if a man has an attractive home to come to after a hard day's work and a good meal daintily prepared he will be satisfied to stay home. Too many of our men come home to disorderly homes and hence there is no incentive to stay home. . . . I have succeeded in enlisting the cooperation of my husband in other areas of family life and I hope one day to succeed in keeping him home at night with his family. The children need to see more of their father.[39]

Such strategies, however, frequently failed. Murray's subjects reported that conflicts over men's social freedoms were causing discord and divorce, especially among the young and American-born. According to Murray, the divorces which ensued from men's extramarital involvements occurred when the men left their wives for other women. Although she does not directly attribute this to women's increasing unwillingness to tolerate infidelity, she does indicate that older and Mexican-born women expressed more support for the ideology of male domination in the family and more tolerance for a sexual double standard mitigated only by the requirement that husbands be discreet and not openly harm their family's well-being. For these women, the expectation that women would remain secluded in the home reinforced the spatial separation between women and men that rendered their husbands' behavior less flagrant and, thus, more tolerable. An increasing number of second-generation women, by contrast, insisted on revising marital norms with the result that their divorce rates were higher than those of their parents' generation.[40]

These women were seeking shared social lives with their husbands, not social autonomy. Indeed, Satterfield's subjects stated that they were willing for their husbands to assume direction over the activities they were to share. A study of Mexicanas done in the late 1960s found that, regardless of generational status, "virtually *no* wives go out alone in the evening." As Constantina Safilios-Rothschild has noted, family "togetherness" is frequently defined so that women are expected to participate in their husbands' interests—sports, for example—in order to claim their time and attention.[41]

One cannot assume, however, that even first-generation women fully accepted the normative power of a repressive gender ideology or conformed exactly to its role prescriptions. Even women who express conventional values have often sought a degree of power in their sexual and family lives. Lupe Serna illustrates the complexities of marital conflicts over power, the tensions between the economic and affective dimensions of marriage for women, and the strength of gender ideology in shaping women's access to resources outside the family. In addition, Serna's struggles at the time of her oral history interview demonstrate the limitations of private, individual strategies to resolve gender conflicts within the family.

Serna decided to move to California in the 1970s, when, at the age of 18, she became pregnant out of wedlock. Her brothers had ostracized her and the United States offered an alternative to the difficulties of remaining in Mexican village society after flouting its norms. She moved in with a sympathetic sister, got a job doing field work, and established a new relationship with a man who soon assumed responsibility for the support of her and her child. She found, however, that he was very jealous and controlling of her, while claiming a great deal of freedom—social and sexual—for himself.[42]

In response, she attempted to express an abstract commitment to Mexican ideas regarding sexuality while enforcing his fidelity to her. She told him that she would like their relationship to be as it had been with her parents—"That I don't *find out*—that's all." At the same time, she expressed her conviction that he did not have the discretion essential to an assertion of the double standard. She stated, "He's a man, so there will naturally be women, but I told him, 'The day I actually see you, I'm leaving.'" In fact, however, she found his philandering painful, threatened to leave whenever she suspected he had been with someone else, and, at one point, extricated a promise of fidelity from him. Linking monogamy to a more companionate marriage, he promised, "I won't do it again. Even better, from now on, we'll always go out together, the two of us." He blamed his actions on women who "offered" themselves to him. "If one is a man, is one going to say no . . . ?" At this point, she retreated to her claim that it was acceptable if she did not know. The problem, of course, was that she did "know" and could no longer live happily with him as long as he claimed sexual license for himself.[43]

When pressed on the issue, he also asserted the prerogatives of a breadwinner, telling her that "he did quite enough in giving Sonia and [herself] food to eat. . . ." Her ambivalence regarding his claim that providing support gave him the right to define the terms of their relationship was expressed in her reluctance to eat. After being told by a doctor that she was underweight because she had a "complex," she concluded, " . . . if I worked, I would eat with more pleasure." Her "complex," of course, derived from a social pathology rather than an individual one.[44]

Indeed, her dissatisfaction with the sexual terms of her common-law marriage was equaled in her frustration over their economic arrangements. He did not give his paycheck to her, but rather held back his spending money, often leaving her with insufficient money to pay household expenses. He objected to her working, although she was bored at home and wanted things for the apartment. She wanted to learn English, but he expressed his fear that she would meet other men at school. She refused to marry him, but her deference to him in the matter of birth control had left her, as she put it, "just at the will of God."[45]

In assessing her life, Serna stated, "The only thing I want is to take away this complex I have. To live my life well, that's all." Hers, however, was, in the words of Dorothy Smith, a rebellion with "no ground to stand on." At that point, her resistance was only partially and privately articulated, but it indicated how profoundly dislocating and painful she found the rupture between her experiences and the discourses her culture provided to interpret them. Although she understood that English-language proficiency, education, and employment might provide her with greater power over some of the circumstances of her life, she perceived only cultural and structural obstacles to their attainment. Her previous deviance had rendered the penalties for nonconformity all too apparent to her and her experience in agricultural work had probably indicated to her the limited occupational possibilities for immigrant women who headed families.[46]

Although scholarship on Mexican women indicates that conflicts over the sexual double standard had been occurring for centuries, many Mexicanas found that American mores offered an important contrast to the conventional expectations they were challenging. Mercedes Espinoza expressed a common perception when she associated her husband's attempts to limit her with Mexican tradition as follows:

> When I got married, I found out that my husband was one hundred per cent Mexican. He was the kind who felt that the wife should stay home—she

does not have a job, she doesn't go out without him, she does not go into the room where her husband and his friends are drinking. Lord! One of those.

Espinoza, who left her husband, commented on the double standard: "I think, if the man is a virgin, he should have a virgin wife. If he's not, why should he be so proud, so strict to want a virgin."[47]

Amelia Villa expressed her disapproval of infidelity somewhat differently, denying that it could occur without damage to the family and stating her claim to resources on the grounds of her contributions as a homemaker. She noted that ". . . there you are in the house, and he's going to be out with some other woman, spending money that he should be spending on you. You cook for him, you wash for him, you do everything for him, and there he is spending money on another who doesn't do anything for him."[48]

Villa, whose husband retained one-fourth of his earnings for his own use, further concluded that women should handle the money because the man "is not going to know what is needed in the house. And I don't like to be asking all the time, give me money for this, give me money for that." She wanted to work in order to save money for emergencies. Ida Gutierrez echoed her sentiments, complaining about having to account to her husband for the money she spent: "Where this dime went, where that dime went! Sometimes I didn't know, and it would drive me crazy. *Hijola!*"[49]

As the cases of Villa, Gutierrez, and many others indicate, women's right to share control of family finances and to leave the household to make purchases was very often contested in Chicano families. According to Murray, the men in the families in her study handled all the money, even including responsibility for grocery shopping. Such economic control, however, was prompting rebellion among some of the younger wives. Thurston, by contrast, reported more egalitarian patterns, although his evidence did not always support that conclusion. In one "egalitarian" couple, the wife controlled the money her husband gave her, but he often spent their money on "excessive drinking sprees in which he [bought] drinks for the whole crowd." His wife attempted to deploy community sentiment against him by complaining about his conduct to others and claiming that they regarded him as a "sucker." Such strategies clearly indicate a lack of marital consensus about who is to control money and how it should be spent. They also exemplify the extent to which Mexicanas' quest for family power in the 1940s and 1950s derived from and was limited by their status as economic dependents at a time when the earnings of Mexicanos was rising.[50]

By the early 1950s, the values of a consumer society had permeated many working-class urban Mexican American households. Thurston concluded that it "is not an overstatement to say that [younger generation] women have burning desires for new homes." They also wanted furniture and appliances to equip them. These women diverged from their mothers in their willingness to purchase ready-made food and clothing rather than spend the time to make them at home.[51]

Many other Mexicanas, however, continued to perform many traditional domestic duties, including food preparation, kin work, child care, and religious observance. As Ruth Schwartz Cowan has noted, women's domestic work often assumes a profound emotional significance in the family. Their household tasks are interwoven with their emotion work for the family. This is especially the case with food preparation. One Mexicana noted: "My husband likes my *tortillas,* and wants them to be fresh and warm, so I just plan to do it each day." Leodoro Hernandez recalled his sister's socialization for her maternal role as follows:

> . . . my sister learned to imitate our mother; she learned to cook, and not only cook for the entire family, but she had to learn how each of the siblings like their eggs cooked, or whether the children like their tortillas barely cooked, well cooked, or slightly toasted.[52]

Such individualized attention provides nurture for other members of the household and maintains their individual identities at the same time. This integration of domestic work with the politics of emotion in the family helps to explain the tenacity of the gender division of labor within the home. The association of household work with expectations of nurture by women precludes an easy or willing assumption of that work by men. Moreover, this allocation of household responsibilities preserves both masculine identity and men's power in the family.[53]

Even within a traditional division of labor, however, women can use their household responsibilities to claim greater autonomy. In order to mediate between the needs of their families and the products provided in the economy, Mexicanas required time for consumer activities and access to money and public spaces. That some had managed to claim increased power in these realms is indicated by the frequent references to shopping trips and material acquisitions on the part of many women in Thurston's study. Indeed, consumption had become a focal point for female sociability, providing the occasion for trips into Los Angeles and for Stanley Jewelry and other parties centered on selling and buying. As was true more generally in American society, women's culture was being linked to consumerism.[54]

Women's desire to make the household a spending priority does not necessarily mean that they had become mindless pawns of the advertising age. Mexicanas generally faced serious problems in this period with housing that was substandard and overcrowded. Such conditions exacerbated family tensions and made domestic labor more onerous and time-consuming. For Mary Ramos, the overcrowding and lack of privacy in migrant worker housing strained family relations—"People yelling, people fighting all the time."[55]

For working-class women, housing adequacy and privacy constitute significant issues in the organization of their work and family lives. Lidia Curiel, for example, stayed with her in-laws for the first three years of her marriage and found the arrangement very difficult, complaining, "I suffered—how I suffered with my mother-in-law." According to Curiel, she was expected to do heavy work, even when pregnant, and did not feel that she could eat all that she wanted. Empathizing with her concerns, her husband built a house for them—18' by 12'. "We all had to fit in there. On the floor, in boxes anyplace, I was tucking children into bed." Curiel's access to household technology mirrored that of many other working-class women—she obtained important labor-saving devices only after her children had grown. She observed, ". . . I used to wash everything by hand, or with one of those old washers with the wringer, but now that I have a small family, *now* I have an automatic machine."[56]

For women in migrant farm work, housing conditions were a major concern. One *toledana* described conditions for migrant workers as follows:

> Most of the places we had to live in weren't fit for animals, even, they would be chicken houses or barns, or little cabins. There were eight of us in our family, three boys, three girls and our parents. Can you imagine us in a three-room cabin? There were full-sized beds. They took up all the space. The boys took one room and we had the other. We all worked in the fields for ten–twelve hours a day, and then had to come back and cook on an old coal stove—and that's pretty hot in August. That was supposed to be good housing. Lots of times there weren't screens in these shacks, 'cause the farmers said we would just tear them up. Well, we didn't get the chance. The flies were really terrible sometimes.[57]

Although Mexicanas were no more immune to the entrapments of consumerism than other women, theirs was not an unthinking appropriation of the values of the dominant culture. According to Ruth Martinez, young Mexicanas took the domestic and consumer values they had learned in home economics classes and elsewhere and sought to adapt them to values and practices derived from their own culture. They selectively adopted those elements which seemed to speak to their needs and to offer the promise of more control in those roles which remained most central in their lives—those of wife and mother.[58]

According to Thurston, the redefinition of familism in the post-1940 period occurred as a result of the desire of younger-generation Mexicanas to reduce social and financial responsibilities to extended kin in order to establish greater independence for the nuclear family. For women generally and Mexicanas particularly, the emotional and financial interconnections of family life created profound dilemmas. Although much of the scholarly literature on women's relationships to extended kin stresses the benefits poor women derive from a broad support system, reliance on extensive kin networks can also exacerbate family tensions and limit women's autonomy. By reducing their financial dependence on relatives, Mexicanas sought to diminish family conflict and establish greater autonomy in the definition of their work and family roles. In order to accomplish this, they altered their attitudes toward some outside institutions—including public assistance and lending agencies—so that they had alternatives to a reliance on relatives; sought to establish a greater geographical distance from close kin; and interacted less with extended family than their parents' generation had.[59]

As Chicanas have sought to redefine the meanings of family in their lives, no relationship has been more emotionally fraught than that between mothers and daughters. As Norma Alarcon has concluded, for the daughter the mother "is part of a cherished and a rejected past." When mothers reproduce and enforce patriarchal power in the lives of daughters, they risk alienating those daughters. To the degree that they seek to undermine men's power in their daughters and other women's lives, they risk the charge of treason to their culture. Cherrie Moraga's comment regarding the double bind encountered by Chicana mothers obtains for all mothers caught between patriarchal cultures: "What I wanted from my mother was impossible."[60]

Over time, the daughters, themselves mothers, began to devise strategic and situated sources of empowerment, often from relationships and resources within their culture. Younger Mexicanas attempted to reduce their emotional load, struggled against the identification of family with masculine reputation, and secured new sources of support by creating more extensive, extrafamilial networks of friends, usually from among coworkers. As Patricia Zavella's studies demonstrate, these friends can offer advice, and sometimes assistance, on family concerns because they are not directly involved and will not further complicate any already difficult situations. Mexicanas may have encouraged an emphasis on family togetherness to improve communication and empathy between fathers and children and, thus, to reduce the stress induced for women by conflicts between distant fathers and rebellious children.[61]

Chicanas continue to maintain, rely on, and value kin relations as a means to enrich their personal lives and to retain a reciprocal system of assistance. As Zavella concludes, "Chicano familism may be women's kin work." Moreover, Chicanas have continued to take responsibility for elderly relatives, especially their mothers. In other cases, as Norma Williams has noted, they have offered assistance to their mothers in ways that enable their mothers' empowerment. As Mexicanas' resources have increased—through paid employment, wider community activities, the revision of gender norms within families, and education—their ability to define the terms of their kin work has grown. As a result, their management of relationships and exchanges within the family increasingly become a cause and consequence of their empowerment. At the same time, a gender-based inequality in emotion work sets limits on that empowerment.[62]

Chicanas have successfully undermined some assumptions regarding sex, gender, and power in their culture. The idea that men should exercise virtually uncontested authority in the family, for example, is less openly or extensively held among Chicanos than in the past. Most of the respondents in Lea Ybarra's 1978 study of Chicano families in Fresno, California, asserted that decision-making power should be shared equally between a husband and wife. They signified the importance of harmony and mutual responsibility by observing that "you need to get your partner's opinion on things because your decisions affect each other's lives," and that "problems are created if decision-making isn't shared." In her oral history interview, Mary Ramos expressed a similar point of view, noting that she and her husband shared companionship and decision-making on purchases "because the woman going one way and the man the other, that shouldn't be."[63]

That some Mexicanos, especially in the second generation, agreed was indicated by some of the men interviewed by Cardenas. Although immigrant fathers often objected when their sons established more egalitarian marriages, some of the sons expressed open support for joint decision-making and the extension of some measure of autonomy to their wives. As one put it: "There is no boss in my home. Most of the time if I want to do something, I do it, or if my wife wants to do something, she does it. . . ." Another concluded more generally, "Maybe that's what the Mexican needs—strong women."[64]

At the same time, male respondents in Ybarra's study did not hold themselves directly accountable for changing their own values and behavior, relying instead on education and women's assertiveness as the means to masculine change. Thus, although Ybarra's subjects indicated that they believed that *machismo* was less common among Chicanos than it had been in the past, they placed most of the burden for effecting and continuing such changes on women. They assumed, as do most people, that empowerment is something that women claim individually, rather than understanding it as a product of a larger social system in which men are central actors.[65]

As a result, they failed to acknowledge the costs, limitations, and impediments to such individualistic strategies. When many interviewees stated that unequal relationships derived from women's failure to assert themselves, they indicated that men's commitment to egalitarianism was situational and that whatever share of familial power women exercised they had to struggle to secure. Although their reports were probably descriptively correct, they obscured the fact that conflict constituted the unassessed cost of such prescriptions. One informant reported that "at the beginning it was stormy because my husband was more hardnosed and both of us wanted to be right. But now we've learned to compromise—unless we get mad." Moreover, the fear that conflict might result in divorce sets limits on women's willingness to "assert themselves." As Ida Gutierrez observed of her conflicts with her husband over money, ". . . you give in if you love the guy. And then sometimes you say to yourself, 'Why, I don't want to be by myself all my life, so I'm going to try.' You know what I mean?"[66]

For Gutierrez and other women, the goal of enhanced power and the desire for more harmony in marriage could undermine one another. The shift to a more companionate form of marriage entailed a new emotional interdependence for both spouses, but did not automatically increase women's marital power. Instead, as Cancian suggests, the emotional politics of companionate marriages may impede women's empowerment in marriage. For Mexicanas it has served as a transitional strategy to increase their autonomy from extended kin, to reduce the sexual double standard, and to extend their access to public spaces.[67]

From Consumer to Breadwinner

In the period since 1960, the pace of change in the lives of Chicanas has accelerated, fueled by a constellation of interrelated developments. Perhaps the most dramatic and important of those changes was the rise in the proportions of Mexicanas working for pay outside the home. This trend derived from and supported others, including improved educational levels, reduced fertility rates, increased political activism, and revised gender norms. These shifts mirror those occurring among other women—especially those of the working class—because women from all groups have confronted similar institutional pressures. But the changes engendered by structural and political shifts in American society did not affect all women in the same ways. Within and across social groups, some women are better placed to create and benefit from change than others.[68]

The motives of Mexicanas who have entered paid employment in recent decades have often been similar to those of other women. Many took jobs in order that they might have more resources for the family and more authority over how they were spent. As Vicki Ruiz has noted, many Chicanas have defined work as an extension of their responsibilities to their family, entering the paid labor force in order to provide better for their children. Lillie Ochoa, who worked while her daughters were in college, explained that she did so "because I wanted their future to be better than mine." One Mexicana reported that she worked in order to move her home off the parental lot, buttressing her attempts to promote familial autonomy with some measure of economic independence. As another Chicana put it, "I think all women should work. It gives them more of a feeling of freedom and they don't have to take so much from their husbands. It doesn't hurt if the kids are taken care of and you're planning something together."[69]

Other Mexicanas have experienced ambivalence regarding their decision to work. Writer Jennie Montoya expressed the conflicts generated by high expectations in dual roles: "I fight with my husband. I ignore my children. And I have all the guilt that comes down upon a woman trying to liberate herself." The working wives interviewed by Lea Ybarra expressed guilt over the effects of their employment on their children. Reflecting the pressures of women's dual responsibilities, one concluded, "If the woman works, the family is not well taken care of, if she doesn't work, there aren't enough things for the home. She doesn't know which way to go." This guilt may be exacerbated by husbands' opposition to their wives' working outside the home. Patricia Zavella found that women's decisions to work caused marital conflict in at least one-third of the families of Mexicana cannery workers she studied.[70]

Many men, however, eventually came to terms with their wives' independent decisions to seek paid employment. Emma Gonzales decided when her children were small that she wanted to work because she was bored at home. Her husband objected on the grounds that her place was in the home. She began working part-time in a furniture store, gradually increasing her hours. When her husband started building their home, they needed her job so they could buy furniture at a discount. By the time she started working full-time, he no longer objected. Indeed, he began preparing meals to assist her, despite ridicule from male relatives who were threatened by his willingness to do "women's work." She concluded that ". . . that's why I'm still working, because he's helped."[71]

For many men, including many Mexicanos, the income added by their wives' paychecks constitutes the main incentive to accept their decision to work. Women's willingness to work outside the home despite conflict with their husbands bespeaks the material and other benefits that employment secured for them. The increasing significance of those benefits to Chicanas and the erosion of opposition to their working was reflected in the large numbers of Chicanas who entered the labor force after 1960. Between 1960 and 1970, the labor force participation rate of Mexican American wives aged 14 to 54 increased from 24 to 35 percent. By 1980 the Mexicana labor force participation rate had virtually converged with that of Anglo and other women. This occurred despite the fact that Chicanas had lower educational levels than other women and faced a more pervasive employment discrimination than Anglo women.[72]

Reproduction was also a domain of conflict, cooperation, and negotiation between women and men. Anne Marie Sorenson's findings on men's roles in fertility decisions helps to explain why lower-income Mexicanas had very large families. Sorenson found that the stronger the ethnic identification of Mexican-origin men the higher were their fertility rates. Children were important to these men as a contribution to "an adult male sex role ideal" which stressed virility. This identification was especially significant to men whose educational and income levels were low, although it affected middle-class men to some degree also. Class mobility, however, reduced the identification of masculinity with virility, as evidenced by a substantial decline in fertility among higher-income Mexicanos. For Mexicanos, then, class and ethnicity interact to define a masculine identity which shapes childbearing patterns.[73]

For some Mexicanas, reproductive freedom has also been denied by the assumptions and practices of the American medical establishment. Many have been sterilized without their consent by Anglo doctors who take it upon themselves to decide how many children poor women should have. Such abuses are most common when the women are dependent on public medical assistance, a situation which gives the state authority and provides the rationale for sterilization—"sparing the taxpayers" the expense of poor children. A study of ten Mexican women sterilized at Los Angeles County Medical Center in the 1970s revealed the consequences of such procedures for poor, rural immigrant women. In eight cases, their marriages were irreparably damaged. According to Carlos Velez-I, this occurred because their husbands believed that their masculine identity was based on their reproductive potential and the political control over their wives which it signified and conferred.[74]

As their situation indicates, for many Mexicanas the possibility of reproductive freedom has been curtailed by the American economy, the Anglo medical establishment, and Mexican and American gender systems. Mexican gender values subordinated women's reproductive rights to men's interrelated claims to masculine identity and power. The prevalence of involuntary sterilization reflects the sexism of the general society in its assumption that women's wishes and well-being in matters of reproduction and sexuality are to be subordinated to the interests of the state and the middle-class men who control it. Because of their dependence on the state, poor women have been especially vulnerable to this form of exploitation.[75]

Gender, Culture, Identity, and Politics

When women are situated between two male-dominated cultures in conflict, questions of women's assimilation and cultural loyalty often become central political issues. Because women have a major role in the socialization of the next generation and because they create the emotional milieu in which identity is formed and experienced, the politics of gender, culture, and identity are emotionally freighted. Mexicanas have, thus, found themselves in ambiguous positions. As mothers, they inevitably have to mediate between two cultures, often with contradictory meanings for themselves, their children, and their husbands. As activists, they have often experienced conflicts between private commitments and public goals. They have found that the question of who is to determine the politics of ethnicity is connected to issues of gender.

Nothing reveals the complex interplay among class, race, and gender relations more directly than the contemporary debate on the meaning of machismo. Some Chicanos have claimed that the oppression of Chicanas has been an important precondition for men's resistance to Anglo domination. Alfredo Mirande expressed this as follows:

> *Machismo* is a symbol of the resistance of Chicanos to colonial control, both cultural and physical. It symbolizes the pride, dignity, and tenacity of the Chicano people as they have resisted the onslaught of colonization. It symbolizes, most importantly, resistance to acculturation and assimilation into Anglo society. If the term is associated with the male and with masculinity, it is not because he has more actively resisted acculturation and assimilation but perhaps his resistance has been more visible and manifest.

Quoting Chicana writers who share his view, he further concludes that women's subordination constitutes a praiseworthy, "knowing," and voluntary abdication of power by women to compensate Chicanos for their struggles and problems. Thus, the idea that Mexicanas have a responsibility to maintain male ego is sanctioned by assumptions regarding men's central role in political interactions with the Anglo political economy.[76]

For Gloria Anzaldua, however, "machismo" is a response to the precepts, practices, and constraints imposed on Mexican American men by the dominant society. In her reading, the historical sanction of Mexican "tradition" goes to a particular form of masculine responsibility, albeit one connected to a protectiveness toward women that she disavows at another point in her text. For Anzaldua,

> The modern meaning of the word "machismo," as well as the concept, is actually an Anglo invention. For men like my father, being "macho" meant being strong enough to protect and support my mother and us, yet being able to show love. Today's macho has doubts about his ability to feed and protect his family. His "machismo" is an adaptation to oppression and poverty and low self-esteem.[77]

When Chicanas fight against oppression they often find that their public activism causes conflict with Chicanos. When Mexicana garment workers organized a union and went out on strike against the Farah company in 1973, some encountered resistance from the men in their lives. Husbands complained that picketing and other union activities took time from families and objected because they believed that it was inappropriate for women to attend public meetings. The northern California cannery workers interviewed by Patricia Zavella reported similar difficulties. Husbands often believed that their wives' political commitments came at the expense of family well-being.[78]

Some husbands came to terms with the changes initiated by their activist wives. One Farah striker described her shift in consciousness and its impact on her marriage as follows:

> Maybe it's just the Mexican woman, maybe it's just that the Mexican woman has been brought up always to do what somebody tells you. . . . For years I wouldn't do anything without asking my husband's permission. . . . I see myself now and I think, good grief, having to ask to buy a pair of underwear! Of course, I don't do this anymore. . . .[79]

Other women chose divorce when they could not find a common ground with their unhappy husbands. Among the California cannery workers, employment at adequate wages and the support of women friends enabled women to leave marriages whose terms had become too confining for them. That such outcomes are not unusual for Chicanas involved in politics was confirmed by New Mexico activist Kathy Alarid, who commented that ". . . a traditional Mexican male does not like the type of woman that I am now. To the Chicanos my age, I'm an abomination. I talk too much. I'm too smart. I'm too strong." From her own experiences, she concluded that ". . . any Chicana that's into something that's an activist, she's divorced."[80]

In the family labor system of field work, however, some Mexicanas found a context within which work, activism, and family unity often reinforced one another. Partnership in the United Farmworkers' Union struggle to improve working conditions and wages, secure racial dignity, and provide a better life for their children sometimes led to greater gender equality in other facets of family and community life. Women like Dolores Huerta, Jessie Lopez de la Cruz, and others assumed leadership positions, enabling the union to broaden its agenda to include issues of importance to women and, thus, helping to ensure the grass-roots unity critical to success. Even in the UFW, though, women's involvement in politics caused divorces.[81]

For Maria Elena Lucas and others in the midwestern farmworkers' movement, however, becoming activists proved to be quite difficult. Facing resistance from their husbands and from some movement leaders reluctant to share power with women, their struggle against grower and corporate power in their lives required for its success a continuing struggle within their families and their union. Despite this, they picketed grocery stores in support of a consumer boycott, lobbied for state laws requiring better conditions in the fields, and organized for the labor union. Lucas's insistence that she be allowed to engage in organizing work rather than the social service work that Cesar Chavez preferred she do derived from her political convictions:

> We can be on welfare forever, we can receive handouts forever, there's enough clothes forever and enough compassionate people out there to be giving handouts, but that's not going to solve our problem. The problem will be solved when we deal with the growers, and they pay better wages, and we have political power.[82]

Similar conclusions were drawn in the early 1980s when the Morenci Miners Women's Auxiliary organized to support copper miners on strike against the Phelps Dodge Corporation in southern Arizona. When a court forbade the striking miners to picket, their wives and other women organized to run the picket line and support their husbands and community during the 18-month strike. In the process, they faced family conflict, impoverishment, community dissension, and violence and intimidation (some of it at the hands of the National Guard and Arizona Department of Public Security officers assigned in large numbers to the small southern Arizona town during the strike).[83]

Women's attachment to their community was a primary motive and means for their activism. They used the managerial and interpersonal skills they had developed as homemakers in order to organize as activists and mediate the multitude of conflicts that develop in such a stressful situation. The women were especially concerned with preserving the union as a locus of power against economic oppression and race and gender discrimination in a company town. As Mary Lou Gonzales put it, "This corporation's past history speaks for itself. . . . The only reason P.D. [Phelps Dodge] started hiring women, Mexican women, especially, was because of the union and federal law."[84]

Because it was able to bring in non-union workers to replace the strikers, the company was able to break the strike and eliminate the union. Despite the defeat, the women felt empowered by their activism. As Judy Aulette and Trudy Mills point out, their work was central to maintaining the strike, although the press usually ignored their political contributions or construed them only as an extension of their domestic work. One Department of Public Security officer noted the women's centrality, remarking: "If we could just get rid of these broads, we'd have it made."[85]

Some women had to fight the opposition of husbands in order to participate in Auxiliary meetings or go on the picket line. At first the picketers were predominantly Anglo. Hispanic husbands objected to their wives attending Auxiliary meetings and picketing, but the exigencies of the political situation and the resistance of Hispanic women to their husbands' attempts at dominance led to accelerating activism on the part of the Mexicanas. In the words of Barbara Kingsolver, "Some of the women had the full support of their families, while others . . . were fighting in several war zones at once."[86]

The women, who were at the heart of the resistance to the company, sometimes had to struggle against the union, which was run by the men and often more responsive to national union headquarters than it was to the community represented by the women. These differences centered on the women's militance and their exclusion from formal decision-making in a political dispute that had become as much theirs as the union's.[87]

Their activism led to a permanent shift in consciousness for many women. Some went back to school; others sought paid employment. Many revised the terms of their marriages. Cleo Robledo, for example, explained the changes in her life as follows: "I just didn't know there could be anything like this. I feel stronger. Before I was just a housewife, now I'm a partner."[88]

When Chicanas become active as feminists, Chicano resistance to their political stance becomes even more pronounced. Many Chicanos have declared that feminism derives from Anglo culture and should be rejected so that women can provide support to a male-directed movement for Chicano liberation. Indeed, Chicanas who advocate greater autonomy and expanded roles for women have been accused of betraying their people and traditions for a dangerous egoism. They have especially been condemned for denying their cultural identity and abandoning *la familia* in selfish pursuit of individual goals. In response to such charges, a group of Chicanas at the 1969 Denver Youth Conference reached the conclusion "that the Chicana woman does not want to be liberated."[89]

Other Chicanas, however, have rejected the assumption that gender inequality can or should be used to end other forms of oppression. Mirta Vidal declared in 1971 that "the appeal for 'unity' based on the continued submission of women is a false one." She further noted the importance of the feminist movement to the accomplishment of goals important to all women, including reproductive freedom, employment opportunities, and educational advancement. Mexicanas' ability to seek cross-cultural alliances among women in order to alter their status has been diminished by the fact that women are, as Darlis Miller and Joan Jensen have perceptively observed, "divided not only by culture but by conflicts among cultures."[90]

It has also been limited by the Anglo domination of the modern women's movement. Chicanas have often been denied a voice in the definition of feminist goals and strategies with the result that both Chicanas and feminism have been short-changed. Racial and ethnic divisions within feminism have centered on racism in the movement, reproductive issues, and the centrality of gender in defining the feminist political agenda. A narrow definition of what constitutes a women's issue impedes the development of a political strategy which can address the problems of women who are also disadvantaged by discrimination on the basis of class, race, or ethnicity.[91]

Patricia Luna, who joined with other minority women at the Houston International Women's Year Conference to develop a unified agenda, articulated their relationship to feminism as follows:

> . . . in the women's movement we were told our problems were no different from the problems of all women. We haven't really had a voice. But now we are saying that we're not going to take a back seat any longer. Either give us a voice or we're going to speak anyway. We will work in the feminist movement, but only if we can keep our cultural feelings, our needs intact. We are going to be in charge of our own destiny. If feminists will not accept this, we will unite outside of the feminist movement. We will keep our unique identity.[92]

Conclusions

What then can we conclude regarding the roles and status of Chicanas? As Diana Valdez and others have observed, they vary enormously, depending on class affiliation, migration status, interactions with Anglos, family structure, age, and other variables. Moreover, they are changing rapidly as Chicanas enter the labor force in larger numbers, have fewer children, improve their educational levels, and participate more widely in community and other activities. Because the patterns of change are intricate, it is often difficult to disentangle causes from consequences or to understand fully their implications for women's empowerment and well-being.[93]

To the extent that they have been able to forge tools for change, Mexicanas have proved to be more enthusiastic innovators than Mexicanos in certain areas of family and community life, including gender role values, acceptance of more freedoms for their children (especially their daughters), and a greater openness to some cross-cultural interactions. Chicanas have developed different views from those of Chicanos on certain issues, including intermarriage, food preferences, and willingness to use social agencies to assist with certain problems. They are also more likely than the men of their group to reject the double standard in sexual norms, to support family planning, and to believe that women should participate actively outside the home.[94]

American-born Mexicanas led the way in creating new family forms in this period. Compared with the immigrant generation, these women had experienced greater exposure to the institutions of American culture. Their familiarity with other gender norms occurred as the institutional basis for male dominance in Mexicano families was eroding somewhat, enabling women to claim more access to resources and to revise norms regarding familism and gender relations. In the postwar period, Mexicanas had a somewhat wider range of opportunity for employment, a marginally improved economic situation, and greater permanence of residence. The latter made it possible for women to establish a more stable women's community and to extent it to include non-kin.

Mexicanos' roles as mediators with Anglo culture were diminishing rapidly in this period. Certain institutional changes—including the rise of the welfare state, the centrality of consumer institutions and activities in postwar America, changes in the schools, and the influence of mass media —facilitated this shift. As a result, women became less dependent on their husbands for resources and for interpretive frameworks with which to define appropriate gender and other relations.[95]

Linda Whiteford's study of Mexicanas in a small, rural border community in Texas illustrates in microcosm many of the processes which promoted change in women's lives. Whiteford found that women in migrant farm-working families were *mujeres abnegadas* (self-denying women), while fathers were authority figures. In the mid-1960s a new pattern developed as agriculture shifted from labor-intensive to capital-intensive techniques, men got new work in smuggling, and federal programs enabled women to obtain new jobs. Because children were not needed as workers, these families were smaller. Moreover, they understood and used federal programs for themselves and their children and modified marital roles as wives become workers and partners in family decisions. They only rarely did migrant work; the women were employed in sales and clerical work, the men in a variety of blue-collar jobs. The women's networks widened to include female coworkers. Other aspects of culture, however, remained intact, bolstered by the overwhelming dominance of Mexicans and Mexican Americans in this border culture. Thus, language, food, and other customs remain Mexican.[96]

As Whiteford demonstrated, not all women could take advantage of structural shifts. Those in the best position to do so had no more than four children (with none younger than five), had been in the United States at least two generations, were over 25 and under 50, and had worked in the fields as children. English-language and other skills less available to recent migrants facilitated access to jobs and federal programs. The absence of preschool children enabled the mother to work with reduced child-care expenses and home responsibilities.[97]

Women who are undocumented aliens face special difficulties. They are subject to exaggerated labor force exploitation and have little access to resources outside the family. In Ramon Salcido's study, 80 percent of the families of undocumented workers were living on or below the poverty line, compared with 56 percent of the documented families. Their economic insecurity, social marginality and isolation, and fear of apprehension place enormous stress on family relations. At the same time, as Salcido has noted, they cannot readily utilize family service or other agencies in the community. Most relied on networks of relatives and friends for assistance.[98]

Moreover, as Fran Buss has observed, poor Mexican Americans "live in a bewildering state of extra-legality that contributes to stress and a high incidence of emotional disability and family problems." Offering rides to friends, neighbors, or strangers can make them unwittingly vulnerable to penalties for illegally assisting aliens or to charges of drug smuggling. Their efforts to assist those in dire need often break laws regarding welfare, immigration, or public housing. When a child is sick, women will lend papers belonging to another child so medical assistance can be provided. On the border between nations and cultures, daily life is necessarily fraught with illegality.[99]

Even when they are living in the United States legally, Mexicanas' willingness to use Anglo-dominated institutions in order to modify authority patterns in the family has been selective. Although resourceful in devising private and informal strategies to undermine some patriarchal family practices, many Mexicanas have been unwilling to resort to outside authorities to aid them in cases of neglect or violence at the hands of men. When one wife in Thurston's study called the police to find her "bar-hopping husband," she was severely criticized by other women in the community.[100]

As in Anglo culture, women often enforce patriarchal authority in the family, even when it subjects other women to physical abuse. Mothers and mothers-in-law, themselves subject to patriarchal authority, sometimes urge their sons to beat their wives in order to assert their authority within the marriage. As Maria Elena Lucas concluded from her own experiences, her husband's abuse of her sustained his authority and that of his mother over her and maintained his reputation in a male peer group.[101]

The public representation of a certain form of patriarchal family life remains linked to masculine identity for Chicanos to some extent. This male dominance is normatively associated with the control of women's sexuality and, thus, their fertility; with men's control of the political relations for the group; and with an insistence that women subordinate their needs to those of men and children within the family in the name of cultural tradition. The continuing importance of this system of masculine identity and power is indicated by the persistence of high fertility rates, Mexicanas' reluctance to use outside authorities to protect against physical abuse, and continuing constraints on the social and political autonomy of married Mexicanas.

In the realm of gender ideology Chicanas have, thus, experienced a complex process whereby their resistances have weakened certain normative constraints while other limitations (often more subtly encoded and enacted) have proved obdurate. Because it shapes the division of power, work, and resources among women and men in families and the general society, gender ideology is contested terrain. Structural shifts have intensified ideological conflict in Chicano families. The fact that women, especially Mexicanas, have begun to claim power over ideology and resources within the family may encourage the view that they have already achieved equality in that domain. Women's exercise of power may appear substantial when it is measured against an expectation of complete subordination.[102]

In fact, however, Mexicanas are assuming a disproportionate amount of the burden of change in their lives. Alterations in women's status are acceptable only as long as they are accomplished with as little disruption to men and to the political economy as possible. As is true in other American families, the gender division of labor in the household has changed only minimally. This means that women have more work responsibilities, more stress deriving from role overload, and less leisure time. Women are expected to pay most of the emotional price for whatever measure of marital power they gain. Expectations centering on women as nurturers remain high and the gender division between affect and authority remains intact in many Chicano families.[103]

Mexicanas have probably made more progress in utilizing the resources made available to them by the American political economy to enhance their familial power than in altering major institutions. Their increased work rates have been especially important in this process of change. Labor force participation does not automatically entail a pronounced alteration in expectations or gender roles, but it does improve women's access to resources by expanding family income, giving women direct access to their own earnings, and providing them with the breadwinner's rationale for a voice in family spending. Paid work has also increased Chicanas' independence and facilitated alterations in their family relations.

At the same time that it has encouraged Mexicanas' struggle for power, the structural context has set limits on their ability to transform their status, particularly in the family. Poverty, discrimination, and job insecurity continue to impose barriers to Chicanas' education, labor force participation, and reproductive control. Moreover, the lack of structural accommodation to women's dual roles has created strains and ambivalences for Mexicanas, as for other women. Their activism in civil rights, feminism, and, especially, union organizing has promoted some improvements in their lives. More important, however, for many Mexicanas it has promoted a shift in consciousness which is essential to the political struggle for full equality in American society.[104]

7

In the Shadow of the Plantation

AFRICAN AMERICAN WOMEN, 1865–1940

THE DEFEAT OF THE SOUTH in the Civil War and the consequent abolition of slavery launched the era in which the meaning of freedom for blacks was defined. During the Reconstruction years, white planters and blacks tested their respective, but unequal, powers and created the institutions that would structure social relations in the South for many decades. The stakes for blacks in this struggle included not only the political content of their freedom but also their economic position and the gender and family relations it would make possible or desirable.

The politics of race and gender in the Reconstruction era starkly reveals the dense interconnections between public status and private life. The black struggle for control over the conditions of their labor and their lives occurred as an integral part of the conduct of daily life. Black women and men used their newly acquired rights to move freely and to withhold their labor in order to improve the conditions of their work and, especially, to secure some measure of family integrity and privacy.[1]

Black women and men together sought to throw off the authority of whites over all facets of their lives. The organization of gender, however, situated them differently with regard to the constraints and choices forged in the postwar South. As a result, white power and the means devised to minimize it often had somewhat different implications for black men and women. Differences in their experiences were particularly pronounced with regard to the ways in which working conditions and the organization of family and sexuality affected each other.

Postwar politics in the South focused especially on the fate of the plantation economy and the social organization of work once blacks had become free wage laborers. Because they believed blacks would work only if forced to do so, whites preferred to maintain the antebellum system of white-directed work under a gang labor system. Although most accepted that the overt use of physical coercion to work had to be moderated, members of the planter elite sought legal and other means to compel black residence and labor on particular plantations under conditions dictated by whites. Planters wanted the right to control family relations in order to reduce the costs of reproducing the labor force and to ensure the availability of a large, tractable, and desperate labor force for the South's staple economy. As their enactment of the Black Codes of 1865–66 indicates, white planters hoped to reduce black freedom to a polite fiction.[2]

Blacks, on the other hand, held to a dream of autonomy based in land ownership. Because they lacked the money and the political clout to accomplish that goal, blacks' only hope was federal land redistribution. The victorious North, however, did not intend such a social revolution. Solicitous of the claims of private property and wary of transferring economic power to a social group which was largely illiterate and inexperienced in property management, federal authorities cooperated with the white South in the maintenance of planter power.[3]

Despite wartime destruction and the political changes of Reconstruction, the planter elite retained control of the land and the major financial and political institutions of the South. The concentration of land ownership in the hands of a few whites drastically limited the ability of blacks to improve their circumstances. By narrowing the range of work available to them, it reduced the leverage their labor power could confer. The lack of industrial jobs in the South and the availability of immigrant labor for low-wage work in the North would confine blacks to the southern plantation system for decades.[4]

Within these constraints, however, blacks deployed their labor power with sufficient success to force whites to replace the gang labor system with one based on tenancy. Under this system, blacks produced a crop (usually cotton) on white-owned land in return for a share of the crop (usually one-half) at the end of the season. In some cases, black tenant farmers were also required to provide wage labor on the lands being cultivated by the white owner. Although the landowners made the cultivation decisions and supervised their workers more than in other renting arrangements, blacks preferred tenancy because it allowed them to live separately from whites and to manage their daily lives with more autonomy than they had in the gang labor system. The planters found that it provided them with a stable labor force throughout the crop cycle because they could defer payment until after the harvest. Planter provision of credit to their tenants, usually at very high interest rates, and control of the bookkeeping increased planter dominance and profits.[5]

The plantation system of farm tenancy, thus, represented a compromise solution to the problem of black labor in the Reconstruction South. More was being compromised than black dreams of land or white reveries about the Old South, however. The revised plantation economy required the maintenance of a social and political order within which virtually all blacks and many whites were to be kept in ignorance and poverty. This precluded the kinds of technological and economic innovations which characterized northern development in the decades after the Civil War. While the North boomed, the South stagnated. As the poorest group in the poorest region of the nation, blacks paid the greatest cost for southern stagnation.[6]

Family and Labor in the Rural South

Black autonomy in family life threatened white control over labor relations in several critical areas. Slavery had enabled planters to wrest the greatest amount of labor out of blacks at the lowest cost feasible. After the war, white owners wanted to regain that level of productivity and profit by controlling the allocation of work time in black families. In order to do so, they tried to dictate the gender division of labor and authority in the household. They also refused responsibility for the support of economically dependent blacks and attempted to expropriate the labor of the most desirable workers. Moreover, planters sought to minimize black parental power because it threatened their authority over the socialization of the labor force and over the terms of child labor.[7]

In the transition to free labor, this issue became one of paramount concern to white southerners. The Atlanta *Constitution* charged in 1883 that "these black parents will only make vagrants and vagrants make thieves." Philip Bruce claimed that children raised in freedom were "much less inclined to work" than their enslaved parents had been, concluding that black parents had become incapable of properly raising their children once the parents and children were no longer under the discipline of white slaveholders.[8]

As a result, blacks experienced great difficulty in establishing the right to discipline and socialize their children without white interference. Caroline Rogers complained to the Freedman's Bureau that her white employer had struck her daughter in her presence. When she told the child to leave, the planter struck her with a board.[9]

In the early Reconstruction period, blacks' right to retain their children was challenged by the actions of whites who kept older children on their plantations in order to take their labor without pay. They used antebellum apprenticeship statutes to claim that they should be awarded custody because the parents were unable to provide support. Sympathetic white judges virtually always found in favor of these white claimants. Because they were more economically oppressed, women were particularly vulnerable to the charge that they were unable to support their children.[10]

Women suffered special harm from these actions. Their economic position meant that they were more dependent on the work and wages of older children, especially sons, than were men. Because they were the primary childrearers, loss of their children also denied women their maternal identity and often severed their most significant relationships. Lucy Lee, whose daughter had been apprenticed in 1860, attempted (unsuccessfully) to claim her after emancipation. For Lee, freedom embodied and entailed her maternal authority:

> . . . God help us, our condition is bettered but little; free ourselves, but deprived of our children, almost the only thing that would make us free and happy. It was on their account we desired to be free. . . .[11]

After Reconstruction, such direct assaults on black parental authority diminished, although the southern caste system took its toll on black mothers in many ways. High infant and child mortality rates, coupled with the labor requirements of the tenancy system, reinforced a high fertility strategy by black women. They often saw many of their children die and others leave—sometimes without further communication—as they tried to find better circumstances for themselves. Lizzie Fant Brown, for example, outlived seven of her eight children. Minnie Moody had eleven children, seven of whom had died. Commenting on the lack of assistance from the others, she said, "My children ain't no service to me now; they're all married or dead or workin' up No'th. None hain't been back since they left 'bout two year ago."[12]

White planters also sought, with less success, to shape marital relationships among blacks. They paid men less than a family wage and charged women's absences from work against the wages of their husbands in order to coerce black women into field work. Some believed that the replacement of the slave quarters with individual family residences for blacks wasted resources and women's labor in cooking for their families. A committee of planters told a northern representative that their authority over blacks as workers should include the right to prohibit "fighting and quarrelling . . . , especially husbands whipping their wives."[13]

Despite these efforts at control, black women reduced their hours in the agricultural labor force and service work after the Civil War, prompting hostile comment from many whites. One planter, for example, complained, "The female laborers are almost invariably idle—[they] do not go to the field but desire to play the lady & be supported by their husbands 'like the white folk do.'" He, and others like him, assumed that the labor power of all blacks—men, women, and children—should be at the disposal of the white custodians of the staple economy of the South and that such control required white power over family relations. Although there were some attempts to deploy the state actively in service to that goal, most planters relied on blacks' need for work and income to enforce the labor of all able-bodied members of their families.[14]

Women and Work in the Rural South

Indeed, the destruction of war, heightened racial conflict, and economic disorganization had reduced most blacks to a state of dire destitution. The most pressing necessity for all blacks after emancipation was to find work to support themselves and their dependents. For black women, the situation was especially difficult. Most were part of family economies where the earnings of all were critical to survival. Many were solely responsible for the support of children and the elderly.[15]

Immediate postwar circumstances made women's ability to make do essential. Ebenezer Brown remembered his mother's resourcefulness as follows:

> I remember afte' de war my mammy wud roast corn cobs an' take de inside out uf it an' use dat soda, an' it wud make de bread rise jes' like soda. We parched tater peelin' an' made coffee, an' we dug up de dirt in smoke house an' dripped dat through er hopper an' biled dat ter git salt.

Such strategies not only enabled many blacks to endure the extreme poverty caused by joblessness, but they allowed some to withhold their labor when the conditions offered by whites were too onerous. Women's unpaid domestic skills were, thus, a political resource at a time when labor relations were being contested.[16]

Rina Brown's account of her mother's work history exemplifies the range of possibility for most black women in the southern postwar economy. Brown described the occupational sojourn of her mother, a woman who had sole responsibility for the support of her children, as follows:

> When we left Miss Atlanta's she give us nuffin to take wid us an' ebery thing we got we had to buy it on credit an' den de white man got whut we made [from field work]. Times wus mi'ty hard afte' de war; nearly starvation. My

mammy wus a good washer an' ironer an' she went from house to house
an' done up de fine clothes fur de white ladies an' dey paid her in older
clothes an' lit'l sumthing to eat.[17]

Women's ability to secure rural work was hampered by white preferences for male labor, the danger of sexual exploitation in jobs which entailed working under direct white supervision, and women's responsibility
for the care of others. Women had difficulty negotiating tenancy arrangements—the main form of rural labor—unless they had husbands or older
sons to assist in farm work. The Freedman's Bureau often allocated less
land to female-headed households than to those headed by men. If they
were to remain in the rural sector, many had to rely on wage labor, the bottom of the economic ladder in the rural economy.[18]

The wage structure in agricultural work, however, impeded women's
ability to support families on their own. Women generally got from one-
half to two-thirds of the wages of men for performing the same labor. The
imperatives of the crop cycle made it important to planters that rural laborers showed up for work as needed. In order to ensure this, they assessed
stiff wage penalties—"deducts"—against those who missed work. These
wage reductions, which amounted to more than a day's wages for a day's
absence, inflicted special damage on women supporting families. They were
more likely to have to miss work and could ill afford reductions in their already inadequate wages. Because of the exorbitant charges for absence
levied by her employer, one black woman ended up "owing" him for labor
she missed while caring for her mother. These practices and the wage gap
between women and men indicate the formal way in which the costs of reproducing the labor force were being assessed against women. Because they
reduced women's incentives for field work, these policies sometimes had
unintended consequences. The deducts and meager wages with which
planters penalized women for their reproductive work served, under certain conditions, to discourage women's field work.[19]

Most historians have concluded that black women reduced their hours
in commercial agriculture primarily because they had made domestic activities, especially childrearing, a priority. It is important to note that most
black women had little choice regarding their need to generate resources
for the family and that they deployed their labor in response to employment conditions as well as family concerns. Indeed, family priorities cannot be understood separately from economic structures. To a degree, the
withdrawal of women from the formal sector reflected the policies of white
planters, who assumed that women would continue to reproduce, socialize, and service the labor force while assuming a heavy burden of field
work. The dual burden imposed on black women by the structures of the
southern rural economy created intense contradictory pressures for them.[20]

To the extent that their families' straitened economic circumstances allowed, black women tried to organize their paid work so that it accommodated their other duties to their families. In some ways, postwar family patterns made it more difficult for women to combine paid and domestic work. Blacks' desire to maintain separate residences for nuclear families, rather than stay in the old slave quarters, meant that older children and elderly women were less likely to be available for child care than in the past. Tenancy partially resolved this problem because it enabled women to combine their domestic and breadwinner responsibilities more readily than they could when employed in wage labor.

Women's limited withdrawal from the staple economy was also predicated on their continuing responsibility for labor-intensive domestic work. As often occurs in situations where women assume breadwinning responsibilities, the allocation of homemaking to women was taken for granted in the gender division of labor. This work was not relieved by modern household technologies. Doing the washing or cooking entailed carrying water and tending a fire—usually after doing farm chores and work in the fields. Consequently, black women had less leisure time than men and, whatever their preferences, spent most of their time in arduous labor in the decades following the Civil War.[21]

It is not surprising, then, that many women spent fewer hours working on the land than they had under slavery or that they preferred to do so under the tenancy system rather than as wage laborers. Black women's motives for withholding their labor from the South's staple economy varied and derived from a structural position different from that of white women or black men. Like black men, they sought some easing of the onerous burden of work which had been imposed under slavery. As tenants they toiled within a family economy which offered them the opportunity to earn under terms more of their own choosing and provided some protection from sexual exploitation.[22]

The tenancy system also removed some of their labor from the formal sectors which define workers as "employed." As is often the case in a rural economy, women's productive labor became difficult to measure. Some of their resource-generating labor—such as maintaining a garden to contribute to subsistence—would not count directly as agricultural production. Yet, given planter expropriation of much of the return on the crops grown by tenant farmers, such work often created more use value for their families than did field work. Although it is clear that black women did shift some of their labor from agricultural work to domestic tasks after emancipation, whether they did so to the extent that scholars have claimed cannot be conclusively established. Indeed, overreaction to change may have caused white observers to overstate the degree to which black women withdrew from the staple economy.[23]

Black women with families commonly took work that enabled them to remain in the home, a choice dictated in part by the customary delegation of domestic duties to them and in part by the lack of better options for paid work outside the home. For that reason, home laundry was a very important occupation for women who were married or mothers. In 1900, some 215,000 black women took in laundry; 41 percent of them were married, another 34 percent were widowed. Because so many women tried to earn a living as laundresses, the supply exceeded the demand, drastically reducing the wages and amount of such work.[24]

Moreover, the work was hot, heavy, and arduous, contributing to general health problems and probably to miscarriages and other reproductive difficulties. In the winter, the amount of work decreased while the difficulties compounded. One laundress said that the work was good in the summer, "But in winter, Lawd, hit's hard. I is had my hands split wide open and my foots might' nigh froze washing outdoors at de wash pot in Winter."[25]

Those who could take work outside the home found that the jobs available to them were generally limited to domestic service and other service occupations. Black women found that work in a private household involved considerable disadvantage to them. Their work was closely supervised by their employers, who accorded them little control over the organization of the work or over the terms of their relationship. They found that "correct" racial comportment was as important a job requirement as the ability to put in long hours cleaning and cooking. Because they were often paid in room and board, hand-me-down clothes, or leftover food, black domestics received less money for their labor than other workers.[26]

The hours were long and often interfered with family and personal life. Margaret Turner, for example, would not take work as a domestic because it meant working on Sundays, thus interfering with her religious observance. Others found that their husbands objected to their working in service or that it conflicted too much with other family obligations. They often took in laundry instead. Despite the fact that their dispersion as workers made organization difficult, black women were able to resist employer preferences for live-in servants and establish live-out housework as the dominant pattern by the 1920s. Married women's decision to work, thus, took place within a context that severely limited their possibilities.[27]

Indeed, understanding the degree to which black women "chose" domesticity is further complicated by the fact that black women and men sometimes disagreed regarding women's work roles. An employed Tennessee woman noted that her husband did not want her to work, questioning her decision on the grounds that he "was doing all he could to give me what I wanted." She told him, however, that she wanted to share the work in order to reduce his burden: "If you put a load on one horse it will pull him down, but two horses can pull it jest as easy." Sometimes husbands insisted that their wives do field work, despite the women's preferences for other work. In other cases, women and men agreed that wives had to work to contribute essential resources. Indeed, the rural men interviewed by Charles Johnson in the 1930s stressed industry, deference, and attractiveness as the attributes most important in a wife.[28]

Rather than a product of consensual choice by women and men, as Jacqueline Jones claims, the gender division of labor in black families derived from white power, the demographic composition of families, and from conflicts and negotiations between black women and men. Whites' ability to control economic conditions virtually ensured black women's availability for paid labor in the southern economy. Economic clout was sometimes backed by physical coercion. E. Franklin Frazier reported the case of a single mother with a sick infant who had been beaten by her landlord in order to force her to leave her baby unattended and work in the fields. In many tenant households, the amount of time a woman could spend with her young children depended on the presence of older children to replace her in field work. This may have been the case in urban economies as well. A Women's Bureau study of women workers in 1920 revealed that employed black women in Jacksonville were less likely to have employed children over the age of 18 in the household than white women workers.[29]

The need to secure an income sometimes required that family members, including women who were married or mothers, leave to seek work elsewhere. These women often contributed to the support of others outside their households, but such responsibilities cannot be documented fully by examining only census records of household composition. Personal narratives, however, reveal complex patterns of assistance between households whose links were forged by women.[30]

Scholars and contemporary observers have often claimed that black women were advantaged over black men in securing employment in both the rural and urban economies. After the Reconstruction crisis had passed, for example, some whites concluded that black women surpassed black men in industry and reliability, a view conditioned not only by racism but also by expectations regarding appropriate gender roles. Unemployment data reveal a more ambiguous gender pattern and underscore the importance of race in disadvantaging all blacks. Census returns from 1900 showed that, among blacks, slightly more women (30 percent) than men (28 percent) reported that they had been unemployed some time during the previous year. In the area of wages, black women suffered an indisputable disadvantage based on both race and sex.[31]

Neither the structure of the economy nor the organization of gender relations enabled black women to rely solely on the nuclear family for support. The inadequate and insecure wages of women and men, the migration of child earners, the death of husbands, and failed marriages prompted black women to turn to other kin for assistance. In a complex system of reciprocity, they often brought dependents into their families and shared resources with others outside their households. As black women negotiated the interconnections between affective and economic relationships within the family, they sought power commensurate with their needs and their material and other contributions to family welfare. In so doing, they altered and extended the mutable family system they had helped to devise under slavery.

Women, Gender, and Family

For black women, the legacy of slavery was complex. It included family and gender systems which resembled those found in other social groups in significant ways. The gender division of labor and authority within black families prescribed domestic work, child nurture, and the maintenance of kin relations for women and an attempt by men to serve as protectors and providers. Men used the leverage they had in the economy to provide some resources to their families and enhance their familial power. Enslaved black men, however, lacked the institutional basis to carry out their role expectations fully or to secure the degree of male dominance prevalent among free whites. Within these limits, black norms sanctioned some level of deference to male authority, especially in interactions with outsiders, and required that black women provide ego support to black men.[32]

Black values and practices diverged substantially from those of whites, especially regarding sexuality and women's work. Under slavery, arduous daily work characterized black women's lives, providing uncongenial soil for the development of mores stressing feminine weakness or incompetence. The politics of race and sex—expressed in the systematic sexual abuse of black women by white men—also precluded the enforcement by black men of norms of premarital chastity for black women. Black values sanctioned premarital sexual experimentation for women, with the result that women often bore their first child before marriage. Enslaved women usually waited until they had entered a stable, monogamous marriage to bear subsequent children. Whether they relied on birth control or sexual abstinence in this intervening period is not clear.[33]

For both women and men, the assumption of parental or marital responsibilities signified their entry into the adult community. For men, this occurred after marriage, which served more to institutionalize the paternal role in the family than to legitimize sexual unions. In addition to providing a father, marriage linked slave children to a larger kin network which could provide nurture if the mother was sold or died. Given that its economic foundations were weak, the slave family derived its strength from the emotional benefits it provided to its members.

After the abolition of slavery, blacks found that the context within which they were to create and sustain family life had changed substantially. Slavery had bequeathed to blacks a complex pattern of family structures that included a substantial number of families broken by sale, military service, and wartime dispersions. At the same time, emancipation meant that black women and men were assuming greater economic functions in the allocation of labor and the distribution of resources within families. Thus, black women found that the affective and economic dimensions of family life were connected in new and sometimes disconcerting ways. These interconnections simultaneously strengthened and undermined postwar families. Moreover, the joint effort by black women and men to wrest more autonomy from whites and its partial success had created ambiguity in gender roles and expectations.

As Herbert Gutman and others have shown, family ties were strong. When the war ended, blacks acted to repair some of the damages inflicted on their families under slavery. They searched for lost spouses, children, and other relatives in order to re-establish family relationships. Many blacks also legalized their marriages in order that their families might be more fully secured from intervention and that they might live "respectably." They also created a family economy in order to pool scarce resources.[34]

This does not mean, however, that the family was egalitarian or without conflict. Suzanne Lebsock found considerable discord between free black women and men in her study of antebellum Petersburg. According to Lebsock, this derived from women's willingness to assert their prerogatives in a context in which deference to their men brought little benefit. Observing that family harmony and integrity are sometimes predicated on women's subordination, Lebsock concluded, "Insofar as conflict grew out of leverage and assertiveness on the part of women, it was a sign of health. . . ."[35]

When emancipation changed the conditions of male-female relations among blacks, a complex pattern of cooperation and conflict ensued. Under slavery, husbands and wives frequently lived on different plantations, had many decisions about family made for them, and often experienced white intervention in marital conflicts. As a result, the sources and degree of male authority in black households were both unclear and contested in the postwar period. One freedman, angry over his wife's infidelity, wrote to the Freedman's Bureau and asked: "Can I not by *moderate* chastisement compel her to obey me? If she insists on leaving me can I not keep the children?" Such threats were carried out often enough by men that black women voiced their interrelated complaints in a work song: "black men beat me, white men cheat me."[36]

Black men were not the only ones to go to the Freedman's Bureau to resolve marital problems. Women often brought complaints, especially regarding physical abuse, to northern officials. Betty Ellington, for example, lodged a complaint with the Freedmen's Bureau when her husband abandoned her and their three children. He had previously assaulted her after she caught him in bed with another woman. After the Freedman's Bureau was ended in 1869, black women had little recourse to outside legal assistance against abuse. One such woman explained her unwillingness to go to court against her abusive husband: "But I wouldn't run to no white man nor no white man's court with my troubles."[37]

As a result, many women fought back against abuse individually. Freedwoman Sarah Fitzpatrick described her husband's only attempt to beat her as follows:

> He come in one night jes' as hot as he could be; got some switches to whup me, but I cot'im, took his switches 'way f'om 'im an' th'owed 'im down, an' choked 'im, 'tel he hollered fer ma' sister to come an' take me up off'im. I told'im, "Willie you can't whup me, you whup chillun, you don't whup grown folks. I'm grown."[38]

A similar resolve was demonstrated later by Nancy White, who explained her views as follows: "Nancy Sawyer Tucker White is not going to have no man beating on her after she is out from under her parents' rule! That is my law and I live by that law first!" She decided to end her marriage after her husband "made the mistake of putting his hands on me like I might have been his child, not his wife."[39]

Men's abusive behavior was indirectly reinforced by the counsels of whites (especially men) regarding the appropriateness of patriarchal family patterns. Laura Towne, a white who went south to teach blacks, observed that speakers had been advising black men to assert their will in families and establish their right to keep their "concerns" as men to themselves in order "to get the women into their proper place." As a result, the men had concluded that masculine domestic power was an "inestimable privilege." According to Towne, the ideas of male superiority were "inflating the conceit of the males to an amazing degree."[40]

Men's claims to marital power received some support from institutional arrangements and postwar conditions. The age gap common between black husbands and wives and the young age at which some black women married increased men's marital authority. Minnie Folkes, who married at the age of 14 in the 1870s, recalled her understanding of marriage as follows: ". . . I didn't know what marriage meant. I had an idea when you loved de man, you an' he could be married an' his wife had to cook, clean up, wash, an' iron fer him was all." Another young bride echoed her understandings: "I didn't know what marriage was for; it jes' meant another home and another somebody to take care o' me and to work for in de field to draw my money—dat's all it meant to me. I didn't know one kind o' love from another."[41]

One older black man, who had married a girl of 16 in the 1870s, indicated the complex pattern of reciprocity and inequality which characterized their marriage as follows:

> I found her a girl of good character, well-behaved and sensible, so she and I talked the matter over and she told me she liked me well enough to try to take care of me, and I promised to do the same for her. She does as I direct. What is my pleasure seems to be hers. She listens to my counsels and I think strives to do right.[42]

Although economic arrangements promoted a family system of labor in agriculture, women's economic dependence on men was pronounced, given men's greater access to the land. Some women married in order to have a livelihood in hard times. Anne Evans found herself without shoes, lodging, or work in the aftermath of emancipation. A friend bought her shoes and some clothes and arranged for her to stay with an older man. Within a few weeks, she married him. She later recalled, ". . . I was might glad to marry him to get a place to stay." In more settled times, also, women often found that marriage enabled them to secure a livelihood for themselves and their children better than the alternatives. A middle-aged single mother expressed the priority of economics in her view of marriage by observing: "What I wants now is a husband not a man. I wants somebody to help me take keer of these children." Indeed, women's expectation that men would work to contribute to their material well-being was often a precondition for marital success.[43]

This expectation did not signify an acceptance of norms prescribing women's withdrawal from productive work as much as it expressed women's need for men's assistance in breadwinning. Sarah Fitzpatrick separated from her husband, Willie, in part because his only contribution to their subsistence came from hunting and fishing. She had expected him to shoulder more of the breadwinning burden: "I told him I mar'ied him to take care o' me, not me to take care o' him." She then entered two common-law relationships, one of which was ended by death, the other by a separation for unspecified reasons after many years together. In each union she continued to work in the fields. For Fitzpatrick, the love of a woman for a man was conditional: it depended on his behavior toward her. As she put it, "I loves a man when he treats me right but I ain't never had no graveyard love fer no man." The economic constraints on her marital power are suggested by the fact that her separation occurred only after her oldest son was able to take over as head of the sharecropping family.[44]

The complaints of black women seeking the return of children "apprenticed" by whites after emancipation reflected their acceptance of breadwinning responsibilities. Mothers, married and single, defined themselves as breadwinners and claimed their children on those grounds. One single mother, who resided in the city of Baltimore, asked for the return of her daughter, stating, "I feel myself perfectly able to support her." Similarly, Mary Ann Ran stated, "I am able to provide for them and with the aid of my husband the father of them to protect them." A Maryland woman married to a Union soldier sought her young children, stating, "I [am] able to support them with the assistance of my father and sister." Female identity was defined in terms of a congruence between maternal values and breadwinning, a compatibility predicated on women's ability to secure a place in a family support system.[45]

Women's work responsibilities were reinforced by the economic position of black men and its effects on their family roles. When confronted with the closed system under which they were expected to earn a livelihood, some black men grew discouraged and abandoned the support responsibility to women. Others left when their inability to secure work created family strains. From the point of view of many black women, it constituted an evasion of an onerous responsibility that was then shifted solely to them. In Zora Neale Hurston's novel, *Their Eyes Were Watching God*, Nanny explained it to her granddaughter, Janie, as follows:

> Honey, de white man is de ruler of everything as fur as Ah been able tuh find out. . . . So de white man throw down de load and tell de nigger man tuh pick it up. He pick it up because he have to, but he don't tote it. He hand it to his womenfolks. De nigger woman is de mule uh de world so fur as Ah can see.[46]

The strains that economic oppression created even for strong marriages were revealed in the correspondence of a man who had left his family in rural North Carolina in 1932 in order to secure work in the city. Writing to his wife, he explained his continuing absence and his inability to send money to them:

> I am very sorry that you can't understand about the way work is in Winston and I tell you every time that I write that we are not doing anything. . . . You ought to know that if I was making any money I would send you some that is what I am trying to work for. . . .[47]

The affection and concern in his letters suggest one of the reasons why this couple was able to weather their crisis. Similarly, a Georgia carpenter tried to ensure his family's well-being if he had to leave to find work and arranged suitable housing for them in his new location if his work was to keep him out of town for long. He concluded, regarding their twenty-five years together: "I'll tell you one thing: I wouldn't swap my wife for no other woman I ever saw, for I couldn't get another to take her place."[48]

Conflicts over money occurred frequently. Minnie Dunn found that her frugality clashed with her husband's generosity. He was always willing to give money to others, while she tried to save it for their own needs. "I'd try to tell him about it, I'd say 'if you save the pennies the dollars will take care of themselves.'" When she decided to buy a house, his family persuaded him not to help with the payments because she had the savings she had eked out from her work as a domestic and a laundress.[49]

The family economy, thus, assumed various forms, as family members negotiated their material and emotional relationships within a context of extreme economic oppression. The lack of a normative consensus between women and men regarding appropriate authority patterns in the household and the contradictory implications of southern economic structures for family power dynamics created a pattern of conflict and relative instability in black family lives. This was exacerbated by high rates of widowhood and by the decisions of older children to leave in order to search for better work opportunities, to establish their own families, or to gain some autonomy from the nuclear family.

The sparse data on household structures offer only a suggestive glimpse of the flexibility and variability of black family structures or of the extent of women's responsibility for the support of others. Knowing how many households are male-headed or how many are extended does not enable us to describe very specifically the dynamics of household composition. They do not reveal the compatibilities and tensions between the affective and economic relationships within families or the connections among women's kin work, their productive work, and their family status.[50]

Family structures derived from the choices made by blacks in a context in which virtually no other institutions provided assistance in the care of dependents and family property and incomes were exceedingly low. Extraordinary poverty and family instability among blacks made a system of extended kinship ties and responsibilities an imperative. Black women often adopted orphaned children and those whose parents could not offer adequate support or care. Although black families tried to support aging parents whenever possible and were more likely to take in such dependents than workers who produced income, they could not always balance their income and their responsibilities to others.[51]

As a result, many black women found themselves responsible for the support of their children and other dependents. After emancipation, many were unable or unwilling to continue or re-establish their slave marriages. Some women could not locate their husbands or found that they had remarried. For others freedom meant the right to renounce husbands whom they found incompatible. Those who had borne children by their masters could expect little assistance from them in providing for their offspring. A few attempted to get the Freedman's Bureau to enforce child support payments from the white fathers, but they usually did not succeed. Others found it impossible to marry because so many black men had died during the Civil War.[52]

Not surprisingly, then, black women were more likely to head families and to do so at a younger age than was true of white women. Herbert Gutman's data from representative southern communities in the 1880 census revealed that women headed 13 to 18 percent of rural black families and 26 to 31 percent of urban black families. Black women in their twenties were two to four times more likely to be family heads than white women of the same age. As Gutman points out, most black families included adult men, but many black women assumed the full breadwinner burden for extended periods in their lives.[53]

The persisting pattern of marriage to older men and the mortality rates caused by poverty contributed to high rates of widowhood for black women. A 1938 study revealed that 48 percent of the wives of black Georgia men aged 65 were under the age of 55. Such arrangements worked to the economic disadvantage of middle-aged women, who were often burdened with aging husbands unable to work or widowed at a young age with little means to secure a livelihood in the rural economy unless they had older children present in the household. One such married woman complained to sociologist Charles Johnson that ". . . my old man won't do. He ain't no count now nohow. He's so old he can't do nothing. Can't even see."[54]

Not only did black women experience high rates of widowhood, they experienced desertion more often than white women, and, whatever the cause, they lost their husbands at a substantially earlier age than whites. In their study of families in Philadelphia, 1850–80, Furstenberg, Hershberg, and Modell found that at least one-fourth of married black women with children reported themselves as widowed by the time they reached their forties. It is probable that many of these women were living separately from their husbands, as Elizabeth Pleck's more detailed work has revealed for Boston in this period. Data from the 1940 census confirms the persistence of these patterns over time. In 1940, 16 percent of black women were reported as widowed, compared with 11 percent of white women. Among those aged 50 to 54 years, 32 percent of black and 15 percent of white women were reported as widowed. Of those who reported themselves as married in 1940, 4 percent of white and 14 percent of black women had husbands absent. In the urban areas, 5 percent of white and 19 percent of black married women did not live with their husbands.[55]

At the same time, marriage rates were higher among blacks than whites, especially at young ages. In 1940, 60 percent of nonwhite women aged 20 to 24 had not married, while 74 percent of white women in the same age group remained single. The combination of high marriage rates and high rates of female-headed families reflects a pattern of serial monogamy and the effects of a normative system that did not require marriage to legitimize pregnancies. Although single black women were more likely to have children than whites, many of these women later married. As one mother said of her daughter who had borne a child outside of marriage: "She started to get married, but didn't; liable to marry after while." As the frequency of remarriage indicates, black women sought marriage, rather than the long-term maintenance of female-headed households. Marriages frequently failed as a consequence of external pressures and black women's willingness to struggle for greater compatibility and egalitarianism in their unions.[56]

The black families of rural Alabama studied by Charles Johnson in 1931 revealed the persistence of these dynamics. Premarital sexuality was common and no stigma attached to a woman who bore a child out of wedlock. Although virtually all adults had been married and most were married at the time, the legal formalities of marriage and divorce were not followed as carefully as the conventions of the larger society required. Legal divorce was rare, although separation and remarriage were quite common. The 612 families included 231 couples in which each spouse was married for the first time, 173 couples in which at least one spouse had been married previously, and 52 households headed by a person separated from her or his spouse.[57]

The community condemned those who remained in an unhappy union more than those who separated. These mores reflected and reinforced women's marital power by sanctioning women's refusal to remain in oppressive marriages. The reasons most commonly given by women for ending their marriages were marital violence and the failure of their husbands to contribute to their support. Several women told Johnson that they left their husbands because they were "jest too mean." One separated from her mate because "he fight so I jest couldn't live with him. He treat me so bad."[58]

Much of the violence in these households stemmed from disputes over the degree of masculine authority, especially in establishing norms for sexual conduct. Many couples reported disputes over the wife's infidelity—real and perceived. In some cases, the threat of violence from husbands supported the sexual double standard within marriage. In others it contributed to marital instability and to women's preference for informal liaisons. Some women found that men's expectations of dominance increased after marriage: "Soon as you marry a man he starts mistreating you, and I'm not going to be mistreated no more." Couples who had established stable unions reported that they had successfully placed jealousy behind them. One man, married for forty years, concluded, "When you jealous you don't live long."[59]

The persistence of the problem of wife abuse over such a long period of time bespeaks the inability of men to establish the kind of dominance they expected. Poverty and racism strained family relations and reduced men's ability to establish an uncontested authority. They lacked the status and income advantage over women that characterized white marriages and sustained their stable but unequal unions. The frequency with which black women chose to fight back and/or to leave abusive husbands indicates that black men's domestic power was neither ideologically nor economically secured.[60]

Men's inability to dictate the terms of gender relations in black families did not mean that these families were either matriarchal or egalitarian. Instead, a complex pattern of deference and assertion characterized black women's unions. Della Harris observed: "You promised to 'bey the man, but before you finish it's cussing, honey." Despite their efforts to secure greater marital power, black women faced marital inequality because they did not have sufficient power outside of marriage to create relationships on their terms. They were able to shape the normative structure of gender relations in the black community enough to secure support from others when they decided to forgo marriage, but not enough to enforce egalitarian relationships on would-be patriarchs.[61]

Black women's willingness to leave oppressive marriages derived from and necessitated a flexible family system that would provide a safety net for female-headed households. The contested nature of gender relations among blacks thus contributed to the development of a family system in which women chose to rely on their own labor and on their kin work to secure multiple sources of support for their dependents. Because black women often could not earn enough to support themselves and others, even at the most minimal level, the organization of family earning and consumption patterns fundamentally affected their well-being.[62]

Older children were a critical component of the support system of unmarried women. If they were reliant on wage labor to support their families, women had to combine their earnings with that of others to survive. As a result, child labor was common in female-headed households. An older woman who had taken in her niece's orphaned children when they were small typified the combination of generosity and economic vulnerability that marked family practices. After her husband's death, she had to rely on the children's labor for support. She described their straitened circumstances as follows:

> I jest make 'nough ter barely pay my taxes. . . . Sometimes I don't git food, go widout eating all day so's ter leave hit fer them ter eat 'cause they hafta work. I been had them in school, though I has a tough time I send them.[63]

When women had older sons, they stood a better chance of contracting as tenant farmers. Given that most single mothers did not own property, their ability to compel the labor of their children, especially their sons, was sustained only by moral authority, not by economic inducements. The implications of women's dependence on their children was epitomized in the assertion of one woman that "I can't let dat boy marry. He all I got to help me."[64]

Elizabeth Pleck has noted, "It was personally trying to belong to a family system that made so many demands." Although they provided security in the face of poverty, complex networks of kin also created competing demands for resources and emotional support. Obligations to extended kin strained some marriages. The incorporation of new people into the household often added to family conflict, especially when that new person was a stepfather. One woman remembered, "my stepfather was so mean to us, Mamma's children, that we had to go stay with my grandmother. He wouldn't let Mamma keep us."[65]

Stepfathers' authority in matters of labor and money could also create conflict. Minnie Dunn left her family in the 1910s and took up live-in work as a domestic servant after a dispute with her stepfather over her share of the family's return for their cotton crop. After working in the fields for her stepfather and turning over most of the wages she earned picking cotton for others, she resented the fact that she got only $5 out of the $500 he cleared that year. He saw his stepchildren, however, as a drain on resources that he wanted to save for his own children: "I don't want 'em sitting around here eating up what I done worked for me and my chaps."[66]

Women found themselves constantly reweaving the fabric of a family system strained by the exigencies of black life and by their own quest for some measure of domestic power and personal autonomy. That quest also entailed the attempt to construct a positive sexual identity and experience from the margins of the dominant race/gender system. Because the custodians of southern white power sought primarily to police the borders of race through the prohibition of liaisons between black men and white women, the implications of their system for black women were ambiguous and often contradictory.[67]

Gender, Race, and Sexuality

As they had under slavery, black women experienced a special vulnerability to violence, especially rape, at the hands of white men. As Jacqueline Dowd Hall has observed, that vulnerability was heightened by the contested nature of race relations in the reconstruction south. In the aftermath of the Civil War, black men and women were often victimized by the displaced anger of northern troops and of the vanquished white southerners, especially when their conduct was perceived to be threatening to the "appropriate" reconstruction of race relations in the new South. For women this meant that sexual assault was added to the other forms of assault, theft, and harassment experienced by black men. White men's use of rape as a form of control over black women continued long after Reconstruction ended.[68]

Assessing the implications of sexual exploitation by white men for black women's relationships to black men is especially difficult. Rennie Simson has claimed that black women's experiences of victimization often caused them to avoid intimacy with men altogether and to construct a sexual self based on self-reliance and, implicitly, repression. According to Simson, this construction of a female identity was encouraged by black women's greater access to employment and by black men's abusive behavior in marriage. Simson's assumption that the sexual oppression of black women under the southern caste system affected their sexual identity and experiences offers a promising perspective on the question of sexuality. In drawing her conclusions, however, she oversimplifies the response of free black women to this dynamic. Although the possibility and/or the experience of such harassment undoubtedly affected their relationships to black men, those effects were contradictory.[69]

In order to justify the sexual license they had claimed, white men perpetuated the myth of the "sexually loose" black woman whose purported sexual appetites constituted an automatic "consent" to their advances and, implicitly, to the system which secured their power. The continuing vulnerability of black women—and the violence visited upon black men who fought to defend them—militated against the imposition of ideologies within the black community that stressed men's obligations to protect women from a "feminine" moral incapacity. Because black women and men were both victimized by the sexual politics of race, they defined a politics of racial resistance that secured the self-esteem of black women and men and reduced gender conflict over this explosive issue. By holding white men accountable for their actions, black norms indirectly affirmed a more positive view of black women's moral capacity.[70]

Ironically, the sexual vulnerability of black women relative to white men opened a space for the assertion of different sexual expectations in their relations to black men. That assertion, however, had to occur in a context of public reticence about issues of gender and sexuality in African American lives. As Darlene Clark Hine observed, black women developed a "culture of dissemblance" in which they protected their sexual reputations and the possibilities of alternative sexualities from white view by a public emphasis on African American women's moral respectability. Although Hine sees this strategy as important to black women's survival, Paula Giddings concluded that "this [discursive] void was a potentially life-threatening one in a time of adjustment to nonslavery. . . ." Their apparently different readings on the "culture of dissemblance" reflect its contradictory meanings in the lives of black women—it offered some protection from the moralizing gaze of whites, but little from the power exercised by white men. Moreover, as Kimberle Crenshaw's analysis of the Clarence Thomas hearings suggests, it contributed to the "contemporary marginalization of black female sexual abuse within black political discourse."[71]

At the same time, African American women's vulnerability to sexual exploitation by white men impeded the development of egalitarian sexual norms. Although black mores mitigated the tendency to blame black women for this system, the men resented what they perceived as black women's sexual license relative to white men. Moreover, white men's sexual privilege became a visible symbol of black men's dispossession as men in a patriarchal culture. As a result, sexuality remained a focal point for gender conflict.[72]

Black men's resentment of that dispossession was expressed in a folk belief that "the only people who were really free was the white man and the black woman." Nancy White noted that when her father said this, "he was generally mad. White men were always messing with black girls." White, however, who had to put up with sexual harassment at the hands of white men and who lost earnings when she quit such abusive employers, understood that black women did not have sexual license in this system. She observed, "When you lose control of your body, you have just about lost all you have in this world!"[73]

What might appear as sexual license to some, moreover, often derived from the constraints created by extreme poverty and the moral revisions they necessitated. A 38-year-old laundress, for example, traded sex with white prisoners for food and relied on assistance from boyfriends as she attempted to support six children and three elderly dependents during the Depression. When her teenage daughter became pregnant, she was angry: ". . . I told her dat I'd worked like a dog to raise her and had talked my tongue pretty near out, trying to show her de pitfalls of sin." The real source of her anger, however, was her concern that the girl had been involved with a white man without receiving any return except another child to feed.[74]

The desire to protect daughters and other women from conditions that would give white men opportunities to exploit them sexually magnified men's domestic power. Although black men were not able to confront white power directly, marriage did offer black women some measure of distance and protection from the menace of sexual and other violence perpetrated by white men. In the rural areas, daughters usually lived with their natal family until they married.

Many women tried to keep their daughters from work in domestic service, often by going to work themselves instead. Speaking at the 1893 World Columbian Exposition, Anna Julia Cooper drew attention to "the painful, patient, and silent toil of mothers to gain title to the bodies of their daughters" confronted by abusive white men. Another African American woman affirmed that

> ... there is no sacrifice I would not make, no hardship I would not undergo rather than allow my daughters to go in service where they would be thrown constantly in contact with Southern white men for they consider the colored girl their special prey.

Other blacks tried to marry their daughters at a young age to men who were responsible earners in order to reduce the likelihood that they would work outside the family while single and to avert the extreme destitution after marriage that could result in their exploitation by white men.[75]

Zora Neale Hurston personified the subtle dynamics of gender, race, and sexuality in the rural South in her 1937 novel *Their Eyes Were Watching God*. The protagonist, Janie Crawford, was raised by her grandmother, Nanny. Above all else, Nanny sought to provide Janie with security from destitution and devaluation, telling her, ". . . Ah can't die easy thinkin' maybe de menfolks white or black is makin' a spit cup outa you. . . ." After Janie's sexual awakening became apparent, Nanny acted to ensure that Janie did not establish a relationship based on love or sexual attraction: she arranged the adolescent Janie's marriage to an older man who owned sixty acres of land. When Janie complained that she couldn't love him, Nanny warned her that

> Dat's de very prong all us black women gits hung on. Dis love! Dat's just what's got us uh pullin' and uh haulin' and sweatin' and doin' from can't see in de mornin' till can't see at night.[76]

Through that marriage and two others, Janie struggled to find her identity, voice, and place in southern black culture. In her first marriage, she learned that the price for protection was an expectation of gratitude, deference, and hard work dictated by her husband. When she left him for a well-dressed and ambitious man who made her "Mrs. Mayor Starks," she found that the "privileges" of middle-class status her husband conferred on her were "the rock she was battered against." He expected her to contribute her labor to his store while remaining mute and distanced from the "mess uh commonness" in their small black community. When her husband's requirements that she serve simultaneously as a helpmeet and as a sexualized symbol of his status and power created tensions, he attempted to mediate them by ordering her to cover her long hair and, thus, cool the ardor of the men who patronized the store.[77]

As she struggled within these relationships, Janie came to realize that she could not renounce love, self-esteem, and autonomy for material security. As she struggled over her decision to marry a third time for love, she realized how difficult it was to trust in love, especially when she had some money and he did not. Once she developed that trust, "her soul crawled out of its hiding place." In Hurston's account, mutual respect and love created and sustained egalitarian patterns of authority and work, despite difficulties posed by jealousy and economic hardship.[78]

As Hurston's account conveys, the emotional and economic significance of black men in the lives of black women often created profound dilemmas. The economic marginality of black women and men created a material interdependence, but not a mutually acceptable normative structure that defined their economic or emotional obligations to one another. Moreover, the contested nature of gender relations made the establishment of unions that were harmonious, emotionally rewarding, and egalitarian very difficult.

Crisis in the Rural South

In the decades between 1890 and 1940, the southern political economy faced economic crisis and political challenge. In the rural areas, blacks and poor whites responded to volatile cotton prices, the ravages of the boll weevil, and increasing poverty with attempts at political mobilization, migration to the cities, and efforts to increase their production for subsistence. After the initial successes of interracial organizing under the Populist umbrella in the 1890s, southern leaders used race to divide the poor and to secure the continuing power of white elites. For blacks, the results of southern Progressivism included violence, disfranchisement, and segregation. In the 1930s, the Great Depression culminated decades of declining economic conditions with massive displacement of blacks from the rural sector and dire destitution.[79]

For decades, black farm owners had been losing their land in the wake of the boll weevil and fluctuating cotton prices. Already on the margin, they had no resources to weather the bad years. During the Depression, a drastic decline in the cotton market and federal policies designed to improve the farmer's lot operated together to force many black tenants and croppers off the land. The crop allotment policies of the Agricultural Adjustment Act promoted the removal of tenants from land being withheld from cultivation, while the subsidies paid to landowners who participated in the crop reduction effort were pocketed largely by whites. When the federal government required owners to pay more of these supports to tenants, many substituted wage laborers for tenants.[80]

Although they paid the greatest cost for the implementation of federal agricultural policies, blacks did not receive any special treatment to cushion the blows inflicted by economic transformation. Indeed, in the rural South, racism in relief policies coexisted with a desperate need on the part of the vast majority of blacks. The desire of employers and politicians to maintain wage and occupational structures segmented by race and gender precluded an equitable welfare policy. This meant that blacks were denied access to relief if officials assumed that work was available in traditional areas of employment, especially agricultural. The Works Projects Adminis-

tration eliminated projects for blacks whenever agriculture needed seasonal workers. Relief authorities also reduced benefits for black families, often below the subsistence level, in order to prevent the withdrawal of workers from low wage jobs. In many cases, blacks were denied assistance
altogether, despite very low income levels.[81]

Many black women confronted the loss of work in traditional categories. The depression in agriculture reduced their incomes drastically. At
the same time, the number of domestic service jobs declined as middle-class
employers discharged household help in order to economize and unemployed white women became increasingly willing to accept such work.
Laundresses faced increasing competition from washing machines and
power laundries. Even when they retained their traditional work, black
women faced deteriorating working conditions and even lower wages
as employers sought to retain their profit levels in the face of a depressed
economy.[82]

Since emancipation, black women had been turning to the city when the
rural economy and family could not provide them with support. Because
unmarried women had very limited employment options in the rural South,
many of them migrated to cities in search of work. As Reiff, Dahlin, and
Smith have noted, the large numbers of female-headed households in many
southern cities derived not from the disorganizing effects of city life, but
rather from the inability of the countryside to provide a living for unmarried women. Although blacks generally preferred to support their aging
mothers, rather than have them continue in employment, poverty often precluded this choice. Many rural widows had no living children; others could
not secure support from children already living in destitution.[83]

By the 1930s, the situation had grown even more desperate. A widow
who had returned to the countryside in order to be near her family found
it almost impossible to survive. She discussed her alternatives as follows:

> It's mighty tight on me to have to go working in dese fields half starved, and
> I ain't had a bit of money to buy a piece of cloth as big as my hand since I
> been back. I washed fer white people in Birmingham, and dey was good to
> me. I am jest gitting long by the hardest. . . . I don't see no money on time.
> Dey gives me a little something to eat 'cause I works wid dem and dey gives
> me a little groceries. I never was in this fix before in my life.[84]

In response to rural unemployment, southern racism, and urban opportunities (especially in the North), black women migrated in increasing
numbers to large cities. By the twentieth century, many black women decided to take the longer sojourn north. The outbreak of World War I in
1914, the decline of immigration, and the expansion of industry in the
north created more favorable conditions for black workers. Black women
also sought the social space provided them by the more covert racism of

the north and by the growth of large black communities in northern cities. A teacher who moved north to find that the only work she could get was in sewing assessed her constrained choice as follows:

> I just couldn't stand the treatment we got in the south, so I came north to escape humiliation and to live a fuller and freer life. And I'm happier, even though I'm finding it harder to make enough to live on.[85]

The disadvantages of service work were starkly revealed when World War I opened up new work options for some urban black women. Given a choice, they left their traditional employment in great numbers. Those who quit household work were especially glad to leave the long hours, confinement, and personalized racial and class conflict that often characterized their relationship to employers. Many entered traditional female-dominated industrial work, especially in garment-making, as white women shifted to jobs vacated by men entering the military. A few fortunate black women also obtained such work, often in jobs that were particularly unpleasant, heavy, and hazardous. They did so, as one put it, for the sake of the "Almighty dollar." In Philadelphia, for example, black women employed in the railroads earned double the income of those working in laundries and hotels. The median income for the black women interviewed by the Consumers' League was less than $10 a week; in the railroads, it ranged from $20 to $24.[86]

Black women's structural position within the American economy also made them vulnerable to racial displacement in times of economic stress. During the Depression, they faced the loss of work in all job categories. According to William Connor, executive director of the Cleveland Urban League, the problem of unemployment was even more serious for black women than for black men. The women had lost positions as hotel maids, elevator operators, and domestic servants to white competitors. In Tuscaloosa, Alabama, black women were losing their laundry business to mechanized laundries that hired white women. In order to promote the change, the laundries ran an advertising campaign featuring a black woman leaning over her washtub in an alley surrounded by dirty children.[87]

As a result, the labor force participation rate of black women declined and their occupational distribution was slightly altered. The proportion of black women aged 14 and over who were in the labor force declined from 43 percent in 1930 to 38 percent in 1940. This change measured not black women's decision to leave the labor force as an expression of their preference for domesticity, as Carl Degler has claimed, but their ejection from work that had historically placed a floor under black destitution.[88]

Letters from unemployed black women to the Roosevelts indicate the despair and privation caused by depression and discrimination. One 20-year-old woman responsible for the support of her mother and her child wrote the President that she was without work or any other source of income, concluding that "you are the only one I know to ask for help except the lord." Cerena Harris, noting the total lack of jobs for black women in the middle range of the female labor force, pointed out to Eleanor Roosevelt that "we can't all be nurses & school teachers—there's not enough schools and hospitals." She asked that the First Lady "please try to help us get work like other girls."[89]

For a variety of reasons, the Democratic administration of Franklin Roosevelt was not able to improve work opportunities for workers like Harris. The New Deal coalition did include blacks to an unprecedented degree, giving them some voice in its policies and extending desperately needed federal aid to them. The political priorities of the administration, however, dictated a neglect of overt civil rights activities, and the design of new programs often created structural disadvantages for minorities. Nevertheless, it did enable blacks to turn to the federal government for help for the first time in American history.[90]

That help, however, had to be offered within the constraints imposed by a racially segmented labor force. In order to ensure that blacks would be forced to take all work deemed appropriate for them, eligibility requirements were stricter for blacks than for whites and benefits were lower. Officials required blacks to seek aid from collateral relatives more often than whites, enforcing an extended family system in order to ensure that meager wages would be stretched as far as possible. Moreover, blacks were more likely to be assisted through direct relief rather than work relief because the latter conferred more dignity and support. This occurred in part because local communities had to provide some support for WPA work projects, and southern leaders, who were generally hostile to welfare, were particularly unwilling to aid blacks.[91]

When welfare officials did provide work relief for black women, they limited it to the kinds of work in which they were usually employed. Most black women who were enrolled in federal projects worked as seamstresses, laundresses, laborers, and domestic servants. Despite the considerable evidence to the contrary, white officials often concluded that black women's unemployment and desperately low wages were caused by their lack of training in domestic service and similar work.[92]

Even minimal assistance could enable women and their families to survive the oppressive conditions of the Depression. One woman household head found the commodities program a real help: "A woman came around once a week with pork, butter, eggs, and a lot of other things, so we eat de best we ever had."[93]

Black women's access to welfare varied by region. In the urban North, racial discrimination was much less pronounced than in the South. As a result, very poor black families were almost as likely as their white counterparts to receive some public assistance. According to Gunnar Myrdal, approximately one-half of black families in northern cities were receiving some public subsidy.[94]

Welfare encompasses more than the assistance provided to the unemployed. During the Depression, the relief system also subsidized low-wage employers by supplementing the incomes of their workers. In the South, for example, hundreds of families of tobacco workers were receiving welfare payments. A November 1934 study of these relief families revealed that 55 percent of black and 28 percent of white families earned less than $28 a month from their processing jobs. Among blacks employed in the leaf houses, most of whom were women, 87 percent earned less than $28 a month. Government policies regarding tobacco worker access to relief and benefit levels reflected and reinforced racial differentials in pay in the industry.[95]

The provision of benefits under the Social Security Act operated to maintain a segmented labor force. Its unemployment compensation program tied eligibility and the level of benefits to a worker's past employment record, benefiting most those who had stable employment patterns and higher wages. The exclusion of domestic service and agricultural work from coverage altogether indicated the degree to which workers for those sectors had to be secured by the elimination of other income options. These provisions of the law also excluded the vast majority of black women workers from the "safety net" created by the Social Security Act.[96]

By 1937, differential access to Social Security was reflected in the numbers who had gained wage credits under the system. Of those aged 15 to 64, 50 percent of white men, 40 percent of black men, 20 percent of white women, and 8 percent of black women had accumulated wage credits. Because these statistics include those who are not in the labor force, the racial differentials between black and white women workers are understated.[97]

The most important source of disadvantage for black women in the labor force came from their exclusion from all but the lowest-paying, least desirable jobs. The strategies available to white women workers to improve their workplace status—protective legislation and unionization—often failed to benefit black women because their location in the labor market precluded effective organization and made it difficult to regulate wages and working conditions. Depression-era unemployment and wage levels, as well as New Deal policies, revealed and reinforced the precarious position of black women in the American economy. Although their access to welfare, especially in northern cities, cushioned the impact of economic change to some degree, they continued to occupy the most vulnerable and exploited segment of the American economy. As the declining employment rates of black women confirm, New Deal programs offered few solutions to the problems created by black women's structural location in the economy.[98]

City Life and the Family

Beginning with the Great Migration of the 1910s, blacks poured into northern cities, fleeing the destitution of the rural South. The conditions of urban life for blacks worsened as more and more people squeezed into the confined areas reserved to blacks by urban developers and politicians. The overcrowding was compounded by the fact that the recreation and vice prohibited in white, middle-class neighborhoods was increasingly located in poor and non-white communities. This pattern derived from and contrasted with the separation between family and the "public" world signified by the growth of the white suburbs in this period. The implications of this for the black community generally and for women particularly were complex.[99]

Black women had to struggle against high rents, poor housing conditions, overcrowding, and lack of privacy as they tried to support and raise their families. The 1910s migration to Pittsburgh, for example, prompted the conversion of sheds, warehouses, and abandoned buildings to housing in the black ghetto. In 1930s Chicago, enterprising landlords divided up apartment buildings into kitchenettes—one-room flats with an ice-box, a bed, and an occasional hotplate. These apartments served as home to thousands of desperate black families.[100]

Overcrowding in housing promoted a lively street culture as blacks sought space to escape domestic pressures and to express their individuality. That street culture, however, occupied the intersection of various systems of power where possibilities for oppression and liberation coexisted. Because it fragmented families by gender and generation and because it offered commercial and sexual temptations, ghetto life challenged black women's moral authority as mothers and as managers of a family economy.[101]

Those temptations posed various threats to family integrity and well-being, including those of infidelity, squandering of family resources, and desertion. They also eroded parental authority in a context in which adult women's need for assistance from older children was growing. For daughters coming of age in urban ghettos, the new commercialized sexuality could mean new possibilities for their sexual exploitation in a masculinist urban culture.

Many women attempted to use religion as a protection against the attractions and dangers of city life. For them, religion was a means to uphold women's moral authority and to secure men's loyalty to family on terms congruent with women's interests. Religious ideology stressed men's financial responsibility to women and children and protected against the dangers of street culture. While women's religious faith created meaning and community in their lives, in some circumstances it also supported their domestic authority and material well-being.[102]

Religion played important and sometimes contradictory roles in the lives of African American women. Evelyn Brooks Higginbotham's study of women in the National Baptist Convention (NBC), the largest African American denomination, shows that women's authority in the church was based on their social contributions as mothers and teachers. Women active in the NBC constructed an ideology of racial self-help and pride based on the assumption that the assimilation of middle-class values, including those of domesticity, would enable black acceptance by whites and an improvement in their status. In rural areas and cities, for example, women missionaries created mothers' training schools to improve the domestic skills and values of black women.[103]

An important component of this strategy was the deployment of a politics of respectability that emphasized the ability of individuals to transcend racial derogation and poverty in order to construct moral lives and end racial oppression. At the same time, Higginbotham noted that "respectability's emphasis on individual behavior served inevitably to blame blacks for their victimization and, worse yet, to place an inordinate amount of blame on black women." Church women supported more than individual interventions, however. They also actively sustained the church's construction of alternative institutions, including schools, newspapers, charitable efforts, and youth facilities.[104]

In the urban setting, some mothers tried to use religion and an ideology of "respectability" to protect their daughters from the exploitation threatened by the sexual economy of American cities. After her daughter went into a prostitute's flat in their building, an urban mother asserted: "I ain't raisin' you to be a goddammed whore! Why I send you to Sunday school? Why I try to raise you right?" When their daughters and granddaughters took jobs in entertainment, many black women sounded warnings that their entry into a world of commercialized sexuality threatened them with a dangerous loss of respectability. Pianist Olivia Charlot recalled that her decision to enter the world of New Orleans jazz caused her grandmother to "put up a big fuss. She said, 'I think it's terrible. Those men are gonna disrespect you. . . .'"[105]

Neither family, church, nor community, however, provided an antidote to urban attractions. The anonymity of urban life, the availability of social and recreational activities outside the supervision of church and family, and individual access to money in a wage economy reduced the importance of kin relations and increased the significance of peer groups in social life. As in other working-class households in this period, the rise of a consumer culture altered family relations.[106]

Integration into an urban wage economy increased pressures on black marriages. Greater instability in black men's employment patterns coupled with the diminished social controls of urban life promoted marital instability. As in the countryside, marriages often foundered as women and men disagreed about issues of economic obligation, fidelity, and physical abuse. These tensions were greatly exacerbated by the Depression. As Jacqueline Jones notes, it is impossible to disentangle the economic roots of family conflict and disintegration in this period, although male unemployment and women's access to welfare and other sources of support outside of marriage both contributed to family instability. Despite changes in work roles imposed by the urban economy, men and women continued to create a livelihood and seek emotional support in an interdependent, but fragile, family system.[107]

Women's relationship to the new urban culture entailed more than vulnerability to masculinist peer culture, sexual exploitation, or family instability. For some women, it offered social freedoms, expanded work possibilities, an opportunity for political participation, sexual agency, and a new cultural voice. That voice received its strongest expression in the urban blues and jazz traditions of the 1920s and 1930s.[108]

Within those traditions, black women expressed their desires and confronted their disappointments, especially those experienced in relationships with men. Their songs explored the tensions between sexual and emotional dependence on men and their desire for some measure of autonomy, security, and dignity within and outside of heterosexual relationships. From Bessie Smith's assertion in "I Ain't Gonna Play No Second Fiddle" that "I'm used to playing lead" to Ma Rainey's "Prove It on Me Blues," where she declares that her lovers "must've been women, cause I don't like no men," African American women expressed their sexual desires and their disaffection with heterosexual relationships that were unequal and unsatisfying.[109]

Politics

Women, however, did not play lead within the civil rights movement. From Booker T. Washington to W. E. B. Dubois, leadership in the effort to improve black status and conditions rested in the hands of men. Women's political initiative and contributions, however, did enable them to stake out a critical role for themselves. This was especially the case in the movement to end the political crime of lynching in the American South. Led by Ida Wells-Barnett, the anti-lynching movement became the vehicle for black women's most radical critique of the race/gender system they confronted.

Wells analyzed the multiple political meanings in the oft-made charge that black men raped white women. According to Wells-Barnett, the myth of a pure white womanhood endangered by a bestial black manhood served to provide southern whites with carte blanche in their use of extralegal violence against blacks and to preclude northern criticism of southern racial politics. When power is conflated with masculine sexuality, any form of resistance becomes a sexual threat. Thus, the mythic structure of the South legitimated the murder of blacks regardless of their purported offense against the racial system. Wells-Barnett further observed that that system required the policing of white women's desires as well as the murder of blacks in order to sustain its own credibility. By their vigilance in attempting to prevent and obscure consensual liaisons between black men and white women, the custodians of southern honor acknowledged the possibility of that choice by white women.[110]

Wells-Barnett also exposed white men's sexual exploitation of black women, but implicitly rejected any extension to black women of the politics of sexual protection and constraint required of white women. As had Anna Julia Cooper before her, she concluded that southern "chivalry" was grounded in inequality and damaging to all women as well as to blacks. Wells-Barnett simultaneously acknowledged women's sexual desires and their right to sexual autonomy, rejecting Victorian passionlessness and claiming black women's right to refuse white men's "advances".[111]

Wells-Barnett's analysis of southern sexual politics was threatening not only to the southern caste system, but also to middle-class feminists' definition of their sexual politics. Frances Willard, for example, interpreted her suggestion that southern white women would consent to unions with blacks as an attack on womanhood generally and as a threat to middle-class women's efforts to control men's sexuality. Having premised their politics on the repression of women's desires, Victorian feminists would not surrender the informal powers they had wrested through sexual denial for the dangers and uncertainties of claims of sexual autonomy in a still-patriarchal world.[112]

This did not mean, however, that black and white feminists occupied no common ground. Black women supported woman suffrage and other measures sustaining human rights. For them feminist arguments claiming equality of rights in a democratic system provided support for their claims to gender and racial equality. Although some black women sought to justify women's rights on the grounds of "feminine" attributes and responsibilities, they were more wary of such arguments than white feminists.[113]

Conclusions

Emancipation and the evolution of the plantation system had mixed implications for black women's roles and status. The erosion of white authority over black family and work relations and the legal protection of black families enhanced the security and autonomy of black women relative to whites. By reducing the amount of contact between black women and white men, these changes provided some protection against sexual exploitation.

Moreover, the sexual politics of race created a dissonance between extremely patriarchal ideologies and the politics of racial resistance. Because the protector role was only indirectly available to black men, their ability to claim women's subordination was weakened. In addition, the economic oppression of black men and black women's definition of their family roles to include a substantial support responsibility precluded a gender inequality founded on wide disparities in work, income, and status.

But black women and men were, to some extent, at odds over the terms under which they were to create the conditions for material and psychological survival as they confronted the American racial caste system. Those tensions derived, at least in part, from a gender division of labor that made women more responsible for the support of children than men and implicitly defined black men's oppression in terms of the loss of masculine prerogatives.

Many men expected to be able to dictate the household division of labor and to enforce a double standard in marital norms regarding sexuality. For some, violence served as a tool of last resort, the weapon of those for whom material, political, and ideological dominance were not fully available. Women's resistance to masculine authority was occasioned by those same circumstances. Their economic position, however, did not offer them advantage over men or enable them to secure egalitarian relationships. The decades of struggle over the terms of gender relations reveal the structural dimension of black family patterns and the inadequacy of private struggles in securing full domestic equality for women.[114]

Black women's place in the American economy did not change significantly in the period before World War II. In 1940, 90 percent of employed black women worked in agriculture or service occupations. The deterioration of the southern rural economy in the preceding two decades had promoted displacement and migration, but America's cities offered only poverty and continuing economic insecurity. Although the contours of black women's work and family roles in modern America were being shaped in these processes of change, their full implications would be determined in the succeeding decades.

8

Progress and Protest

AFRICAN AMERICAN WOMEN SINCE 1940

IN THE YEARS SINCE 1940, African American women have experienced important changes in their work, family, and community roles. An accelerated urban migration, economic changes, the development of the welfare state, and a changed political and legal context have dramatically altered the conditions of their lives. Nothing, however, was more important for the transformation of African American status in the United States than the dismantling of the plantation economy in the South. Although that system had been eroding for decades, economic changes initiated during World War II provided the impetus for its destruction, ending its stranglehold on black workers and black lives.[1]

The birth of the "New South" required a significant and often troubling revision of social relations. The caste politics and overt racism that had long characterized the south became a liability for a region seeking industrial capital. As Jessie Daniel Ames noted in 1939:

> We have managed to reduce lynchings not because we've grown more law abiding or respectable but because lynchings become such bad advertising. The South is going after big industry at the moment, and a lawless, lynch-mob population isn't going to attract very much outside capital. And this is

the type of attitude that can be turned to advantage much more speedily than the abstract appeal to brotherly love.[2]

Economic considerations did not prevent violence and disregard for law on the part of many white southerners in the wake of a growing civil rights movement. In 1957, the specter of white mobs trying to keep African American children from attending Central High School in Little Rock haunted the national conscience, raising questions regarding the legitimacy and stability of southern political institutions. Thereafter, violent resistance to black activism deepened the crisis.[3]

The successes and visibility of the mass-based civil rights movement enabled African Americans to press their claims in regional and national politics. Through their activism, African American women contributed enormously to American political change, securing for themselves and others increased rights and opportunities. As a result, they entered new job categories, received better wages than in the past, and participated more directly in national decision-making. Greater legal protection against discrimination in the labor force, mandated by the 1964 Civil Rights Act, combined with expansion in the tertiary sector of the economy to improve black women's economic status substantially.[4]

African American women and men found that they needed whatever assistance they could get in their struggle to secure a livelihood in the postwar economy. Millions moved to the cities in this period with little cushion against the vicissitudes of an urban wage economy. They had virtually no savings and were entirely dependent on wage work for support. Moreover, racism and their late entry into competition for urban jobs impeded their mobility. As a result, black women and men have faced chronic unemployment and all the problems associated with urban poverty.[5]

Reduced demand for workers in the rural sector and discrimination in urban jobs created a new class of black dependents—many of them women and children—whose claims to support strained traditional welfare and employment practices in the North as well as the South. The increasing reliance of Afro American women on public assistance as a source of support in a discriminatory economy has fueled a backlash and provided a convenient scapegoat for those attempting to stem the tide of change. The "welfare mother" has joined the "black rapist" as a central mythic figure in America's racial politics, revealing their changed character.[6]

In the last few decades, public officials have subjected African Americans to heightened scrutiny and regulation of their private lives, especially in the areas of gender relations, sexuality, and reproduction. Teenage motherhood and the rise of female-headed families have become convenient explanations for the persistence of black poverty, despite the fact that the pregnancy rates of black teens have decreased consistently since the 1950s. Politicians who have directed their attention to the problem of welfare—

rather than those of education, jobs, and wages for women and men—have often obscured and exacerbated problems in the African American family, while professing to solve them. Not coincidentally, they have also capitalized politically by heaping abuse on women whose public dependence has come to be defined as a private failure with dangerous social consequences.[7]

The family and economic problems confronting African American women in the postwar era did not originate in welfare policies, however. Their causes were multiple, deriving from historic and continuing patterns of racism and discrimination, the legacy of earlier black family traditions, and the intensified pressures confronting blacks in an urban environment. For Afro-American women, especially, the ghetto has been hostile terrain. Marked culturally as masculine space, the streets of the ghetto have signified the denial of their maternal authority and of their personal autonomy.[8]

Most important, they have symbolized conflicts between women and men as they try to establish the norms whereby they are to provide economic security, emotional support, and dignity to one another in a society unwilling to provide regular jobs and adequate incomes for African Americans. The debate over black "matriarchy" and male "absence" from families has obscured the profound economic and emotional interdependence between black women and men and the heightened tensions over the terms of their mutual needs in recent decades. Poor African American men's increasing loyalty to a peer group and a masculine identity defined in street culture has conflicted with women's attempts to enforce a stronger domestic orientation by men. These conflicts have worsened as life in inner-city America has become more precarious and dangerous.[9]

The economic opportunities that define respectable masculinity and men's relationships to women and children in American society have been denied to African American men, who have internalized dominant norms sufficiently to interpret their experiences either as personal failures or imposed powerlessness. As a result, some have redefined masculinity in terms of the aggression, violence, and materialism that also receives a kind of ambivalent sanction for men in the dominant culture. As bell hooks has observed, poor men and men of color "often suffer from blindly and passively acting out a myth of masculinity that is life-threatening."[10]

When African American men engage in activities and work that are illegal, dangerous, and stigmatized, they encounter consequences more severe than those meted out to whites in similar circumstances. In addition, popular media and politicians offer a stream of negative representations of African American men as prone to violence and unable to participate responsibly in the economy and society. In short, racial oppression is gendered for men as well as women. Racism constructs some oppressions shared by African American women and men and some specific to each gender.[11]

The result of heightened gender conflict has been an increase in marital dissolution among blacks accompanied by a growing reluctance on the part of black women to marry at all. By the 1980s, two-thirds of adult African American women were living without husbands and the majority of African American children were living apart from their fathers. This rise in female-headed families has meant an increase in black women's bread-winning responsibilities that has far outstripped their gains in income in the postwar era.[12]

At the same time, African American family structures—and women's roles and position within them—have become more varied as some African Americans have experienced occupational mobility in the postwar period. Black family dynamics vary with the migration status, place of residence, region, education, and income of family members. Across the social spectrum, however, black families have been affected by public policy decisions often taken without regard for their effects on the well-being of African Americans.

Many of the changes experienced by blacks in the decades since 1940 were exemplified and accelerated during World War II. These included the abandonment of the plantation South for cities throughout the nation; discrimination in employment, housing, and access to basic public services; ghettoization; and family separations and disruptions. In one regard, however, World War II was different: the economic boom it caused revealed the possibilities and limitations created for African Americans in a "full employment" economy whose new jobs often carried high wages and the benefits of unionization.

War and Postwar

Because it withdrew millions of men from the civilian economy and required the production of vast amounts of war material, American entry into World War II created an unprecedented labor shortage. The demand for workers occurred in all sectors of the economy, but was especially pronounced in durable goods manufacturing. Because jobs in this sector had traditionally been held by white males and because workers had organized successful unionization drives in many basic industries in the 1930s, wages and other benefits were much better in durable goods than in the occupations usually held by blacks and women. As a result, the war years challenged traditional patterns of segregation in work and income, creating the possibility for radical alterations in employer practices and in social relations generally.[13]

Wartime demand also dramatically altered the plantation economy of the rural South. By drawing workers off the land, the war economy rapidly accelerated the mechanization of southern agriculture. The organization of rural production shifted from a labor-intensive system dependent on large numbers of unskilled and impoverished sharecroppers to one characterized by low numbers of semi-skilled wage workers. As a result, African American women's place in the southern and national economies was dramatically altered.[14]

Those alterations did not occur without political pressure. In order to secure their rights in the expanding wartime economy, blacks organized to ensure that defense jobs were open to minorities as well as whites. Beginning with A. Philip Randolph's March on Washington Movement of 1940–41, they pressured the Roosevelt administration to outlaw discrimination in defense industries. Reluctantly, Roosevelt signed an executive order prohibiting discrimination on the grounds of race or religion and establishing the Fair Employment Practice Committee to monitor federal contractors' compliance with the order.[15]

The FEPC lacked real enforcement authority and had to rely more on persuasion than coercion. As a result, the occupational gains experienced by blacks derived more from economic expansion than from federal pressure. As the War Manpower Commission expressed it, "we cannot afford the luxury of thinking in terms of white men's work. It isn't white men's work we had to do—it's war work and there's more than enough of it."[16]

African American women, however, faced an especially deep-seated discrimination in the workplace even when white male workers were in short supply. Employers in industries like shipbuilding, where the preference for male labor was very strong, turned to black men before they hired women in significant numbers. Those who turned to women workers to remedy their wartime labor scarcity resisted hiring black women. Moreover, those who did employ African American women often assigned them to work that was hot, dirty, disagreeable, and hazardous. Afro-American women were also more likely to be hired for jobs in which substandard wages and working conditions prevailed. In Baltimore, for example, many black women in manufacturing categories worked in munitions or in the canneries, where employment was seasonal and insecure even during the war.[17]

Maya Angelou's challenge to racial barriers in San Francisco mirrored that of other black women seeking war work. When Angelou applied for a job as a streetcar conductor, the receptionist told her that they were only accepting applicants referred by agencies. Undeterred, Angelou reminded her that they had run an ad in the morning paper and demanded to see the personnel manager. The woman claimed that he was out for the day. Angelou noted in her autobiography that she and the receptionist "were firmly joined in the hypocrisy to play out the scene," a scene "stale with familiarity" even though she had never enacted it before and, in all probability, neither had her counterpart. She departed, but returned with "the frequency of a person on salary," until the company relented and hired her.[18]

With few refinements, that scene was replayed thousands of times across the continent during the war years. Some Afro-American women returned time and again to the same gatekeepers seeking work in labor-short occupations. Some, like Angelou, wore the opposition down and secured the jobs they wanted; many failed to obtain work commensurate with their abilities and training. Some of them turned to collective strategies. At one Detroit plant African American women lined up at the gate and told the white women who appeared there that the company was hiring blacks only. Others joined with civil rights organizations in staging protests against discrimination or filed complaints with the FEPC. As Josephine Blackwell observed in her FEPC complaint, proving discrimination was hard because "no factory is going to have the nerve to tell you 'we do not hire colored.'"[19]

Despite continuing discrimination, wartime demand gave African American women their first important break out of work in agriculture and domestic service. They responded with alacrity, moving to war-boom communities and entering the labor force in large numbers. In Detroit, for example, the black female labor force rate jumped from 32 percent in 1940 to 49 percent in 1944. Nationally, the proportion of the black female labor force employed in industrial work increased from 7 to 18 percent, in jobs as laborers from 6 to 17 percent. At the same time, the percentage employed in domestic service dropped from 60 to 45 percent. By contrast, African American women made little progress in entering clerical and sales work during the war.[20]

Discrimination in other areas of American society contributed to the problems of African American women workers. Continued segregation in housing limited blacks to increasingly overcrowded neighborhoods in central cities, often located at a considerable distance from war plants. As Fanny Christina Hill has noted, the overcrowding required cooperation:

> We were accustomed to shacking up with each other. We had to live like that because that was the only way to survive. Negroes, as a rule, are accustomed to a lot of people around. They have lived like that from slavery time on. We figured out how to get along with each other.[21]

Local officials frequently ignored the needs of black areas in determining transportation priorities in a time of shortages of personnel and equipment for public transit systems. In Los Angeles, for example, the transit company made no runs to Watts at night, seriously complicating the transportation arrangements of shift workers. For women, who frequently had family as well as work responsibilities, the transportation problems could limit work options.[22]

Moreover, the disadvantages experienced by African Americans in gaining access to war-curtailed commercial services—including laundries, restaurants, and stores—posed special difficulties for women shouldering a double burden. Segregation in federally funded day care facilities limited the access of black women to an essential service and contributed to absenteeism and turnover.[23]

Although their wage levels were considerably higher than they had been before the war, black women still had difficulty making ends meet because they were often supporting or aiding relatives and were much more likely than white women to have small children to care for. In some cases, transportation and day care expenses took a disproportionate amount of their earnings. A woman employed at the Edgewood Arsenal in Baltimore earned $25 a week, of which she spent $7.50 to $9.00 on child care and $2.50 on transportation.[24]

Discrimination in housing, day care, transportation, and commercial establishments affected African American women's family decisions. Facing uncertain employment circumstances and lacking adequate housing and day care, many women workers chose to leave their children with relatives when they migrated to new communities. Although this practice had deep historical roots, its persistence during the war years derived from the lack of institutional support for black family integrity.[25]

African American women's labor force attachment was also reflected in the postwar plans expressed by women employed in defense industries. In eight of the nine cities surveyed for racial differences, at least 88 percent of the African American women workers declared their intention to continue working. Whatever their aspirations, black women faced discriminatory policies in firing, rehiring, and seniority as employers re-established sex and race segregation in the postwar workplace. Margaret Turner, for example, found herself reassigned to the cleaning crew after her wartime stint as a production worker in the cigarette industry.[26]

The Myth of African American Women's Labor Force Advantage

African American women workers discharged from their war jobs could not return wholesale to their traditional work, however. The reduction of jobs in the rural areas accelerated as southern landowners continued to mechanize many facets of agricultural production in the postwar era. In the process, they evicted many black tenant farmers, replacing them with smaller numbers of wage laborers, mostly men. In addition, the growth of mechanized laundries cost many women their jobs as home laundresses. Displaced from traditional sources of employment, black women increasingly crowded into the lowest paid sectors of the urban economy.[27]

The decline of home-based employment, most notably in agriculture and as laundresses, necessitated a movement of married women workers into jobs outside the home. As a result of these structural shifts, the historic tension between their responsibilities as breadwinners and as homemakers was intensified. Consequently, the employment rates of African American married women grew more slowly than those of white wives in the postwar period. In order to balance their support and caretaking duties, some black women went on welfare; many relied even more heavily on the family networks that had sustained them under the plantation system.

Others, however, were able to capitalize on the widening opportunities provided by postwar prosperity, urbanization, the industrialization of the South, and, after 1964, by more effective legal protection against discrimination. Various circumstances have contributed to the pattern of mobility, some operating to greater effect than others at different points in time. Throughout the period, improving levels and quality of education, urban migration, and a generally expanding economy have promoted some expansion of opportunity.

In the 1940s black women workers experienced their first substantial break with historic employment patterns, moving out of domestic service and agricultural work in large numbers and into some categories of service and manual work. By the 1950s the continuing migration of blacks from the rural South to cities and the growing demand for women workers in service, sales, and clerical work enabled increasing numbers of black women to move into new kinds of work.

In the period from 1940 to 1964 African American women tested the possibilities for economic advance in a time of urban migration and general prosperity. Because their educational levels improved dramatically and their movement to the cities substantially widened their job possibilities, black women had reason to expect appreciable job mobility. What they experienced, however, was a complex pattern of economic improvement and relative stagnation as they advanced primarily into occupations vacated by white women.[28]

Among African Americans generally, this period was marked by somewhat higher incomes, some occupational mobility, increasing insecurity of employment, and little improvement in family incomes relative to those of whites. Most income advance occurred during the war years. In urban areas, the average African American family earned 66 percent of the money income received by the average white family in 1945. By 1949, urban black families' income was 58 percent of that of white families.[29]

The changes created since the Depression had also created a generational divide among African American women, with a large proportion of older women among those still working in agriculture and household service. By contrast, those who had found jobs in clerical, sales, and factory work tended to be much younger. Among African American women in 1960, only 9 percent of clerical workers were over the age of 45, compared with 57 percent of those employed in agriculture.[30]

A victim of this process of selective change, Hannah Nelson reflected on the system that confined her to domestic service despite her considerable abilities:

> I am a woman of sixty-one years old and I was born into this world with some talent. But I have done the work that my grandmother's mother did. It is not through any failing of mine that this is so. . . . I have grown to womanhood in a world where the saner you are, the madder you are made to appear.[31]

Those who, like Hannah Nelson, remained in domestic service in the postwar period found that conditions had not improved substantially. The work was still characterized by low wages, long hours, and few benefits. Moreover, workers were vulnerable to sexual harassment, lack of privacy, and psychological exploitation by employers who required deference while they set the terms for the personal relationship entailed in working in someone else's home. Mabel Lincoln succinctly summarized the risks for household workers: "Now, if you are a woman slinging somebody else's hash and busting somebody else's suds or doing whatsoever you might do to keep yourself from being a tramp or a willing slave, you will be called out of your name [insulted] and asked out of your clothes."[32]

Despite the decline of agricultural employment, many African American women remained in rural areas during this period. Some continued to work in sharecropping families or agricultural wage labor. The latter work generally went to men, however, limiting rural women's ability to support themselves. Blacks often found that the only land available to them was the least desirable. Anne Moody remembered her stepfather's anger and fear when he realized that the land he had rented after the war was filled with shrapnel, grenades, and other remnants of its recent history as an army camp. She noted, "From then on Raymond plowed very carefully." He also insisted, however, that all family members work in the fields.[33]

Some African American women supplemented meager farm earnings with traditional sources of income—like domestic service—while others commuted to nearby towns and cities to take jobs in occupations made available to them by white mobility, civil rights legislation, and improved access to transportation. Even so, domestic responsibilities and conventional mores kept women closer to home in their job searches, limiting some to part-time and temporary work. Hylan Lewis's study of a rural black South Carolina community in the mid-1950s revealed that those women who were employed full-time, year-round earned about $500 a year. The men, who were employed less regularly, earned somewhat less than $1000 a year.[34]

Because of the deep-seated prejudice that African American women have encountered at the hands of employers, economic expansion alone has never been sufficient to improve their relative labor force status, much less to ensure them equality of opportunity at work. During the "full employment" economies of World War II and the Korean War, for example, other groups of workers improved their occupational and income status much more dramatically than did African American women. Because prosperity does not "trickle down" to them as rapidly as to some others, equal opportunity policies have been critical to advancing African American women's workplace status.[35]

The passage of the 1964 Civil Rights Act was especially important because it forced many businesses to remove racial barriers to Afro-American women for the first time. Affirmative action thus created expanded opportunities for them in certain clerical, sales, and manufacturing categories and raised their income levels. According to Paul Burstein, the earnings of non-white women relative to white men remained largely unchanged before the passage of equal opportunity legislation. Between 1964 and 1978, however, they jumped from 28 percent of white men's earnings to 47 percent.[36]

The initial gains from the outlawing of discrimination were not equally available to all African American women. In the first decade of affirmative action efforts, those who were younger and better educated experienced more employment advances than others. Because discriminatory practices had been especially pervasive in the South, legal guarantees promoted more immediate changes for black women there than elsewhere as previously "white" jobs in the textile, tobacco, communications, retail, and other industries were opened to blacks. At the same time, discriminatory practices remained more systematic in the South than elsewhere.[37]

Within a year of the enactment of the Civil Rights Act, the number of South Carolina textile companies that would not hire African American women had declined from 24 to 4. In that same period, black women made up 44 percent of the new women hired in the North Carolina textile mills. The southern subsidiaries of AT&T also abandoned policies barring black women from work in operator and other clerical positions. By 1969, 17 percent of the women hired by South Central Bell were African American. As a result of a 1971 consent decree, Southern Bell was forced to rescind its ban against the hiring of unwed mothers—a policy that had especially disadvantaged black women.[38]

As a result of improved education, northern migration, urbanization, and, especially, the Civil Rights Act, African American women experienced substantial occupational mobility in the 1960s and 1970s. During the 1960s, the proportions of black women workers employed as domestic servants declined from 34 to 14 percent. In 1965 about 24 percent found work in white-collar categories. By 1978, that figure had increased to 46 percent. Much of that change was accounted for by younger African American women taking jobs in the clerical sector.[39]

Black women's gains have occurred almost entirely through the integration of job categories historically assigned to women, not because "men's" jobs have been opened to them to any great degree. By contrast, African American men have moved more slowly into new categories in the male labor force. The structure of the female labor force may facilitate a more rapid integration than the male labor force allows because the stakes are smaller (in income, power, and prestige) and because white women cannot translate racism into discrimination as effectively as white men through such devices as union apprenticeship systems, legal stalling, and political challenges to affirmative action. Moreover, many low-wage women's categories have experienced rapid growth since World War II, facilitating an expansion of minority women's access to those fields.[40]

For a long time, scholars and others have interpreted African American women's access to any jobs as yet another form of economic advantage over African American men. Gerda Lerner, for example, has stated that there is a "sex loophole" in race discrimination, a result of the willingness of white society to make jobs available for black women rather than black men. According to Lerner, black men were thus "deprived of the gap in status opportunity and economic advancement over black women, which white men take for granted in regard to white women." Daniel Moynihan took the idea of African American female advantage to its most egregious extreme, arguing that black women had greater educational and employment opportunities than black men, received greater encouragement to succeed within their families, and utilized their "superior" position to dominate black men.[41]

Lerner correctly concludes that men's structural superiority over women is less pronounced among African Americans than among whites. Black men's advantage relative to black women, however, is still substantial. African American women have higher unemployment rates and substantially lower incomes than African American men. In 1969, 20 percent of black men workers earned less than $3000 a year, while more than half of black women workers labored for so little. Moreover, sex discrimination in the workplace disadvantages all women, radically limiting their ability to translate educational achievements into occupational and income improvements. The postwar economy offered African American women neither adequate wages nor regular work. In order to support their families, most had to have assistance—from men or the state or both.[42]

Women, Power, and Poverty

Their lives marked by inadequate incomes and onerous support responsibilities, African American women have pieced together a livelihood for themselves and others through paid work, kin exchanges, marriage, liaisons with men, and public support. Through their kin networks, they have circulated goods and services to each other, providing food, clothing, furniture, loans, child care, transportation, and other necessary items to those in greatest need. The problem for many African American women is that no one source of income—whether it is work, welfare, kin, or men—can provide all that their families require on a regular basis. Therefore, poor women must keep their options open to the greatest degree possible.

Each economic strategy employed by women implies its own restrictions and reciprocities; balancing their often competing claims while preserving an essential measure of personal autonomy requires enormous resourcefulness. For many years, for example, welfare officials would cut off benefits under the Aid to Families with Dependent Children program if they believed that the mother was involved with a man who might be contributing resources to the family.

African American women's efforts to meet their obligations to a matrifocal kin network have often conflicted with their desire to maintain relationships with boyfriends or husbands. Many women have found it difficult to provide support for relatives when their husbands expect resources to remain within the nuclear family. A young black woman described the conflicts she experienced trying to balance the claims of her kin and her desire to marry:

> They don't want to see me married! Magnolia knows that it be money getting away from her. I couldn't spend the time with her and the kids and be giving her the money that I do now. I'd have my husband to look after. I couldn't go where she want me to go. I couldn't come every time she calls me. . . . They broke me and Otis up. They kept telling me that he didn't want me and that he didn't want the responsibility.[43]

Reliance on a kin network for critical support means that emotional and economic dependencies are closely connected, generating great tensions in family relations. Managing those tensions becomes an essential component of women's breadwinning work. Poor African American women, thus, often compensate for their lack of material resources by using the skills and leverage available to them from traditional women's roles. They deploy their domestic, nurturing, and interpersonal skills, and, at times, their sexuality, with their economic circumstances in mind. Their family power (and its limitations), thus, derives at least as much from their kin and domestic work as it does from their access to paid work or welfare.

In order to maintain their support system, however, they have often had to subordinate individual preferences and needs to group requirements as well as work to maintain harmony in the family group. Others have had to relinquish some control over important areas of their lives in order to increase their economic security. This is sharply revealed in the sharing of authority over children in matrifocal kin networks. Women leave their children with grandmothers, aunts, and others when their life circumstances dictate. When the mother finds that her kin do not share her views on proper childrearing, she has to defer to their authority as long as she accepts their assistance. Indeed, matrifocal kin networks, rather than the biological mother, have sometimes made the decision about who is to serve as the primary parent to a child.[44]

This complex pattern of interdependence and individual assertion means that poor African American women must both strain and strengthen the relationships that are central to their well-being. It is no wonder that a woman described by Lee Rainwater as one of the most successful practitioners of this great balancing act felt that "her family was continually on the edge of a precipice. . . ." For those with less skill and luck in this high-risk enterprise, the precipice looked like safe terrain.[45]

Not surprisingly, many African American women sought assistance from the state in their attempts to support their families. Their interactions with welfare officials were shaped by the general exigencies of their circumstances and by the other strategies they had developed to survive. In addition, the terms of black women's access to welfare were highly contested in the postwar period.

The welfare system responded only haltingly to the needs of African American women and others disadvantaged by structural inequities in the economy. Until the 1960s, the AFDC program served only a small proportion of those actually eligible for its benefits, giving preferential treatment to widows and whites. As a result, most unmarried African American mothers did not receive support from AFDC. Moreover, welfare officials remained responsive to the needs of local employers, especially in the rural economy, removing mothers from eligibility whenever demands for workers increased.[46]

Over time, however, the AFDC program came to include more minority women, unmarried mothers, and women who were divorced or deserted. In 1936–37 only 2 percent of children receiving ADC were those of unmarried parents; by 1961 that figure had reached 21 percent. As its client population changed, however, AFDC became more costly, visible, and controversial. As Grace Marcus noted, the social stigmas attached to the new AFDC population "undermined the appeal that a category for children might otherwise carry" and "diverted attention from the children's needs."[47]

Moreover, politicians, social workers, and other "experts" constructed highly racialized interpretations of unwed motherhood and welfare dependency in the postwar period. By the late 1950s, southern politicians had launched a vendetta against black welfare mothers, especially those with illegitimate children. By invoking deeply rooted stereotypes associating black women with profligate sexuality, reproductive excess, and economic parasitism, these politicians sought not only to renounce public responsibility for impoverished African American women and children, but also to discredit the black civil rights movement. In response, welfare officials used vague provisions of the law to remove thousands of families from the AFDC rolls. They charged that the women were not providing suitable homes for their children or that the mothers' sexual partners were "substitute fathers" and, thus, the children were not "deprived of parental support" as the law required.[48]

These actions culminated years of efforts on the part of welfare officials either to compel support of children from the biological fathers or to locate "substitute fathers" who could be coerced into serving as the family breadwinner. For women recipients of AFDC, the result was midnight raids and social worker inspections to locate signs of men's unauthorized presence in the household. The message to women recipients was clear: they were to be celibate or supported by men.[49]

The "illegitimacy" of African American women's behavior came from their refusal to use their sexuality in service to the goals of the state. Public officials assumed that women should and could secure men's financial responsibility for children by restricting their childbearing to marriage. Many of the women denied welfare did find that their economic dependence on men increased, primarily because the rural economy could not provide them enough work to support their families. That dependence, however, did not promote marriage or reduce the likelihood that they would need public assistance in the future. A study of those removed from AFDC in Mississippi revealed that they were more likely to have illegitimate children in the future than those retained in the program. The women denied benefits had even less leverage with men than before, were more likely to use their sexuality to secure assistance from them, and were more subject to exploitation from all quarters.[50]

Ironically, these very women whose power is so limited and contingent have been defined in American culture as "matriarchs" who wield great and damaging power in their families and, indirectly, in American society. The myths of the black matriarch and of the welfare mother have been used to rationalize the unequal status of women and minorities while supporting claims that the American political economy promotes equal opportunity. These views were propounded most effectively by Daniel Moynihan in a 1965 report for the Department of Labor entitled *The Negro Family: The Case for National Action*. More than any other document, the Moynihan Report has set the terms for the debate over African American poverty in recent decades.[51]

It attributed African American poverty to family structure, concluding that "the Negro community has been forced into a matriarchal structure . . . which . . . seriously retards the progress of the group as a whole, and imposes a crushing burden on the Negro male. . . ." Although Moynihan did differ with many conservatives regarding the importance of providing adequate jobs for black men in order that they might have the means to assume the breadwinning role, his emphasis on black family "pathologies" gave government and employers a powerful excuse for continued inaction against discriminatory practices.[52]

In *The Negro Family* and in his 1986 book, *Family and Nation*, Moynihan has located the roots of those "pathologies" in African American women's violation of the "principle of legitimacy." That principle requires not only marital legitimation of sex and offspring, but masculine authority in the home and in public institutions. According to this view, women who exercise family authority drive husbands from the household and destroy their sons' ability to perform effectively as adults.[53]

The fact that women serve as breadwinners in many African American families confounds the assumptions on which our political economy has relied for a very long time. Historically, employers and policy-makers have assumed that men will be workers ("employables") and women will be dependents ("unemployables"). The welfare and wage practices of American society have taken for granted that women will spend most of their lives in stable marriages and that men will willingly serve as providers for women and children. Welfare programs for female-headed families were created to provide assistance for the infrequent exceptions to this rule—primarily women who had lost the support of a husband as a result of his death or disability.[54]

The contradictory stereotypes used to describe poor African American women reveal the confusion engendered by the woman breadwinner in a society that views her as a contradiction in terms. Vilified as castrating matriarchs if they attempt to become self-reliant, poor black women have also been condemned as parasitic dependents if they rely on public assistance. In either case, they are castigated as incompetent mothers whose autonomy from men threatens social disorder. As Wahneema Lubiano notes, this ideology leaves African American women no culturally sanctioned roles or meanings outside of marital dependence and makes them the scapegoats for the failures of the American political economy and the frustrations of African American men:

> Whether by virtue of *not achieving* and thus passing on bad culture as welfare mothers, or by virtue of *managing to achieve* middle-class success via education, career, and/or economic successes (and thus, I suppose, passing

on genes for autonomous female success?), black women are responsible for the disadvantaged status of African Americans.[55]

The denunciation of black women has focused particularly on those decisions regarding work, sexuality, and reproduction that result in their autonomy from marriage. Conservatives charge that they are having babies without husbands in order to secure welfare benefits, promoting indolence and immorality in women and men alike. Liberals have focused either on their refusal or inability to marry, agreeing that male-headed families are essential to the material and psychological well-being of the African American community. Some, including William Wilson, have concluded that black women would gladly give up independence for economic support from husbands. Although liberals do stress the importance of expanded job opportunities for black men, their conclusion that female-headed families "cause" poverty increases the credibility of those who would blame blacks for their own condition.[56]

At the same time, attacks on poor African American women derive much of their power from sexist archetypes of ancient vintage. The idea that the subversion of masculine authority unleashes women's sexual excess, reproductive chaos, and social danger is a common cultural theme. It derives much of its contemporary meaning and credibility not only from the politics of race, but also from the highly contested relations of gender in the postwar era. By interpreting black poverty as a result of unregulated sexuality and gender inversion, white males can represent their own particularistic claims to rights, privileges, and power as though they served the interests of all and can undermine the legitimacy of African American claims to economic empowerment and of women's right to equality.

African American poverty—defined by whites for a century as inevitable and acceptable—has become a political "problem" in the United States only since the civil rights movement gave some clout to black efforts to secure economic equality. As visible symbols of the shortcomings of the American political economy, poor African Americans represent a threat to existing practices unless their claims to opportunity and support can be discounted.

Women, Men, and the Crisis in African American Family Relations

However androcentric and racist Moynihan's understandings of the causes and consequences of marital instability among African Americans were, his sense that African American families were experiencing heightened stresses was correct. The movement of blacks to the cities, their placement in the secondary sector of the urban labor force, and the systematic frustration of their attempts to enter the American mainstream took an enormous toll on black family life. Increased dependence on wage work for a livelihood in a context of pervasive discrimination intensified economic pressures in the lives of women and men.

At the same time, urbanization and the increasing importance of the mass media in their lives dramatically increased African American interaction with a national culture. This exposure to middle-class possibilities heightened black expectations but did not offer a means for the elimination of barriers to their achievement. According to Kenneth Clark, the contrast between ghetto realities and media-sponsored aspirations had a profoundly demoralizing effect on many blacks, who interpreted "their predicament as a consequence of personal disability or as an inherent and imposed powerlessness which all Negroes share." Family life became a major theater within which black despair was enacted and reproduced, prompting Paula Giddings to conclude that "giving Blacks half a loaf in exchange for acculturation into American society had a more dire impact on the Black family than slavery, war, or racial violence."[57]

Whereas the rural economy had encouraged marriage by linking women's access to agricultural work to a family system of labor and making manifest men's breadwinning efforts, the postwar urban environment intensified marital conflict and instability. As a hedge against masculine failure, many poor black men attempted to limit their affective and economic commitments to families. Many African American women experienced that distancing as a betrayal and concluded that men were unreliable as partners and providers. Inevitably, men who chose to limit their family commitments found that their strategies had backfired as their marital performance fell short of their wives' expectations, contributing to high rates of separation and divorce. The result for many poor men and women was that they had become, in the words of Jean Carey Bond and Pat Peery, "hateful partners in a harrowing dance."[58]

As a result of their own experiences, many African American mothers convey deeply contradictory messages to their daughters. Virtually all socialize their daughters to a primary emotional and sexual orientation to men—a message reinforced in black popular culture. At the same time, many also encourage them to view men with great suspicion and to develop some independence in case their heterosexual relationships do not work out. They label men's abuse as wrong to a greater degree than is true in many other social groups, while conveying the message that it is unrealistic to expect real respect or mutuality from men.[59]

From their first adolescent courtships through their adult encounters, poor African American women and men warily negotiate the meanings of sexuality and parenthood for their emotional and economic ties to one an-

other. Among adolescents, young men pressure women for sexual relationships in order to affirm their masculinity and adult status. At all ages,
many women seek commitment in their sexual relationships for the sake of
their emotional and economic security. Men, however, are often reluctant
to assume the risks associated with the breadwinner role and approach
marriage and fatherhood ambivalently.[60]

Those men who marry find that the vagaries of the secondary labor
market exert enormous pressures on them. The low wages and high unemployment rates in secondary sector jobs constantly threaten their ability to support their families adequately. Many men experience the loss of a
job as a serious blow to their self-esteem. By virtue of their economic and
emotional ties to men, women become the inevitable witnesses to masculine failure. Because women symbolize and press the families' claims to
men's earnings, men usually turn to street culture for ego support when
frustrated by their inability to meet their wives' expectations. There they
can seek out other women or their masculine peer group for uncritical ap-
proval. As Elliot Liebow observed, the latter defines a lesser standard of
masculine worth and offers a man relationships in which he can be "a person in his own right . . . noticed by the world he lives in . . . ." These
friends, however, stand "unrevealed to one another," able to offer support
only to the degree that they maintain distance.[61]

Some men have treated their income as an individual asset unavailable
to the family except as a "gift," expecting their wives to support the children. Others have given their children little time or attention. It is hardly
surprising that some black women have concluded that "men are no good"
and have experienced men's tenuous ties to their families as a betrayal. One
such woman discounted men's professions of concern for their children as
follows: "They say they love them. Shit. If they love them, would they let
them go hungry? In raggedy-ass clothes? They don't love them. Children
are just a tie to a man." Gail Stokes articulated the anger of women forced
to assume the main breadwinning responsibility:

> My belly rose and swelled year after year from the implantations of your
> seed, while you cursed my pregnancies, forgetting that they were all main-
> ly the product of your sexual pleasures. But you didn't mind letting the con-
> sequences rain heavily upon *my* nappy head. . . . Yes, I know your pay
> isn't much and your opportunities are limited, but when you squander away
> what little you do make and the same little that I count on so desperately,
> how else can I react?[62]

Sarah Webster Fabio has criticized

> the mistaken notion that a gift to black men meant improving the lot of
> black women and children—this, of course has been proven a lie. Giving
> money to black men gives money to black men. . . . Giving money to black

women trickles down to black children, if they are smart enough not to give it away to black men.[63]

Their anger suggests the toll taken by chronic poverty and gender conflicts over economic responsibilities. Their despair exacerbated by racism, many African Americans find the maintenance of relationships difficult. That this is not true in all cases is important, however. Examining stable African American families in this period reveals the meanings of mobility for black families and the structural supports essential to family cohesion.

Dorothy Bolden, for example, attributed the success of her second marriage to the fact that she and her husband were jointly responsible for breadwinning and child care. Her husband was fortunate in that his employment was steady, although poorly paid. She worked in domestic service and his schedule at work enabled him to supervise their children in the afternoons. She explained: "I was lucky. My husband always got off at one or two o'clock during the daytime, and I have a wonderful husband. I was lucky to have a husband to share the responsibility."[64]

Their relationship exemplified several elements critical for family integrity and economic well-being among blacks—regular work for men, women's employment, and relatively egalitarian gender practices. Those African American families in which men have jobs that offer more security and higher incomes experience greater marital stability. Families with incomes above the poverty line experienced less stress and deprivation with the result that marital harmony and stability was enhanced.[65]

A significant component of that stability was the sense that crises were temporary and that family members could cope. One working-class black mother of four described her response to her husband's hospitalization after he sustained a serious injury at work:

> I worked three days [a week] then, but the Welfare Department, the State, they helped us, and we kept our bills paid up. When I look back on it, I don't really think it was a bad time. You know, we still had our needs, and we had everything paid, our rent, and we kept everything going, but we didn't get anything else. . . . 'Cause you know, time be worse at that time, but then it's gone and then you look back at it, and then you say, "Well, I was really blessed in a way because . . . he was not paralyzed."

That family's ability to manage was predicated on its previous strength, the probability that the husband could return to his job as a construction foreman, and the availability of welfare to see them through the crisis.[66]

At the same time, economic mobility has not eased the dual burden of employment and family work for most working-class and middle-class African American women. Indeed, black mobility rests firmly on the two-earner family. Women's employment outside the home, even when their children are young, has been essential to black mobility as well as to the maintenance of middle-class status. Maternal employment, especially when adequately compensated, has increased the economic well-being and stability of African American families.[67]

Social mobility for blacks, however, does not automatically create nuclear families supported by men. Jesse Bernard's study of marital status differences by race and class found that black men's rates of marital stability increased with economic mobility but that they were significantly less likely to be living in stable first marriages than whites with comparable occupational or income status. This is partly because many upwardly mobile African Americans bring with them distrust and conflicts rooted in their previous poverty and have to manage the tensions generated between nuclear families and other kin when some relatives remain impoverished.[68]

Economics alone, however, cannot explain the origins of female-headed families. Labor force discrimination against minority men can contribute to the emergence of female-headed families, but does not fully account for it. Women's active assertion of their prerogatives in heterosexual unions, a dynamic that has either been overlooked or condemned by most scholars, has also promoted the rise of families headed by women.[69]

As in the past, African American women have defined norms of reciprocity in their relationships that they expect men to honor. Indeed, Robert Blood and Donald Wolfe found in their 1960 study that black women of all social classes expressed greater dissatisfaction with the emotional, companionate, and financial dimensions of their marriages than did white women in the same income groups. Although Blood and Wolfe implied that black women were not sufficiently grateful to their husbands, one might conclude instead that they held to a higher standard of mutual responsibility in marriage than prevailed among whites of the same social classes. Audre Lorde has noted, "Female-headed households in the Black community are not always situations by default."[70]

African American women's willingness to leave unions in which that standard has been breached derives in part from their faith in their ability to support themselves. May Anna Madison explained, "A black man can't do any more to me than I will let him do because I can and have taken care of myself." Blanche Scott, who had worked for pay all her life, left her husband in 1946 because "he was wild. He's run around with women and drink. He had done me so bad, I just left him." Maya Angelou left her white husband in the 1950s, despite the fact that she would have to seek employment, having concluded that ". . . women who accepted their husbands' inattention and sacrificed all their sovereignty for a humiliating marriage [were] more unsavory than the prostitutes who were drinking themselves awake in the noisy bar."[71]

Many African American women have viewed employment as a means to set some limits on the power of men in their lives. Janie Cameron Riley stated that she could not understand why white women put up with their husbands' liaisons with black women, given that they had more employment opportunities than black women. For Riley, it was inconceivable that a woman would put up with such conduct when she could support herself. Others also concluded that white women were more willing than African Americans to accept oppressive conditions in their marriages. Nancy White observed:

> When you come right down to it, white women just *think* they are free. Black women *know* they ain't free. Now, that is the most important difference between the two. . . . The white women would be all right if they would just stop paying any attention to them sorry menfolks of theirs.[72]

In all social classes, married African American women are more likely than white women to work for pay, whether their husbands are opposed to, neutral about, or in favor of their employment. Their decisions to work for pay do not necessarily indicate power over their husband's actions or an equal voice in other marital decisions regarding the gender division of labor, money, sexuality, or companionship. Indeed, their decisions to work may derive in part from their lack of power over other domains of their marriages and in part from their willingness to assert themselves in those areas of the marriage where they can act autonomously. Their low marriage rates testify to their inability to impose their standards of marital reciprocity in a society hostile to their implementation.[73]

Unable to compel the full emotional allegiance or economic assistance of the men they loved, some found themselves settling for "love on men's terms." Those terms sometimes included the requirement that women tolerate infidelity. In a social group where the number of men is lower than the number of women, some women have decided, however reluctantly, to "share" their men with others. Others stayed in oppressive unions while they tried to tame their husbands' "wildness."[74]

Poor men's terms usually included a willingness to contribute to the support and nurture of families, but to do so on a voluntary and often limited basis. In fact, Liebow found that poor men were often most willing to do so in contexts where the formal claims on their support were weakest—as stepfathers or "boyfriends" in the household—rather than within marriage. When the expectations of them were low, their participation garnered them more credit. Non-marital unions, thus, have offered men a way to realize the rewards of family life—and contribute to family well-being—with less pressure and stress.[75]

Given these dynamics, it is not surprising that the number of black women heading families has increased dramatically, especially since the 1960s. The proportion of African American women who are married and living with their husbands declined from 52 percent in 1947 to 34 percent in 1980. Compared with white women, black women were less likely to marry, more likely to be divorced or separated, and less likely to remarry after a divorce. As African American women's marriage and remarriage rates have declined, marital pregnancy rates have fallen more rapidly than non-marital pregnancy rates. By the 1980s, most black babies were born outside of wedlock and the majority of black children were not living with their fathers. To an even greater extent than in the past, African American women had become breadwinners.[76]

Even more so than for other women, heading a family means poverty for black women. Limited work opportunities have kept most black female-headed families well below the official poverty line. Moreover, their ability to use the law to secure financial assistance from the fathers of their children has been hampered by their high rates of illegitimacy and the poverty of the children's fathers. In 1978, only 29 percent of unmarried African American mothers had court orders mandating child support payments, compared with 44 percent of Hispanics and 71 percent of whites.[77]

As a result, poor black women often had to rely on "street corner strategies" to secure some support from the fathers of their children and other men in their lives. This has often entailed entering men's spaces—the streets, for example—in order to ask them for money. These strategies worked to some degree; 69 percent of the AFDC fathers in Carol Stack's study contributed some financial and nurturing assistance to their children. In order to wrest money from men who were otherwise reluctant to volunteer their help, African American women have had to sacrifice dignity and privacy.[78]

Supporting their children was not the only dilemma African American mothers faced in the postwar era. As in the past, they confronted the contradictory tasks assigned them as mothers in a racist society: to ensure their children's survival while also enabling them to develop autonomy and self-esteem in a society that feared and often punished such attributes in blacks. Moreover, African American mothers did so in a social environment that had erected new barriers to their goals. Yula Moses assessed her efforts to guide and protect her daughter as follows:

> The street is a pit and there are ten thousand hands ready to undo what you have done. You can only do so much and then it is with the child you are trying to help whether they will go your way or follow the street ways. I am not so big a fool that I imagine that I can stand between my daughter and evil, which is everywhere.

For those women trying to raise children to be hopeful, thoughtful, and healthy in a ghetto environment that breeds disillusionment, cynicism, and self-destructive behaviors, Moynihan's conclusions regarding African American women's excessive maternal power must seem willfully obtuse.[79]

Some black women have also faced the anger of sons who, even as adults, could not accept the limitations of their mothers' power against racist oppression. Calvin Hernton wrote of his anger at his grandmother, on whom he was solely dependent for his support and survival, because she accepted humiliation rather than confront a system she could not change: "There arose in me an incipient resentment towards my grandmother, indeed, towards all Black women—because I could not help but compare them with White women." African American psychiatrists William Grier and Price Cobbs charged that black mothers had blunted the "assertiveness and aggression" of their sons, who then developed "considerable hostility toward Black women as inhibiting instruments of an oppressive system."[80]

This further manifestation of the divisive effects of the culture and politics of race in postwar American prompted Paula Giddings to wonder "what Black women would have been charged with had they permitted their sons to be lynched . . . ?" Many African American women, including Audre Lorde, have concluded that black men's displaced rage promotes gender conflict and diverts attention from the real causes of black men's oppression, most notably capitalism. In addition, Lorde called attention to the harm inflicted on black women by black men who have absorbed "the dominant white male disease of sexism":

> History and popular culture, as well as our personal lives, are full of tales of Black women who had "compassion for misguided black men." Our scarred, broken, battered and dead daughters and sisters are a mute testament to that reality. . . .
> No reasonable Black man can possibly condone the rape and slaughter of Black women by Black men as a fitting response to capitalist oppression. And destruction of Black women by Black men clearly cuts across all class lines.[81]

As Lorde understood, many women who lived in the inner cities found that isolation, fear, and danger marked their daily lives. Janet McRae told interviewer John Gwaltney in the 1970s:

> Drugs is the heaviest thing we have to bear. I don't know very many people who are into drugs and there probably are not many, but there are enough to make life hell for everybody. We might as well be in jail, John. I do everything I have to do before dark and then I generally stay here, locked in. . . .

The situation worsened in the 1980s with the introduction of crack cocaine and the escalation of the power of a relatively small number of ghetto residents (mostly young men) to create fear and danger for all in the community.[82]

As the foregoing suggests, poor African American women often found it difficult to translate the shadow work of survival strategies into moral authority within the family or power over their own lives. The depressive style of adaptation noted by Lee Rainwater in his study of Pruitt-Igoe Housing Projects in St. Louis reflected the emotional costs paid by women in this system. The cumulative effect of the hazards and defeats encountered on a daily basis prompted many poor women to isolate themselves, to sacrifice hope and engagement with life in order to minimize the level of risk and stress in their lives.[83]

Others turned to politics for answers to their plight. Hannah Nelson, who was the victim of three burglaries, two attempted muggings, and one mugging during which she was stripped in the street, understood her difficulties to derive from a social system in which she and other African Americans had no real power:

> Each day that we live like this, with more responsibility than any other people and no authority at all, our people become more disorganized. TV, movies, drugs and school make our young men into walking disgraces, and we can do nothing about it so long as we live among white people. Do you think I would tolerate a school like that one Kwame goes to if I were running a school? Do you imagine I would create a welfare system which degrades women and children? What have I lost in Chile or Cuba or Southeast Asia?[84]

Women and Activism

Many African American women asked the same questions in the postwar era. Some organized to change the conditions in which they and other Americans lived, despite the resistances and intimidations they encountered at the hands of hostile whites. Because the specificities of their place in American society created unique problems and perspectives, African American women struggled to define a politics that addressed their particular needs. They marched, lobbied, picketed, boycotted, and litigated in order to secure the dignity, rights, and opportunities accorded to others. Their activism shaped a multitude of social movements, including those for civil rights, welfare reform, reproductive freedom, workers' rights, feminism, and others.[85]

Their struggle was made even more difficult by increasing disagreements with black men over the appropriate roles and legitimate political claims of black women in the black movement. As Beverly Guy-Sheftall has noted, this gender conflict represents a substantial break with the past. At the inception of the modern civil rights movement, the contributions and concerns of African American women occupied a less contested place in movement politics. Indeed, notable African American leaders, including W. E. B. DuBois, supported women's rights and encouraged women's participation in civil rights activism.[86]

Shifts in the historical context for the movement—including the altered gender politics of the white middle class, changes in the economic conditions of American blacks, and the sexual revolution—contributed to the emergence of overt gender conflict among black activists. As has already been noted, external pressures on African American family life—material, ideological, and psychological—increased dramatically with the urbanization and proletarianization of millions of American blacks. Movement dynamics reflected the heightened tensions between black women and men, while generating new sources of conflict and misunderstanding.[87]

This dynamic was especially pronounced during the civil rights movement of the early 1960s. Some of the difficulties women experienced in that movement—a near monopoly of decision-making authority and public leadership by men and the assignment of women to traditional tasks like typing, filing, cooking, and maintaining male egos—mirrored those confronted by other women, white and African American, in various political movements. What distinguished the interracial civil rights movement was its emotionally freighted confrontation with the sex/gender system that had derived from and sustained racial hatreds and inequalities for many generations.[88]

Nothing symbolized the flouting of southern racial/sexual mores more than sexual relationships between black men and white women. As the movement for racial equality grew in the South, many African American men saw the toppling of this taboo as the measure of white commitment to egalitarianism within the movement. That test of "commitment," however, rested only with white women and entailed pressures on them to renounce control over their sexuality in service to the cause. Moreover, some black men used it to express their racial antagonisms, signifying white women's role as scapegoats in a movement fraught with tension. One black activist put it:

> So, in a sense, what passes itself off as desire quite often . . . is probably a combination of hostility and resentment, because he resents what the society has done to him, and he wants to take it out on somebody who symbolizes the establishment of that society. And at the same time it's a search for his own personhood, for his own freedom.[89]

Some white women found themselves with the choice of consenting to the advances of African American men or being called racist—the worst epithet imaginable in a movement for racial equality. Because they did not want to jeopardize the movement, those who did not welcome such advances made up "boyfriends" or switched projects in order to avoid conflicts over race and sexuality. Moreover, they were keenly aware of the retribution that awaited black men accused of "taking liberties" with white women. Mary Rothschild has noted, "The horror of the southern lynching tradition kept them silent."[90]

That this confrontation was only partially understood by those who experienced it contributed to their pain and disillusionment, while deepening political divisions based on race and gender. One white woman recalled:

> I always dreaded Saturday nights, because we'd all meet in our apartment and drink wine and then when the black guys got a little drunk, they'd pour out all their hatred—racial hatred—at us. But the white guys never got it— sometimes they'd join them—it was always directed at us "white bitches." I couldn't deal with it, not at all. It was just so painful. It tore me up inside.[91]

Some African American women experienced the sexual politics of the movement as a sexual rejection by African American men. Victimized for centuries by a white standard of beauty, they saw sexual liaisons between black men and white women as an expression of racist sexual values. A black woman explained in 1965:

> Sex is one thing; The Movement is another. And the two shouldn't mix. There's an unhealthy attitude in The Movement toward sex. The Negro girls feel neglected because the white girls get the attention. The white girls are misused. There are some hot discussions at staff meetings.

Many African American women felt angry at both white women and African American men. Given the social fabric created by the politics of race, gender, and sexuality in the South, it is no wonder that a movement that attempted to change race relations would face emotionally charged internal divisions. That it did so without a political analysis of those connections between race and the sex/gender system heightened the conflict and pain.[92]

Significantly, it was African American women who first challenged the sexism within the movement. In 1964 several conducted a sit-in at the Student Nonviolent Coordinating Committee headquarters to protest its relegation of women to secondary status. After consulting with Ruby Doris Smith Robinson and other black women regarding the problem of sexism in the movement, Casey Hayden and Mary King, both white, drafted a position paper on the status of women in SNCC. It condemned the discriminatory treatment of women and sexist attitudes in the movement, observing that "women are the crucial factor that keeps the movement running on a day to day basis," but "they are not given equal say-so when it comes to day to day decision making."[93]

Despite the sexism, African American women participated in the movement of the 1950s and 1960s in a variety of ways. They served as leaders of civil rights organizations, especially at the local level. Many worked as grass-roots organizers, drawing from the authority and relationships they had developed as members of families, neighborhoods, churches, and work groups. Within SNCC especially, the critical role of local activism empowered women to act on behalf of their community. "There is always a 'mama,'" wrote Charles Sherrod, SNCC activist, in 1962. "She is usually a militant woman in the community, outspoken, understanding, and willing to catch hell, having already caught her share."[94]

Indeed, their centrality in the movement often derived from the changed political significance of their traditional roles and activities. Ella Baker noted, "The movement of the fifties and sixties was carried largely by women, since it came out of the church groups. . . . It's true that the number of women who carried the movement is much larger than that of the men." Women also contributed in many subtle ways—through their provision of homes, food, and emotional support to organizers and through their daily acts of courage in the face of threats and reprisals from angry whites.[95]

The vision and possibilities for change sustained by the movement drew black activists together for the sake of their common cause. Many African American women and men found that the direct confrontation with racism gave them dignity, hope, and confidence in themselves. Bernice Johnson Reagon described it as follows:

> There was a sense of power, in a place where you didn't feel you had any power. There was a sense of confronting things that terrified you, like jail, police, walking in the street—you know, a whole lot of black folks couldn't even walk in the street in those places in the South. So you were saying in some basic way, "I will never again stay inside those boundaries."[96]

The civil rights movement of the 1950s and early 1960s forced a reluctant white political establishment to pass landmark legislation that dismantled segregation and gave African Americans in the South the right to vote. It also provided pressure in favor of legislation to fight poverty, improve the education of the poor, and provide free legal assistance to the poor. The courage, dedication, and political skills of black women contributed enormously to those successes.

Despite this, their political activity has often remained "invisible" to scholars who focus on formal positions of leadership in national associations and on the issues and actions men have deemed important. Women's activism, by contrast, occurs on the local level and often centers on issues scholars have deemed peripheral—like welfare or education. According to Ida Susser, the political efforts of working-class women have shifted in recent decades in response to the increasing instability of the labor market and their heightened dependence on public assistance for support. Their political commitments reflect the effects of public policies on the conditions of their private lives.[97]

African American women's political consciousness and strategies have derived from their concerns as mothers, breadwinners, and community members. Many entered politics by working to improve the schools for their children or to claim more access to city services—like regular garbage pick-ups or safer neighborhoods—and then expanded their concerns. Drawing from a long tradition of civic activism, they have organized and acted to improve the conditions of their lives in ways that have been visible to their community, if not to academics.[98]

In some cases, local mobilization led to national actions. One expression of that dynamic was the creation of the National Welfare Rights Organization in the mid-1960s. Although its executive director was George Wiley, a black man, most leadership positions, especially at the grass-roots level, were in the hands of black women. Leaders like Johnnie Tilmon, a welfare mother from Los Angeles who served as the first president of the NWRO, worked effectively to increase benefits, reduce government snooping and harassment of welfare recipients, and ensure that more of those whose poverty made them eligible for public programs actually received assistance. Many of the members of NWRO and beneficiaries of its successes were white women.[99]

Because it found its political base among the poor, the NWRO had to struggle for resources and to establish the legitimacy of its goals. The desperate poverty of its members made it dependent on liberal organizations for support. The stigma attached to the poor in America—especially when they include large numbers of minorities, women, and children—made many such organizations reluctant to endorse NWRO. Because it was an interracial movement in a separatist era and a woman-led movement in a time when the politics of patriarchal protest dominated the African American movement, NWRO also found it difficult to raise money among other African American activists.[100]

By the mid-1970s, the NWRO had a dwindling membership and serious financial problems. Its very successes had made it seem less necessary to its constituency. In addition, the conservative trend in American politics had reduced its external base of support, reducing its ability to organize and to lobby effectively on behalf of its members. Originally a community-based movement, by the late 1970s welfare activism had returned to the local level, kept alive by those women who knew from experience that many American women are, in the words of Johnnie Tilmon, "one man away from welfare."[101]

The Politics of Patriarchal Protest

By the mid-1960s, many black women shared black men's disillusionment with the possibilities of interracial cooperation. For years they had lived with the hatred and violence of southern whites afraid of change and the paternalistic behavior of northern white liberals. Many therefore endorsed the shift to a Black Power movement based on separatism and, when necessary, violent confrontations with white power. They welcomed the emphasis on black pride and black political and economic autonomy from whites.[102]

At the same time, the rise of black power had somewhat different meanings for women and men. Many African American men came to view racial oppression as a form of masculine dispossession and to claim their rights to jobs, political power, and dignity as masculine, rather than human, entitlements. African American women, they argued, should be subordinated and domestic, their roles confined to supporting men's endeavors and bearing and rearing children for the movement. As Paula Giddings has observed, "ironically, the most nationalist groups were also the most sexist. . . ."[103]

The rhetoric of community and equality of the early 1960s had allowed women more ideological leverage to make claims to power and resources than did the appeal to black power and autonomy of the late 1960s. African American women experienced a great tension between their nationalism and their feminism (however inchoate) as they sought to situate themselves in a political and cultural space that was not "white." Male leaders assumed that men should define African American identity and take charge of the confrontation with white power.

The militaristic and confrontational politics of black separatism not only appealed to a martial masculinity, it elicited the subliminal fears associated with the woman warrior. Those fears were especially potent in the context of the debate over black "matriarchy." The militant movement provided black men a means to assume the masculine roles of protectors and rulers and, thus, to claim the privileges white men expected from those roles.[104]

While black men defined their struggle as one for "manhood," some black women saw the goal of militant separatism as black nationhood. After thirty years of interracial work for civil rights, Dara Abubakari declared herself a separatist, concluding, "Black people have to get freedom for themselves; it cannot be given to them. The only thing you can aspire to is nationhood." She and many other African American women had concluded that economic and political self-determination for blacks was possible only if they separated from whites.[105]

The patriarchal politics of black power thus confronted them with a difficult dilemma. Although some openly disagreed with the misogyny of militant leaders, many found that they were expected to choose between racial equality and empowerment as women. The fact that the feminist movement was dominated by white middle-class women who defined its agenda out of their experiences and concerns made it unappealing to many African American women.[106]

Throughout the postwar era, many black women believed that it was more important to fight to eradicate racial oppression than to struggle against black men for gender equality within their community. Septima Clark, for example, noted that Ella Baker ". . . was concerned about not being recognized in a man-made world, and it didn't bother me." According to Clark, women active in the Southern Christian Leadership Conference discussed the problems they had with male leaders among themselves, but did not complain openly.[107]

Fannie Lou Hamer, a sharecropper activist who endured job loss and physical violence in the struggle for justice in Mississippi and the nation, also gave priority to the African American struggle:

> . . . I'm not hung up on this about liberating myself from the black man, I'm not going to try that thing. I got a black husband, six feet three, two hundred and forty pounds, with a 14 shoe, that I don't *want* to be liberated from. But we are here to work side by side with this black man in trying to bring liberation to all people.[108]

Indeed, the meanings given to ideas of exploitation and liberation by white feminists often seemed unrelated to the experiences and conditions of African American women. When middle-class white women spoke of employment as liberation, they did not expect to be working in other women's kitchens. May Anna Madison noted:

> White women have done more bad things to me than black men ever thought of doing. Black men will make a fool out of me if I let them, but it was a white woman who had me crawling around her apartment before I was thirteen years old, cleaning places she would never think of cleaning with a toothbrush and toothpick! It was a female chauvinist sow that worked me a full day for seventy-five cents![109]

Even after the successful repression of the black power movement by the federal government, the politics of masculine protest retained their appeal for many African American men. The charges of matriarchal dominance put many activist black women in a defensive posture regarding their place in the black family, their roles in the movement, and their claims as beneficiaries of black activism. As the crisis in African American gender relations accelerated and right-wing attacks on African American families grew more savage, some black women became increasingly convinced that sexism provided a poor foundation for a civil rights movement.

They responded by exploring black feminism as a means to understand their unique dilemmas and to define a political agenda responsive to their needs. Some came to view their empowerment as women as their most urgent and difficult goal. Pauli Murray, whose adult experiences of sex discrimination reached from Howard University to Harvard University and from the practice of law to the ministry, concluded:

I have reached that point in my conviction where being a woman is perhaps a more complex and more difficult status than being a black. First of all, it is the oldest, the most continuous, the most recalcitrant, the most stubborn kind of prejudice and oppression. . . . It is thoroughly supported by the most authoritative kind of thing that can be drawn to support it, namely, Holy Scriptures.[110]

Many African American women have chosen fiction, drama, and poetry as the means to explore issues of womanhood, sexuality, and power. Writers like Ntozake Shange, Alice Walker, Toni Morrison, and Gloria Naylor have offered powerful and sophisticated representations of the ways in which the politics of race and gender interact to construct gender oppression within African American communities. Their explorations of the need for black women "to love themselves," in the words of Ntozake Shange, have elicited hostile reactions from many black men (and black women), who regard their criticisms of black men as treasonable vilifications that play into the hands of hostile whites.[111]

The degree to which the acceptance of male dominance by African American women had become the precondition for racial solidarity became particularly visible in the 1991 confirmation hearings for Clarence Thomas, then a nominee for the U.S. Supreme Court. Thomas was a self-proclaimed black conservative whose nomination by President George Bush was designed to ensure that the Supreme Court would no longer serve as an institutional base of support for African Americans and others fighting discrimination in the workplace and elsewhere. Despite the political and administrative record established by Thomas that justified Bush's confidence in his conservative credentials, Thomas successfully cloaked himself in the mantle of the experiences and struggles of African Americans during his confirmation hearings.[112]

Once the Senate Judiciary Committee reluctantly made public Anita Hill's charges of sexual harassment by Thomas, the nominee and his very powerful supporters "conjured up a grand drama of male victimization," in the words of historian Christine Stansell. That drama

. . . swept back and forth between ancient misogynist themes—the scorned woman, the woman as pawn—to Thomas's irresponsible and confused representations of Afro-American history, featuring himself as a martyred lynch victim.

As Nell Painter observed, those representations and their gendered underpinnings enabled him to create "a tableau of white-black racism that allowed him to occupy the position of 'the race.'"[113]

His initial claim to African American sympathies was achieved in the hearings when he recounted his own past, a story of poverty, racism, individual struggle, and family support that resonated with the historical and contemporary experiences of many African Americans. For him and for them, his life history contained possibilities for transcending and subverting racism and its consequences in African American lives. Many blacks invested such accounts of oppression with oppositional political meanings that entailed claims on the state and on each other. Thomas, by contrast, interpreted his past as an individual mobility tale, concluding that civil rights activism and legislation were damaging to black progress. His denial of connection to the social relations, political entitlements, and communities that had enabled his survival and success is essential to the construction of "self-made men" and their multiple entitlements in American society.[114]

As Gayle Pemberton noted, Thomas created this "sentimentalized portrait of himself and his history that satisfie[d] white power," while simultaneously compelling black sympathy. Thomas offered the American public a tale of masculine mobility that stressed the role of individual initiative and patriarchal authorities in his rise from poverty to power and affluence. His grandfather, about whom he talked at length, offered paternal guidance, and the Catholic Church provided moral frameworks. As Wahneema Lubiano cogently observed:

> Thomas and his grandfather became . . . the bringers of order, of law—against chaos, against anarchy—the male figures so desperately needed in (and missing from) Moynihan's "black family."

Without mentioning Moynihan, Thomas distanced himself from the female-centered kin networks that have offered emotional and economic support to many African Americans and erased the labor women provided to enable his "independent" success.[115]

As early as 1989, he had distorted the circumstances and actions of his sister, Emma Mae Martin, by denouncing her as a welfare dependent before a conservative white audience. Playing to their stereotypes of African American women for his own career advantage, he stated that she was so dependent on the state "that she got mad when the [welfare] check was late." His account ignored the fact that she was on AFDC only for a short period of time, when she had to take care of *their* sick aunt, and that she normally worked two minimum-wage jobs in order to support herself and others in their family, all without any assistance from her successful and affluent brother. As Michael Thelwell noted, this exposed "not only a failure of character but the shallowness of his public rhetoric about traditional family values."[116]

When Anita Hill testified regarding Thomas's workplace harassment of her when he was chair of the Equal Employment Opportunity Commission, he charged the Senate Judiciary Committee with conducting a "high-tech lynching," adroitly shifting from a politics of racial denial to one in which he occupied center stage in the long history of African American oppression. Kimberle Crenshaw observed, "Cases involving sexual accusations against black men have stood as hallmarks of racial injustice." With this charge Thomas mobilized political support for him among blacks accustomed to privileging the racial oppression of black men over the race and gender victimization of black women.[117]

He also shifted attention from his interactions with Anita Hill to his relations with the men on the Senate committee, with whom he shared a tacit understanding that defined racism as a form of masculine dispossession to be exorcised from their particular fraternity by the preservation of his credibility and reputation. A patriarchal bargain was struck and executed: he was confirmed as an Associate Justice of the Supreme Court and all the men involved were able to deny their complicity in the various systems of dominance they enacted in the hearings.[118]

Anita Hill paid part of the price for this "bargain" with her credibility and reputation. Many African Americans viewed her as a traitor to the race for failing to enact the sacrificial role expected of African American women when the public discussion of gender oppression among blacks threatens the advancement of an African American man and/or the solidarity and reputation of African Americans generally. Her treason was greatly compounded by the sexual nature of the charges she brought before a national audience. Gayle Pemberton noted, "Many a black man [and woman] felt that Thomas was collectively defending black manhood as he routinely answered senators' questions."[119]

In this context the race and gender oppressions of African American women, including Anita Hill, were rendered invisible and unintelligible. Many scholars have noted that Hill had no discourse available to convey her experiences and their complex meanings. The long history of sexual victimization of African American women, including that of systematic and racialized sexual harassment at work, does not embody racial oppression or gender oppression in the American imagination. As a successful black woman, her class privileges were visible and salient, while Thomas's were obscured. Moreover, her narrative of mobility as an unmarried middle-class African American woman positioned her as a threat to male dominance in all communities and institutions.[120]

Feminist perspectives on sexual harassment in the workplace were simultaneously marginalized (by the exclusion of expert testimony from the hearings) and demonized. At the same time, feminist defenders of Hill effaced her identity and oppressions as an African American woman. This reinforced the convictions of some blacks that Hill was merely a pawn of white feminists, while raising the threat that her individual narrative of harassment might legitimize women's accounts of oppression and force political change.[121]

As in the civil rights movement, the absence of a public discourse about the connections between race, gender, and sexuality affected political mobilization. In this case, it precluded effective opposition to Thomas's confirmation. Many African American and white women were so enraged by the hearings and their result, however, that they organized to articulate their anger and, in some cases, to unseat the senators who had vilified Hill in order to place Thomas on the court. The political effects and meanings of this historic event continue to unfold.

Conclusions

In the years since World War II, African American women have experienced and helped to create dramatic changes in their social position and political roles. The destruction of the southern plantation system created new economic opportunities and new forms of economic oppression in their lives. As blacks moved to the wage economy of the cities, some found new jobs open to them while many faced unemployment and systematic racial discrimination. For women, urbanization meant increased support responsibilities and heightened conflicts between their dual roles as breadwinners and homemakers.

These changes in their economic roles and needs have not been accompanied by the wider employment opportunities they necessitate. Black women's economic dependence (on men and the state) therefore has increased. At the same time, the urban wage economy has provided only low wages and insecure employment for most black men. As a result, neither black women nor men have the structural supports necessary to enact their role responsibilities in the family.

Moreover, economic oppression dramatically heightens gender conflict among blacks. Women's efforts to keep their marriages intact often founder in the face of their husbands' unemployment and the temptations of street culture for discouraged men. As in the past, black women's willingness to forgo unpromising marriages or to leave bad relationships has not created egalitarianism in gender roles and has probably diminished their material well-being.[122]

African American women's dependence on men extends beyond the material. Most also desire and expect strong sexual and emotional ties to black men. Many, however, remain convinced that ". . . the terms that they want to enter our lives are just not acceptable. Not workable. Not in our best interests." As in the past, they have been willing to struggle with their men in order to secure more egalitarian relationships. The disparity between their gender ideals and the terms of their relationships bespeak black women's limited power in the domestic realm. It also reveals the inadequacies of individualistic strategies unsupported by the values or practices of the larger society.[123]

Those strategies have been undermined at every turn by the persistence of racism and sexism in American society. Only when good jobs and public power are as available to black women and men as to others can the pressures on their families be eased sufficiently so that they can define a gender system based on shared responsibility and mutual trust. Until then, the "harrowing dance" will continue, orchestrated by those who believe that neglect can be benign and that subordination is the price women must pay for economic well-being and marital stability.

Notes

Chapter 1. *"Changing Woman" and the Politics of Difference*

1. The term racial ethnic, borrowed from Bonnie Thornton Dill, is used to stress the co-existence of racialized identities imposed by the dominant culture with ethnic (and national, in the case of American Indians) cultures constructed by and within semi-autonomous communities. Bonnie Thornton Dill, "Our Mothers' Grief: Racial Ethnic Women and the Maintenance of Families," *Journal of Family History* 13 (1988): 415–31; Cornel West, "Race and Social Justice in a Multicultural Democracy," *Liberal Education* 80 (Summer 1994): 32–39.

2. Kimberle Crenshaw, "Whose Story Is It, Anyway? Feminist and Antiracist Appropriations of Anita Hill," in Toni Morrison, ed., *Race-ing Justice, En-gendering Power: Essays on Anita Hill, Clarence Thomas, and the Construction of Social Reality* (New York: Pantheon, 1992), 404; bell hooks, *Yearning: Race, Gender, and Cultural Politics* (Boston: South End Press, 1990); Patricia Hill Collins, *Black Feminist Thought: Knowledge, Conciousness, and the Politics of Empowerment* (New York: Routledge, 1991); Gloria Anzaldua, *Borderlands, La Frontera: The New Mestiza* (San Francisco: Spinsters/Aunt Lute, 1987); Cherrie Moraga and Gloria Anzaldua, eds., *This Bridge Called My Back: Writings by Radical Women of Color* (Watertown, Mass.: Persephone Press, 1981); Combahee River Collective, "A Black Feminist Statement," in Gloria T. Hull, Patricia Bell Scott, and Barbara Smith,

222 *Notes*

eds., *All the Women Are White, All the Blacks Are Men, But Some of Us Are Brave: Black Women's Studies* (New York: Feminist Press, 1982), 13–22; Paula Gunn Allen, *The Sacred Hoop: Recovering the Feminine in American Indian Traditions* (Boston: Beacon Press, 1986); Nancy A. Hewitt, "Compounding Differences," *Feminist Studies* 18 (Summer 1992): 313–26.

3. Robert Berkhofer stressed the importance of balancing respect for the diverse experiences of heterogeneous Indian nations with the need to elucidate "common trends and repetitive processes." Although it suggests some of the complexities in American Indian cultures and their gender systems, this study focuses primarily on experiences shared by many Indian women, particularly in their confrontations with white authorities. Robert F. Berkhofer, Jr., "The Political Context of a New Indian History," *Pacific Historical Review* 40 (Aug. 1971): 357–82.

4. Vron Ware, *Beyond the Pale: White Women, Racism, and History* (London: Verso, 1992), 37. Chandra Mohanty further concludes that the ". . . particular constructions of morality to which third world women are subject inform their notions of self, their organizing, and their day-to-day resilience." Chandra Talpade Mohanty, "Cartographies of Struggle: Third World Women and the Politics of Feminism," in Chandra Talpade Mohanty, Ann Russo, and Lourdes Torres, eds., *Third World Women and the Politics of Feminism* (Bloomington: Indiana Univ. Press, 1991), 30.

5. Evelyn Brooks Higginbotham, "African-American Women's History and the Metalanguage of Race," *Signs* 17 (Winter 1992): 251–74.

6. Higginbotham, "African-American Women's History and the Metalanguage of Race," 266–73; Elizabeth V. Spelman, *Inessential Woman: Problems of Exclusion in Feminist Thought* (Boston: Beacon Press, 1988), 124–25.

7. Morrison, ed., *Race-ing Justice, En-gendering Power.*

8. hooks, *Yearning*, 58; Gunn Allen, *Sacred Hoop.*

9. Ramon A. Gutierrez, "Community, Patriarchy and Individualism: The Politics of Chicano History and the Dream of Equality," *American Quarterly* 45 (March 1993): 44–72; Crenshaw, "Whose Story Is It, Anyway?," 402–40; Catharine A. MacKinnon, *Feminism Unmodified: Discourses on Life and Law* (Cambridge: Harvard Univ. Press, 1987), 63–69; Cherrie Moraga, "From a Long Line of Vendidas: Chicanas and Feminism," in Teresa de Lauretis, ed., *Feminist Studies/Critical Studies* (Bloomington: Indiana Univ. Press, 1986), 173–90; Alma M. Garcia, "The Development of Chicana Feminist Discourse, 1970–1980," in Ellen Carol Dubois and Vicki L. Ruiz, eds., *Unequal Sisters: A Multi-Cultural Reader in U.S. Women's History* (New York: Routledge, 1990), 418–31.

10. Micaela di Leonardo, *The Varieties of Ethnic Experience: Kinship, Class, and Gender Among California Italian-Americans* (Ithaca: Cornell Univ. Press, 1984), 221.

11. [Daniel P. Moynihan], U.S. Department of Labor, *The Negro Family: The Case for National Action* (Washington, D.C.: U.S. Government Printing Office, 1965); Jacqueline Dowd Hall, "'The Mind That Burns in Each Body': Women, Rape, and Racial Violence," in Ann Snitow, Christine Stansell, and Sharon Thompson, eds., *The Powers of Desire: The Politics of Sexuality* (New York: Monthly Review Press, 1983), 328–49.

12. Elsa Barkley Brown, "'What Has Happened Here': The Politics of Differ-

ence in Women's History and Feminist Politics," *Feminist Studies* 18 (Summer 1992): 295–312; Hazel V. Carby, *Reconstructing Womanhood: The Emergence of the Afro-American Woman Novelist* (New York: Oxford Univ. Press, 1987), 108–16; Spelman, *Inessential Woman*.

13. Hall, "'The Mind That Burns in Each Body,'" 328–49.

14. Crenshaw, "Whose Story Is It, Anyway?," 402–40; Belinda Bozzoli, "Marxism, Feminism and South African Studies," *Journal of Southern African Studies* 9 (April 1983): 139–71; Aida Hurtado, "Relating to Privilege: Seduction and Rejection in the Subordination of White Women and Women of Color," *Signs* 14 (Summer 1989): 833–55. Patricia Hill Collins conceptualizes race, class, and gender as "interlocking systems of oppression." Collins, *Black Feminist Thought*, 222.

15. As Hurtado also notes, differences between white women and women of color in their relationships to white men foster different (and sometime incompatible) political understandings and agendas. Hurtado, "Relating to Privilege," 833–55.

16. Gutierrez, "Community, Patriarchy and Individualism" 44–72; Norma Alarcon, "What Kind of Lover Have You Made Me, Mother?: Towards a Theory of Chicanas' Feminism and Cultural Identity Through Poetry," in Audrey T. McCluskey, ed., *Women of Color: Perspectives on Feminism and Identity* 1 (Bloomington: Indiana Univ. Women's Studies Program, 1985), 85–110; Moraga, "From a Long Line of Vendidas," 173–190. Mother/daughter dynamics have developed somewhat differently in African American culture. Patricia Hill Collins, "The Meaning of Motherhood in Black Culture and Black Mother/Daughter Relationships," *Sage* IV (Fall 1987): 3–10.

17. Bozzoli, "Marxism, Feminism and South African Studies," 139–71; Moraga, "From a Long Line of Vendidas," 173–90. George Sanchez has offered a cogent critique of binary models of culture in Chicano history in *Becoming Mexican American: Ethnicity, Culture and Identity in Chicano Los Angeles, 1900–1945* (New York: Oxford Univ. Press, 1993), 3–14.

18. Nancy A. Hewitt, "Beyond the Search for Sisterhood: American Women's History in the 1980s," in Dubois and Ruiz, eds., *Unequal Sisters*, 1–14.

19. Hewitt, "Beyond the Search for Sisterhood," 1–14; Crenshaw, "Whose Story Is It, Anyway?," 402–40; Combahee River Collective, "A Black Feminist Statement," 13–22.

20. Gunn Allen, *Sacred Hoop*, 222; Hazel V. Carby, *Reconstructing Womanhood: The Emergence of the Afro-American Woman* (New York: Oxford Univ. Press, 1987); Combahee River Collective, "A Black Feminist Statement," 13–22; Elsa Barkley Brown, "Womanist Consciousness: Maggie Lena Walker and the Independent Order of Saint Luke," in Ruiz and Dubois, eds., *Unequal Sisters*, 208–23.

21. White working-class and middle-class women have been subject to systematic regulation in service to the racial and class order, but this is beyond the purview of this book. See Hall, "'The Mind That Burns in Each Body,'" 328–49; Ann Stoler, "Carnal Knowledge and Imperial Power: Gender, Race, and Morality in Colonial Asia," in Micaela di Leonardo, ed., *Gender at the Crossroads of Knowledge: Feminist Anthropology in the Postmodern Era* (Berkeley: Univ. of California Press, 1991), 51–101; Hurtado, "Relating to Privilege," 849.

22. Ann Stoler, *Carnal Knowledge and Imperial Power* (Berkeley: Univ. of California Press, forthcoming); Mary E. Young, "Women, Civilization, and the Indian Question," in Purdy, ed., *Clio Was a Woman*, 98–110; George J. Sanchez, "'Go After the Women': Americanization and the Mexican Immigrant Woman," in Dubois and Ruiz, eds., *Unequal Sisters*, 250–63; Hurtado, "Relating to Privilege," 833–55; Collins, "The Meaning of Motherhood in Black Culture," 3–10; Theda Skocpol, *Protecting Soldiers and Mothers: The Political Origins of Social Policy in the United States* (Cambridge: Harvard Univ. Press, 1992); Linda Gordon, ed., *Women, the State, and Welfare* (Madison: Univ. of Wisconsin Press, 1990). Gwendolyn Mink, Eileen Boris, and Sonya Michel particularly notice the contradictory meanings of the welfare state for poor and racial ethnic women. Gwendolyn Mink, "The Lady and the Tramp: Gender, Race, and the Origins of the American Welfare State," in Gordon, ed., *Women, the State, and Welfare*, 92–122; Eileen Boris, "The Power of Motherhood: Black and White Activist Women Redefine the 'Political,'" in Seth Koven and Sonya Michel, eds., *Mothers of a New World: Maternalist Politics and the Origins of Welfare States* (New York: Routledge, 1993), 213–45; Sonya Michel, "The Limits of Maternalism: Policies Toward American Wage-Earning Mothers During the Progressive Era," in Koven and Michel, eds., *Mothers of a New World*, 277–320.

23. Hurtado, "Relating to Privilege," 853; Lorde, *Sister Outsider: Essays and Speeches* (Trumansburg, NY: Crossing Press, 1984), 119; Rickie Solinger, *Wake Up Little Susie: Single Pregnancy and Race Before Roe v. Wade* (New York: Routledge, 1992).

24. Vicki L. Ruiz, *Cannery Women, Cannery Lives: Mexican Women, Unionization, and the California Food Processing Industry, 1930–1950* (Albuquerque: Univ. of New Mexico Press, 1987); Higginbotham, "African-American Women's History and the Metalanguage of Race," 251–74; Sanchez, "'Go After the Women,'" 250–63; Buss, ed., *Forged Under the Sun*, 16.

25. Jacqueline Jones, *Labor of Love, Labor of Sorrow: Black Women, Work, and the Family from Slavery to the Present* (New York: Basic Books, 1985). Arlie Hochschild defines emotion work as follows: "I use the term *emotional labor* to mean the management of feeling to create a publicly observable facial and bodily display; emotional labor is sold for a wage and therefore has *exchange value*. I use the synonymous terms *emotion work* or *emotion management* to refer to these same acts done in a private context where they have *use value*." Arlie Hochschild, *The Managed Heart: Commercialization of Human Feeling* (Berkeley: Univ. of California Press, 1983), 7. Micaela Di Leonardo defines kin work as "the conception, maintenance, and ritual celebration of cross-household kin ties, including visits, letters, telephone calls, presents, and cards to kin; the organization of holiday gatherings; the creation and maintenance of quasi-kin relations; decision to neglect or to intensify particular ties; the mental work of reflection about all these activities; and the creation and communication of altering images of family and kin vis-a-vis the images of others, both folk and mass media." Micaela Di Leonardo, "The Female World of Cards and Holidays: Women, Families, and the Work of Kinship," *Signs* 12 (Spring 1987): 440–53.

26. Rayna Rapp, "Family and Class in Contemporary America: Notes Toward an Understanding of Ideology," in Barrie Thorne with Marilyn Yalom, eds., *Re-*

thinking the Family: Some Feminist Questions, rev. ed. (New York: Longman, 1992), 168–87; Di Leonardo, "The Female World of Cards and Holidays," 440–53.

27. Laura Balbo, "The Servicing Work of Women and the Capitalist State," *Political Power and Social Theory* 3 (1982): 251–70; Gunn Allen, *Sacred Hoop*, 207.

28. Fran Buss, ed., *Forged Under the Sun: Forjada Bajo El Sol: The Life of Maria Elena Lucas* (Ann Arbor: Univ. of Michigan Press, 1993), 18; Maureen Fitzgerald, personal communication.

29. Ronald Takaki, *A Different Mirror: A History of Multicultural America* (Boston: Little, Brown, 1993); Derrick Bell, *And We Are Not Saved: The Elusive Quest for Racial Justice* (New York: Basic Books, 1987); David Mura, "Strangers in the Village," in Rick Simonson and Scott Walker, eds., *The Graywolf Annual Five: Multicultural Literacy* (St. Paul: Graywolf Press, 1988), 151.

30. Toni Morrison, *Playing in the Dark: Whiteness and the Literary Imagination* (New York: Vintage Books, 1993), 64.

31. Claudia Brodsky Lacour has noted the links between a masculinized citizenship, gender, and racism: "For to deny man his rights as a citizen is, historically and actually, to treat him as 'woman,' that genre of 'man' whose rights are forgotten instantly without that oversight even being noticed. . . ." Claudia Brodsky Lacour, "Doing Things with Words: 'Racism' as Speech Act and the Undoing of Justice," in Morrison, ed., *Race-ing Justice, En-gendering Power*, 146; Mink, "The Lady and the Tramp," 92–122.

32. Mink, "The Lady and the Tramp," 92–122.

33. Ibid. The effectiveness of middle-class women's mothering was often assisted by the availability of racial ethnic women for low-wage employment in domestic service. While women of color cared for white children, their own children were subject to makeshift arrangements. Mura, "Strangers in the Village," 135.

34. Mohanty, "Cartographies of Struggle," 21.

35. Sanchez, "'Go After the Women'"; Balbo, "The Servicing Work of Women," 251–70;

36. Christine Stansell, *City of Women: Sex and Class in New York 1789–1860* (Urbana: Univ. of Illinois Press, 1987); Patricia Zavella, *Women's Work and Chicano Families: Cannery Workers of the Santa Clara Valley* (Ithaca: Cornell Univ. Press, 1987); Laurie Coyle, Gail Hershatter, and Emily Honig, "Women at Farah: An Unfinished Story," in Joan N. Jensen and Sue Davidson, eds., *A Needle, a Bobbin, a Strike: Women Needleworkers in America* (Philadelphia: Temple Univ. Press, 1984); Barbara Kingsolver, *Holding the Line: Women in the Great Arizona Mine Strike of 1983* (Ithaca: ILR Press, 1989); Sonya O. Rose, "'Gender at Work': Sex, Class and Industrial Capitalism," *History Workshop: A Journal of Social and Feminist Historians* (Spring 1986): 113–31.

37. Karen Brodkin Sacks, "What's a Life Story Got to Do with It?" in Personal Narratives Group, ed., *Interpreting Women's Lives: Feminist Theory and Personal Narratives* (Bloomington: Indiana Univ. Press, 1989), 85–95; Mary Pardo, "Creating Community: Mexican American Women in Eastside Los Angeles," *Aztlan* 20 (Spring and Fall 1991): 39–71; Martha Ackelsberg and Irene Diamond, "Gender and Political Life: New Directions in Political Science," in Beth B. Hess and Myra Marx Ferree, eds., *Analyzing Gender: A Handbook of Social Science Research* (Beverly Hills: Sage Publications, 1987), 504–25.

38. Balbo, "The Servicing Work of Women," 267.

39. Anthony Giddens, *Central Problems in Social Theory: Action, Structure and Contradiction in Social Analysis* (London: Macmillan, 1979), 148–49.

40. Hill Collins, *Black Feminist Thought,* 237. As Michelle Fine has warned, feminist scholars should not "collude in the more general tendency to hold women personally responsible for their life circumstances." Michelle Fine, "Reflections on a Feminist Psychology of Women: Paradoxes and Prospects," *Psychology of Women Quarterly* 9 (1985): 167–83.

41. Linda Gordon, *Heroes of Their Own Lives: The Politics and History of Family Violence* (New York: Penguin Books, 1988); Gordon, "What's New in Women's History," 20–30; Linda Gordon, "What Is Women's History?," *History Today* (June 1985): 46; Smith-Rosenberg, *Disorderly Conduct;* Judith R. Walkowitz, *Prostitution and Victorian Society: Women, Class, and the State* (Cambridge: Cambridge Univ. Press, 1980); Virginia Scharff, *Taking the Wheel: Women and the Coming of the Motor Age* (New York: Free Press, 1991); Nancy F. Cott, *The Grounding of Modern Feminism* (New Haven: Yale Univ. Press, 1987); Rosalind Pollack Petchesky, *Abortion and Woman's Choice: The State, Sexuality, and Reproductive Freedom* (Boston: Northeastern Univ. Press, 1984); Judith Stacey, "Can There Be a Feminist Ethnography?," *Women's Studies International Forum* 11 (Jan. 1988): 21–27.

42. Anzaldua, *Borderlands/La Frontera,* 79–80. As Chandra Mohanty notes, Anzaldua's invocation of the borderlands is not abstract; it is a "notion of agency born of history and geography." Mohanty, "Cartographies of Struggle," 37.

43. Joan W. Scott, "Multiculturalism and the Politics of Identity," *Bulletin of the Conference Group on Women's History* 23 (Oct./Nov. 1992): 6.

44. Ruth Roessel, *Women in Navajo Society* (Rough Rock, Ariz.: Navajo Resource Center, 1981).

45. Jacqueline Dowd Hall, "Partial Truths," *Signs* 14 (1989): 902–11.

Chapter 2.   American Indian Women and Cultural Conflict

1. Calvin Martin, "Ethnohistory: A Better Way to Write Indian History," *Western Historical Quarterly* 9 (Jan. 1978): 41–56.

2. Joan M. Jensen, "Native American Women and Agriculture: A Seneca Case Study," *Sex Roles* 3 (Oct. 1977): 423–41; Petition, To the Washington Chiefs from the Moqui Villages, March, 1894, Records of the Bureau of Indian Affairs, Letters Received 1881–1907, Record Group 75, National Archives.

3. Catherine L. Albanese, *Nature Religion in America from the Algonkian Indians to the New Age* (Chicago: Univ. of Chicago Press, 1990), 16–34; Calvin Martin, "The Metaphysics of Writing Indian-White History," in Calvin Martin, ed., *The American Indian and the Problem of History* (New York: Oxford Univ. Press, 1987), 27–34.

4. Paula Gunn Allen, *The Sacred Hoop: Recovering the Feminine in American Indian Traditions* (Boston: Beacon Press, 1992); Patricia Albers and Beatrice Medicine, eds., *The Hidden Half: Studies of Plains Indian Women* (Lanham, Md.: Univ. Press of America, 1983); Jensen, "Native American Women and Agriculture," 423–41; Theda Perdue, "Cherokee Women and the Trail of Tears," *Journal of*

Women's History 1 (Spring 1989): 14–30; Mona Etienne and Eleanor Burke Leacock, eds., *Women and Colonization: Anthropological Perspectives* (New York: Praeger, 1990). For a different view, see Katherine M. Wiest, "Plains Indian Women: An Assessment," in W. Raymond Wood and Margot Liberty, eds., *Anthropology on the Great Plains* (Lincoln: Univ. of Nebraska Press, 1980), 255–71.

5. Paula Petrik, "Commentary," in Lillian Schlissel, Janice Monk, and Vicki Ruiz, eds., *Western Women: Their Land, Their Lives* (New Haven: Yale Univ. Press, 1988), 247–52; Christine Bolt, *American Indian Policy and American Reform: Case Studies of the Campaign to Assimilate the American Indians* (London, 1987), 252–69; K. N. Llewellyn and E. Adamson Hoebel, *The Cheyenne Way: Conflict and Case Law in Primitive Jurisprudence* (Norman: Univ. of Oklahoma Press, 1978), 180–211.

6. Allen, *Sacred Hoop*, 4–5.

7. Aihwa Ong, "Colonialism and Modernity: Feminist Representations of Women in Non-Western Societies," *Inscriptions* (1988): 79–92. For a list of Indian autobiographies, see H. David Brumble, *An Annotated Bibliography of American Indian and Eskimo Autobiographies* (Lincoln: Univ. of Nebraska Press, 1981).

8. Patricia C. Albers, "Autonomy and Dependency in the Lives of Dakota Women: A Study in Historical Change," *Review of Radical Political Economics* 17 (1985): 109–34; Jensen, "Native American Women and Agriculture," 423–41; Perdue, "Cherokee Women and the Trail of Tears," 14–30.

9. Bolt, *American Indian Policy and American Reform*, 252–69; Teresa L. Amott and Julie A. Matthaei, *Race, Gender, and Work: A Multicultural Economic History of Women in the United States* (Boston: South End Press, 1991), 31–61; Martin, "Ethnohistory: A Better Way to Write Indian History," 41–56.

10. Jensen, "Native American Women and Agriculture," 423–41; Carol Devens, "Separate Confrontations: Gender as a Factor in Indian Adaptation to European Colonization in New France," *American Quarterly* 38 (1986): 461–80; Perdue, "Cherokee Women and the Trail of Tears," 14–30.

11. Theda Perdue, "Cherokee Women and the Trail of Tears," 14–30; Devon A. Mihesuah, *Cultivating the Rosebuds: The Education of Women at the Cherokee Female Seminary, 1851–1909* (Urbana: Univ. of Illinois Press, 1993), 3. Indeed, the retrospective nature of personal narratives always poses a dilemma for historians, but it is especially significant in interpreting Native American women's history.

12. Devens, "Separate Confrontations," 461–80; Alice Kehoe, "The Shackles of Tradition," in Albers and Medicine, eds., *The Hidden Half*, 53–73.

13. Sherry B. Ortner, "Theory in Anthropology Since the Sixties," *Comparative Studies in Society and History* 26 (Jan. 1984): 143 [126–66]. This interpretive problem is more pronounced among anthropologists than among historians. Robert F. Berkhofer, Jr., "The Political Context of a New Indian History," *Pacific Historical Review* 40 (1971): 357–82.

14. For an example of the difficulty of attempting to reconstruct the remote precontact past, see Irene Silverblatt, *Moon, Sun, and Witches: Gender Ideologies and Class in Inca and Colonial Peru* (Princeton: Princeton Univ. Press, 1987).

15. Carolyn Niethammer, *Daughters of the Earth: The Lives and Legends of American Indian Women* (New York: Macmillan, 1977), 105–37; Anna Moore Shaw, *A Pima Past* (Tucson: Univ. of Arizona Press, 1974), 28–30, 47–52, 70–74;

Lalla Scott, *Karnee: A Paiute Narrative* (Reno: Univ. of Nevada Press, 1966), 21–25; Leslie Spier, "Problems Arising from the Cultural Position of the Havasupai," *American Anthropologist* 31 (April-June 1929): 213–22.

16. Harriet Whitehead, "The Bow and the Burden Strap: A New Look at Institutionalized Homosexuality in Native North America," in Sherry B. Ortner and Harriet Whitehead, eds., *Sexual Meanings: The Cultural Construction of Gender and Sexuality* (Cambridge: Cambridge Univ. Press, 1981), 80–115; Spier, "Problems Arising from the Cultural Position of the Havasupai," 213–22; Niethammer, *Daughters of the Earth*, 105–85.

17. Shaw, *A Pima Past*, 28, 47–52, 69–74; Whitehead, "The Bow and the Burden Strap," 80–115.

18. Bolt, *American Indian Policy and the American Reform*, 252–69; Niethammer, *Daughters of the Earth*, 37–55; Keith H. Basso, ed., *Western Apache Raiding and Warfare* (Tucson: Univ. of Arizona Press, 1971), 267–69; Scott, *Karnee: A Paiute Narrative*, 30–31.

19. Lucille Jake, Evelyn James, and Pamela Bunte, "The Southern Paiute Woman in a Changing Society," *Frontiers* 7 (1983): 44–49; Scott, *Karnee: A Paiute Narrative*, 18, 75; Nancy Oestreich Lurie, ed., *Mountain Wolf Woman, Sister of Crashing Thunder: The Autobiography of a Winnebago Indian* (Ann Arbor: Univ. of Michigan Press, 1961), 29–30; Llewellyn and Hoebel, *Cheyenne Way*, 169–80.

20. Scott, *Karnee: A Paiute Narrative*, 18–19; Niethammer, *Daughters of the Earth*, 96–99; Llewellyn and Hoebel, *Cheyenne Way*, 180–87.

21. Albers, "Autonomy and Dependency in the Lives of Dakota Women," 109–34; Perdue, "Cherokee Women and the Trail of Tears," 14–30; Genevieve Chato and Christine Conte, "The Legal Rights of American Indian Women," in Lillian Schlissel, Janice Monk, and Vicki Ruiz, eds., *Western Women: Their Land, Their Lives*, 229–46; Devens, "Separate Confrontations," 461–80; Bolt, *American Indian Policy and American Reform*, 252–69; Niethammer, *Daughters of the Earth*, 215–24; Howard L. Harrod, *Mission Among the Blackfeet* (Norman: Univ. of Oklahoma Press, 1971), 8, 10; Lurie, ed., *Mountain Wolf Woman*, 129–30.

22. Niethammer, *Daughters of the Earth*, 57–69; Mary E. Young, "Women, Civilization, and the Indian Question," in Mabel E. Deutrich and Virginia Cardwell Purdy, eds., *Clio Was a Woman: Studies in the History of American Women* (Washington: Howard Univ. Press, 1980), 98–110; Ely McClellan, *Obstetric Practices Among the Aborigines of North America* (Louisville: John P. Morton, 1873), 6, 9; Charlotte Johnson Frisbie, *Kinaalda: A Study of the Navaho Girls' Puberty Ceremony* (Middletown, Conn.: Wesleyan Univ. Press, 1967), 7; Flora L. Bailey, *Some Sex Beliefs and Practices in a Navaho Community* (Cambridge: Peabody Museum of American Archeology and Ethnology, 1950), 7; Clara Sue Kidwell, "The Power of Women in Three American Indian Societies," *Journal of Ethnic Studies* 6 (Fall 1978): 113–21.

23. Evelyn Blackwood, "Sexuality and Gender in Certain Native American Tribes: The Case of Cross-Gender Females," *Signs* 10 (Autumn 1984): 27–42; Oscar Lewis, "Manly-Hearted Women Among the North Piegan," *American Anthropologist* 43 (April-June, 1941): 173–87; Whitehead, "The Bow and the Burden Strap," 80–115; Walter Williams, *The Spirit and the Flesh: Sexual Diversity in American Indian Culture* (Boston, 1986); Will Roscoe, *The Zuni-Man Woman*

(Albuquerque: Univ. of New Mexico Press, 1991); Will Roscoe, "The Zuni Man-Woman," *Out/Look* 1 (Summer 1988): 56–67; Ramon A. Guttierez, "Must We Deracinate Indians to Find Gay Roots," *Out/Look* 1 (Winter 1989): 61–67; John D'Emilio and Estelle B. Freedman, *Intimate Matters: A History of Sexuality in America* (New York: Harper & Row, 1988), 6–9. "Two-spirits" is the usage preferred by American Indians to refer to individuals who are gay, lesbian, or transgendered (including transvestites and transsexuals).

24. Niethammer, *Daughters of the Earth*, 139–46; Jensen, "Native American Women and Agriculture," 423–41; Perdue, "Cherokee Women and the Trail of Tears," 14–30.

25. Jensen, "Native American Women and Agriculture," 423–41; Perdue, "Cherokee Women and the Trail of Tears," 14–30; Devens, "Separate Confrontations," 461–80.

26. Devens, "Separate Confrontations," 461–80; Jensen, "Native American Women and Agriculture," 423–41.

27. Jensen, "Native American Women and Agriculture," 423–41; Devens, "Separate Confrontations," 461–80; Polingaysi Qoyawayma, *No Turning Back: A True Account of a Hopi Indian Girl's Struggle to Bridge the Gap Between the World of Her People and the World of the White Man* (Albuquerque: Univ. of New Mexico Press, 1964); Berkhofer, "The Political Context of a New Indian History," 357–82; Graham D. Taylor, *The New Deal and American Indian Tribalism: The Administration of the Indian Reorganization Act, 1934–45* (Lincoln: Univ. of Nebraska Press, 1980), 39–62; Mihesuah, *Cultivating the Rosebuds.*

28. Many Indian nations rapidly assimilated the horse into their economic and cultural order. The market system was also selectively adapted in many nations. Richard White, *The Roots of Dependency: Subsistence, Environment, and Social Change Among the Choctaws, Pawnees, and Navajos* (Lincoln: Univ. of Nebraska Press, 1983); Mary C. Wright, "Economic Development and Native American Women in the Early Nineteenth Century," *American Quarterly* 33 (Winter 1981): 525–36.

29. Loretta Fowler, *Shared Symbols, Contested Meanings: Gros Ventre Culture and History, 1778–1984* (Ithaca: Cornell Univ. Press, 1987). In some nations, the acculturated held a great deal of the formal power, so the appeal to tradition had less political force. The Cherokees who were forced to move to Indian Territory were one such case. Mihesuah, *Cultivating the Rosebuds.*

30. Jensen, "Native American Women and Agriculture," 423–41.

31. Ibid.

32. Dolores Janiewski, "Learning to 'Live like White Folks': Gender, Ethnicity and the State in the Inland Northwest," in Dorothy O. Helly and Susan M. Reverby, eds., *Gendered Domains: Rethinking Public and Private in Women's History* (Ithaca: Cornell Univ. Press, 1991): 167–80; Jensen, "Native American Women and Agriculture," 423–41; Terry P. Wilson, "Osage Indian Women During a Century of Change, 1870–1980," *Prologue* 14 (Winter 1982): 185–201. Colonizing powers sometimes present exaggerated and outmoded gender systems as models for the colonized. Helen Callaway, *Gender, Culture and Empire: European Women in Colonial Nigeria* (Houndmills, Basingstoke, Hampshire: Macmillan Press, 1987).

33. Robert A. Trennert, Jr., *Alternative to Extinction: Federal Indian Policy and*

the Beginnings of the Reservation System (Philadelphia: Temple Univ. Press, 1975), 1–31.

34. Trennert, *Alternative to Extinction*, 193–95.

35. Francis Paul Prucha, ed., *Documents of United States Indian Policy* (Lincoln: Univ. of Nebraska Press, 1990), 14.

36. Francis Paul Prucha, *American Indian Policy in Crisis: Christian Reformers and the Indian, 1865–1900* (Norman: Univ. of Oklahoma Press, 1976), 30–71; Francis Paul Prucha, *The Great Father: The United States Government and the American Indian* (Lincoln: Univ. of Nebraska Press, 1984), II: 693.

37. Prucha, *Great Father*, II: 707.

38. William T. Hagan, "The Reservation Policy: Too Little and Too Late," in Jane F. Smith and Robert M. Kvasnicka, eds., *Indian-White Relations: A Persistent Paradox* (Washington: Howard Univ. Press, 1976), 157–69; Harrod, *Mission Among the Blackfeet*, 39–48.

39. Hagan, "The Reservation Policy," 157–69; Sarah Winnemucca Hopkins, *Life Among the Piutes: Their Wrongs and Claims* (New York: G. P. Putnam's Sons, 1883). Some nations fared better than most in the transition to farming in this period. Leonard A. Carlson, *Indians, Bureaucrats, and Land: The Dawes Act and the Decline of Indian Farming* (Westport, Conn.: Greenwood Press, 1981), 115–62.

40. David H. Getches, Daniel M. Rosenfelt, and Charles F. Wilkinson, *Federal Indian Law: Cases and Materials* (St. Paul: West Publishing, 1978), 69–77.

41. Chato and Conte, "The Legal Rights of American Indian Women," 229–46; Janiewski, "Learning to 'Live like White Folks,'" 167–80; Albers, "Autonomy and Dependency in the Lives of Dakota Women," 109–34; Perdue, "Cherokee Women and the Trail of Tears," 14–30.

42. Imre Sutton, *Indian Land Tenure: Bibliographical Essays and a Guide to the Literature* (New York: Clearwater Publishing, 1975), 125–29; Otis, *The Dawes Act and the Allotment of Indian Lands*, ed. Prucha, 44–45; Kenneth R. Philp, "Termination: A Legacy of the Indian New Deal," *Western Historical Quarterly* 14 (April 1983): 165–80.

43. Carlson, *Indians, Bureaucrats, and Land*, 133–61.

44. Larry W. Burt, *Tribalism in Crisis: Federal Indian Policy, 1953–1961* (Albuquerque: Univ. of New Mexico Press, 1982), 2; Janiewski, "Learning to 'Live like White Folks,'" 167–80; Janet A. McDonnell, *The Dispossession of the American Indian, 1887–1934* (Bloomington: Indiana Univ. Press, 1991), 124; Father Berard Haile, *Women versus Men: A Conflict of Navajo Emergence* (Lincoln: Univ. of Nebraska Press, 1981), 17.

45. Frederick E. Hoxie, *A Final Promise: The Campaign to Assimilate the Indians, 1880–1920* (Lincoln: Univ. of Nebraska Press, 1984), 165–66; Felix S. Cohen, *Handbook of Federal Indian Law* (Albuquerque: Univ. of New Mexico Press, 1970), 226; McDonnell, *The Dispossession of the American Indian*, 87–102; Thomas Biolsi, *Organizing the Lakota: The Political Economy of the New Deal on the Pine Ridge and Rosebud Reservations* (Tucson: Univ. of Arizona Press, 1992), 14–15.

46. Hoxie, *A Final Promise*, ix–xv, 115–45.

47. Prucha, *Great Father*, II: 814, 828–29.

48. Even before the Dawes Act, Indians were forced to cede much of their land

to the federal government. Hoxie, *A Final Promise*, 41–53, 147–87; Walter Hart Blumenthal, *American Indians Dispossessed: Fraud in Land Cessions Forced upon the Tribes* (Philadelphia: George S. MacManus, 1955), 158–59; Prucha, *Great Father*, II: 867, 889–96; William T. Hagan, "Justifying Dispossession of the Indian: The Land Utilization Argument," in Christopher Vecsey and Robert W. Venables, eds., *American Indian Environments: Ecological Issues in Native American History* (Syracuse: Syracuse Univ. Press, 1980), 65–80.

49. Catherine A. MacKinnon, *Feminism Unmodified: Discourses on Life and Law* (Cambridge: Harvard Univ. Press, 1987), 63–69; other cites, Prucha, *Great Father*, II: 759–813; Hoxie, *A Final Promise*, 147–87, 211–8.

50. Hagan, "Justifying Dispossession of the Indian," in Vecsey and Venables, eds., *American Indian Environments*, 65–80; Hoxie, *A Final Promise*, 187; Prucha, *The Great Father*, II: 879–80.

51. Hoxie, *A Final Promise*, 147–87; United States, House of Representatives, Committee on Indian Affairs, Hearings on the Condition of Various Tribes of Indians, Indians of the U.S., 66th Cong., 1st sess., 1919, Pt. 4, pp. xxxii–xxxiii.

52. Prucha, *Great Father*, II: 762, 780.

53. Hoxie, *A Final Promise*, 211–38.

54. Prucha, *Great Father*, II: 882–84; Hoxie, *A Final Promise*, 181–82, 223. Prior to the decision in *Sandoval*, the Pueblos' autonomy had been established by the Treaty of Guadalupe Hidalgo as interpreted in an 1876 case, *United States v. Joseph*. John R. Wunder, *"Retained by the People": A History of American Indians and the Bill of Rights* (New York: Oxford Univ. Press, 1994), 42–44.

55. Gerald Sider, "When Parrots Learn to Talk, and Why They Can't: Domination, Deception, and Self-Deception in Indian-White Relations," *Comparative Studies in Society and History* 29 (Jan. 1987): 3–23.

56. Carlson, *Indians, Bureaucrats, and Land*, 115–62.

57. Prucha, *Great Father*, II: 757, 897–916; Richard White, *Roots of Dependency*, 212–314.

58. Biolsi, *Organizing the Lakota*; Taylor, *The New Deal and American Indian Tribalism*; Clayton R. Koppes, "From New Deal to Termination: Liberalism and Indian Policy, 1933–1953," *Pacific Historical Review* 46 (Nov. 1977): 543–66; Kenneth Philp, *John Collier's Crusade for Indian Reform, 1920–1954* (Tucson: Univ. of Arizona Press, 1977).

59. Taylor, *The New Deal and American Indian Tribalism*, 66; Koppes, "From New Deal to Termination," 543–66.

60. Prucha, *Great Father*, II: 993–1012.

61. Alison R. Bernstein, *American Indians and World War II: Toward a New Era in Indian Affairs* (Norman: Univ. of Oklahoma Press, 1991), 89–111.

62. Evon Z. Vogt, "Between Two Worlds: Case Study of a Navajo Veteran," *American Indian* 5 (1949): 13–21; John Adair and Evon Vogt, "Navaho and Zuni Veterans: A Study of Contrasting Modes of Culture Change," *American Anthropologist* 51 (Oct.–Dec. 1949): 547–61; Annual Report, Office of Indian Affairs, 1945.

63. Burt, *Tribalism in Crisis*, 125; Prucha, *Great Father*, II: 1013–84; Philp, "Termination: A Legacy of the Indian New Deal," 165–80. The creation of the Indian Claims Commission in 1946 to settle outstanding disputes between various

nations and the U.S. government was also supposed to facilitate the ending of the Indians' special status under American law.

64. Burt, *Tribalism in Crisis;* Prucha, *Great Father,* II: 1013–84; Kenneth R. Philp, "Termination: A Legacy of the Indian New Deal," 165–80; Wunder, *"Retained by the People,"* 107–11.

65. Nancy Oestreich Lurie, "Menominee Termination: From Reservation to Colony," *Human Organization* 31 (Fall 1972): 257–69.

66. Ibid.; Nicholas C. Peroff, *Menominee Drums: Tribal Termination and Restoration, 1954–1974* (Norman: Univ. of Oklahoma Press, 1982). A similar fate befell the Klamath Indians. Susan Hood, "Termination of the Klamath Indian Tribe of Oregon," *Ethnohistory* 19 (Fall 1972): 379–92.

67. Prucha, *Great Father,* II: 1005–9, 1043–44, 1074–79.

68. Ibid., II: 1079–84.

69. U.S. House of Representatives, "Rehabilitation of the Navajo and Hopi Tribes of Indians," Report No. 1474, 81st Cong., 2d Sess., 1950; U.S. House of Representatives, "Promoting the Rehabilitation of the Standing Rock Sioux Tribe of Indians and Better Utilization of the Resources of the Standing Rock Indian Reservation," Report No. 412, 81st Cong., 1st Sess., 1949.

70. Prucha, *Great Father,* II: 1011, 1085–90;

71. Ibid.; *Los Angeles Times,* Jan. 13, 1972.

72. *Los Angeles Times,* May 2, 1971, Jan. 13, 1972.

Chapter 3.   An Expensive Luxury

1. Frederick E. Hoxie and Joan T. Mark, eds., *With the Nez Perces: Alice Fletcher in the Field, 1889–1992* (Lincoln: Univ. of Nebraska Press, 1981), 35.

2. Dolores Janiewski, "Learning to Live 'Just Like White Folks': Gender, Ethnicity and the State in the Inland Northwest," in Dorothy O. Helly and Susan M. Reverby, eds., *Gendered Domains: Rethinking Public and Private in Women's History* (Ithaca: Cornell Univ. Press, 1991), 167–80.

3. Brookings Institution, Institute for Government Research, *The Problem of Indian Administration* (Baltimore: Johns Hopkins Univ. Press, 1928), 572.

4. Mary E. Young, "Women, Civilization, and the Indian Question," in Virginia Cartwell Purdy and Mabel E. Deutrich, eds., *Clio Was a Woman: Studies in the History of American Women* (Washington, D.C.: Howard Univ. Press, 1980), 98–110; Brookings Institution, *Problem of Indian Administration,* 499, 547–663.

5. These relations, however, were far from private. Michel Foucault, *The History of Sexuality: An Introduction,* vol. 1 (New York: Vintage Books, 1990).

6. Malcolm McDowell, "Landless Indians of California and Nevada," April 17, 1917, Special Reports, Board of Indian Commissioners, RG 75, NA, vol. I (hereafter cited as SR, NA); Malcolm McDowell, "Mescalero Indian Reservation, New Mexico," May 1, 1918, SR, NA, vol. 2; Flora Warren Seymour, "Report on the Jicarilla Apache Indian Reservation, New Mexico," Oct. 19, 1923, SR, NA, vol. 4; Indian Rights Association, Annual Report, 1921, p. 9. The Meriam Report, however, blamed the government for practices that "have operated against the development of wholesome family life" and concluded that "to say . . . that the backwardness of the Indian race is due to the unprogressive character of the women, is

to over-simplify the diagnosis of the problem and to obscure the deeper causes." Brookings Institution, *Problem of Indian Administration,* 6, 574, 547–663. For evidence of persistence and adaptation of Indian cultures and power in men's domains, see Peter Iverson, ed., *The Plains Indians of the Twentieth Century* (Norman: Univ. of Oklahoma Press, 1987); Omer Stewart, *Peyote Religion* (Norman: Univ. of Oklahoma Press, 1988); and Fred W. Voget, *The Shoshoni-Crow Sun Dance* (Norman: Univ. of Oklahoma Press, 1984).

7. Hoxie and Mark, eds., *With the Nez Perces,* 35; Estelle Aubrey Brown, *Stubborn Fool: A Narrative* (Caldwell, Idaho: Caxton Printers, 1952); Janiewski, "Learning to Live 'Just Like White Folks,'" 167–80.

8. Brookings Institution, *Problem of Indian Administration,* 6, 568, 604.

9. Peggy Pascoe, *Relations of Rescue* (New York: Oxford Univ. Press, 1990); Kathy Peiss, *Cheap Amusements: Working Women and Leisure in Turn-of-the-Century New York* (Philadelphia: Temple Univ. Press, 1986); Mari Jo Buhle, *Women and American Socialism, 1870–1920* (Urbana: Univ. of Illinois Press, 1983); Mary Ryan, *Womanhood in America: From Colonial Times to the Present,* 3d ed. (New York: Franklin Watts, 1983), 167–252; Elizabeth Ewen, *Immigrant Women in the Land of Dollars: Life and Culture on the Lower East Side, 1890–1925* (New York: Monthly Review Press, 1985); Carroll Smith-Rosenberg, *Disorderly Conduct: Visions of Gender in Victorian America* (New York: Oxford Univ. Press, 1985), 245–96.

10. Carrie Niethammer, *Daughters of the Earth: The Lives and Legends of American Indian Women* (New York: Collier Books, 1977), 105–37; Patricia C. Albers, "Autonomy and Dependency in the Lives of Dakota Women: A Study in Historical Change," *Review of Radical Political Economics* 17 (1985): 109–34.

11. Sherry B. Ortner, "The Virgin and the State," *Feminist Studies* 4 (Oct. 1978): 19–35.

12. Ibid.

13. Hearings on H.R. 7902 Before the House Committee on Indian Affairs, 73d Cong., 2d sess., pt. 9, pp. 428–89, quote on p. 430.

14. Francis Paul Prucha, *The Great Father: The United States Government and the American Indian,* 2 vols. (Lincoln: Univ. of Nebraska Press, 1984), II: 611–86, quote on 621; Smith-Rosenberg, *Disorderly Conduct.*

15. Francis Paul Prucha, ed., *Documents of United States Indian Policy* (Lincoln: Univ. of Nebraska Press, 1990), 50; Prucha, *Great Father,* II: 671, 615, 678.

16. United States, House of Representatives, Committee on Indian Affairs, Hearings on the Condition of Various Tribes of Indians. Indians of the United States, 66th Cong., 1st sess., 1919, pt. 6, p. 65. An 1888 federal law had already established that Indian women who married white men became U.S. citizens, "with all the rights, privileges, and immunities of any such citizen, being a married woman. . . ." The latter clause qualified her political claims, given the 1874 Supreme Court decision in *Bradwell v. Illinois,* limiting married women's rights under the Fourteenth Amendment. Prucha, ed., *Documents of United States Indian Policy,* 176–77. The passage of the Indian Citizenship Act in 1924 conferred citizenship on all Indians who had not previously received it. Prucha, *Great Father,* II: 793–94. In 1896 it was decided that the children of mixed marriages could not receive allotments—it seems to have been applied only to Indian women marrying

whites. S. M. Brosius, "The Insecurity of an Allotment," 20th annual Lake Mohonk Conference of the Friends of the Indian, 1902.

17. Hoxie and Mark, eds., *With the Nez Perces,* 48; Lawrence C. Kelly, *The Navajo Indians and Federal Indian Policy, 1900–1935* (Tucson: Univ. of Arizona Press, 1968), 49–50. Indeed, laws frequently required the consent of the majority of adult Indian males before tribal land could be alienated. Whether this conferred real power can be disputed: federal officials often employed deceit and coercion to obtain that "consent."

18. Hoxie and Mark, eds., *With the Nez Perces,* 54–55, 82. In 1885, former U.S. Supreme Court Justice William Strong supported alloting land to a male head of household in order that "Indians [be] brought together in families." Francis Paul Prucha, ed., *Americanizing the American Indians: Writings by the "Friends of the Indian," 1880–1900* (Cambridge: Harvard Univ. Press, 1973), 40.

19. Susan Hardy Aiken, *Isak Dinesen and the Engendering of Narrative* (Chicago: Univ. of Chicago Press, 1990), 4.

20. Young, "Women, Civilization, and the Indian Question," 98–110; Hoxie and Mark, eds., *With the Nez Perces,* 54; W. E. Gates, Opening Address, 18th Annual Lake Mohonk Conference of the Friends of the Indian, 1900; Thomas Biolsi, *Organizing the Lakota: The Political Economy of the New Deal on the Pine Ridge and Rosebud Reservations* (Tucson: Univ. of Arizona Press, 1992), 7–12.

21. Petition, To the Washington Chiefs from the Moqui Villages, March, 1894, Records of the Bureau of Indian Affairs, Letters Received 1881–1907, Record Group 75, National Archives.

22. U.S., House of Representatives, Report #1700 on H.R. 8905, 51st Cong., 1st sess., 1890, pp. 2–3; D. S. Otis, *The Dawes Act and the Allotment of Indian Lands,* Francis Paul Prucha, ed. (Norman: Univ. of Oklahoma Press, 1973), 106–23; J. P. Kinney, *A Continent Lost—A Civilization Won: Indian Land Tenure in America* (London: Oxford Univ. Press, 1937), 241. Moreover, as Dolores Janiewski has noted, policy-makers "attempted to deprive . . . feminist and socialist critics of subversive examples that might suggest that [dominant] arrangements could and should be changed." Janiewski, "Learning to Live 'Just Like White Folks,'" 180.

23. Alice Fletcher supported this act. Hoxie and Mark, eds., *With the Nez Perces,* 82. U.S., House of Representatives, Report #1700 on H.R. 8905, 51st Cong., 1st sess., 1890, pp. 2–3; Otis, *Dawes Act and the Allotment of Indian Lands,* 106–23; Kinney, *A Continent Lost—A Civilization Won,* 241. Janiewski cogently noted, "Having denied women the education and skills necessary for farming, they proceeded to define women as unable to farm." Janiewski, "Learning to Live 'Just Like White Folks,'" 174–75.

24. Otis, *Dawes Act and the Allotment of Indian Lands,* 106–23.

25. S. 4713, 56th Cong., 1st Sess., RG 75, Entry 1395, NA.

26. W. A. Jones to United States Indian Agents and School Superintendents in Charge of Agencies, April 5, 1901, RG 75, Entry 1395.

27. Law, Regulating Marriages and Divorces Among Allotted Indians, March 12, 1897, Territory of Oklahoma, RG 75, Entry 1395; Legislature of Nebraska, 32d sess., House roll No. 285, 1911, RG 75, Entry 1395; Laws, Joint Resolutions, and Memorials Passed by the Legislature of the State of Nebraska at the Thirty-second Session (York, Nebraska: York Blank Book Company, 1911).

28. Malcolm McDowell, "Landless Indians of California and Nevada," April 17, 1917, SR, NA, vol. I; Report of Field Matron, Neah Bay Agency in Report of the Commissioner of Indian Affairs, 1903; Superintendent's Report, Oklahoma Cantonment (Arapaho and Cheyenne), 1907, Annual Narrative and Statistical Reports, RG 75, Microfilm Publication M1011 (hereafter cited as ANSR).

29. Letter, Charles H. Burke to Chauncy S. Goodrich, March 9, 1929, General Services (hereafter cited as GS), RG 75, Box 1117, NA; Biolsi, *Organizing the Lakota*, 7–12.

30. Letter, Aug. F. Duclos, Superintendent, to Commissioner of Indian Affairs, May 21, 1926, RG 75, Classified Files (hereafter cited as CF), box 172, NA; Letter, [?] Wright, to Malcolm McDowell, June 26, 1918, RG 75, E1395; 1926 hearings.

31. Letter, Peter Paquette to Commissioner of Indian Affairs, March 26, 1909, RG 75, CF, box 11. Paquette also suggested that the daughters be kept in school until they reached the age of 20.

32. Samuel A. Eliot, "Report on the Pima Indian Reservation, Arizona," May, 1917, SR, BIA, vol. I; Shaw, *A Pima Past.*

33. Samuel A. Eliot, "Report on the Fort Hall Indian Reservation, Idaho," April 15, 1920, SR, BIA, vol. 3; Frank Knox, "Report on the Fort Apache Indian Reservation, Arizona," Oct. 10, 1920, SR, BIA, vol. 3; Malcolm McDowell, "Mescalero Indian Reservation, New Mexico," May 1, 1918, SR, BIA, vol. 2; Flora Warren Seymour, "Report on the Jicarilla Apache Indian Reservation, New Mexico," Oct. 19, 1923, SR, BIA, vol. 4.

34. Margaret Connell Szasz, *Education and the American Indian: The Road to Self-Determination Since 1928*, 2d ed. (Albuquerque: Univ. of New Mexico Press, 1977); Hearings Before a Subcommittee of the Committee on Indian Affairs of the U.S. Senate, 71st Congress, 3rd sess., 1930, pp. 4481–83; Fran Leeper Buss, ed., *Dignity* (Ann Arbor: Univ. of Michigan Press, 1985), 150–68; Interview with Lydia, Fran Buss Oral History Collection; Testimony of As-ton-pia at St. Michaels Mission, Arizona, Sept. 6, 1932 [?], Papers of the Franciscans, St. Michaels, Arizona, Special Collections, University of Arizona Library (hereafter cited as UA). The number and power of acculturated Cherokees in Oklahoma meant that they established their own institutions based on white models, although their decision to do so was a subject of continuing dispute by "traditionals." Devon A. Mihesuah, *Cultivating the Rosebuds: The Education of Women at the Cherokee Female Seminary, 1851–1909* (Urbana: Univ. of Illinois Press, 1993).

35. Frank Knox, "Report on the Ute Indians of Utah and Colorado," Oct. 15, 1915, SR, BIA, vol. I; Polingaysi Qoyawayma, *No Turning Back: A Hopi Indian Woman's Struggle to Live in Two Worlds* (Albuquerque: Univ. of New Mexico Press, 1964), 17–25. In the late nineteenth century, poor Catholic and Jewish immigrants were also vulnerable to the loss of their children, who were placed with Protestant families. Maureen Fitzgerald, "Irish-Catholic Nuns and the Development of New York City's Welfare System, 1840–1900" (Ph.D. diss., University of Wisconsin, 1992).

36. Oral history, Cynthia Dakota, Fran Buss collection, Special Collections, University of Arizona Library.

37. Letter, As-ton-pia to U.S. Indian Commissioner, July 11, 1932, and As-

ton-pia testimony, Sept. 6, 1932, Franciscan Papers, Special Collections, UA, box 41.

38. Ibid.

39. Ibid., and letter, Rt. Rev. Msgr. William Hughes to Rev. Arnold Heinzmann, Nov. 18, 1932, Franciscan Papers, Special Collections, UA, box 41. Federal officials disputed her claim of lost sheep and refused to compensate her. Letter, Commissioner of Indian Affairs to Rev. Arnold Heinzmann, Feb. 15, 1933, Franciscan Papers, Special Collections, UA, box 41.

40. As-ton-pia testimony, Sept. 6, 1932, Franciscan Papers, Special Collections, UA, box 41.

41. Mary Logan Rothschild and Pamela Claire Hronek, *Doing What the Day Brought: An Oral History of Arizona Women* (Tucson: Univ. of Arizona Press), 39.

42. Robert A. Trennert, Jr., *The Phoenix Indian School: Forced Assimilation in Arizona, 1891–1935* (Norman: Univ. of Oklahoma Press, 1988), 65–66.

43. K. Tsianina Lomawaima, "Domesticity in the Federal Indian Schools: The Power of Authority Over Mind and Body," *American Ethnologist* 20 (May 1993): 227–40; Szasz, *Education and the American Indian*, 16–88; Ann Metcalf, "From Schoolgirl to Mother: The Effects of Education on Navajo Women," *Social Problems* 23 (June 1976): 535–44; David Wallace Adams, "Schooling the Hopi: Federal Indian Policy Writ Small, 1887–1917," *Pacific Historical Review* 48 (Aug. 1979): 335–56; Flora W. Seymour, "Report on the Zuni Indians of New Mexico," June 7, 1924, SR, BIA, vol. 5, p. 158; Qoyawayma, *No Turning Back*, 59; Moore, *A Pima Past*, 127. Parents did not always oppose their children's attendance in boarding schools. Trennert, *Phoenix Indian School*, 48–51.

44. Szasz, *Education and the American Indian*, 27, 64–65; Trennert, *Phoenix Indian School*, 9, 20, 29–37, 52–54, 70–75, 87–101, 138.

45. Brookings Institution, *Problem of Indian Administration*, 610–18; Lomawaima, "Domesticity in the Federal Indian Schools," 230–31.

46. William Ketcham, "Report on the Eufala Boarding School, Eufala, Oklahoma," Feb. 20, 1917, SR, BIA, vol. 1, p. 249; Malcolm McDowell, "Report on the Sherman Institute, Riverside, California," SR, BIA, vol. 1, pp. 539–40; Letter, Carrie A. Lyford to the Commissioner of Indian Affairs, Feb. 6, 1931, Office Files of Carrie A. Lyford, Records of the Bureau of Indian Affairs, Record Group 75, National Archives (hereafter cited as CAL, BIA); Rapid City Indian School, Rapid City, South Dakota, Nov. 1–6, 1930, CAL, BIA; Lomawaima, "Domesticity in the Federal Indian Schools," 230–231; Trennert, *Phoenix Indian School*, 20, 51–54, 70–73, 87–92.

47. Flora Warren Seymour, "Bismarck Indian School—North Dakota," Sept. 14, 1927, SR, BIA, vol. 1, p. 336; Mary Vaux Walcott, "Report on the California Outing Centers," Sept. 25, 1929, SR, BIA, vol. 8, pp. 158–69.

48. Buss, ed., *Dignity*, 156.

49. Frances Page to Ida Bahl, Feb. 15, 1975, Virginia Brown, Ida Bahl, and Lillian Watson Collection, Special Collections, Northern Arizona University Library.

50. Trennert, *Phoenix Indian School*, 70–73, 88–101; McDowell, "Report on the Sherman Institute, Riverside, California," 539–40; Walcott, "Report on the California Outing Centers," Sept. 158–69.

51. William H. Ketcham, "Schools Among the Five Civilized Tribes of Oklahoma," June 1, 1919, SR, BIA, vol. 1, pp. 331–33.

52. Trennert, *Phoenix Indian School*, 49–50, 133–36. K. Tsianina Lomawaima particularly emphasizes the importance of analyzing student resistance. Lomawaima, "Domesticity in the Federal Indian Schools," 227–240. The Cherokee Female Seminary, which was operated solely by the Cherokee Nation, also enforced serious limits on contacts between male and female students. Mihesuah, *Cultivating the Rosebuds*, 77–79.

53. Lomawaima, "Domesticity in the Federal Indian Schools," 227–40.

54. Trennert, *Phoenix Indian School*, 133–36.

55. Brookings Institution, *Problem of Indian Administration*, 567; Qoyawayma, *No Turning Back*, 69; Trennert, *Phoenix Indian School*, 56, 145–46.

56. Qoyawayma, *No Turning Back*, 67–76.

57. Ibid.

58. Flora Warren Seymour, "Report on the Mescalero Indian Reservation, New Mexico," June 6, 1932, SR, BIA, vol. 10; Flora Warren Seymour, "Indian Service Educational Activities in the Southwest," July 28, 1932, SR, BIA, vol. 10; Ketcham, "Report on the Eufala Boarding School."

59. Dane Coolidge, Testimony to the Indian Investigation Committee of the U.S. Senate, Nov. 12, 1930. Indeed, the Meriam Report urged that boarding schools be replaced with day schools on the grounds that preadolescent children should not be separated from their parents. Brookings Institution, *Problem of Indian Administration*, 550.

60. Hearings Before a Subcommittee of the Committee on Indian Affairs, U.S. Senate, 71st Cong., 3rd sess., 1930, pp. 4481–83.

61. Qoyawayma, *No Turning Back*, 67–76; Smithson, "The Havasupai Woman," 95–96, 101; Carroll Smith-Rosenberg, *Disorderly Conduct*, 245–96.

62. Earl Y. Henderson, "Report on the Truxton Canyon Indian Agency, Arizona," Feb. 1, 1928, BIC, SR, vol. 6, BIA; Smithson, "The Havasupai Woman," 95–96, 101; Truman Michelson, *The Autobiography of a Fox Indian Woman*, Annual Report of the Bureau of American Ethnology, 1918–1919 (Washington: GPO, 1925), 313–15.

63. Qoyawayma, *No Turning Back*, 69–71; Rothschild and Hronek, *Doing What the Day Brought*, 54–55.

64. Lalla Scott, *Karnee: A Paiute Narrative* (Reno: Univ. of Nevada Press, 1966), 18, 75–78.

65. Ely McClellan, *Obstetric Practices Among the Aborigines of North America* (Louisville: John P. Morton, 1873), 6, 9; Charlotte Johnson Frisbie, *Kinaalda: A Study of the Navaho Girls' Puberty Ceremony* (Middletown, Conn.: Wesleyan Univ. Press, 1967), 7; Flora L. Bailey, *Some Sex Beliefs and Practices in a Navaho Community* (Cambridge: Peabody Museum of American Archeology and Ethnology, 1950), 7; Carma Lee Smithson, "The Havasupai Woman," Anthropological Papers, University of Utah, April 1959, pp. 74–75; Gordon MacGregor, *Warriors Without Weapons: A Study of the Society and Personality Development of the Pine Ridge Sioux* (Chicago: Univ. of Chicago Press, 1946), 62; Flora Warren Seymour, "Report on the Red Lake Chippewa Indians of Minnesota," Sept. 26, 1927, BIC, SR, NA, vol. 6.

66. Melissa MacKinnon, "The Sexual Politics of Native American Assimilation: Native American Domestic Workers and Red Slavery in Tucson, Arizona," paper presented at the Reworking Labor History Conference, Madison, April 9–11, 1992; Peiss, *Cheap Amusements.*

67. MacKinnon, "The Sexual Politics of Native American Assimilation." This is similar to the reconstitution of the perpetrator of incest from a family member to a "dirty old man" in the same time period. Linda Gordon, *Heroes of Their Own Lives: The Politics and History of Family Violence* (New York: Penguin Books, 1988), 204–49.

68. William J. Ketcham, "Indians in Oklahoma, Idaho, Washington, Oregon and other States," June 3, 1918, SR, BIA, vol. 2; Malcolm McDowell, "Landless Indians of California and Nevada," April 17, 1917, SR, BIA, vol. I.

69. Letter, Hubert Work to Hon. Scott Leavitt, Jan. 15, 1926, in Hearings on H.R. 7826, Committee on Indian Affairs, House of Representatives, 69th Cong., 1st sess., 1926, pp. 2–3.

70. Letter, Bill Shelton to BIA, Oct. 1, 1910, GS, BIA, box 1116; Letter, Fred A. Possehl to Honorable Fred H. Abbott, Feb. 21, 1912, GS, BIA, box 1116; Lalla Scott, *Karnee: A Paiute Narrative* (Reno: Univ. of Nevada Press, 1966), 35–58; Hearings on H.R. 7826, Committee on Indian Affairs, House of Representatives, 69th Cong., 1st sess., 1926.

71. Hearings on H.R. 7826, Committee on Indian Affairs, House of Representatives, 69th Cong., 1st sess., 1926; Trennert, *Phoenix Indian School,* 133–36.

72. Young, "Women, Civilization, and the Indian Question," 98–110; George Vaux, Jr., to Henry Ashurst, 1918, Entry 1387, RG 75, NA; Board of Indian Commissioners, Bulletin 138, Releasing Indians from Government Supervision, April 27, 1921, Entry 1395, RG 75, NA; Law and Order Survey, 1929–1930, Entry 1393, RG 75, NA.

73. Hearings on H.R. 7826, Committee on Indian Affairs, House of Representatives, 69th Cong., 1st sess., 1926.

74. Letter, C. H. Asbury to Malcolm McDowell, June 18, 1918, RG 75, E1395; Bureau of Indian Commissioners, Bulletin 138, Releasing Indians from Government Supervision.

75. Hearings on H.R. 7826, Committee on Indian Affairs, House of Representatives, 69th Cong., 1st sess., 1926.

76. Ibid.

77. The C.W.A. Social and Economic Survey of Selected Indian Reservations, Oct. 1934, Entry 792, RG 75, NA; Albers, "Autonomy and Dependency in the Lives of Dakota Women," 109–34.

78. Clara Sue Kidwell, "The Power of Women in Three American Indian Societies," *Journal of Ethnic Studies* 6 (Fall 1978): 113–21; Joan M. Jensen, "Native American Women and Agriculture: A Seneca Case Study," *Sex Roles* 3 (Oct. 1977): 423–41; Albers, "Autonomy and Dependency in the Lives of Dakota Women," 109–34; Patricia Albers and Beatrice Medicine, eds., *The Hidden Half: Studies of Plains Indian Women* (Washington, D.C.: Univ. Press of America, 1983).

79. Teresa L. Amott and Julia A. Matthaei, *Race, Gender, and Work: A Multicultural Economic History of Women in the United States* (Boston: South End Press, 1991), 31–61; Mary C. Wright, "Economic Development and Native Amer-

ican Women in the Early Nineteenth Century," *American Quarterly* 33 (Winter 1981): 525–36. Some note women's selective appropriations of white technologies. Young, "Women, Civilization, and the Indian Question," 98–110; Jensen, "Native American Women and Agriculture," 423–41.

80. Chato and Conte, "The Legal Rights of American Indian Women," 229–46; Janiewski, "Learning to 'Live like White Folks,'" 13; Albers, "Autonomy and Dependency in the Lives of Dakota Women," 109–34; Perdue, "Cherokee Women and the Trail of Tears," 14–30.

81. *Madonna Swan, a Lakota Woman's Story,* as told through Mark St. Pierre (Norman: Univ. of Oklahoma Press, 1994), 181; Superintendent's Report, Cantonment Agency, Oklahoma, 1907, ANSR, roll 1; Rayna Rapp, "Family and Class in Contemporary America: Notes Toward an Understanding of Ideology," in Barrie Thorne with Marilyn Yalom, eds., *Rethinking the Family: Some Feminists Questions,* rev. ed. (Boston: Northeastern Univ. Press, 1992), 49–70.

82. Malcolm McDowell, "Fort Totten Indian School, Devils Lake Reservation, North Dakota," Sept. 14, 1921, SR, BIA, vol. 4; F. H. Abbott, "Report on the Fort Peck Indian Reservation, Montana," Nov. 1914, SR, BIA, vol. I.; Earl Y. Henderson, "Report on the Havasupai Indian Agency, Arizona," Jan. 20, 1928, SR, BIA, vol. 6.

83. Many whites had viewed Native American women as drudges whose work responsibilities resulted from men's default. Amott and Matthaei, *Race, Gender, and Work,* 34. Bolt concludes that this became pronounced only after industrialization.

84. Helen Bannan, "'True Womanhood' on the Reservation: Field Matrons in the United States Indian Service," Working Paper No. 18, Southwest Institute for Research on Women, 1984; Sandra K. Schackel, "'The Tales Those Nurses Told!': Public Health Nurses Among the Pueblo and Navajo Indians," *New Mexico Historical Review* 65 (April 1990): 225–49.

85. Report of Field Matron at Bishop in Report of the Commissioner of Indian Affairs, 1906; Report of Field Matron, Cherry Creek, South Dakota, Aug. 10, 1896, in Report of the Commissioner of Indian Affairs, 1896; Report of Field Matron, Fort Berthold Agency, Aug. 15, 1906, in Report of the Commissioner of Indian Affairs, 1906; Report of Field Matron, Shoshoni Reservation, Aug. 14, 1902, in Report of the Commissioner of Indian Affairs, 1902.

86. Report of Field Matron, Shoshoni Reservation, Aug. 14, 1902, in Report of the Commissioner of Indian Affairs, 1902; Report of Field Matron at Yakima Agency, Aug. 30, 1892, in Report of the Commissioner of Indian Affairs, 1892; Report of Female Industrial Teacher, Cherry Creek, South Dakota, Aug. 10, 1906, in Report of the Commissioner of Indian Affairs, 1906.

87. Hugh L. Scott, "Report on the Blackfeet Indian Reservation, Montana," Aug. 16, 1919, SR, BIA, June 1, 1919, vol. 2; Malcolm McDowell, "Report on the Papago Indians, Arizona," April 8, 1919, SR, BIA, vol. 2; Earl Y. Henderson, "Report on the Havasupai Indian Agency, Arizona," Jan. 20, 1928, SR, BIA, vol. 6; Shaw, *A Pima Past,* 28–30, 47–52, 70–74, 228.

88. Report of Field Matron, Fort Berthold Reservation, Aug. 25, 1896, in Report of the Commissioner of Indian Affairs, 1896; Report of Field Matron at Bishop, in Report of the Commissioner of Indian Affairs, 1906; Report of Field Matron, Yakima Agency, Aug. 19, 1892, in Report of the Commissioner of Indian

Affairs, 1892; Report of Field Matron, Fort Berthold Reservation, Aug. 14, 1900, in Report of the Commissioner of Indian Affairs, 1900; Report of Field Matron, Zuni Pueblo, July 16, 1903, in Report of the Commissioner of Indian Affairs, 1903.

89. Report of the Commissioner of Indian Affairs, 1931. Sarah Deutsch noted a similar faith in technology among Anglos seeking to acculturate New Mexico Hispanics. Sarah Deutsch, *No Separate Refuge: Culture, Class, and Gender on an Anglo-Hispanic Frontier in the American Southwest, 1880–1940* (New York: Oxford Univ. Press, 1987), 77.

90. Catherine L. Albanese, *Nature Religion in American: From the Algonkian Indians to the New Age* (Chicago: Univ. of Chicago Press, 1990), 16–34.

91. Report of Field Matron, Zuni Pueblo, July 16, 1903, in Report of the Commissioner of Indian Affairs, 1903.

92. Lynn Gray, "Making the Spirit Whole: An Interview with Clara Sue Kidwell," *EastWest* 16 (Nov. 1986): 46–47; David E. Jones, *Sanapia: Comanche Medicine Woman* (New York: Holt, Rinehart and Winston, 1972). Report of Field Matron at Bishop, in Report of the Commissioner of Indian Affairs, 1906; Report of Field Matron at Navajo Agency in Report of the Commissioner of Indian Affairs, 1892; Report of Field Matrons on Fort Berthold Reservation, Aug. 15, 1906, in Report of the Commissioner of Indian Affairs, 1906.

93. Malcolm McDowell, "Report on the Zuni Indian Reservation, New Mexico," May 15, 1919, SR, BIA, vol. 2; Report of Field Matron, Moqui Reservation, Aug. 1896, in Report of the Commissioner of Indian Affairs, 1896; Report of Field Matron, Zuni Pueblo, July 16, 1903, in Report of the Commissioner of Indian Affairs, 1903; Report of Female Industrial Teacher, Cherry Creek, South Dakota, Aug. 10, 1906, in Report of the Commissioner of Indian Affairs, 1906.

94. Report of Field Matron, Fort Berthold Agency, North Dakota, Aug. 15, 1905, in Report of the Commissioner of Indian Affairs, 1905; Earl Y. Henderson, "Report on the Havasupai Indian Agency, Arizona," Jan. 20, 1928, SR, BIA, vol. 6; Report of Field Matron at Navajo Agency in Report of the Commissioner of Indian Affairs, 1892; Gladys A. Reichard, *Social Life of the Navajo Indians* (New York: Columbia Univ. Press, 1928), 52; Narrative Annual Report, Kiowa Indian Agency, July 1, 1929, Indian Surveys (hereafter cited as IS), Records of the BIA, RG 75; Industrial Survey, Cherokee, North Carolina, 1923, IS, BIA.

95. Barbara A. Babcock, "'A New Mexican Rebecca': Imaging Pueblo Women," *Journal of the Southwest* 32 (Winter 1990): 400–437.

96. Robert Fay Schrader, *The Indian Arts and Crafts Board: An Aspect of New Deal Indian Policy* (Albuquerque: Univ. of New Mexico Press, 1983), 18–20; Laura Thompson and Alice Joseph, *The Hopi Way* (New York: Russell & Russell, 1965), 22–24.

97. Report of Field Matron, Fort Berthold Agency, North Dakota, Aug. 15, 1905, in Report of the Commissioner of Indian Affairs, 1905; Earl Y. Henderson, "Report on the Havasupai Indian Agency, Arizona," Jan. 20, 1928, SR, BIA, vol. 6; Report of Field Matron at Navajo Agency, in Report of the Commissioner of Indian Affairs, 1892; Babcock, "'A New Mexican Rebecca,'" 400–437; Schrader, *Indian Arts and Crafts Board.*

98. Report of Field Matron at Navajo Agency, in Report of the Commissioner of Indian Affairs, 1892; *Indians at Work,* July-Sept. 1942.

99. Report of Field Matron at Bishop, in Report of the Commissioner of Indian Affairs, 1906; Report of Field Matron, Puyallup Agency, July 1, 1899, in Report of the Commissioner of Indian Affairs, 1899; Report of Field Matron at Bishop, in Report of the Commissioner of Indian Affairs, 1906.

100. Scott, *Karnee: A Paiute Narrative;* Qoyawayma, *No Turning Back,* 62–64.

101. Albers, "Autonomy and Dependency in the Lives of Dakota Women," 109–34; Annual Report of the Secretary of the Interior, Office of Indian Affairs, 1935, p. 127; Joan M. Jensen, "Canning Comes to New Mexico: Women and the Agricultural Extension Service 1914–1919," in Joan M. Jensen and Darlis A. Miller, eds., *New Mexico Women: Intercultural Perspectives* (Albuquerque: Univ. of New Mexico Press, 1986), 201–26; Biolsi, *Organizing the Lakota,* 109–25.

102. McDowell, "Report on the Zuni Indian Reservation, New Mexico," Earl Y. Henderson, "Report on the Havasupai Indian Agency, Arizona," Jan. 20, 1928, SR, BIA, vol. 6; Richard White, *Roots of Dependency;* Reports of Field Matrons, 1911–14, Leech Lake Agency, BIA, Entry 1091.

103. Annual Report of the Secretary of the Interior, Office of Indian Affairs, 1935, p. 127; Flora Warren Seymour, "Report on the Jicarilla Apache Indian Reservation, New Mexico," Oct. 19, 1923, SR, BIA, vol. 4; Annual Report of Extension Workers, Blackfeet Agency, Dec. 1, 1931–Nov. 30, 1932, BIA; Annual Report of Extension Workers, Cheyenne River Reservation, South Dakota, Dec. 1, 1932–Nov. 30, 1933, BIA. Similar disasters affected the drought-stricken Lakotas. Biolsi, *Organizing the Lakota,* 111–12.

104. Edward E. Ayer, "Report on California and Arizona Indians," Aug. 11, 1915, SR, BIA, vol. 1; Malcolm McDowell, "Landless Indians of California and Nevada," April 1917, SR, BIA, vol. 1; Nancy Oestreich Lurie, ed., *Mountain Wolf Woman, Sister of Crashing Thunder: The Autobiography of a Winnebago Indian* (Ann Arbor: Univ. of Michigan Press, 1961), 44, 104; "Report of Agent for Kiowa Agency," Aug. 30, 1907; ANSR, M1011, roll 1.

105. McDowell, "Landless Indians of California and Nevada," and "Indian Employment in Arizona," Nov. 6, 1923, SR, BIA, vol. 4.

106. Report of Field Matron at Yakima Agency, Aug. 30, 1892, in Report of the Commissioner of Indian Affairs, 1892; Albers, "Autonomy and Dependency in the Lives of Dakota Women," 109–34.

107. Albers, "Autonomy and Dependency in the Lives of Dakota Women," 109–34.

108. McDowell, "Landless Indians of California and Nevada"; Earl Y. Henderson, "Report on the Truxton Canyon Indian Agency, Arizona," Feb. 1, 1928, SR, BIA, vol. 6; Albers, "Autonomy and Dependency in the Lives of Dakota Women."

109. Sarah M. Nelson, "Widowhood and Autonomy in the Native-American Southwest," in Arlene Scadron, ed., *On Their Own: Widows and Widowhood in the American Southwest, 1848–1939* (Urbana: Univ. of Illinois Press, 1988), 22–41; Alice Schlegel, "Hopi Family Structure and the Experience of Widowhood," in ibid., 42–64; Warren K. Moorehead, "Choctaw Indians of McCurtain County, Oklahoma," [n.d., probably 1914], SR, BIA, vol. I; Industrial Surveys, Western Navajo, [1920s], BIA; A General Survey of the Jicarilla Apache Reservation, March 28, 1939, RG 75, Entry 788, NA.

110. Henderson, "Report on the Havasupai Indian Agency." By the 1950s, some women were inheriting land, although their claims were always subject to dispute. Three of the four widows who had inherited land had not remarried. Carma Lee Smithson, "The Havasupai Woman," Anthropological Papers, University of Utah (April 1959): 43, 140–43.

Chapter 4.   From the Indian New Deal to Red Power

1. Annual Report, Commissioner of Indian Affairs, 1947.

2. Catharine A. MacKinnon, *Feminism Unmodified: Discourses on Life and Law* (Cambridge: Harvard Univ. Press, 1987), 63–69; Genevieve Chato and Christine Conte, "The Legal Rights of American Indian Women," in Lillian Schlissel, Vicki L. Ruiz, and Janice Monk, eds., *Western Women: Their Land, Their Lives* (Albuquerque: Univ. of New Mexico Press, 1988), 227–46.

3. Donald L. Parman, *The Navajos and the New Deal* (New Haven: Yale Univ. Press, 1976); Laurence M. Hauptman, *The Iroquois and the New Deal* (Syracuse: Syracuse Univ. Press, 1981).

4. "The C.W.A. Social and Economic Survey of Selected Indian Reservations," Oct. 1934, RG 75, Entry 792, NA; Parman, *Navajos and the New Deal,* 33, 126; Hauptman, *Iroquois and the New Deal,* 73–74.

5. "The C.W.A. Social and Economic Survey of Selected Indian Reservations."

6. Alison Bernstein, "A Mixed Record: The Political Enfranchisement of American Indian Women During the Indian New Deal," *Journal of the West* 23 (July 1984): 13–20.

7. U.S., Department of the Interior, *Federal Indian Law* (Washington: GPO, 1958), 423–28.

8. Bernstein, "A Mixed Record," 13–20; Minutes of the All-Pueblo Council, March 15, 1934, RG 75, Entry 1011, NA; Annual Report of the Secretary of the Interior, 1935; Hauptman, *Iroquois and the New Deal,* 62–63.

9. Bernstein, "A Mixed Record," 13–20; Gretchen M. Bataille, *Native American Women: A Biographical Dictionary* (New York: Garland, 1993), 42–44, 78–80, 203–4.

10. Hauptman, *Iroquois and the New Deal,* 12–14, 34–55, 62–63; Parman, *Navajos and the New Deal,* 169.

11. Ramon Gutierrez, *When Jesus Came the Corn Mothers Went Away* (Stanford: Stanford Univ. Press, 1991), 79; Bernstein, "A Mixed Record," 16; John R. Wunder, *"Retained by the People": A History of American Indians and the Bill of Rights* (New York: Oxford Univ. Press, 1994), 153–56.

12. Hauptman, *Iroquois and the New Deal,* 73–74, 124–26; Bernstein, "A Mixed Record," 13–20. Bernstein's conclusion that these programs represented a break with white notions of appropriate gender roles is not supported by the evidence.

13. Clyde Kluckhohn and Dorothea Leighton, *The Navaho* (Garden City, N.Y.: Doubleday, 1962), 73–76; Laila Sayid Shukry, "The Role of Women in a Changing Navaho Society" (Ph.D. diss., Cornell University, 1954), 72–73, 140, 182; Chato and Conte, "The Legal Rights of American Indian Women," 227–246; Parman, *Navajos and the New Deal,* 62–67, 175, 256.

14. Elizabeth Ward, *No Dudes, Few Women: Life with a Navaho Range Rider* (Albuquerque: Univ. of New Mexico Press, 1951), 44, 88–94; Station KTGM, Navajo Service Broadcast, Feb. 21, 1939, Van Valkenburgh Collection, RG 831, Arizona Historical Society (hereafter cited as VVC); Parman, *Navajos and the New Deal*, 87–89.

15. Hauptman, *Iroquois and the New Deal*, 136–63.

16. Ibid.; Parman, *Navajos and the New Deal*, 23.

17. Annual Report of Extension Workers, Cherokee Indian Agency, Dec. 1, 1931–Nov. 30, 1932, and Dec. 1, 1932–Nov. 30, 1933, Entry 788, Box 2, RG 75; Parman, *Navajos and the New Deal*, 210. Other New Deal policies increased trader power. Parman, *Navajos and the New Deal*, 35–36; A General Survey of the Jicarilla Apache Reservation, March 28, 1939, RG 75, Entry 788.

18. Ruth Milkman, "Women's Work and the Economic Crisis: Some Lessons from the Great Depression," in Nancy F. Cott and Elizabeth H. Pleck, eds., *A Heritage of Her Own: Toward a New Social History of American Women* (New York: Simon & Shuster, 1979), 507–41; Joan M. Jensen, "'I've Worked, I'm Not Afraid of Work': Farm Women in New Mexico, 1920–1940," in Joan M. Jensen and Darlis A. Miller, eds., *New Mexico Women: Intercultural Perspectives* (Albuquerque: Univ. of New Mexico Press, 1986), 227–55; Annual Report of Extension Workers, Report of Pawnee Indian Agency, Pawnee, Oklahoma, Dec. 1, 1933–Nov. 30, 1934; Rayna Rapp, "Family and Class in Contemporary America: Notes Toward an Understanding of Ideology," in Barrie Thorne with Marilyn Yalom, eds., *Rethinking the Family: Some Feminist Questions*, rev. ed. (Boston: Northeastern Univ. Press, 1992), 49–70.

19. Annual Report, Secretary of the Interior, 1940; Annual Report, Commissioner of the Office of Indian Affairs, 1941.

20. Milkman, "Women's Work and the Economic Crisis," 507–41.

21. Karen Anderson, *Sex Roles, Family Relations, and the Status of Women During World War II* (Westport, Conn.: Greenwood Press, 1981); Alison R. Bernstein, *American Indians and World War II: Toward a New Era in Indian Affairs* (Norman: Univ. of Oklahoma Press, 1991), 64–88; Robert Anderson, "The Northern Cheyenne War Mothers," *Anthropological Quarterly* 29 (July 1956): 82–90.

22. Bernstein, "Walking in Two Worlds," 124–26; Jeanne Clark, "Indian Women Harness Old Talents to New War Jobs," *Indians at Work* (July–Sept. 1942); 25–28; Indians in the War, U.S., Department of Interior, Office of Indian Affairs, Nov. 1945; Gordon MacGregor, *Warriors Without Weapons: A Study of the Society and Personality Development of the Pine Ridge Sioux* (Chicago: Univ. of Chicago Press, 1946), 46; Annual Report, Secretary of the Interior, 1943; John Adair, "The Navajo and Pueblo Veteran: A Force for Culture Change," *American Indian* 4 (1947): 5–11; Annual Report, Office of Indian Affairs, 1945; *Indians at Work* (July–Sept. 1942), 50.

23. Annual Report, Secretary of the Interior, 1943; Annual Report, Office of Indian Affairs, 1945; Robert Ritzenhaler, "The Impact of War on an Indian Community," *American Anthropologist* 45 (April–June 1943): 325–326; *Indians at Work* (April 1942): 10–14.

24. Kluckhohn and Leighton, *The Navaho*, 132–34.

25. Shukry, "The Role of Women in a Changing Navaho Society," 219; Cara

Elizabeth Richards, "The Role of Iroquois Women: A Study of the Onondaga Reservation" (Ph.D. diss., Cornell University, 1957), 112; Untitled document, including Civil Complaint, Fannie Slim vs. Tom Slim, [1943?], Franciscans papers, RG 500, Arizona Historical Society, (hereafter cited as FP); Annual Report, Office of Indian Affairs, 1945.

26. "Industrial Parks in Indian Areas: A Guide for Businessmen," 1970, Records of Presidential Committees, Commissions, and Boards, RG 220, NCIO, box 17, NA; Indian Aid, Inc., Records of Presidential Committees, Commissions, and Boards, RG 220, NCIO, Box 29, NA.

27. Patricia C. Albers, "Autonomy and Dependency in the Lives of Dakota Women: A Study in Historical Change," *Review of Radical Political Economics* 17 (1985): 109–34.

28. Annual Report, Commissioner of Indian Affairs, 1949; American Indian Policy Review Commission, Final Report, "Report on Urban and Rural Non-Reservation Indians" (Washington: GPO, 1976), 79.

29. Annual Report, Commissioner of Indian Affairs, 1947.

30. Juvenile Delinquency Among the Indians, Report of the Committee on the Judiciary, U.S. Senate, 84th Cong., 2d sess.

31. Elaine M. Neils, *Reservation to City: Indian Migration and Federal Relocation* (Chicago: Univ. of Chicago Department of Geography, 1971), 43, 90–94; Joan Crofut Weibel, "Native Americans in Los Angeles: A Cross-Cultural Comparison of Assistance Patterns in an Urban Environment" (Ph.D. Diss., UCLA, 1977), 97, 147, 209–16; Joan Weibel, "The American Indian Family in Los Angeles: A Comparison of Premigration Experience, Postmigration Residence and Employment Mobility, and Coping Strategies," in Jerry N. McDonald and Tony Lazewski, eds., *Geographical Perspectives on Native Americans: Topics and Resources* (Washington, D.C.: Association of American Geographers, 1976), 121–45.

32. Neils, *Reservation to City,* 116–17; Cleveland American Indian Family Development Program, "Development Program for the Indian Wife, Mother, or Single Girl," n.d. [1971?], Record Group 220, Presidential Committees, Commissions, and Boards, NA; Jackson *News,* March 12, 1969, Record Group 381, Office of Employment Opportunity, NA; Choctaw Conference on Early Childhood Development, Dec. 7–8, 1971, Philadelphia, Mississippi, RG 220, PCCB, NA.

33. Weibel, "The American Indian Family in Los Angeles," 121–45; Lawrence Clinton, Bruce A. Chadwick, and Howard M. Bahr, "Vocational Training for Indian Migrants: Correlates of 'Success' in a Federal Program," *Human Organization* 32 (Spring 1973): 17–28.

34. Alan L. Sorkin, *The Urban American Indian* (Lexington, Mass.: Lexington Books, 1978), 28, 32, 34, 143.

35. Weibel, "The American Indian Family in Los Angeles," 121–45; Shirley Fiske, "Rules of Address: Navajo Women in Los Angeles," *Journal of Anthropological Research* 34 (Spring 1978): 72–91.

36. Joseph H. Stauss and Bruce A. Chadwick, "Urban Indian Adjustment," *American Indian Culture and Research Journal* 3 (1979): 23–38; Arthur Margon, "Indians and Immigrants: A Comparison of Groups New to the City," *Journal of Ethnic Studies* 4 (Winter 1977): 17–28.

37. Ruth Mulvey Harmer, "Uprooting the Indians," *Atlantic* 197 (1956):

54–57; Virginia Cloud to Chairman Raymond Nakai, Aug. 28, 1968, Records of the Office of Economic Opportunity, RG 381, NA; Joan Ablon, "American Indian Relocation: Problems of Dependency and Management in the City," *Phylon* 26 (1965): 362–71.

38. Carole E. Goldberg, *Public Law 280: State Jurisdiction Over Reservation Indians* (Los Angeles: UCLA American Indian Culture and Research Center, 1975).

39. U.S., Department of the Interior, *Federal Indian Law*, 286–87; Letter, Selene Gifford to William O. Roberts, Nov. 4, 1952, RG 75, Entry 57A185; John Leiper Freeman, Jr., "A Program for Indian Affairs, Summary of the Report of the Hoover Commission Task Force on Indian Affairs," *American Indian* 7 (Spring 1954): 48–62.

40. Juvenile Delinquency Among the Indians. These attacks against AFDC recipients, particularly when they were women of color, were common in this period. Winifred Bell, *Aid to Dependent Children* (New York: Columbia Univ. Press, 1965).

41. Juvenile Delinquency Among the Indians.

42. Ibid.; *Menominee News*, March 25, 1958, RG 75, Entry 68A-4937.

43. Juvenile Delinquency Among the Indians; Minutes of the Regular Meeting of the Menominee Advisory Council, July 13, 1954, RG 75, Entry 68A-4937. For the origins of the term "political voyeurs," see Teresa De Lauretis, *Alice Doesn't: Feminism, Semiotics, Cinema* (Bloomington: Indiana Univ. Press, 1984), 91.

44. U.S., Department of the Interior, *Federal Indian Law*, 423–33.

45. Memo, Murray L. Crosse, Area counsel to Harry A. Sellery, Jr., Chief Counsel, Aug. 8, 1953; Memo, Crosse to Sellery, Aug. 30, Oct. 3, Nov. 30, 1953, Jan. 22, Feb. 22, 1954, RG 75, Entry 57A125; Richards, "The Role of Iroquois Women," 71; North American Indian Women's Association, *Special Needs of Handicapped Indian Children and Indian Women's Problems* (Washington: BIA, 1978).

46. Shukry, "The Role of Women in a Changing Navajo Society," 116; Kluckhohn and Leighton, *The Navajos*, 53–61.

47. Shukry, "The Role of Women in a Changing Navajo Society," 121–23, 145–63; MacGregor, *Warriors Without Weapons*, 57.

48. Carma Lee Smithson, "The Havasupai Woman," in University of Utah, *Anthropological Papers* 38 (April 1959): 43, 140–43.

49. S. Lyman Tyler, "The Recent Urbanization of the American Indian," in Thomas G. Alexander, ed., *Essays on the American West, 1973–1974* (Provo: Brigham Young Univ. Press, 1975), 43–62; Necah Furman, "Technological Change and Industrialization Among the Southern Pueblos," *Ethnohistory* 22 (Winter 1975): 1–14.

50. Irene Stewart, *A Voice in Her Tribe: A Navajo Woman's Own Story*, Doris Ostrander Dawdy, ed. (Socorro, N.M.: Ballena Press, 1980); Stan Steiner, *The New Indians* (New York: Harper & Row, 1968), 215–30.

51. Steiner, *New Indians*, 215–30;

52. Ibid.; Alvin M. Josephy, Jr., *Red Power: The American Indians' Fight for Freedom* (New York: McGraw-Hill, 1971).

53. Nicholas C. Peroff, *Menominee Drums: Tribal Termination and Restoration, 1954–1974* (Norman: Univ. of Oklahoma Press, 1982), 163–232; Deborah Shames, ed., *Freedom with Reservation: The Menominee Struggle to Save Their*

Land and People (Madison: National Committee to Save the Menominee People and Forests, 1972), 67–110.

54. *New York Times,* Jan. 2, 20, 1975.

55. *New York Times,* Jan. 10, 29, 1975; George D. Spindler and Louise S. Spindler, "Identity, Militancy, and Cultural Congruence: The Menominee and Kainai," *Annals of the American Academy of Political and Social Science* 436 (March 1978): 73–85.

56. *New York Times,* Jan. 7, 20, 1975. The occupation ended in February 1975 when the Alexian Brothers agreed to give the novitiate to the Menominees; the agreement was later abrogated. *New York Times,* July 5, 1975, April 22, 1976; George Spindler and Louise Spindler, *Dreamers with Power: the Menominee* (Prospect Heights, Ill.: Waveland Press, 1984), vii–viii.

57. Mary Crow Dog and Richard Erdoes, *Lakota Woman* (New York: Grove Weidenfeld, 1990), 113, 131, 137.

58. Robert Burnette and John Koster, *The Road to Wounded Knee* (New York: Bantam Books, 1974), 231; Paula Gunn Allen, *The Sacred Hoop: Recovering the Feminine in American Indian Traditions* (Boston: Beacon Press, 1992), 200.

59. Crow Dog and Erdoes, *Lakota Woman; Akwesasne Notes,* Late Spring 1974, Early Autumn 1974, Early Winter 1974, Early Summer 1976.

60. Ibid.

61. *Jacobson v. Forest County Potawatomi Community,* 389 F. Supp. 994 (E.D. Wis. 1974); Dennis R. Holmes, "Political Rights Under the Indian Civil Rights Act," *South Dakota Law Review* 24 (1979): 419–46.

62. MacKinnon, *Feminism Unmodified,* 63–69; *New York Times,* Nov. 30, 1977.

63. Wunder, *"Retained by the People,"* 125–28, 132–56; Andra Pearldaughter, "Constitutional Law: Equal Protection: *Martinez v. Santa Clara Pueblo*—Sexual Equality Under the Indian Civil Rights Act," *American Indian Law Review* 6 (1978–79): 187–204; Holmes, "Political Rights Under the Indian Civil Rights Act," 419–46.

64. W. W. Hill, *An Ethnography of Santa Clara Pueblo New Mexico,* Charles H. Lange, ed. (Albuquerque: Univ. of New Mexico Press, 1982), 154–56; Elsie Clews Parsons, "The Social Organization of the Tewa of New Mexico," *Memoirs of the American Anthropological Association* 36 (1929): 31–32.

65. Of those Santa Clara women who married others, all married other Indians. The later claim by some Pueblos that the issue was the loss of land to whites who married Santa Clara women is not sustained by the ethnographic evidence. Catherine MacKinnon's analysis reflects this misconception. Parsons, "The Social Organization of the Tewa," 31–40; Hill, *An Ethnography of Santa Clara Pueblo New Mexico,* 19–21, 154–56; MacKinnon, *Feminism Unmodified,* 63–69.

66. *Santa Clara Pueblo v. Martinez,* 436 U.S. 49 (1978); MacKinnon, *Feminism Unmodified,* 63–69; Letters re amicus briefs in RG 267, Records of the U.S. Supreme Court, file 85477, NA; *Akwesasne Notes,* Early Autumn 1975.

67. *Martinez v. Santa Clara Pueblo,* 540 F. 2d 1039, 1048 (10th Cir. 1976). In Canada, the amended Indian Act of 1951 raised very similar issues. *Wassaja,* April–May 1973; Montreal *Star,* Feb. 3, 1970; Kathleen Jamieson, *Indian Women and the Law in Canada: Citizens Minus* (Ottawa, 1978), 79–92.

68. MacKinnon, *Feminism Unmodified,* 63–69.

69. Ibid., 66.

70. Brint Dillingham, "Indian Women and IHS Sterilization Practices," *American Indian Journal* 3 (Jan. 1977): 27–28; Dillingham, "Sterilization of Native Americans," *American Indian Journal* 3 (July 1977): 16–19; Linda Gordon, *Woman's Body, Woman's Right: Birth Control in America,* 2d ed. (New York: Penguin Books, 1990), 431–36; Rosalind P. Petchesky, *Abortion and Woman's Choice: The State, Sexuality, and Reproductive Freedom* (New York: Longman, 1984), 83–89, 159–60, 178–81; *Akwesasne Notes,* Early Summer 1974, Early Winter 1974, September 1977.

71. Dillingham, "Indian Women and IHS Sterilization Practices," 27–28; Dillingham, "Sterilization of Native Americans," 16–19.

72. *Akwesasne Notes,* Sept. 1977.

73. Petchesky, *Abortion and Woman's Choice,* 180; Gordon, *Woman's Body, Woman's Right,* 433–36; Brint Dillingham, "Sterilization: A Conference and a Report," *American Indian Journal* 4 (Jan. 1978): 13–16.

74. Dillingham, "Sterilization: A Conference and a Report," 13–16; Crow Dog and Erdoes, *Lakota Woman,* 16; *Akwesasne Notes,* Sept. 1977.

75. Dillingham, "Sterilization: A Conference and a Report," 13–16; Manual P. Guerrero, "Indian Child Welfare Act of 1978: A Response to the Threat to Indian Culture Caused by Foster and Adoptive Placements of Indian Children," *American Indian Law Review* 7 (1979): 51–77; Russel Lawrence Barsh, "The Indian Child Welfare Act of 1978: A Critical Analysis," *Hastings Law Journal* 31 (1980): 1287–1336; *Akwesasne Notes,* Early Summer 1974, Sept. 1977.

76. Guerrero, "Indian Child Welfare Act of 1978," 51–77; Barsh, "The Indian Child Welfare Act of 1978," 1287–1336.

77. Ibid.

78. Michael Dorris, *The Broken Cord* (New York: Harper & Row, 1989); Ernest L. Abel, *Fetal Alcohol Exposure and Effects: A Comprehensive Bibliography* (Westport, Conn.: Greenwood Press, 1985), ix–xv.

79. Dorris, *Broken Cord,* 164, 217–18, 238.

80. Ibid.

81. Ibid., 214.

82. Petchesky, *Abortion and Woman's Choice,* 241–85.

83. Dorris, *Broken Cord,* 238.

84. Ibid., 86–87; North American Indian Women's Association, *Special Needs of Handicapped Indian Children and Indian Women's Problems;* Marla N. Powers, *Oglala Women: Myth, Ritual, and Reality* (Chicago: Univ. of Chicago Press, 1986), 173–78.

85. Allen, *Sacred Hoop;* Crow Dog and Erdoes, *Lakota Woman,* 68–70.

86. Powers, *Oglala Women,* 126–27, 149–54; Allen, *Sacred Hoop,* 224; Gretchen M. Bataille and Kathleen Mullen Sands, *American Indian Women: Telling Their Lives* (Lincoln: Univ. of Nebraska Press, 1984), 129.

87. Allen, *Sacred Hoop,* 194–221.

88. Ibid.

89. Wynne Hanson, "The Urban Woman and Her Family," *Social Casework: The Journal of Contemporary Social Work* 61 (Oct. 1980): 476–83; Ruth Roessel,

Women in Navajo Society (Rough Rock, Ariz.: Navajo Resource Center, 1981),
51–63.
    90. Crow Dog and Erdoes, *Lakota Woman*, 65–66.
    91. Ibid.
    92. Ibid., 69, 105.
    93. Powers, *Oglala Women*, 194–99.

Chapter 5. Mexicanas: The Immigrant Experience

    1. Richard Griswold del Castillo, *La Familia: Chicano Families in the Urban
Southwest, 1848 to the Present* (Notre Dame: Univ. of Notre Dame Press, 1984);
Rosalinda Gonzalez, "Chicanas and Mexican Immigrant Families, 1920–1940:
Women's Subordination and Family Exploitation," in Lois Scharf and Joan M.
Jensen, eds., *Decades of Discontent: The Women's Movement, 1920–1940* (West-
port, Conn.: Greenwood Press, 1983), 59–84; Julia Kirk Blackwelder, "Women in
the Work Force: Atlanta, New Orleans, and San Antonio, 1930–1940," *Journal of
Urban History* 4 (May, 1978): 331–58; Julia Kirk Blackwelder, *Women of the Depression: Caste and Culture in San Antonio, 1929–1939* (College Station: Texas A
& M Univ. Press, 1984).
    2. William Chafe, *The Paradox of Change: The American Woman in the Twen-
tieth Century* (New York: Oxford Univ. Press, 1991); Mary Ryan, *Womanhood in
America from Colonial Times to the Present*, 3d ed. (New York: J. Watts, 1983),
167–252; Sheila Rothman, *Woman's Proper Place: A History of Changing Ideals
and Practices, 1870 to the Present* (New York: Basic Books, 1978).
    3. The expression "dynamic hybrid" was coined by Griswold del Castillo, *La
Familia*, xiii.
    4. George J. Sanchez, *Becoming Mexican American: Ethnicity, Culture, and
Identity in Chicano Los Angeles, 1900–1945* (New York: Oxford Univ. Press,
1993).
    5. Oscar Lewis, *Tepoztlan: Village in Mexico* (New York: Holt, Rinehart and
Winston, 1960), 54–59; Nadia Haggag Youssef, *Women and Work in Developing
Societies* (Berkeley: Univ. of California Institute of International Studies, 1974),
82–94; Kristina Lindborg and Carlos Julio Ovando, *Five Mexican-American
Women in Transition: A Case Study of Migrants in the Midwest* (San Francisco: R
& E Research Associates, 1977), 9–23; Ramon Guiterrez, *When Jesus Came, the
Corn Mothers Left* (Stanford: Stanford Univ. Press, 1991); Georgie Anne Geyer, *The
New Latins: Fateful Change in South and Central America* (Garden City, N.Y.:
Doubleday, 1970), 86–103. Although relatively accurate regarding its implications
for family relations, Geyer's discussion of machismo overstates its political and eco-
nomic effects considerably.
    6. Lindborg and Ovando, *Five Mexican-American Women in Transition*,
84–88; Anna-Britta Hellbom, *La Participacion cultural de las mujeres: indias y mestizas en el Mexico precortesiano y postrevolucionario* (Stockholm: Ethnographical
Museum, 1967). These values were institutionalized in the nineteenth-century Mexican legal system. Silvia Marina Arrom, *The Women of Mexico City, 1790–1857*
(Stanford: Stanford Univ. Press, 1985), 55, 64–65, 70–72, 85–87; Sylvia M. Arrom,

"Changes in Mexican Family Law in the Nineteenth Century,: The Civil Codes of 1870 and 1884," *Journal of Family History* 10 (Fall 1985): 307–8.

7. Lewis, *Tepoztlan*, 59–63; Griswold del Castillo, *La Familia*, 3, 26–29, 41; Evelyn Stevens, "Marianismo: The Other Face of Machismo in Latin America," in Ann Pescatello, ed., *Female and Male in Latin America: Essays* (Pittsburg: Univ. of Pittsburg Press, 1973): 89–101; Jane Jacquette, "Literacy Archetypes and Female Role Alternatives: The Woman and the Novel in Latin America," in Pescatello, ed., *Female and Male*, 3–27. Some scholars, including Jacquette and Stevens, believe that marianismo—the veneration of the virgin Mary—gave women substantial power, but in the Catholic culture of Mexico the idea that women might have the capacity for moral vigilance over themselves, much less over men, never caught hold. See Arrom, *Women of Mexico City*, 259–68.

8. Alfredo Mirande and Evangelina Enriquez, *La Chicana: The Mexican-American Woman* (Chicago: Univ. of Chicago Press, 1979), 24–33, 241.

9. The Virgin of Guadalupe has been used as a symbol of resistance during the Mexican War of Independence, the Mexican Revolution, and in the United Farm Workers strikes of the 1960s. Wolf, "The Virgin of Guadalupe: A Mexican National Symbol," *Journal of American Folklore* 71 (1958): 34–39; Arthur F. Corwin, "The Study and Interpretation of Mexican Labor Migration: An Introduction," in Arthur F. Corwin, ed., *Immigrants—and Immigrants: Perspectives on Mexican Labor Migration to the United States* (Westport, Conn.: Greenwood Press, 1978), 10.

10. Nan Elsasser, Kyle MacKenzie, and Yvonne Tixier y Vigil, eds., *Las Mujeres: Conversations from a Hispanic Community* (Old Westbury, N.Y.: Feminist Press, 1980), 23.

11. William B. Taylor, *Drinking, Homicide, and Rebellion in Colonial Mexican Villages* (Stanford: Stanford Univ. Press, 1979), 85; Arrom, *The Women of Mexico City*, 232–38.

12. John Tutino, "Family Economies in Agrarian Mexico, 1750–1910," *Journal of Family History* 10 (Fall, 1985): 258–71; Taylor, *Drinking, Homicide, and Rebellion*, 116, 124, 127, 138. Women also took an active part in the War of Independence. Arrom, *Women of Mexico City*, 32–38.

13. Taylor, *Drinking, Homicide, and Rebellion*, 107; Elsasser et al., eds., *Las Mujeres*, 13–14; Michaelson and Goldschmidt, "Female Roles and Male Dominance Among Peasants," *Southwestern Journal of Anthropology* 27 (Winter 1971): 330–52.

14. Lawrence Cardoso, *Mexican Emigration to the United States, 1897–1931: Socio-Economic Patterns* (Tucson: Univ. of Arizona Press, 1980); Gonzalez, "Chicanas and Mexican Immigrant Families," 59–84.

15. Eric Wolf, *Peasants* (Englewood Cliffs, N.J.: Prentice-Hall, 1966), 13–16, 45; Margaret Towner, "Monopoly Capitalism and Women's Work During the Porfiriato," in *Women in Latin America: An Anthology from Latin American Perspectives* (Riverside, Calif.: Latin American Perspectives, 1979), 47–62. George Sanchez concludes that these changes necessitated "flexibility and adaptability" by Mexican families and undermined "rigid gender roles." Sanchez, *Becoming Mexican American*, 132.

16. Oscar Lewis, *Tepoztlan: Village in Mexico* (New York: Holt, Rinehart and

Winston, 1960), 22; Robert Redfield, *Tepoztlan: A Mexican Village* (Chicago: Univ. of Chicago Press, 1930), 49. Lewis does not indicate how the women managed to accomplish their revolt.

17. Tutino, "Family Economies in Agrarian Mexico, 1750–1910," 258–71; Towner, "Monopoly Capitalism and Women's Work," 56; Arrom, *Women of Mexico City*, 154–205; Cardoso, *Mexican Emigration*, 14.

18. Louise Tilly and Joan Scott, *Women, Work, and Family* (New York: Holt, Rinehart and Winston, 1978); Alice Kessler-Harris, *Out to Work* (New York: Oxford Univ. Press, 1982); Arrom, *Women of Mexico City*, 191; Towner, "Monopoly Capitalism and Women's Work During the Porfiriato," 47–62; Anna Macias, *Against All Odds: The Feminist Movement in Mexico to 1940* (Westport, Conn.: Greenwood Press, 1982), 8–13, 44. The age group 15 to 30 was chosen because 95 percent of the documented prostitutes were in that age bracket. Arrom, *Women of Mexico City*, 201. George Sanchez stresses the variability in Mexican family and gender arrangements and the effects of industrial capitalism in transforming the gender relations of Mexican village society. Sanchez, *Becoming Mexican American*, 131–132.

19. Macias, *Against All Odds*, 40–44; Cardoso, *Mexican Emigration*, 39–41, 71–75; Elizabeth Salas, *Soldaderas in the Mexican Military: Myth and History* (Austin: Univ. of Texas Press, 1990), 36–41, 72. Labor recruiters also encouraged Mexican migration to the U.S. Camille Guerin-Gonzales, *Mexican Workers and American Dreams: Immigration, Repatriation, and California Farm Labor, 1900–1939* (New Brunswick: Rutgers Univ. Press, 1994), 25–47.

20. Mario Barrera, *Race and Class in the Southwest: A Theory of Racial Inequality* (South Bend: Univ. of Notre Dame Press, 1979); Mark Reisler, *By the Sweat of Their Brow: Mexican Immigrant Labor in the United States, 1900–1940* (Westport, Conn.: Greenwood Press, 1976); Gonzalez, "Chicanas and Mexican Immigrant Families," 59–84; Albert Camarillo, *Chicanos in a Changing Society: From Mexican Pueblos to American Barrios in Santa Barbara and Southern California, 1848–1930* (Cambridge: Harvard Univ. Press, 1979); Sigurd Arthur Johansen, *Rural Social Organization in a Spanish-American Culture Area* (Albuquerque: Univ. of New Mexico Press, 1948), 26; Carey McWilliams, *Factories in the Fields: The Story of Migratory Farm Labor in California* (Boston: Little, Brown, 1939); Carey McWilliams, *Ill Fares the Land: Migrants and Migratory Labor in the United States* (Boston: Little, Brown, 1944), 16–29, 37.

21. Barrera, *Race and Class in the Southwest*, 58–104; Gonzalez, "Chicanas and Mexican Immigrant Families," 59–84. For a discussion of third world migrant women in the modern global economy, see Annie Phizacklea, "Introduction," in *One Way Ticket: Migration and Female Labour*, Annie Phizacklea, ed. (London: Routledge & Kegan Paul, 1983), 1–11, and Mirjana Morokvasic, "Women in Migration: Beyond the Reductionist Outlook," in ibid., 13–31.

22. U.S., Bureau of the Census, *Seventeenth Census of the U.S.: 1950*, Special Report P-E, No. 3A, *Nativity and Parentage* (Washington, D.C.: GPO, 1953); Pima County, Arizona, Census, 1910; Vicki L. Ruiz, *Cannery Women, Cannery Lives: Mexican Women, Unionization, and the California Food Processing Industry, 1930–1950* (Albuquerque: Univ. of New Mexico Press, 1987), 5; Sanchez, *Becoming Mexican American*, 136–37.

23. Manuel Gamio, *The Life Story of the Mexican Immigrant* (New York: Dover Publications, 1971), vii, 64, 159–62, 237–42, 247; Sanchez, *Becoming Mexican American,* 138.

24. Ruth A. Allen, "Mexican Peon Women in Texas," *Sociology and Social Research* 16 (Nov.–Dec. 1931): 131–42; Reports of the Immigration Commission, "Immigrants in Industries," 61st Cong., 2d session., 1909–10, Senate Documents, vol. 85, part 3 (Washington, D.C.: GPO, 1911), 19, 39, 127, 568.

25. Allen, "Mexican Peon Women," 131–42.

26. Vicki Ruiz notes, "In many instances, women's wage labor provided the safety net or extra edge in their families' day-to-day confrontation with poverty." Ruiz, *Cannery Women, Cannery Lives,* 9.

27. Sanchez, *Becoming Mexican American,* 129–50.

28. Ruiz, *Cannery Women, Cannery Lives,* 11–12, 16–17.

29. Ibid., 3–20. In addition, racial segregation further isolated Mexicanas. Sanchez, *Becoming Mexican American,* 144.

30. Cardoso, *Mexican Emigration,* 64; Gonzalez, "Chicanas and Mexican Immigrant Families," 59–84; U.S., Bureau of the Census, *Fifteenth Census of the U.S.,* 1930, Population, vol. III, pt. 1, pp. 12, 20.

31. Richard G. Thurston, "Urbanization and Sociocultural Change in a Mexican-American Enclave" (Ph.D. Diss., UCLA, 1957), 100.

32. Louise Ano Nuevo Kerr, "Chicanas in the Great Depression," in Adelaida Del Castillo, ed., *Between Borders: Essays on Mexicana/Chicana History* (Encino, Calif.: Floricanto Press, 1990), 257–68.

33. Reisler, *By the Sweat of Their Brow,* 2–3; Gonzalez, "Chicanas and Mexican Immigrant Families," 59–84; Barrera, *Race and Class in the Southwest,* 58–103; Camarillo, *Chicanos in a Changing Society,* 221. As George Sanchez has documented, Americanization programs directed at women had the goal of increasing their employment in these fields. Sanchez, *Becoming Mexican American,* 104.

34. Lloyd Fellows, *Economic Aspects of Mexican Rural Population in California with Special Emphasis on the Need for Mexican Labor in Agriculture* (1929; rpt., San Francisco: R and E Research Associates, 1971); Gonzalez, "Chicanas and Mexican Immigrant Families," 59–84; Adaljiza Sosa Riddell, "Chicanas and El Movimiento," *Aztlan* 5 (Spring and Fall 1974): 159; Allen, "Mexican Peon Women," 137.

35. Paul S. Taylor, *Mexican Labor in the United States: Valley of the South Platte, Colorado* (Berkeley: Univ. of California Press, 1929), 140–45; Paul S. Taylor, *Mexican Labor in the United States: Dimmit County, Winter Garden District, South Texas* (Berkeley: Univ. of California Press, 1931), 324; Letter, Patrick Abaseal to Frances Perkins, n.d. [1930s], Governor's Papers, Arizona State Archives, box 6.

36. Allen, "Mexican Peon Women," 135, 137.

37. Gonzalez, "Chicanas and Mexican Immigrant Families," 59–84; Taylor, *Mexican Labor: Valley of the South Platte, Colorado,* 97, 104–5, 130, 134, 154; Taylor, *Mexican Labor: Dimmit County,* 297; Blackwelder, *Women of the Depression,* 9, 83–85; Ruiz, *Cannery Women, Cannery Lives,* 21–25; Final Disposition Report, Case No. 10-BR-186, Records of the Fair Employment Practice Committee, Record Group 228, box 795, National Archives (hereafter cited as NA).

38. Blackwelder, *Women of the Depression,* 62, 77; Allen, "Mexican Peon Women," 131–42; Rosaura Sanchez, "The Chicana Labor Force," in Rosaura Sanchez and Rosa Martinez Cruz, eds., *Essays on La Mujer* (Los Angeles: UCLA Chicano Studies Center, 1977), 7; Taylor, *Mexican Labor: Dimmit County,* 356. A study of 90 Mexican working-class families in Los Angeles in 1935 revealed that 28 of the wives generated income for the household, but only 3 of these wives were employed as domestic servants (one of them counted as a domestic servant/nurse). Records of the Bureau of Labor Statistics, Record Group 257, boxes 27–30, NA. According to the 1950 U.S. Census, foreign-born Mexicanas were more likely to work in service than the native-born. See Table II. U.S., Bureau of the Census, *Seventeenth Census of the U.S.,* 1950, Special Report, P-E, No. 3A, Nativity and Parentage, pp. 160–61.

39. Mario Garcia, *Desert Immigrants: The Mexicans of El Paso, 1880–1920* (New Haven: Yale Univ. Press, 1981), 199–201; U.S., Children's Bureau, "Welfare of Families of Sugar-Beet Laborers," Publication No. 247 (Washington, D.C.: GPO, 1939), 25, 57, 60, 79–80; Taylor, *Mexican Labor in the United States: Chicago and the Calumet Region* (Berkeley: Univ. of California Press, 1932), 198–200. This does not necessarily mean that Russian German women were "liberated," as they were not able to translate their economic contributions into equally shared family or social power. Elmer Reisch, "Tradition and Transition: Volga German Women on the Great Plains," paper presented at the Women's West Conference, Park City, Utah, July 13, 1984.

40. Blackwelder, "Women in the Work Force," 350–51; Records of the Bureau of Labor Statistics, Record Group 257, boxes 27–30, NA. George Sanchez concluded that some wives also worked to enable families to buy a home, but that this work was regarded as temporary. Sanchez, *Becoming Mexican American,* 201–3.

41. Blackwelder, "Women in the Work Force," 339; Records of the Bureau of Labor Statistics, Record Group 257, boxes 27–30, NA; Sanchez, *Becoming Mexican American,* 201–3.

42. Ruiz, *Cannery Women, Cannery Lives;* Blackwelder, *Women of the Depression;* Adelaida R. del Castillo and Magdalena Mora, "Sex, Nationality, and Class: La Obrera Mexicana," in Magdalena Mora and Adelaida R. del Castillo, eds., *Mexican Women in the United States: Struggles Past and Present* (Los Angeles: UCLA Chicano Studies Research center, 1980), 1–4; Theresa Aragon de Valdez, "Organizing as a Political Tool for the Chicana," *Frontiers* 5 (1980): 7–12; George N. Green, "ILGWU in Texas," *Journal of Mexican-American History* 1 (1971): 144–69; Melissa Hield, "'Union-Minded': Women in the Texas ILGWU, 1933–1950," *Frontiers* 4 (Summer 1979): 59–70. As del Castillo and Mora point out, the idea that Mexican women were passive (or apolitical) requires that the scholar overlook the tradition of activism in Mexicana history. David M. Gordon, Richard Edwards, and Michael Reich, *Segmented Work, Divided Workers: The Historical Transformation of Labor in the United States* (Cambridge: Cambridge Univ. Press, 1982), offers an analytical and historical framework for interpreting labor market segmentation.

43. U.S., Women's Bureau, "Women in Texas Industries," (Washington, D.C.: GPO, 1930); Blackwelder, *Women of the Depression,* 90–108.

44. Sanchez, *Becoming Mexican American,* 209–26; Abraham Hoffman, *Un-*

wanted Mexican Americans in the Great Depression: Repatriation Pressures, 1929–1939 (Tucson: Univ. of Arizona Press, 1974); Cardoso, *Mexican Emigration,* 144–51; Guerin-Gonzales, *Mexican Workers and American Dreams,* 77–94.

45. Sanchez, *Becoming Mexican American,* 209–26; Hoffman, *Unwanted Mexican Americans in the Great Depression;* Cardoso, *Mexican Emigration,* 144–51; Ruth Milkman, "Women's Work and the Economic Crisis: Some Lessons from the Great Depression," in Nancy F. Cott and Elizabeth H. Pleck, eds., *A Heritage of Her Own: Toward a New Social History of American Women* (New York: Simon & Shuster, 1979) 507–41.

46. Ruiz, *Cannery Women, Cannery Lives,* 8–9; Blackwelder, *Women of the Depression,* 10, 14, 29.

47. Blackwelder, *Women of the Depression,* 7; Hoffman, *Unwanted Mexican Americans;* Reisler, *By the Sweat of Their Brow,* 227–57.

48. Harold Shapiro, "Pecan Shelling in San Antonio," *Social Science Quarterly* 32 (1951): 233–42; Selden C. Menefee and Orin C. Cassmore, *The Pecan Shellers of San Antonio* (1940; rpt., Westport, Conn.: Greenwood Press, 1978), 7–22.

49. Ibid., Roberto R. Calderon and Emilia Zamora, "Manuela Solis Sager and Emma B. Tenayuca: A Tribute," in Del Castillo, ed., *Between Borders,* 269–79; Blackwelder, *Women of the Depression,* 141–43.

50. Camarillo, *Chicanos in a Changing Society,* 66, 78, 91–99, 120, 137. Richard Griswold del Castillo similarly labels female-headed households "matriarchal." Griswold del Castillo, "A Preliminary Comparison of Chicano, Immigrant and Native Born Family Structures, 1850–1880," *Aztlan* 6 (Spring 1975): 87–94. These female-headed households, however, are not "matriarchies." As Suzanne Lebsock has observed, the label of matriarch is often applied when the amount of power exercised by a woman is regarded as inappropriate. Suzanne Lebsock, *The Free Women of Petersburg: Status and Culture in a Southern Town* (New York: W. W. Norton, 1984), 89–90.

51. Garcia, *Desert Immigrants,* 199; U.S., Bureau of the Census, *Fourteenth Census of the U.S., 1920,* Population, vol. II, p. 568.

52. William John Knox, *The Economic Status of the Mexican Immigrant in San Antonio, Texas* (1927; rpt., San Francisco: R and E Research Associates, 1971), Donna J. Guy, "The Economics of Widowhood in Arizona, 1880–1940," in Arlene Scadron, ed., *Widowhood and Aging in the American Southwest, 1847–1939* (Champaign-Urbana: Univ. of Illinois Press, 1988), 195–223; Garcia, *Desert Immigrants,* 199; Blackwelder, *Women of the Depression,* 72.

53. Records of the Bureau of Labor Statistics, Record Group 257, boxes 27–30, NA; Guy, "The Economics of Widowhood," 195–223; Martha Loustaunau, "Hispanic Widows and Their Support Systems in the Mesilla Valley of Southern New Mexico, 1910–1940," paper presented at the Conference of the Western Social Science Association, Albuquerque, April 29, 1983; U.S., Bureau of the Census, *Fifteenth Census of the U.S., 1930,* Population, Vol. IV, p. 82; Adaljiza Sosa Riddell, "Chicanas and El Movimiento," *Aztlan* 5 (Spring and Fall 1974): 159.

54. Mary Kidder Rak, "A Social Survey of Arizona," University of Arizona Bulletin No. 111 (Tucson, Ariz.: University Extension Division, 1921), 37–38; J. C. Brodie to B. B. Moeur, Sept. 4, 1934, Governor's Papers, box 6, Arizona State Archives, Phoenix; Valente Soto et al. to B. B. Moeur, Aug. 13, 1934, Governor's

Papers, box 6, Arizona State Archives; Winifred Bell, *Aid to Dependent Children* (New York: Columbia Univ. Press, 1965); Karl H. McBride to W. C. Ferguson, Nov. 15, 1938, Governor's Papers, box 10, Arizona State Archives; Menefee and Cassmore, *Pecan Shellers of San Antonio,* 37–43; Migratory Labor, July 1940, Records of the Department of Health, Education, and Welfare, Record Group 47, box 34, NA; Norman D. Humphrey, "Employment Patterns of Mexicans in Detroit," *Monthly Labor Review* 61 (Nov. 1945): 913–24.

55. Savilla Simons, "A Study of Child Labor in Industrialized Agriculture in Hidalgo County, Texas," *Social Service Review* 16 (Sept. 1942): 414–35; Valente Soto et al. to Honorable B. B. Moeur, Aug. 13, 1934; Sanchez, *Becoming Mexican American,* 223–24.

56. Letter, Patrick Abaseal to Frances Perkins, Governor's Papers, box 6, Arizona State Archives; Cletus E. Daniel, *Bitter Harvest: A History of California Farmworkers, 1870–1941* (Ithaca: Cornell Univ. Press, 1981), 271–72.

57. United States Department of Labor, Children's Bureau, Welfare of Families of Sugar-Beet Laborers, Publication 247, 1939; Simons, "A Study of Child Labor," 429–30.

58. Works Progress Administration Report, Women's, Professional, and Service Projects, Colorado, May 1, 1936, Records of the Works Progress Administration, Record Group 69, box 556, NA.

59. J. C. Brodie to Governor B. B. Moeur, Sept. 4, 1934; H. A. Clark to H. H. Hotchkiss, July 9, 1934, Governor's Papers, box 6, Arizona State Archives.

60. Blackwelder, *Women of the Depression,* 7–10, 20, 24. Blackwelder's contention that Mexicanas' familism deterred them from the creation of charitable organizations is probably true, but that does not mean that such groups would have measurably improved their situation, given her observation that they had proved totally inadequate even in the Anglo community.

61. Hoffman, *Unwanted Mexican Americans.*

62. Ibid.; U.S., Bureau of the Census, *Sixteenth Census of the U.S., 1940,* Population, Nativity and Parentage of the White Population, pp. 87–88; U.S., Bureau of the Census, *Seventeenth Census of the U.S., 1950,* Special Report, P-E, No. 3A, Nativity and Parentage, pp. 160–61; Vicki L. Ruiz, "'Star Struck': Acculturation, Adolescence, and the Mexican American Woman, 1920–1950," in Adela de la Torre and Beatriz M. Pesquera, eds., *Building with Our Hands: New Directions in Chicana Studies* (Berkeley: Univ. of California Press, 1993), 109–29.

63. Blackwelder, *Women of the Depression,* 33, 66; Allen, "Mexican Peon Women," 139; U.S., Bureau of the Census, *Seventeenth Census of the U.S., 1950,* Special Report, P-E, No. 3A, Nativity and Parentage, pp. 57, 161. By contrast, only 20 percent of the women over 14 in the general population were single, although some of that difference can be accounted for by differences in the age structures of the populations. Allen's conclusions are not necessarily corroborated by the census data which show that Mexican American men over 14 were much more likely to be single (48%) than the sons of immigrants from all groups (27%), although that might have occurred as a result of young women's inability to marry as well as sons' economic responsibilities in families.

64. Sherna Gluck, "Interlude of Change: Women and the World War II Work Experience," *International Journal of Oral History* 3 (1982): 92–113; Office of

War Information Report No. 24, Spanish-Americans in the Southwest and the War Effort, Oct. 18, 1942, Records of the Fair Employment Practice Committee, Record Group 228, box 371, NA: Locality Report, Denver, Colorado Defense Area, April 1942, Records of the Office of Community War Services, Record Group 215, Community Reports, box 13, NA; Memo, Will W. Alexander to War Manpower Commission, Oct. 1, 1942, Records of the Fair Employment Practice Committee, Record Group 228, box 367, NA.

65. Memo, Frank D. Reeves to Bruce Hunt, Nov. 1, 1944, Records of the Fair Employment Practice Committee, Record Group 228, box 790, NA; Memo, Carlos Castenada to Will Maslow, May 8, 1944, Records of the Fair Employment Practice Committee, Record Group 228, box 790, NA; Complaint of Josephine Alaman and Pala Flores against Juvenile Manufacturing Company, San Antonio; Final Disposition Report, April 28, 1945, Records of the Fair Employment Practice Committee, Record Group 228, box 810, NA; Karen Anderson, "Last Hired, First Fired: Black Women Workers During World War II," *Journal of American History* 69 (June 1982): 82–97; Ruth Tuck, *Not with the Fist: Mexican-Americans in a Southwest City* (New York: Harcourt, Brace, 1946), 140, 174–77.

66. Ernesto Galarza, *Merchants of Labor: The Mexican Bracero Story* (San Jose, Calif.: Rosicrucian Press, 1964), 46–57; Richard B. Craig, *The Bracero Program: Interest Groups and Foreign Policy* (Austin: Univ. of Texas Press, 1971); Richard Mines and Ricardo Anzaldua, *New Migrants vs. Old Migrants: Alternative Labor Market Structures in the California Citrus Industry,* Monographs in U.S.-Mexican Studies, No. 9 (San Diego: Program in United States-Mexican Studies, Univ. of California at San Diego, 1982), 24; Lloyd H. Fisher, *The Harvest Labor Market in California* (Cambridge: Harvard Univ. Press, 1953), 117–38.

67. Galarza, *Merchants of Labor,* 46–57; Craig, *Bracero Program,* 44.

68. U.S., Bureau of the Census, *Seventeenth Census of the U.S.,* 1950, Special Report, P-E, No. 3A, Nativity and Parentage, pp. 160–61.

69. Barrera, *Race and Class,* 139–40.

70. Lindborg and Ovando, *Five Mexican-American Women in Transition;* Ellen Cantarow, *Moving the Mountain: Women Working for Social Change* (Old Westbury, N.Y.: Feminist Press, 1980), 109; Riddell, "Chicanas and El Movimiento," 159; Ruiz, "'Star Struck,'" 109–29.

71. Emory Bogardus, *The Mexican in the United States* (1934; rpt., New York: Arno Press and the *New York Times,* 1970), 28.

72. Garcia, *Desert Immigrants,* 200–201; Beatrice Griffith, *American Me* (Boston: Houghton Mifflin, 1948), 76–80. Obviously, familial control of young girls also gave parents some control over a daughter's choice of a husband by allowing for relaxed vigilance when an acceptable suitor appeared.

73. William Jones Wallrich, "Some Variants of the 'Demon Dancer,'" *Western Folklore 9* (April 1950): 144–46.

74. "El Enganchado" from Taylor, *Mexican Labor: Chicago,* vi–vii; Manuel Gamio, *Mexican Immigration to the United States* (New York: Dover Publications, 1971); Maria Herrera-Sobek, "The Acculturation Process of the Chicana in the *Corrido,*" *De Colores 6* (1982): 7–16; Ruiz, "'Star Struck,'" 109–29.

75. Herrera-Sobek, "The Acculturation Process of the Chicana," 7–16.

76. Rene Cardenas, "Three Critical Factors That Inhibit Acculturation of Mex-

ican Americans" (Ph.D. diss., University of California, 1970), 95. Cardenas chose for his study only families whose heads believed in patriarchal traditions.

77. Cardenas, "Three Critical Factors That Inhibit Acculturation of Mexican Americans," 101–102.

78. Ibid., 99–102.

79. Beatrice Griffith, *American Me* (Boston: Houghton Mifflin, 1948), 76.

80. Taylor, *Mexican Labor: Chicago,* 201–3; Sanchez, *Becoming Mexican American,* 141; Ruiz, "'Star Struck,'" 109–29.

81. Taylor, *Mexican Labor: Chicago,* 192–214; Norman D. Humphrey, "Employment Patterns of Mexicans in Detroit," *Monthly Labor Review* 61 (Nov. 1945): 921.

82. Taylor, *Mexican Labor: Chicago,* 204–8; Winifred M. Murray, "A Sociocultural Study of 118 Mexican Families in a Low-Rent Public Housing Project in San Antonio, Texas," (1954; rpt., New York: Arno Press, 1976), 39; Richard G. Thurston, "Urbanization and Sociocultural Change in a Mexican-American Enclave," (1957; rpt., San Francisco: R and E Research Associates, 1974), 30–35. Thurston collected his data in 1951.

83. "The Mexicans of Jerome, Impressions of 1929," in WPA, box 8, Arizona State Archives; Murray, "A Sociocultural Study," 30, 38.

84. Ruth Schwartz Cowan, *More Work for Mother: The Ironies of Household Technology from the Open Hearth to the Microwave* (New York: Basic Books, 1983); Johansen, *Rural Social Organization,* 58, 72–73. The families in Johansen's sample were 89 percent Hispanic. United States Department of Labor, Children's Bureau, "Children Engaged in Farm Labor in the United States," Records of the Children's Bureau, Record Group 102, box 984, NA; Ruth Lucretia Martinez, *The Unusual Mexican: A Study in Acculturation* (1942; rpt., San Francisco: R and E Research Associates, 1973).

85. Savilla Simons, "A Study of Child Labor in Industrialized Agriculture in Hidalgo County, Texas," *Social Service Review* 16 (Sept. 1942): 433; Griffith, *American Me,* 132–37.

86. Taylor, *Mexican Labor,* II: 183, 195; Simons, "A Study of Child Labor," 414–35.

87. Johansen, *Rural Social Organization,* 116; Joan M. Jensen, "Women Teachers, Class, and Ethnicity: New Mexico, 1900–1950," *Southwest Economy and Society* 4 (Winter 1978–79): 3–13; Taylor, *Mexican Labor: Valley of the South Platte,* 220.

88. George J. Sanchez, "'Go After the Women': Americanization and the Mexican Immigrant Woman, 1915–1929," in Ellen Carol Dubois and Vicki L. Ruiz, eds., *Unequal Sisters: A Multi-Cultural Reader in U.S. Women's History* (New York: Routledge, 1990), 250–63.

89. Gonzalez, "Chicanas and Mexican Immigrant Families," 59–84; Taylor, *Mexican Labor: Imperial Valley, California* (Berkeley: Univ. of California Press, 1928), 92–93; Ruth Allen, "Mexican Peon Women in Texas," *Sociology and Social Research* 16 (Nov.–Dec. 1931): 131–42. Many Mexican women did not learn to drive because they did not have the language and literacy skills required to pass written tests. Thurston, "Urbanization and Sociocultural Change," 104.

90. Many of these rural-based first-generation Mexican women faced circum-

stances very similar to those of the Japanese immigrant women of this period. Yuji Ichioka, "*Amerika Nadeshiko:* Japanese Immigrant Women in the United States, 1900–1924," *Pacific Historical Review* 49 (May 1980): 339–57.

91. Rose Pesotta, *Bread Upon the Waters* (New York: Dodd, Mead, 1944), 34–63, 332–68; Shapiro, "Pecan Shelling in San Antonio," 233–42; Blackwelder, *Women of the Depression,* 33, 60–89. Blackwelder's contention that second-generation Mexicanas sought individualistic liberty misstates the situation. Instead, they wanted a somewhat greater degree of autonomy in their lives, especially as single women, but expected to assume a substantial degree of responsibility for the well-being of others.

92. Ovando and Lindborg, *Five Mexican-American Women in Transition;* Elsasser et al., eds., *Las Mujeres;* Taylor, *Mexican Labor: Chicago,* 205.

93. Barrera, *Race and Class in the Southwest,* 58–104.

94. Vicki Ruiz, "'And Miles to Go...': Mexican Women and Work, 1930–1950," *Western Women: Their Land, Their Lives* (Albuquerque: Univ. of New Mexico Press), 117–35; Richard Griswold del Castillo, "A Preliminary Comparison of Chicano, Immigrant and Native Born Family Structure, 1850–1880," *Aztlan* 6 (Spring 1975): 87–94; U.S., Bureau of the Census, *Seventeenth Census of the U.S.,* 1950, Special Report, P-E, No. 3A, Nativity and Parentage, pp. 160–61; Ruiz, "'Star Struck,'" 109–29. George Sanchez has argued that Mexican born wives had higher labor force rates than American-born Chicanas, but he relies on a sample of naturalization records that is probably not representative of Mexicanas as a whole. Sanchez, *Becoming Mexican American,* 142.

Chapter 6.   Border Women: Gender, Culture, and Power

1. William H. Chafe, *The Paradox of Change: American Women in the 20th Century* (New York: Oxford Univ. Press, 1991), 175–238; Joan Smith, "The Paradox of Women's Poverty: Wage-Earning Women and Economic Transformation," *Signs: Journal of Women in Culture and Society* 10 (Winter 1984): 291–310; Sara Evans, *Personal Politics: The Roots of Women's Liberation in the Civil Rights Movement and the New Left* (New York: Vintage Books, 1979).

2. Anna-Britta Hellbom, *La Participacion cultural de las mujeres: indias y mestizas en el Mexico precortesiano y postrevolucionario* (Stockholm: Ethnographical Museum, 1967), 192–7, 201, 300–301; Fernando Penalosa, "Mexican Family Roles," *Journal of Marriage and the Family* 30 (Nov. 1968): 680–89.

3. Susan Christopherson, "Parity or Poverty? The Spatial Dimension of Income Inequality," Southwest Institute for Research on Women, Working Paper, Number 21; Patricia Zavella, "The Impact of 'Sun Belt Industrialization' on Chicanas," *Frontiers* 8 (1984): 21–28; Judith Stacey, *Brave New Families: Stories of Domestic Upheaval in Late Twentieth Century America* (New York: Basic Books, 1990); Sheldon L. Maram, *Hispanic Workers in the Garment and Restaurant Industries of Los Angeles County,* Working Papers in the United States-Mexico Studies, 12, Program in United States-Mexico Studies, University of California at San Diego, 1980; James B. Greenberg, "Economic Sectors and Household Composition Among Mexican Families on the Border," Bureau of Applied Research in Anthropology, University of Arizona, n.p., 1985.

4. Sylvia Gonzales, "La Chicana: An Overview," in U.S., Department of Education, National Institute of Education, "Conference on the Educational and Occupational Needs of Hispanic Women," 1980, pp. 200–201.

5. A. M. Saragoza, "Mexican Children in the U.S.: The Central San Joacquin Valley," *De Colores* 6 (1982): 64–74. According to Saragoza, ". . . the relationship of the Chicano child to his family, peers and 'Anglo' society was dynamic, variable and increasingly tense by the late 1950s."

6. Maria Herrera-Sobek, "The Acculturation Process of the Chicana in the Corrido," *De Colores* 6 (1982): 7–16; Cherrie Moraga, "From a Long Line of Vendidas: Chicanas and Feminism," in Teresa de Lauretis, ed., *Feminist Studies/Critical Studies* (Bloomington: Indiana Univ. Press, 1986), 173–90; Gloria Anzaldua, *Borderlands/La Frontera, the New Mestiza* (San Francisco: Spinsters/Aunt Lute, 1987), 17. Micaela di Leonardo has noted that Italian American women must negotiate their ethnic identities, given the fact that "ethnicity itself is seen to belong to men: they arrogate to themselves (and identify with) those ethnic characteristics maintained by women to whom they are connected." Micaela di Leonardo, *The Varieties of Ethnic Experience: Kinship, Class, and Gender Among California Italian-Americans* (Ithaca: Cornell Univ. Press, 1984), 219–28.

7. Anzaldua, *Borderlands/La Frontera,* 79; Fran Leeper Buss, ed., *Forged Under the Sun/Forjada bajo el sol* (Ann Arbor: Univ. of Michigan Press, 1993), 10, 17–20.

8. Maxine Baca Zinn, "Political Familism: Toward Sex Role Equality in Chicano Families," *Aztlan* 6 (Spring 1975): 13–26; Maxine Baca Zinn, "Employment and Education of Mexican-American Women: The Interplay of Modernity and Ethnicity in Eight Families," *Harvard Educational Review* 50 (Feb. 1980): 47–62.

9. Alfredo Mirande and Evangelina Enriquez, *La Chicana: The Mexican-American Woman* (Chicago: Univ. of Chicago Press, 1979), 234–43; Moraga, "From a Long Line of Vendidas," 173–90.

10. Daniel O. Price, "Rural to Urban Migration of Mexican Americans, Negroes and Anglos," *International Migration Review* 5 (Fall 1971): 281–91; Audie Lee Blevins, Jr., "Rural to Urban Migration of Poor Anglos, Mexican Americans, and Negroes" (Ph.D. diss., University of Texas, 1970), 47, 162.

11. Anne Marjorie Brunton, "The Decision to Settle: A Study of Mexican-American Migrants" (Ph.D. diss., Washington State University, 1971), 8, 14, 84; Linda C. Majka and Theo J. Majka, *Farm Workers, Agribusiness, and the State* (Philadelphia: Temple Univ. Press, 1982), 165; Victor Paul Salandini, "The Short-Run Socio-economic Effects of the Termination of Public Law 78 on the California Farm Labor Market for 1965–1967" (Ph.D. Diss., Catholic University, 1969), 211–12.

12. Barbara June Macklin, "Structural Stability and Culture Change in a Mexican-American Community" (Ph.D. diss., University of Pennsylvania, 1963), 33; Buss, ed., *Forged Under the Sun,* 73.

13. Maram, *Hispanic Workers in the Garment and Restaurant Industries.*

14. Christopherson, "Parity or Poverty?"; Zavella, "The Impact of 'Sun Belt Industrialization' on Chicanas," 21–28.

15. Alan Bernstein, Bob DeGrasse, Rachel Grossman, Chris Paine, and Lenny Siegel, "Silicon Valley: Paradise or Paradox?," in Magdalena Mora and Adelaida

R. Del Castillo, eds., *Mexican Women in the United States: Struggles Past and Present* (Los Angeles: UCLA Chicano Studies Research Center, 1980), 105–12.

16. Smith, "The Paradox of Women's Poverty," 291–310; Maram, *Hispanic Workers in the Garment and Restaurant Industries;* Maria Patricia Fernandez-Kelly, *For We Are Sold, I and My People: Women and Industry in Mexico's Frontier* (Albany: State Univ. of New York Press, 1983), 20, 22; Robert C. Stone et al., "Ambos Nogales: Bi-cultural Urbanism in a Developing Region," *Arizona Review of Business and Public Administration* 12 (Jan. 1963): 1–29.

17. Greenberg, "Economic Sectors and Household Composition"; *New York Times,* March 19, 1984; Cameron Duncan, "The Runaway Shop and the Mexican Border Industrialization Program," *Southwest Economy and Society* 2 (Oct.–Nov. 1976): 4–25.

18. Greenberg, "Economic Sectors and Household Composition"; *New York Times,* March 19, 1984; Fernandez-Kelly, *For We Are Sold,* 28;

19. Greenberg, "Economic Sectors and Household Composition"; *New York Times,* March 19, 1984; Fernandez-Kelly, *For We Are Sold;* Duncan, "The Runaway Shop," 4–25.

20. Fernandez-Kelly, *For We Are Sold,* 47–69; Susan Tiano, "Women's Work and Unemployment in Northern Mexico," in Vicki L. Ruiz and Susan Tiano, eds., *Women on the U.S.-Mexico Border* (Boston: Allen & Unwin, 1987), 17–39; Susan Tiano, "Maquiladoras in Mexicali: Integration or Exploitation?," in *Women on the U.S.-Mexican Border,* 77–101.

21. Fernandez-Kelly, *For We Are Sold,* 60–69; Maram, *Hispanic Workers in the Garment and Restaurant Industries;* Arthur F. Corwin, "A Story of Ad Hoc Exemptions: American Immigration Policy Toward Mexico," in Arthur F. Corwin, ed., *Immigrants—and Immigrants: Perspectives on Mexican Labor Migration to the United States* (Westport, Conn.: Greenwood Press, 1978), 138–40.

22. Corwin, "A Story of Ad Hoc Exemptions," 138–40; Lamar B. Jones, *Mexican-American Labor Problems in Texas* (1965; rpt., San Francisco: R and E Research Associates, 1971), 18–54, 84–91; Brian Scott Rungeling, "Impact of the Mexican Alien Commuter on the Apparel Industry of El Paso, Texas" (Ph.D. diss., University of Kentucky, 1969), 2, 12, 62; Vicki Ruiz, "By the Day or the Week: Mexicana Domestic Workers in El Paso," in *Women on the U.S.-Mexico Border,* 61–76. INS officials do not attempt to arrest illegals working in domestic service as they are not regarded as a threat to "American" jobs.

23. Rungeling, "Impact of the Mexican Alien Commuter," 25, 56–58, 62, 70, 86, 93, 98. According to Rungeling, about 65 percent of the sewing machine operators in El Paso were receiving the minimum wage.

24. Corwin, "A Story of Ad Hoc Exemptions," 140; Leo Grebler, *Mexican Immigration to the United States: The Record and Its Implications* (Los Angeles: Univ. of California at Los Angeles, Mexican-American Study Project, Advance Report 2, 1966), 59–67.

25. Ina R. Dinerman, "Patterns of Adaptation Among Households of U.S.-Bound Migrants from Michoacan, Mexico," *International Migration Review* 12 (Winter 1978): 485–501.

26. Macklin, "Structural Stability and Culture change in a Mexican-American Community," 36–37. This is probably more true of long-distance migration than

of movement to the border area. Vicki Ruiz and Susan Tiano, *Women on the U.S.-Mexico Border: Responses to Change* (Boston: Allen & Unwin, 1987).

27. Rosalia Solorzano-Torres, "Female Mexican Immigrants in San Diego County," in *Women on the U.S.-Mexico Border*, 41–59.

28. Ruiz, *Cannery Women, Cannery Lives*; Patricia Zavella, "'Abnormal Intimacy': The Varying Work Networks of Chicana Cannery Workers," *Feminist Studies* 11 (Fall 1985): 541–57; Adelaida R. Del Castillo and Magdalena Mora, "Sex, Nationality, and Class: La Obrera Mexicana," in Mora and Del Castillo, eds., *Mexican Women in the United States*, 1–4; Mario F. Vazquez, "The Election Day Immigration Raid at Lilli Diamond Originals and the Response of the ILGWU," in ibid., 145–50.

29. Denise Segura, "Labor Market Stratification: The Chicana Experience," *Berkeley Journal of Sociology* 29 (Spring 1984): 57–91.

30. Much of the literature on the Chicano family shares the shortcomings of marital power literature and fails to take into account feminist theory, thus omitting important empirical and analytical possibilities.

31. Carolyn Weesner Matthiasson, "Acculturation of Mexican-Americans in a Midwestern City" (Ph.D. diss., Cornell University, 1968), 113–14. Similarly, a 1968 study using personal standardized interviewing found it difficult to secure information from Mexican American men and so focused exclusively on the women. Roland G. Tharp, Arnold Meadow, Susan G. Lennhoff, and Donna Satterfield, "Changes in Marriage Roles Accompanying the Acculturation of the Mexican-American Wife," *Journal of Marriage and the Family* 30 (Aug. 1968): 404–12. Nies also had great difficulty securing interviews with the husbands, whose actual values and goals regarding birth control could not be ascertained. Charles Michael Nies, "Social Psychological Variables Related to Family Planning Among Mexican-American Females" (Ph.D. diss., University of Texas, 1974), 76. Given this reticence by Mexicanos, scholars have problems generalizing about their reactions and contributions to change.

32. Richard G. Thurston, *Urbanization and Sociocultural Change in a Mexican-American Enclave* (1957; rpt., Saratoga, Calif.: R and E Research Associates, 1974), 39–41, 52, 98, 103, 106–7, 117, 125–9; Alfredo Mirande, "Machismo: Rucas, Chingasos y Chingaderas," *De Colores* 6 (1982): 17–31.

33. Ronald E. Cromwell, Ramon Corrales, and Peter M. Torisello, "Normative Patterns of Marital Decision Making Power and Influence in Mexican and the United States: A Partial Test of Resource and Ideology Theory," *Journal of Comparative Family Studies* 4 (Autumn 1973): 177–96; Hyman Rodman, "Marital Power and the Theory of Resources in Cultural Context," *Journal of Comparative Family Studies* 3 (Spring, 1972): 50–69; Thurston, "Urbanization and Sociocultural Change," 129; Norma Williams, *The Mexican American Family: Tradition and Change* (Dix Hills, N.Y.: General Hall, 1990), 95.

34. Mirande, "Machismo," 17–31; Baca Zinn, "Employment and Education of Mexican-American Women," 52; Ovando and Lindborg, *Five Mexican-American Women in Transition*, 54. This did not necessarily mean that traditional patterns promoted women's confidence in their domestic competence in the American setting. Tharp found that Spanish-speaking women rated themselves as poor-

er mothers and housekeepers than English-speaking Mexicanas. Tharp et al., "Changes in Marriage Roles," 404–12.

35. Rene Cardenas, "Three Critical Factors That Inhibit Acculturation of Mexican Americans" (Ph.D. diss., University of California at Berkeley, 1970), 101, 125; Thurston, "Urbanization and Sociocultural Change," 117.

36. Winifred M. Murray, "A Socio-Cultural Study of 118 Mexican Families Living in a Low-Rent Public Housing Project in San Antonio, Texas" (1954; rpt., New York: Arno Press, 1976), 50. Norman Humphrey concluded in 1945 that traditional restrictions on Mexican American girls were causing discord. Norman Diamond Humphrey, "The Stereotype and the Social Types of Mexican-American Youths," *Journal of Social Psychology* 22 (Aug. 1945): 75–78.

37. Thurston, "Urbanization and Sociocultural Change," 106–8, 125, 129. Companionate marriage was not necessarily egalitarian; see Ryan, *Womanhood in America*, 217–52, 259–78.

38. Thurston, "Urbanization and Sociocultural Change," 106–7. For a description of a rural woman's efforts to secure a family recreational pattern, see "Jessie Lopez de la Cruz: The Battle for Farmworkers' Rights," in Ellen Cantarow, ed., *Moving the Mountain: Women Working for Social Change* (Old Westbury, N.Y.: Feminist Press, 1980), 111, 114.

39. Murray, "A Socio-Cultural Study of 118 Mexican Families," 41. These themes obviously reflect many contained within the "feminine mystique" of the 1950s. Chafe, *Paradox of Change*, 175–93. The point is not to argue that this ideology spoke realistically or fairly to the needs of women, but rather that it offered some mechanisms for negotiation within the family. The idea of family togetherness provided a mechanism for retaining the assistance and resources of men for women and children. Lillian Rubin has speculated that bar culture is appealing to men because drinking reduces the inhibitions and enables men to express emotions otherwise proscribed by their culture. Lillian B. Rubin, *Intimate Strangers: Men and Women Together* (New York: Harper & Row, 1983), 140.

40. Murray, "A Socio-Cultural Study of 118 Mexican Families," 22, 30, 42, 48, 57. In Murray's sample, almost one-third of the families were headed by women who were divorced or separated. Thurston et al. also found first-generation women to be more conservative on these questions. The Spanish-speaking women in Tharp's study believed in the inevitability of the double standard, expected less sexual consideration from their husbands, and reported less sexual pleasure than did the English-speaking. Thurston, "Urbanization and Sociocultural Change," 106–10; Macklin, "Structural Stability and Culture Change," 162–65; Tharp et al., "Changes in Marriage Roles."

41. Tharp et al., "Changes in Marriage Roles," 404–12; Constantina Safilios-Rothschild, *Love, Sex, and Sex Roles* (Englewood Cliffs, N.J.: Prentice Hall, 1977), 68–69.

42. Lindborg and Ovando, *Five Mexican-American Women in Transition*, 25–32.

43. Ibid., 32–41.

44. Ibid.

45. Ibid.

46. Ibid.; Edwin M. Schur, *Labelling Women Deviant: Gender, Stigma, and Social Control* (New York: Random House, 1984), 34–47; Dorothy Smith, "A Sociology for Women," in Julia Sherman and Evelyn Beck, eds., *The Prism of Sex: Essays in the Sociology of Knowledge* (Madison: Univ. of Wisconsin Press, 1979), 135–87.

47. Lindborg and Ovando, *Five Mexican-American Women in Transition,* 68–83.

48. Ibid., 68.

49. Ibid., 66–68; Nan Elsasser, Kyle MacKenzie, and Yvonne Tixier y Vigil, eds., *Las Mujeres: Conversations from a Hispanic Community* (Old Westbury, N.Y.: Feminist Press, 1980), 69–70.

50. Murray, "A Socio-Cultural Study of 118 Mexican Families," 48; Thurston, "Urbanization and Sociocultural Change," 100–102.

51. Thurston, "Urbanization and Sociocultural Change," 57–59. Dolores Hayden and Susan Strasser discuss the emphasis placed on women's consumerism by custodians of American capitalism in the early decades of the century. Dolores Hayden, The *Grand Domestic Revolution: A History of Feminist Designs for American Homes, Neighborhoods, and Cities* (Cambridge: MIT Press 1981), 281–89; Susan Strasser, *Never Done: A History of American Housework* (New York: Pantheon Books, 1982), 242–81.

52. Macklin, "Structural Stability and Culture Change in a Mexican-American Community," 61, 120–25; Leodoro Hernandez, "The Socialization of a Chicano Family," *De Colores* 6 (1982): 80; Beatriz M. Pesquera, "'In the Beginning He Wouldn't Lift Even a Spoon': The Division of Household Labor," in Adela de la Torre and Beatriz M. Pesquera, eds., *Building with Our Hands: New Directions in Chicana Studies* (Berkeley: Univ. of California Press, 1993), 181–95; Ruth Schwartz Cowan, "The 'Industrial Revolution' in the Home: Household Technology and Social Change in the Twentieth Century," in Linda K. Kerber and Jane DeHart-Mathews, eds., *Women's America: Refocusing the Past* (New York: Oxford Univ. Press, 1987), 328–42.

53. Sarah Fenstermaker Berk, *The Gender Factory: The Apportionment of Work in American Households* (New York: Plenum Press, 1985). Berk has documented the persistence of traditional responsibilities within families and concludes that the reproduction of the gender division of labor within the household occurs because it secures the reproduction of the gender system. She does not specify the content or dynamics of gender except as a system wherein men are to be dominant and women submissive.

54. Thurston, "Urbanization and Sociocultural Change," 57–59; Laura Balbo, "The Servicing Work of Women and the Capitalist State," *Political Power and Social Theory* 3 (1982): 251–70.

55. Frank G. Mittlebach and Grace Marshall, *The Burden of Poverty* (Los Angeles: Univ. of California at Los Angeles, Mexican-American Study Project, Advance Report 5, 1966), 43–47; Lindborg and Ovando, *Five Mexican-American Women in Transition,* 55–63.

56. Lindborg and Ovando, *Five Mexican-American Women in Transition,* 45, 54.

57. Macklin, "Structural Stability and Culture Change in a Mexican-Ameri-

can Community," 34–35. For a more positive account of camp housing see Lindborg and Ovando, *Five Mexican-American Women in Transition*, 63–68.

58. Ruth Lucretia Martinez, *The Unusual Mexican: A Study in Acculturation* (1942; rpt., San Francisco: R and E Research Associates, 1973), 48–49; Ruth D. Tuck, *Not with the Fist: Mexican-Americans in a Southwest City* (New York: Harcourt, Brace, 1946), 103–9.

59. Thurston, "Urbanization and Sociocultural Change," 39, 40, 61, 62, 107, 125. Carol Stack, for example, has noted the importance of kin networks to African American women's ability to support themselves and their children. Carol Stack, *All Our Kin: Strategies for Survival in a Black Community* (New York: Harper & Row, 1974); Dair L. Gillespie, Richard S. Krannich, and Ann Leffler, "The Missing Cell: Amiability, Hostility, and Gender Differentiation," *Social Science Journal* 22 (April 1985): 17–30.

60. Norma Alarcon, "What Kind of Lover Have You Made Me, Mother?: Towards a Theory of Chicanas' Feminism and Cultural Identity Through Poetry," in Audrey T. McCluskey, ed., *Women of Color: Perspectives on Feminism and Identity* (Indiana University, Women's Studies Program, Occasional Papers Series, 1985), vol. 1, p. 91; Norma Alarcon, "Chicana Feminist Literature: A Re-Vision Through Malintzin/or Malintzin: Putting Flesh Back on the Object," in Cherrie Moraga and Gloria Anzaldua, eds., *This Bridge Called My Back: Writings by Radical Women of Color* (New York: Kitchen Table: Women of Color Press, 1981), 182–90; Cherrie Moraga, "From a Long Line of Vendidas: Chicanas and Feminism," in Teresa de Lauretis, ed., *Feminist Studies/Critical Studies* (Bloomington: Indiana Univ. Press, 1986), 173–90.

61. Patricia Zavella, "Support Networks of Young Chicana Workers," paper presented at the Western Social Science Association, Albuquerque, April 29, 1983; Zavella, "'Abnormal Intimacy,'" 541–57.

62. Zavella, "Support Networks of Young Chicana Workers"; Zavella, "'Abnormal Intimacy,'" 541–57; Norma Williams, *The Mexican American Family: Tradition and Change* (Dix Hills, N.Y.: General Hall, 1990), 93; Susan Emley Keefe, "Urbanization, Acculturation and Extended Family Ties: Mexican Americans in Cities," *American Ethnologist* (Spring 1979): 349–65; Micaela di Leonardo, "The Female World of Cards and Holidays: Women, Families, and the Work of Kinship," *Signs* 12 (Spring 1987): 440–53; Rosie the Riveter Revisited: Women and the World War II Work Experience, San Diego State University Library, interviews, vol. 37, Alicia Shelit; vol. 12, Maria Fierro, vol. 35, Lupe Purdy. Senour, "Psychology of the Chicana," 335. For the implications of such patterns for marital power, see Francesca M. Cancian, "The Feminization of Love," *Signs* 11 (Summer 1986): 692–709. Men benefit materially and emotionally from women's emotion work, but often do not acknowledge their dependence. As a result, women cannot claim reciprocal benefits from men.

63. Lea Ybarra, "Marital Decision-Making and the Role of *Machismo* in the Chicano Family," *De Colores* 6 (1982): 32–47; Lindborg and Ovando, *Five Mexican-American Women in Transition*, 55–63; Williams, *Mexican American Family*.

64. Cardenas, "Three Critical Factors That Inhibit Acculturation," 98–102, 125, 160, 184.

65. Ybarra, "Marital Decision-Making and the Role of *Machismo*," 32–47.

66. Ibid.; Elsasser et al., eds., *Las Mujeres,* 70. This problem is hardly unique to Mexicanas. Cancian, "The Feminization of Love," 692–709. Lillian Rubin concluded that ". . . there's a complex interaction between economic and emotional dependency and that, with any adult, a prolonged and profound economic dependency will soon *become* an emotional one as well." Lillian B. Rubin, *Intimate Strangers: Men and Women Together* (New York: Harper & Row, 1983), 143.

67. Constantina Safilios-Rothschild, "The Study of Family Power Structure: A Review 1960–1969," *Journal of Marriage and the Family* (Nov. 1970): 539–52; Marie LaLiberte Richmond, "Beyond Resource Theory: Another Look at Factors Enabling Women to Affect Family Interaction," *Journal of Marriage and the Family* (May 1976): 257–66; Kathleen Gerson, *Hard Choices: How Women Decide About Work, Career, and Motherhood* (Berkeley: Univ. of California Press, 1985), 29; Cancion, "Feminization of Love," 692–709.

68. Zavella, "The Impact of 'Sun Belt Industrialization' on Chicanas," 21–28; Maxine Baca Zinn, "Ethnic Identity Among Chicanos," *Frontiers* 5 (Summer 1980): 18–24; Fernando Penalosa and Edward C. McDonagh, "Social Mobility in a Mexican-American Community," *Social Forces* 44 (June 1966): 498–505.

69. Thurston, "Urbanization and Sociocultural Change," 40, 93, 100; Vicki L. Ruiz, "Obreras y madres: Labor Activism Among Mexican Women and Its Impact on the Family," *Renato Rosaldo Lecture Series Monograph* I (Summer 1985): 19–38.

70. Elsasser et al., eds., *Las Mujeres,* 115; Ruiz, "Obreras y madres," 29; Ybarra, "When Wives Work," 169–78; Zavella, "'Abnormal Intimacy,'" 541–57; Rosie the Riveter Revisited, vol. 8, Beatrice Morales Clifton, 30–32; vol. 35, Lupe Purdy, 38, 60–61.

71. Elsasser et al., eds., *Las Mujeres,* 53–55. This pattern of men's resistance and subsequent accommodation to women working for pay probably typified many twentieth-century families. Karen Anderson, *Wartime Women: Sex Roles, Family Relations, and the Status of Women During World War II* (Westport, Conn.: Greenwood Press, 1981); Sherna Gluck, *Rosie the Riveter Revisited: Women, the War, and Social Change* (Boston: Twayne Publishers, 1987); Rosie the Riveter Revisited, vol. 8, Beatrice Morales Clifton, 30–32.

72. Rosemary Cooney, "Changing Labor Force Participation of Mexican American Wives: A Comparison with Anglos and Blacks," *Social Science Quarterly* 56 (Sept. 1975): 252–61; Frank D. Bean, Russell L. Curtis, Jr., and John F. Marcum, "Familism and Marital Satisfaction Among Mexican Americans: The Effects of Family Size, Wife's Labor Force Participation, and Conjugal Power," *Journal of Marriage and the Family* 39 (Nov. 1977): 759–67.

73. Ann Marie Sorenson, "Ethnicity and Fertility: The Fertility Expectations and Family Size of Mexican-American and Anglo Adolescents and Adults, Husbands and Wives" (Ph.D. diss., University of Arizona, 1985), 10–21, 78–79, 94, 107–19, 160, 172, 211. Sorenson used Spanish-language use at home as a measure of ethnic identification for Mexicanos. She also found that Spanish language use at home increased fertility expectations of the young, especially for boys. Nies, "Social Psychological Variables Related to Family Planning Among Mexican-American Females," vii, viii, 76, 104, 115. Thurston, "Urbanization and Sociocultural Change," 35.

74. Antonia Hernandez, "Chicanas and the Issue of Involuntary Sterilization: Reforms Needed to Protect Informed Consent," *Chicano Law Review* 3 (1976): 3–37; Carlos G. Velez-I, "*Se me acabo la cancion:* An Ethnography of Non-Consenting Sterilizations Among Mexican Women in Los Angeles," in Magdalena Mora and Adelaida R. Del Castillo, eds., *Mexican Women in the United States: Struggles Past and Present* (Los Angeles: UCLA Chicano Studies Research Center, 1980), 71–91.

75. Rosalind Pollack Petchesky, *Abortion and Woman's Choice: The State, Sexuality, and Reproductive Freedom* (Boston: Northeastern Univ. Press, 1984), 83–89, 178–81.

76. Mirande, "Machismo," 17–31. As studies by Baca Zinn and Thurston demonstrate, even women who exercise some measure of family power and/or participate in public politics often feel that they must give lip service to the idea of male dominance. Thurston, "Urbanization and Sociocultural Change in a Mexican-American Enclave," 86; Baca Zinn, "Employment and Education of Mexican-American Women," 47–62; Williams, *Mexican American Family,* 87.

77. Anzaldua, *Borderlands, La Frontera,* 83.

78. Ruiz, "Obreras y madres," 19–38; Laurie Coyle, Gail Hershatter, and Emily Honig, "Women at Farah: An Unfinished Story," in Magdalena Mora and Adelaida R. Del Castillo, eds., *Mexican Women in the United States: Struggles Past and Present,* 117–43; Zavella, "'Abnormal Intimacy,'" 551.

79. Ruiz, "Obreras y madres," 19–38; Coyle, Hershatter, and Honig, "Women at Farah," 133.

80. Elsasser et al., eds., *Las Mujeres,* 61. Such outcomes are probably not unusual in Anglo families either.

81. "Jessie Lopez de la Cruz," 94–151; Baca Zinn, "Political Familism," 13–26; Ruiz, "Obreras y madres," 29. That women's participation may increase men's commitment to undertake the risks of union activism is indicated by the fact that a 1970 strike in the California citrus industry failed when single males refused to join families in the walkout. Richard Mines and Ricardo Anzaldua, *New Migrants vs. Old Migrants: Alternative Labor Market Structures in the California Citrus Industry* (San Diego: University of California-SD Program in United States-Mexican Studies, 1982), 43.

82. Buss, ed., *Forged Under the Sun,* 20–24, 181–241, quote on 223.

83. Barbara Kingsolver, *Holding the Line: Women in the Great Arizona Mine Strike of 1983* (Ithaca, N.Y.: ILR Press, 1989); Judy Aulette and Trudy Mills, "Something Old, Something New: Auxiliary Work in the 1983–1986 Copper Strike," *Feminist Studies* (Summer 1988): 251–68.

84. Kingsolver, *Holding the Line,* quote on 84; Aulette and Mills, "Something Old, Something New," 251–68.

85. Aulette and Mills, "Something Old, Something New," 251–68; Kingsolver, *Holding the Line,* 15.

86. Kingsolver, *Holding the Line,* 138, 15; Aulette and Mills, "Something Old, Something New," 251–68.

87. Kingsolver, *Holding the Line,* 134–162; Aulette and Mills, "Something Old, Something New," 251–68.

88. Kingsolver, *Holding the Line,* 175–90, quote on 182; Aulette and Mills, "Something Old, Something New," 251–68.

89. Mirta Vidal, *Chicanas Speak Out, Women: New Voice of La Raza* (New York: Pathfinder Press, 1971), 4–10. This does not differ from the attempts of Anglo men to silence feminist voices in other 1960s social movements. Evans, *Personal Politics*. Alma M. Garcia, "The Development of Chicana Feminist Discourse, 1970–1980," in Ellen Carol Dubois and Vicki L. Ruiz, eds., *Unequal Sisters: A Multi-cultural Reader in U.S. Women's History* (New York: Routledge, 1990), 418–31; Vicki Ruiz, "Mascaras y muros: Chicana Feminism and the Teaching of U.S. Women's History," in Susan Ware, ed., *New Viewpoints in Women's History* (Cambridge: Schlesinger Library, 1994), 53–63.

90. Vidal, *Chicanas Speak Out*, 8.

91. Patricia Zavella, "Reconciling Chicana Studies and Feminist Theory," talk given at the University of Arizona, April 9, 1987; Sonia Saldivar-Hull, "Feminism on the Border: From Gender Politics to Geopolitics," in Hector Calderon and Jose David Saldivar, eds., *Criticism in the Borderlands: Studies in Chicano Literature and Ideology* (Durham: Duke Univ. Press, 1991), 203–20.

92. Elsasser et al., eds., *Las Mujeres*, 92.

93. Valdez, "Mexican American Family Research," 48–63.

94. Matthiasson, "Acculturation of Mexican-Americans," 126–28; Cardenas, "Three Critical Factors That Inhibit Acculturation," 204; Sally J. Andrade, "Family Planning Practices of Mexican Americans," in Margarita Melville, ed., *Twice a Minority: Mexican American Women* (St. Louis: C. V. Mosby, 1980), 22, 25.

95. Balbo, "The Servicing Work of Women and the Capitalist State," 251–70; Colin Bell and Howard Newby, "Husbands and Wives: The Dynamics of the Deferential Dialectic," Diana Leonard Barker and Sheila Allen, eds., *Dependence and Exploitation in Work and Marriage* (London: Longman, 1976), 152–68.

96. Linda Whiteford, "Migrants No Longer: Changing Family Structure of Mexican Americans in South Texas," *De Colores* 6 (1982): 99–107.

97. Whiteford, "Migrants No Longer," 99–107.

98. Ramon M. Salcido, "The Undocumented Alien Family," *De Colores* (1982): 109–119.

99. Buss, ed., *Forged Under the Sun*, 7–8, 267.

100. Thurston, "Urbanization and Sociocultural Change," 24; Griffith, *American Me*, 36, 65. Barbara Macklin cites an example of a woman attempting to mediate between her daughter and her abusive husband in order to persuade him to leave or to stop harming her. Macklin, "Structural Stability and Culture Change," 185.

101. Buss, ed., *Forged Under the Sun*, 25–28, 93–95, 116–24.

102. Gloria Steinem has noted that the perception that women talk more than men when in fact men actually speak more and dominate conversations can be explained when one understands that women's speaking is measured against an expectation of silence. Gloria Steinem, *Outrageous Opinions* (New York: Holt, Rinehart, and Winston, 1983), 179. Lea Ybarra, for example, defined "traditionally male-dominated" families as ones with the "husband never sharing decision-making with his wife or helping her in household activities." Such families are probably extremely rare. Lea Ybarra, "When Wives Work: The Impact on the Chicano Family," *Journal of Marriage and the Family* (Feb. 1982): 169.

103. Pesquera, "'In the Beginning He Wouldn't Lift Even a Spoon,'" 181–95.

According to Beatriz Pesquera, "the only way [Chicana professionals] have altered the distribution of [household] labor has been through conflict and confrontation." She found similar dynamics in blue-collar marriages.

104. Williams, *Mexican American Family*, 95–96; Zavella, "Reconciling Chicana Studies and Feminist Theory."

Chapter 7.   In the Shadow of the Plantation

1. Charles L. Flynn, Jr., *White Land, Black Labor: Caste and Class in Late Nineteenth-Century Georgia* (Baton Rouge: Louisiana State Univ. Press, 1983), 6–14, 59–62, 78; Michael Wayne, *The Reshaping of Plantation Society: The Natchez District, 1860–1880* (Baton Rouge: Louisiana State Univ. Press, 1983), 45; Roger L. Ransom and Richard Sutch, *One Kind of Freedom: The Economic Consequences of Emancipation* (Cambridge: Cambridge Univ. Press, 1977), 44–45, 65–67.

2. Ransom and Sutch, *One Kind of Freedom*, 65–67, 94; Peter Kolchin, *First Freedom: The Response of Alabama's Blacks to Emancipation and Reconstruction* (Westport, Conn.: Greenwood Press, 1972), 62; Flynn, *White Land, Black Labor*, 6–20, 59–62; Eric Foner, *Nothing but Freedom: Emancipation and Its Legacy* (Baton Rouge: Louisiana State Univ. Press, 1983), 72.

3. Jay R. Mandle, *The Roots of Black Poverty: The Southern Plantation Economy After the Civil War* (Durham: Duke Univ. Press, 1978), 16–27; Ransom and Sutch, *One Kind of Freedom*, 94.

4. Ransom and Sutch, *One Kind of Freedom*, 80; Wayne, *Reshaping of Plantation Society*, 86; Mandle, *Roots of Black Poverty*, 16–27.

5. Mandle, *Roots of Black Poverty*, 16–27, 44–51; Gavin Wright, *The Political Economy of the Cotton South: Households, Markets, and Wealth in the Nineteenth Century* (New York: W. W. Norton, 1978), 162.

6. Ransom and Sutch, *One Kind of Freedom*, xi, 11, 94–95; Mandle, *Roots of Black Poverty*, 3, 52–83.

7. Carl Schurz, "Report on the States of South Carolina, Georgia, Alabama, Mississippi, and Louisiana," document no. 30, in Message of the President of the United States, 39th Cong., 1st sess., Senate Executive Document No. 2. Planters' committee recommendations to the Freedman's Bureau reveal the extent to which they sought to regulate private lives in the service of labor control.

8. See Bruce, *The Plantation Negro as a Freeman: Observations on His Character, Condition, and Prospects in Virginia* (1889; rpt., Northbrook, Ill.: Metro Books, 1972), 1–7.

9. Leon Litwack, *Been in the Storm So Long: The Aftermath of Slavery* (New York: Alfred A. Knopf, 1979), 238; Caroline Rogers complaint to Freedman's Bureau in Dorothy Sterling, ed., *The Trouble They Seen: Black People Tell the Story of Reconstruction* (Garden City, N.Y.: Doubleday, 1976), 50–51. Cited in Flynn, *White Land, Black Labor*, 62.

10. Gutman, *Black Family*, 404–12; Kolchin, *First Freedom*, 63–67.

11. Gutman, *Black Family*, 404–12; Jacqueline Jones, *Labor of Love, Labor of Sorrow: Black Women, Work, and the Family from Slavery to the Present* (New York: Basic Books, 1985), 81.

268 *Notes*

12. George P. Rawick, ed., *The American Slave: A Composite Autobiography* (Westport, Conn.: Greenwood Press, 1977), Supplement, ser. 1, vol. 6, Mississippi Narratives, pp. 260, 279; "Minnie Moody [pseudonym], Negro Farmer," Federal Writers' Project Papers (hereafter cited as FWP), folder 211, Southern Historical Collection, University of North Carolina Library, Chapel Hill (hereafter cited as SHC]; Hortense Powdermaker, *After Freedom: A Cultural Study in the Deep South* (New York: Viking Press, 1939), 209–10.

13. Schurz, "Report."

14. Cited in Kolchin, *First Freedom*, 62; Dolores Janiewski, *Sisterhood Denied: Race, Gender, and Class in a New South Community* (Philadelphia: Temple Univ. Press, 1985), 16, 27–54.

15. Henry L. Swint, ed., *Dear Ones at Home: Letters from Contraband Camps* (Nashville: Vanderbilt Univ. Press, 1966), 160.

16. Rawick, ed., *American Slave*, vol. 6, *Mississippi Narratives*, 253. Similarly, some men hunted, fished, and kept hogs in open-range areas in order to secure a subsistence outside the commercial economy. Foner, *Nothing but Freedom*, 64.

17. Rawick, ed., *American Slave*, vol. 6, *Mississippi Narratives*, 278.

18. Elizabeth Hyde Botume, *First Days Among the Contrabands* (1893; rpt., New York: Arno Press and the New York *Times*, 1968), 151; Flynn, *White Land, Black Labor*, 66; Jones, *Labor of Love, Labor of Sorrow*, 62, 73; Thomas J. Edwards, "The Tenant System and Some Changes Since Emancipation," *Annals of the American Academy of Political and Social Science* 49 (Sept. 1913): 41; Janiewski, *Sisterhood Denied*, 17–18, 38, 42–44.

19. Ransom and Sutch, *One Kind of Freedom*, 57, 60, 236; Janiewski, *Sisterhood Denied*, 38; Wayne, *Reshaping of Plantation Society*, 141; Sterling, ed., *We Are Your Sisters*, 321–31. Ransom and Sutch conclude that the postbellum wage gap between women and men was fair because it reflected sex differences in productivity in field work, but their argument is circular. Their statistical "proof" for a difference in productivity rests on the assumption of a such a difference.

20. Wayne, *Reshaping of Plantation Society*, 135; Jones, *Labor of Love, Labor of Sorrow*, 46–47, 58–60; Flynn, *White Land, Black Labor*, 60–62.

21. Botume, *First Days Among the Contrabands*, 151; Frances Sage Bradley and Margaretta A. Williamson, "Rural Children in Selected Counties of North Carolina," 1918, U.S. Children's Bureau Publication 33, Records of the Children's Bureau (hereafter cited as CB), Record Group 149 (hereafter cited as RG), National Archives (hereafter cited as NA), box L388; Helen M. Dart, "Maternity and Child Care in Selected Rural Areas in Mississippi," U.S. Children's Bureau Publication 88, 1921, RG 149, NA, box L385.

22. Ransom and Sutch, *One Kind of Freedom*, 57, 60; Carl Schurz, "Report."

23. Litwack, *Been in the Storm So Long*, 244; Elizabeth Rauh Bethel, *Promiseland: A Century of Life in a Negro Community* (Philadelphia: Temple Univ. Press, 1981), 47–48; Ransom and Sutch, *One Kind of Freedom*, 232–36. The conclusions of Ransom and Sutch regarding the reductions in black labor are based on white accounts and the census of 1870. They offer no discussion of the reliability of such data nor any analysis of the problems of comparing the labor system under slavery, in which most work was not compensated, with one in which a wage system had been partially introduced.

24. Sharon Harley, "Northern Black Female Workers: Jacksonian Era," in Sharon Harley and Rosalyn Terborg-Penn, eds., *The Afro-American Woman: Struggles and Images* (Port Washington, N.Y.: Kennikat Press, 1978), 5–16; interview with Miss Thomas (Baltimore Colored YWCA), June 29, 1916, CB, RG 102, NA, box 121; U.S. Department of Commerce and Labor, Bureau of the Census, "Statistics of Women at Work," 1907, p. 174; interview with Nancy Grooms, June 15, 1916, CB, RG 102, NA, box 121; Report on Conditions Affecting Baltimore Negroes, n.d. [probably 1916], CB, RG 102, NA, box 121.

25. Report on Conditions Affecting Baltimore Negroes; "My Time Is Mighty Nigh Out," FWP, Folder 111, SHC.

26. David M. Katzman, *Seven Days a Week: Women and Domestic Service in Industrializing America* (New York: Oxford Univ. Press, 1978), 184–222; Judith Rollins, *Between Women: Domestics and Their Employers* (Philadelphia: Temple Univ. Press, 1985), 155–232.

27. Margaret Holmes Turner Oral History, June 2, 1979, and Laura Kirkpatrick Oral History, June 21, 1979, Southern Oral History Project (hereafter cited as SOHP), SHC; "Bea, the Washerwoman," FWP, folder 145, SHC; "The Three Sisters," FWP, folder 145, SHC; Katzman, *Seven Days a Week,* 291–20.

28. Abzug, "The Black Family During Reconstruction," 36; Dorothy Sterling, ed., *We Are Your Sisters: Black Women in the Nineteenth Century* (New York: W. W. Norton, 1984), 322; Frances Hoggan, *American Negro Women During Their First Fifty Years of Freedom* (London: Personal Rights Association, 1913), 5; Charles S. Johnson, *Shadow of the Plantation* (Chicago: Univ. of Chicago Press, 1969), 54–56; Sharon Harley, "For the Good of Family and Race: Gender, Work, and Domestic Roles in the Black Community, 1880–1930," *Signs* 15 (Winter 1990): 336–49.

29. Jones, *Labor of Love, Labor of Sorrow,* 3, 13–14, 36, 38, 41, 46, 57, 59, 62, 78; Dart, "Maternity and Child Care," 35; Bradley and Williamson, "Rural Children in Selected Counties"; E. Franklin Frazier, *The Negro Family in the United States* (Chicago: Univ. of Chicago Press, 1939), 141; Bethel, *Promiseland,* 47, 162; U.S. Women's Bureau, "Family Status of Breadwinning Women in Four Selected Cities," Bulletin 23, US GPO, 1925, pp. 37–38.

30. William Taylor Thom, "The Negroes of Sandy Spring, Maryland: A Social Study," Department of Labor, *Bulletin* 6 (1901): 56–57; Swint, ed., *Dear Ones At Home,* 160; Rawick, ed., *American Slave,* vol. 6, *Mississippi Narratives,* 97, 260; Elizabeth Hafkin Pleck, *Black Migration and Poverty: Boston, 1865–1900* (New York: Academic Press, 1979), 162–96; Clyde Vernon Kiser, *Sea Island to City: A Study of St. Helena Islanders in Harlem and Other Urban Centers* (1932; rpt., New York: Atheneum, 1969), 119–20; "Bachelor Mothers," FWP, folder 183, SHC; Margaret Holmes Turner Oral History, June 2, 1979, SOHP, SHC.

31. These views obviously contradict the white Reconstruction stereotype of indolent and demoralized black women trying to avoid wage labor and live on the wages of men. U.S., Bureau of the Census, Twelfth Census of the United States: 1900, Special Reports, Occupations, p. ccxxvi; Sterling, ed., *We Are Your Sisters,* 323–26; interview with Mamie Jones, June 15, 1916, CB, RG 102, NA, box 121; Rennie Simson, "The Afro-American Female: The Historical Context of the Construction of Sexual Identity," in Ann Snitow, Christine Stansell, and Sharon Thomp-

son, eds., *The Powers of Desire: The Politics of Sexuality* (New York: Monthly Review Press, 1983), 229–35. Gerda Lerner concluded that there was a "sex loophole" in race discrimination that enabled black women to secure jobs more easily than black men. Gerda Lerner, *The Majority Finds Its Past: Placing Women in History* (New York: Oxford Univ. Press, 1979), 75–79.

32. Suzanne Lebsock, *The Free Women of Petersburg: Status and Culture in a Southern Town, 1784–1860* (New York: W. W. Norton, 1984), 87–111; Jones, *Labor of Love, Labor of Sorrow,* 38. Jones claims that slaves chose their gender division of labor, ignoring the role of African custom and of white work allocations and gender assumptions in shaping slave family relations. Claudia Goldin, "Female Labor Force Participation: The Origin of Black and White Differences, 1870 and 1880," *Journal of Economic History* 37 (March 1977): 101; Eugene Genovese, *Roll, Jordan, Roll: The World the Slave Made* (New York: Pantheon Books, 1974), 482–501. Genovese implicitly lauds black women for their willingness to maintain black men's self-esteem without noticing the lack of reciprocity in this arrangement.

33. Herbert G. Gutman, *The Black Family in Slavery and Freedom, 1750–1925* (New York: Vintage Books, 1977), 60–67, 81, 636; Lebsock, *Free Women of Petersburg,* 87–111. According to Lebsock, free black women often chose to establish informal unions rather than marriage in order to preserve their autonomy.

34. Gutman, *Black Family,* 412–431; Litwack, *Been the Storm So Long,* 229–42.

35. Gutman, *Black Family,* 72–73; Lebsock, *Free Women of Petersburg,* 110; Sterling, ed., *We Are Your Sisters,* 315–44.

36. Kolchin, *First Freedom,* 61, 75; Schurz, "Report"; Sterling, ed., *We Are Your Sisters,* 340.

37. Sterling, ed., *We Are Your Sisters,* 338–41; Powdermaker, *After Freedom,* 165.

38. John W. Blassingame, ed., *Slave Testimony: Two Centuries of Letters, Speeches, Interviews, and Autobiographies* (Baton Rouge: Louisiana State Univ. Press, 1977), 644.

39. John Langston Gwaltney, *Drylongso: A Self-Portrait of Black America* (New York: Random House, 1980), 148.

40. Sterling, ed., *We Are Your Sisters,* 318.

41. Jones, *Labor of Love, Labor of Sorrow,* 62; Sterling, ed., *Trouble They Seen,* 95; "I'd Like to Have a Coca Cola," FWP, folder 216, SHC. An age gap also characterized southern white rural marriages, but was even more pronounced among rural blacks. Peter Kolchin has concluded that the sex ratio among young adults enhanced men's power in marriage. It may also have encouraged the custom of women marrying significantly older men. Kolchin, *First Freedom,* 62–63; Frazier, *Negro Family,* 165.

42. Sterling, ed., *Trouble They Seen,* 218.

43. Sterling, eds., *We Are Your Sisters,* 309; Frazier, *Negro Family,* 134–35; Johnson, *Shadow of the Plantation,* 53.

44. Blassingame, ed., *Slave Testimony,* 644–49.

45. Gutman, *Black Family,* 408–9.

46. Jones, *Labor of Love, Labor of Sorrow,* 104–5; Zora Neale Hurston, *Their Eyes Were Watching God* (Urbana: Univ. of Illinois Press, 1979), 29.

47. Letters, James Scott to Mary Scott [pseudonyms], Dec. 3, 13, 23, 30, 1932, Record Group #3860, SHC.

48. "The Carpenter of Lickskillet," FWP, holder 145, SHC.

49. Minnie Lawrence Dunn Oral History, SOHP, SHC.

50. Gutman, *Black Family,* 433; Crandall A. Shifflett, "The Household Composition of Rural Black Families: Louisa County, Virginia, 1880," *Journal of Interdisciplinary History* 6 (Autumn 1975): 235–60. Pleck has shown that longitudinal data reveal more family instability than the data used in most studies. Pleck, *Black Migration and Poverty,* 164–66, 194.

51. Shifflett, "The Household Composition of Rural Black Families," 235–60; Janice L. Reiff, Michel R. Dahlin, and Daniel Scott Smith, "Rural Push and Urban Pull: Work and Family Experiences of Older Black Women in Southern Cities, 1880–1900," *Journal of Social History* 16 (Summer 1983): 39–48.

52. Kolchin, *First Freedom,* 62–63;

53. Gutman, *Black Family,* 489–500.

54. Johnson, *Shadow of the Plantation,* 57, 77–78; memo, W. R. Williamson to Wilbur Cohen, Aug. 24, 1938, Records of the Department of Health, Education, and Welfare (hereafter cited as HEW), RG 47, box 31, SSA, Office of the Commissioner, NA.

55. Frank F. Furstenberg, Jr., Theodore Hershberg, and John Modell, "The Origin of the Female-Headed Black Family: The Impact of the Black Experience," *Journal of Interdisciplinary History* 6 (Autumn 1975): 211–33. Whether the pattern found by Furstenberg et al. explains dynamics in the South remains to be seen. U.S., Bureau of the Census, Sixteenth Census of the United States: 1940, Population, vol. IV, pt. 1, pp. 17, 25. It is difficult to separate the widowed from the deserted because some with absent husbands reported themselves as widows. Pleck, *Black Migration and Poverty,* 161–96.

56. Frazier, *Negro Family,* 114; U.S., Bureau of the Census, Sixteenth Census of the United States: 1940, Population, vol. IV, pt. 1, p. 17. The overall marriage rates (33.2% for white women and 33.5% for black women) appear similar because of differences in the age structure of the populations. When age is taken into account, the proportion of black women who are or have been married is substantially higher than for white women, except between the ages of 30 and 50.

57. Johnson, *Shadow of the Plantation,* 49–50, 71–83.

58. Ibid., 75–80.

59. Ibid., 51–53, 83; Powdermaker, *After Freedom,* 157–74, 192–96.

60. Jacqueline Jones's recourse to the claim that poverty "explains" abuse obscures the fact that violence also occurs in economically secure households and betrays a reluctance to analyze the dynamics of abuse in black households. Jones, *Labor of Love, Labor of Sorrow,* 103–5; Lenore E. Walker, *The Battered Woman* (New York: Harper Colophon Books, 1979), 127–44; Lebsock, *Free Women of Petersburg,* 87–111.

61. Charles L. Perdue, Jr., Thomas E. Barden, and Robert K. Phillips, eds., *Weevils in the Wheat: Interviews with Virginia Ex-Slaves* (Charlottesville: Univ. of Virginia Press), 131.

62. Bethel, *Promiseland,* 52. Bethel's finding that landowning families were more often nuclear when they had an adequate amount of property to convey indicates the importance of land to the retention of the labor power of sons for the natal household.

63. Viola I. Paradise, "Child Labor and the Work of Mothers in Oyster and Shrimp Canning Communities on the Gulf Coast," Children's Bureau Publication no. 98, 1922, p. 46; Frazier, *Negro Family,* 140, 145–50; Johnson, *Shadow of the Plantation,* 61–63. In some cases, black women lost custody of their children to the fathers, who took them to help ensure their own livelihood. Everett Ingram recalled that after emancipation his father ". . . stole both de older chillun . . . and went off." Rawick, ed., *American Slave,* vol. 1., *Alabama Narratives,* 205.

64. Johnson, *Shadow of the Plantation,* 63.

65. Ibid., 78; Pleck, *Black Migration and Poverty,* 196; "Bachelor Mothers," FWP, Folder 183, SHC; "I'd Like to Have a Coca Cola."

66. Minnie Lawrence Dunn Oral History, June 21, 1979, SOHP, SHC.

67. Rayna Rapp, "Family and Class in Contemporary America: Notes Toward an Understanding of Ideology," in Barrie Thorne, ed., *Rethinking the Family: Some Feminist Questions,* rev. ed. (Boston: Northeastern Univ. Press, 1992), 49–70.

68. Gutman, *Black Family,* 25–27, 386–87; Litwack, *Been in the Storm So Long,* 176; Jacqueline Dowd Hall, "'The Mind That Burns in Each Body': Women, Rape, and Racial Violence," in Snitow, Stansell, and Thompson, eds., *Powers of Desire,* 328–49.

69. Simson, "The Afro-American Female," in Snitow, Stansell, and Thompson, eds., *Powers of Desire,* 229–35; Gerda Lerner, ed., *Black Women in White America: A Documentary History* (New York: Vintage Books, 1972), 149–215.

70. Lerner, ed., *Black Women in White America,* 163–71; Hortense J. Spillers, "Interstices: A Small Drama of Words," in Carole S. Vance, ed., *Pleasure and Danger: Exploring Female Sexuality* (Boston: Routledge & Kegan Paul, 1984), 73–100. Spillers has cogently noted that black women's sexuality can be understood only when their agency is acknowledged. Angela Davis, "Reflections on the Black Woman's Role in the Community of Slaves," *Black Scholar* 3 (Dec. 1971): 3–15. Davis (p. 12) has noted that "the slave master's sexual domination of the black woman contained an unveiled element of counter-insurgency."

71. Darlene Clark Hine, "Rape and the Inner Lives of Black Women in the Middle West," *Signs* 14 (Summer 1989): 912–20; Paula Giddings, "The Last Taboo," in Toni Morrison, ed., *Race-ing Justice, En-gendering Power* (New York: Pantheon Books, 1992); Kimberle Crenshaw, "Whose Story Is It, Anyway? Feminist and Antiracist Appropriations of Anita Hill," in ibid., 419.

72. Powdermaker, *After Freedom,* 144–45, 193–96.

73. Gwaltney, *Drylongso,* 143–47.

74. "The Story of a Washwoman, FWP, folder 243, SHC. The mother was relieved when she found that the father of her daughter's child was black.

75. David M. Katzman, *Seven Days a Week: Women and Domestic Service in Industrializing America* (New York: Oxford Univ. Press, 1978), 216–17; Thom, "The Negroes of Sandy Spring," 79; Gunnar Myrdal, *An American Dilemma: The Negro in a White World* (New York: McGraw-Hill, 1964), I: clxiii. Cooper quote

from Paula Giddings, *When and Where I Enter: The Impact of Black Women on Race and Sex in America* (Toronto: Bantam Books, 1984), 87.

76. Hurston, *Their Eyes Were Watching God.*

77. Ibid.; Mary Helen Washington, *Invented Lives: Narratives of Black Women 1860–1960* (Garden City, N.Y.: Anchor Press, 1987), 237–54.

78. Hurston, *Their Eyes Were Watching God.*

79. C. Vann Woodward, *The Strange Career of Jim Crow,* 3d rev. ed. (New York: Oxford Univ. Press, 1974); Steven Hahn, *The Roots of Southern Populism: Yeomen Farmers and the Transformation of the Georgia Upcountry, 1850–1890* (New York: Oxford Univ. Press, 1983); Jack Kirby, *Darkness at the Dawning: Race and Reform in the Progressive South* (Philadelphia: Lippicott, 1972); Myrdal, *An American Dilemma,* I: 205–78.

80. Myrdal, *An American Dilemma,* I: 230–78.

81. Frances Fox Piven and Richard A. Cloward, *Regulating the Poor: The Functions of Public Welfare* (New York: Pantheon Books, 1971), 76–77, 129; FERA News, [n.d.], Records of the Federal Emergency Relief Administration (hereafter cited as FERA), RG 69, Old Subject File, box 74; Negro Project Workers, Jan. 1938, Records of the Works Projects Administration (hereafter cited as WPA), RG 69, NA, box 562.

82. Julia Kirk Blackwelder, "Women in the Work Force: Atlanta, New Orleans, and San Antonio, 1930–1940," *Journal of Urban History* 4 (May 1978): 331–58; "Reckin' I'll Be Washin' an' Ironin' til I Drop Daid," FWP, folder 169, SHC; "Bea, the Washerwoman," FWP, folder 145, SHC; "The Three Sisters," FWP, folder 145, SHC. Ruth Milkman, "Women's Work and the Economic Crisis: Some Lessons from the Great Depression," in Nancy F. Cott and Elizabeth H. Pleck, eds., *A Heritage of Her Own: Toward a New Social History of American Women* (New York: Simon & Schuster, 1979), 507–41. Black women, thus, experienced less protection from unemployment than did white women, whose jobs in female-dominated categories were protected from male takeovers by the ideologies and imperatives of a labor market divided by gender.

83. Arlene Scadron, ed., *Widowhood and Aging in the American Southwest, 1847–1939* (Champaign-Urbana: Univ. of Illinois Press, 1987); Reiff, Dahlin, and Smith, "Rural Push and Urban Pull," 39–48; Shifflett, "Household Composition of Rural Black Families," 235–60. Thus, the conclusion of Pleck and others that the female-headed household was a creation of the city ignores the central role of migration in removing such households from an unsupportive rural setting. Pleck's analysis of the ways that cities exacerbated marital instability, however, remains persuasive. Pleck, *Black Migration and Poverty,* 162–96.

84. Johnson, *Shadow of the Plantation,* 114.

85. Joint Committee to Study the Employment of Colored Women in New York City and Brooklyn, *A New Day for the Colored Woman Worker* (New York: Young, 1919), 11, 13; Myrdal, *An American Dilemma,* I: 182–201.

86. Consumers' League of Eastern Pennsylvania, Colored Women as Industrial Workers in Philadelphia, 1919–20.

87. [George Arthur?] to F. W. Persons, [Oct. 1935?], Records of the Bureau of Employment Security (hereafter cited as BES), RG 183, NA, box 1386.

88. U.S., Bureau of the Census, 16th Census of the United States: 1940, Popula-

tion, vol. II, pt. 1, pp. 25, 50; Carl Degler, *At Odds: Women and the Family in American from the Revolution to the Present* (New York: Oxford Univ. Press, 1980), 391.

89. Katherine Bethea to Franklin D. Roosevelt, May 8, 1934, FERA, RG 69, Old Subject File, NA, box 19; Cerena Harris to Mrs. Roosevelt, April 23, 1938, BES, RG 183, NA, box 1388; Lillie Mae Nixon to First Lady and President, May 11, 1934, FERA, RG 69, Old Subject File, NA, box 19.

90. Harvard Sitkoff, *A New Deal for Blacks: The Emergence of Civil Rights as a National Issue,* vol. I: *The Depression Decade* (New York: Oxford Univ. Press, 1978).

91. Walter White to Eleanor Roosevelt, Nov. 13, 1934, FERA, RG 69, NA, box 19; Nancy E. Rose, "Gender, Race, and the Welfare State: Government Work Programs from the 1930s to the Present," *Feminist Studies* 19 (Summer 1993): 319–42.

92. Many Colored Women Employed on WPA Projects, July 16, 1937, WPA, RG 69, box 562; Summary of Women's and Professional Projects—Alabama, 1936, WPA, RG 69, box 556; A Report on the Availability of the Services of the Cleveland Office of the Ohio State Employment Service to Negro Applicants, Aug. 15, 1936, BES, RG 183, box 1388; A Report on the Availability of the Services of the National Reemployment Service, Affiliated with the U.S. Employment Service, to Negro Applicants, Particularly Birmingham, Dec. 16, 1936, BES, RG 183, box 1385; A Report on the Availability of the Services to Negro Applicants of the Arkansas State Employment Service Office, Dec. 16, 1936, BES, RG 183, box 1385; Cerena Harris to Mrs. Roosevelt, April 23, 1938, BES, RG 183, box 1388.

93. "The Story of a Washwoman," FWP, folder 243, SHC.

94. Myrdal, *An American Dilemma,* I: 353–58.

95. Study of Tobacco Workers Families, Series 286, Records of the National Recovery Administration, RG 9, NA.

96. Rose, "Gender, Race, and the Welfare State," 319–42.

97. Robert J. Myres, Estimates of Persons with 1937 Wage Credits Who Attain Age 65 in Specified Years, HEW, RG 47, box 31, NA.

98. Sitkoff, *A New Deal for Blacks,* 326–35; David R. Goldfield, *Black, White, and Southern: Race Relations and Southern Culture 1940 to the Present* (Baton Rouge: Louisiana State Univ. Press, 1990), 27–29.

99. St. Clair Drake and Horace R. Cayton, *Black Metropolis: A Study of Negro Life in a Northern City,* Vol. II (New York: Harper & Row, 1962), 381–83, 576–81; Abraham Epstein, *The Negro Migrant in Pittsburgh* (1918; rpt., New York: Arno Press and the New York Times, 1969), 8–21; Jones, *Labor of Love, Labor of Sorrow,* 181–95.

100. Epstein, *Negro Migrant,* 8–16.

101. Ibid., 50; Jones, *Labor of Love, Labor of Sorrow,* 181–95.

102. Hortense Powdermaker, *After Freedom,* 232, 236, 254, 272–73; Janiewski, *Sisterhood Denied,* 139–40; Linda Dahl, *Stormy Weather: The Music and Lives of a Century of Jazzwomen* (New York: Pantheon Books, 1984), 103.

103. Evelyn Brooks Higginbotham, *Righteous Discontent: The Women's Movement in the Black Baptist Church, 1880–1920* (Cambridge: Harvard Univ. Press, 1993), 97.

104. Ibid., 171–229, quote on 202. The efforts of Baptist women to change black culture frequently encountered resistance from black women and men.

105. Ibid., 199; Drake and Cayton, *Black Metropolis,* II: 568; Dahl, *Stormy Weather,* 15.

106. Pleck, *Black Migration and Poverty,* 161–96; Kiser, *Sea Island to City,* 201–15; Jones, *Labor of Love, Labor of Sorrow,* 185, 191–92.

107. Drake and Cayton, *Black Metropolis,* II: 581–88; Jones, *Labor of Love, Labor of Sorrow,* 186, 198, 225; Daphne Duval Harrison, "Black Women in the Blues Tradition," in Sharon Harley and Rosalyn Terborg-Penn, eds., *The Afro-American Woman: Struggles and Images* (Port Washington, N.Y.: Kennikat Press, 1978), 61. Elizabeth Pleck has concluded that disease, sterility, urbanization, and poverty caused the black pattern of marital instability and female-headed households in cities. Pleck, *Black Migration and Poverty,* 161–96.

108. Dahl, *Stormy Weather,* 103–20; Harrison, "Black Women in the Blues Tradition," 58–73; Hazel V. Carby, "'It Jus Be's Dat Way Sometime': The Sexual Politics of Women's Blues," in Dubois and Ruiz, eds., *Unequal Sisters,* 238–49.

109. Dahl, *Stormy Weather,* 103–20; Harrison, "Black Women in the Blues Tradition," 58–73; Carby, "'It Jus Be's Dat Way Sometime,'" 238–49.

110. Ida B. Wells-Barnett, *On Lynchings: Southern Horrors, a Red Record, Mob Rule in New Orleans* (New York: Arno Press, and the New York Times, 1969); Hazel V. Carby, *Reconstructing Womanhood: The Emergence of the Afro-American Woman Novelist* (New York: Oxford Univ. Press, 1987), 108–16; Gerda Lerner, *The Majority Finds Its Past: Placing Women in History* (Oxford: Oxford Univ. Press, 1981), 83–93; Hall, "'The Mind That Burns in Each Body,'" 328–49; Giddings, "The Last Taboo," in Morrison, ed., *Race-ing Justice, En-gendering Power,* 441–465.

111. Wells-Barnett, *On Lynching;* Carby, *Reconstructing Womanhood,* 97–116.

112. Carroll Smith-Rosenberg, *Disorderly Conduct: Visions of Gender in Victorian America* (New York: Oxford Univ. Press, 1985); Ellen Carol Dubois and Linda Gordon, "Seeking Ecstasy on the Battlefield: Danger and Pleasure in Nineteenth-Century Feminist Sexual Thought," in Vance, ed., *Pleasure and Danger,* 31–49. Middle-class white women had selectively deployed assumptions regarding women's asexuality and spiritual superiority to men in order to claim a right to control of marital sexuality and reproduction, to establish a women's domain in the public sphere through clubs and other associations, and to legitimize a claim to moral authority in private and public life.

113. Nancy F. Cott, "Feminist Theory and Feminist Movements: The Past Before Us," in Juliet Mitchell and Ann Oakley, eds., *What Is Feminism: A Re-examination* (New York: Pantheon Books, 1986), 49–62; Rosalyn M. Terborg-Penn, "Afro-Americans in the Struggle for Woman Suffrage" (Ph.D. diss., Howard University, 1977); Rosalyn M. Terborg-Penn, "Discontented Black Feminists: Prelude and Postscript to the Passage of the Nineteenth Amendment," in Lois Scharf and Joan Jensen, eds., *Decades of Discontent: The Women's Movement, 1920–1940* (Westport, Conn.: Greenwood Press, 1983), 261–78.

114. Powdermaker, *After Freedom,* 165, 169–74. The experiences of black women in this period confirm Rodman's conclusions that women's marital power

is enlarged when men do not have a substantial material advantage over them and when gender ideologies validate women's claims to power. Rodman, "Marital Power and the Theory of Resources in Cultural Context," 50–69.

Chapter 8. Progress and Protest

1. Jay R. Mandle, *The Roots of Black Poverty: The Southern Plantation Economy After the Civil War* (Durham, N.C.: Duke Univ. Press, 1978), 98–104, 117–22.

2. Jacqueline Dowd Hall, *Revolt Against Chivalry: Jessie Daniel Ames and the Women's Campaign Against Lynching* (New York, 1979), 169.

3. Jill Quadagno, *The Transformation of Old Age Security: Class and Politics in the American Welfare State* (Chicago: Univ. of Chicago Press, 1988), 142–51.

4. Paul Burstein, *Race, Jobs, and Politics: The Struggle for Equal Employment Opportunity in the United States Since the New Deal* (Chicago: Univ. of Chicago Press, 1985), 125–54.

5. Mandle, *Roots of Black Poverty*, 84–104.

6. Ibid., 98–104, 117–22; Ruth Sidel, *Women and Children Last: The Plight of Poor Women in Affluent America* (New York, 1986), 9.

7. Winifred Bell, *Aid to Dependent Children* (New York: Columbia Univ. Press, 1965), 4–13; Bettina Aptheker, *Woman's Legacy: Essays on Race, Sex, and Class in American History* (Amherst: Univ. of Massachusetts Press, 1982), 129–51.

8. William Julius Wilson, *The Truly Disadvantaged: The Inner City, the Underclass, and Public Policy* (Chicago: Univ. of Chicago Press, 1987), 20–62; Ann Petry, *The Street* (Boston: Beacon Press, 1985); Lee Rainwater, *Behind Ghetto Walls: Black Families in a Federal Slum* (Chicago: Aldine Publishing, 1970); Robert Staples, ed., *The Black Family: Essays and Studies* (Belmont, Calif.: Wadsworth Publishing, 1971), 3; Jacqueline Jones, *The Dispossessed: American's Underclasses from the Civil War to the Present* (New York: Basic Books, 1992), 269–84.

9. Robert Staples, "The Dyad," in Staples, ed., *Black Family*, 74–83; Rainwater, *Behind Ghetto Walls*; Carol B. Stack, *All Our Kin: Strategies for Survival in a Black Community* (New York: Harper & Row, 1974), 109–13. Staples has concluded that conflict and hostility are so endemic that "it makes little sense to create a myth about the happiness or stability of Black marriages."

10. bell hooks, *Yearning: Race, Gender, and Cultural Politics* (Boston: South End Press, 1990), 63; Jones, *Dispossessed*, 273–84; William Oliver, *The Violent Social World of Black Men* (New York: Lexington Books, 1994). Philip Corrigan has concluded that masculinity, like femininity, is dichotomized. Success as a monogamous, respectable, responsible "family man" conflicts with "the free-ranging, moving, shifting and the singular concentration upon doing well within the male gaze." The latter occupies the world of the street gang or that of the harassing, womanizing men (and their voyeuristic enablers) from all social classes. Philip Corrigan, "Masculinity as Right: Some Thoughts on the Genealogy of 'Rational Violence,'" in Philip Corrigan, ed., *Social Forms/Human Capacities: Essay in Authority and Difference* (London: Routledge, 1990), 281–83.

11. U.S. Department of Justice, "Race of Prisoners Admitted to State and Federal Institutions, 1926–1986," 1991.

12. Wilson, *Truly Disadvantaged,* 77–92; Andrew J. Cherlin, *Marriage, Divorce, Remarriage* (Cambridge: Harvard Univ. Press, 1981), 93–112.

13. Ruth Milkman, *Gender at Work* (Urbana: Univ. of Illinois Press, 1987); Susan Hartmann, *The Home Front and Beyond: American Women in the 1940s* (Boston: Twayne Publishers, 1982), 78–88; Karen Anderson, *Wartime Women: Sex Roles, Family Relations, and the Status of Women During World War II* (Westport, Conn.: Greenwood Press, 1981); Karen Tucker Anderson, "Last Hired, First Fired: Black Women Workers During World War II," *Journal of American History* 69 (June 1982): 82–97.

14. Mandle, *Roots of Black Poverty,* 84–104, 117–22.

15. Harvard Sitkoff, *A New Deal for Blacks: The Emergence of Civil Rights as a National Issue,* vol. I: *The Depression Decade* (New York: Oxford Univ. Press, 1978), 298–325.

16. Anderson, "Last Hired, First Fired," 82–97; Robert C. Weaver, *Negro Labor: A National Problem* (New York: Harcourt, Brace, 1946), 27; Herbert Hill, *Black Labor and the American Legal System: Race, Work, and the Law,* vol. 1 (Washington: Bureau of National Affairs, 1977), 173–84.

17. Anderson, *Wartime Women,* 36–42; Anderson, "Last Hired, First Fired," 82–97; General Comments of Workers, Baltimore, Md., Records of the Women's Bureau (hereafter cited as WB), RG 86, box 1541, NA.

18. Maya Angelou, *I Know Why the Caged Bird Sings* (New York: Bantam Books, 1969), 225–29.

19. Anderson, *Wartime Women,* 40–41; Anderson, "Last Hired, First Fired," 82–97; Josephine A. Blackwell to G. James Fleming, Feb. 14, 1943, Records of the President's Committee on Fair Employment Practice (hereafter cited as FEPC), RG 228, box 658, NA; Paula Giddings, *When and Where I Enter: The Impact of Black Women on Race and Sex in America* (New York: Morrow, 1984), 235–38. According to Giddings, one-fourth of the complaints to FEPC were lodged by black women.

20. "Trends in Employment of Negroes," *Monthly Labor Review* (Jan. 1945): 3; Employment of Minority Workers During Current Period of Intensive War Production, 1945, FEPC, Box 378, NA; Anderson, "Last Hired, First Fired," 82–97; U.S., Bureau of the Census, *Characteristics of the Detroit-Willow Run Congested Production Area* (Washington, D.C.: GPO, 1944), 16.

21. Sherna Berger Gluck, *Rosie the Riveter Revisited: Women, the War, and Social Change* (Boston: Twayne Publishers, 1987), 39.

22. Alonzo Nelson Smith, "Black Employment in the Los Angeles Area, 1938–1948" (Ph.D. diss., UCLA, 1978), 53, 188.

23. Minutes, Federal Coordinating Committee for Michigan, Oct. 14, 1943, Records of the Office of Community War Services (hereafter cited as OCWS), RG 215, War Area Reports and Correspondence, box 10, NA; Charlotte Moton to Frank Crutsinger, Feb. 25, 1944, OCWS, RG 215, General Classified Files, box 227, NA.

24. General Comments of Workers, Baltimore, Md., WB, RG 86, box 1541, NA.

25. Ibid.

26. Anderson, "Last Hired, First Fired," 82–97; U.S., Department of Labor of

Labor, Women's Bureau, "Women Workers in Ten War Production Areas and Their Postwar Employment Plans," 1946, p. 47; Margaret Holmes Turner Oral History, June 2, 1979, Southern Oral History Project (hereafter cited as SOHP), Record Group 4007, Southern Historical Collection (hereafter cited as SHC), University of North Carolina (hereafter cited as UNC).

27. Anderson, "Last Hired, First Fired," 82–97; U.S., Bureau of the Census, U.S. Summary, Industry, p. 189; U.S. Bureau of the Census, U.S. Census of Population: 1950, Occupational Characteristics, Special Report P-E, No. 1B, vol. 4, Pt. 1, p. 33.

28. Daniel O. Price, *Changing Characteristics of the Negro Population* (Washington: GPO, 1969), 6–11, 28, 72, 117; Gordon F. Bloom, F. Marion Fletcher, and Charles R. Perry, *Negro Employment in Retail Trade* (Philadelphia: Univ. of Pennsylvania Press, 1972), 39.

29. U.S., Department of Labor, Bulletin No. 1119, *Negroes in the United States: Their Employment and Economic Status* (Washington: GPO, 1952), 24.

30. U.S., Bureau of the Census, Census of Population, 1960, p. 1–543; Phyllis A. Wallace, *Black Women in the Labor Force* (Cambridge: MIT Press, 1980), 23–37.

31. John Langston Gwaltney, *Drylongso: A Self-Portrait of Black America* (New York: 1980), 7.

32. Judith Rollins, *Between Women: Domestics and Their Employers* (Philadelphia: Temple Univ. Press, 1985); Gwaltney, *Drylongso*, 68.

33. Anne Moody, *Coming of Age in Mississippi* (New York: Dell Publishing, 1968), 80–81.

34. Molly Crocker Dougherty, *Becoming a Woman in Rural Black Culture* (New York: Holt, Rinehart and Winston, 1978), 21–27; Hylan Lewis, *Blackways of Kent* (Chapel Hill: Univ. of North Carolina Press, 1955), 122.

35. Anderson, "Last Hired, First Fired," 82–97.

36. Burstein, *Discrimination, Jobs, and Politics,* 137; Duran Bell, "Occupational Discrimination as a Source of Income Differences: Lessons of the 1960's," *American Economic Review* 62 (May 1972): 363–72; Richard B. Freeman, "Alternative Theories of Labor-Market Discrimination: Individual and Collective Behavior," in George M. von Furstenberg, Ann R. Horowitz, and Bennett Harrison, eds., *Patterns of Racial Discrimination,* vol. II, *Employment and Income* (Lexington, Mass.: D. C. Heath, Company, 1974), 33–49; Wallace, *Black Women in the Labor Force,* 58–76.

37. Joan Gustafson Haworth, James Gwartney, and Charles Haworth, "Earnings, Productivity, and Changes in Employment Discrimination During the 1960's," *American Economic Review* 65 (March 1975): 158–68; Wallace, *Black Women in the Labor Force,* 50.

38. Phyllis A. Wallace and Maria P. Beckles, "1966 Employment Survey in the Textile Industry of the Carolinas," EEOC, Office of Research and Reports, RR 1966-11, Records of the Equal Employment Opportunity Commission, RG 403, NA (hereafter cited as EEOC); "Negro Employment in the Textile Industries of North and South Carolina," Nov. 21, 1966, EEOC, Office of Research and Reports, RR 1966-10; Exhibit 2-Findings of Facts, Docket No. 19143, EEOC, box 2; Wallace, *Black Women in the Labor Force,* 48–53.

39. Wallace, *Black Women in the Labor Force*, 23–37.

40. Joan Smith, "The Paradox of Women's Poverty: Wage-Earning Women and Economic Transformation," *Signs* 10 (Winter 1984): 291–310.

41. Gerda Lerner, *The Majority Finds Its Past: Placing Women in History* (New York: Oxford Univ. Press, 1979), 75–80; Daniel O. Price, *Changing Characteristics of the Negro Population* (Washington: GPO, 1969), 8; [Daniel P. Moynihan], U.S., Department of Labor, *The Negro Family: The Case for National Action* (Washington, D.C.: GPO, 1965).

42. Lerner, *Majority Finds Its Past*, 75–80; Lewis, *Blackways of Kent*, 122; Charmeynne D. Nelson, "Myths About Black Women Workers in Modern America," *Black Scholar* 6 (March 1975): 11–15; Elizabeth McTaggart Almquist, *Minorities, Gender, and Work* (Lexington, Mass.: Lexington Books, 1979), 59.

43. Stack, *All Our Kin*, 113–15; Hyman Rodman, "The Lower-Class Value Stretch," *Social Forces* 42 (Dec. 1963): 205–15.

44. Stack, *All Our Kin*, 45–49; Patricia Hill Collins, "The Meaning of Motherhood in Black Culture and Black Mother/Daughter Relationships," *Sage* 4 (Fall 1987): 3–10.

45. Rainwater, *Behind Ghetto Walls*, 99.

46. Piven and Cloward, *Regulating the Poor*, 131–37; Solinger, *Wake Up Little Susie: Single Pregnancy and Race Before Roe v. Wade* (New York: Routledge, 1992), 42.

47. Saul Kaplan, "Support from Absent Fathers of Children Receiving ADC," U.S., Department of Health, Education, and Welfare, Public Assistance Report No. 41, 1955, pp. xi, 7, 27, 28; Maurine McKeany, *The Absent Father and Public Policy in the Program of Aid to Dependent Children* (Berkeley: Univ. of California Press, 1960), 1–3; Robert H. Muggs, "Aid to Families with Dependent Children: Initial Findings of the 1961 Report on Characteristics of Recipients," *Social Security Bulletin* 26 (March 1963): 4, 8; Grace M. Marcus, "Reappraising Aid to Dependent Children as a Category," *Social Security Bulletin* 8 (Feb. 1945): 3–5.

48. Winifred Bell, *Aid to Dependent Children* (New York: Columbia Univ. Press, 1965), 57–151; Solinger, *Wake Up Little Susie*, 1–85.

49. Virginia Franks, "Shall We Sneak Up on Our Clients?," *Public Welfare* 9 (May 1951): 106–9, 123; Bell, *Aid to Dependent Children*, 57–151.

50. Bell, *Aid to Dependent Children*, 70, 93–110; Solinger, *Wake Up Little Susie*, 31.

51. [Moynihan], *Negro Family*.

52. Ibid.

53. Ibid.; Daniel P. Moynihan, *Family and Nation* (San Diego: 1986), 38, 168–71.

54. Linda Gordon, "What Does Welfare Regulate?," *Social Research* 55 (Winter 1988): 609–30.

55. Wahneema Lubiano, "Black Ladies, Welfare Queens, and State Minstrels: Ideological War by Narrative Means," in Toni Morrison, ed., *Race-ing Justice, Engendering Power* (New York: Pantheon Books, 1992), 323–63.

56. [Moynihan], *Negro Family*; Wilson, *Truly Disadvantaged*, 82–92; Patricia Hill Collins, "A Comparison of Two Works on Black Family Life," *Signs* 14 (Summer 1989): 875–84; Maxine Baca Zinn, "Family, Race, and Poverty in the Eight-

ies," *Signs* 14 (Summer 1989): 856–74. Liberal willingness to predicate black advance on male-dominated families not only indicates the limits of their liberalism, but also ignores the possibility that their gender politics may preclude a real solution to black poverty.

57. Lewis, *Blackways of Kent*, 30–39; Clark, *Dark Ghetto*, 12; Giddings, *When and Where I Enter*, 256.

58. Lee Rainwater, *Behind Ghetto Walls: Black Families in a Federal Slum* (Chicago: 1970), 150–63, 170–75; Gail A. Stokes, "Black Woman to Black Man," in Staples, ed., *Black Family*, 159–61; Elliott Liebow, *Tally's Corner: A Study of Negro Streetcorner Men* (Boston: 1966), 70–78, 95, 115; Joyce Ladner, *Tomorrow's Tomorrow: The Black Woman* (Garden City, N.Y.: Anchor Books, 1971), 66, 188; Stack, *All Our Kin*, 108–20; Lee Rainwater, "Husband-Wife Relations," in Staples, ed., *Black Family*, 163–66; Sarah Webster Fabio, "Blowing the Whistle on Some Jive," *Black Scholar* 10 (May–June 1979): 57; Kenneth B. Clark, *Dark Ghetto: Dilemmas of Social Power* (New York: Harper Torchbooks, 1965), 70–74; Jean Carey Bond and Pat Peery, "Has the Black Man Been Castrated?," in Staples, ed., *Black Family*, 140–44.

59. Gloria I. Joseph and Jill Lewis, *Common Differences: Conflicts in Black and White Feminist Perspectives* (Boston: South End Press, 1981), 127–48, 178–230; Collins, "The Meaning of Motherhood in Black Culture," 3–10.

60. Ladner, *Tomorrow's Tomorrow*, 201–12, 231; Liebow, *Tally's Corner*, 70, 76–78, 115; Clark, *Dark Ghetto*, 70–74.

61. Liebow, *Tally's Corner*, 60–63, 206–7, 213; Lillian Rubin, *Intimate Strangers: Men and Women Together* (New York: Harper & Row, 1983), 137–40.

62. Lee Rainwater, "Husband-Wife Relations," in Staples, ed., *Black Family*, 163–66; Ladner, *Tomorrow's Tomorrow*, 66, 188; Liebow, *Tally's Corner*, 95; Stokes, "Black Woman to Black Man," 159–61; Dougherty, *Becoming a Woman in Rural Black Culture*, 24.

63. Fabio, "Blowing the Whistle on Some Jive," 57. Similarly, white men's reluctance to support their children after a divorce raises serious questions about policies that assume a "trickle down" pattern from men to women and children. Terry Arendell, *Mothers and Divorce: Legal, Economic, and Social Dilemmas* (Berkeley: Univ. of California Press, 1986).

64. Nancy Seifer, ed., *"Nobody Speaks for Me": Self-Portraits of American Working Class Women* (New York: Simon and Schuster, 1976), 149; Jerry M. Lewis and John G. Looney, *The Long Struggle: Well-Functioning Working-Class Black Families* (New York: Brunner/Mazel, 1983).

65. Jessie Bernard, "Marital Stability and Patterns of Status Variables," *Journal of Marriage and Family* 28 (Nov. 1966): 421–39; J. Richard Udry, "Marital Instability by Race, Sex, Education, and Occupation Using 1960 Census Data," *American Journal of Sociology* 72 (Sept. 1966): 203–9; John H. Scanzoni, *The Black Family in Modern Society* (Boston: Allyn and Bacon, 1971).

66. Lewis and Looney, *Long Struggle*, 2.

67. Harriette Pipes McAdoo, "Factors Related to Stability in Upwardly Mobile Black Families," *Journal of Marriage and the Family* 40 (Nov. 1978): 761–76; Giddings, *When and Where I Enter*, 247–48; Lewis and Looney, *Long Struggle*, 94–95.

68. Bernard, "Marital Stability," 421–39; Udry, "Marital Instability," 203–9; Scanzoni, *Black Family*.

69. Marietta Morrissey, "Female-Headed Families: Poor Women and Choice," in Naomi Gerstel and Harriet Engel Gross, eds., *Families and Work* (Philadelphia: 1987), 302–14. Mexican-American families, by contrast, have relatively low proportions of female-headed families despite high poverty rates.

70. Robert O. Blood, Jr. and Donald M. Wolfe, *Husbands and Wives: The Dynamics of Married Living* (New York: 1960), 108–9, 171, 182, 195, 197, 214–15, 223–24; Scanzoni, *Black Family*, 201–3; Gwendolyn Brooks, "Why Negro Women Leave Home," *Negro Digest* 9 (March 1951): 26–28; Robert Staples; "The Myth of the Black Matriarchy," in Staples, ed., *Black Family*, 157; Audre Lorde, *Sister/Outsider: Essays and Speeches* (Trumansburg, N.Y.: Crossing Press, 1984), 51.

71. Blanche Scott Oral History, July 11, 1979, SOHP, UNC, SHC, RG 4007, H-229; Maya Angelou, *Singin' and Swingin' and Gettin' Merry like Christmas* (Toronto: Bantam Books, 1977), 39; Gwaltney, *Drylongso*, 171.

72. Janie Cameron Riley and Lottie Phillips Oral History, June 6, 1975, B-64, SOHP, UNC, SHC; Gwaltney, *Drylongso*, 147; Rollins, *Between Women*, 175.

73. Bart Landry and Margaret Platt Jendrek, "The Employment of Wives in Middle-Class Black Families," *Journal of Marriage and the Family* 40 (Nov. 1978): 787–97; Ladner, *Tomorrow's Tomorrow*, 44–46, 184–88.

74. Liebow, *Tally's Corner*, 137–60; Audrey B. Chapman, "Male-Female Relations: How the Past Affects the Present," in Harriette Pipes McAdoo, ed., *Black Families*, 2d ed. (Newbury Park, Calif.: Sage Publications, 1988), 195–96; Lewis and Looney, *Long Struggle*, 111.

75. Liebow, *Tally's Corner*, 83–91; Lee Rainwater, "Husband-Wife Relations," in Staples, ed., *Black Family*, 163–66.

76. Given other changes in the patterns of black response to census takers in this period, it is possible that these statistics overstate the change. It is not clear whether black women report their common-law relationships as marriages as readily as they did in the past. Andrew J. Cherlin, *Marriage, Divorce, Remarriage* (Cambridge, Mass.: Harvard Univ. Press, 1981), 93–112; Wilson, *Truly Disadvantaged*, 66–71; Arthur J. Norton and Jeanne E. Moorman, "Current Trends in Marriage and Divorce," *Journal of Marriage and the Family* 49 (Feb. 1987): 3–14. Although female-headed families have also increased among whites, the proportion of black families with children that were headed by women was more than three times the rate for white families in 1983. Ruth Sidel, *Women and Children Last: The Plight of Poor Women in Affluent America* (New York: 1986), 18.

77. U.S., Bureau of the Census, Current Population Reports, Special Studies, "Child Support and Alimony: 1978," Series P-23, no. 106, p. 3.

78. Liebow, *Tally's Corner*, 76; Stack, *All Our Kin*, 71.

79. Fran Leeper Buss, ed., *Dignity: Lower Income Women Tell of Their Lives and Struggles* (Ann Arbor: Univ. of Michigan Press, 1985), 19–51; Gwaltney, *Drylongso*, 181.

80. Giddings, *When and Where I Enter*, 319–20.

81. Ibid., 320; Lorde, *Sister/Outsider*, 60–65.

82. Gwaltney, *Drylongso*, 123; Jones, *Dispossessed*, 273–84. As Jones notes,

gang cultures are found in all racial ethnic groups (including whites) in poor neighborhoods.

83. Rainwater, *Behind Ghetto Walls*, 103, 108–10.

84. Gwaltney, *Drylongso*, 8–9.

85. Jacqueline Jones, *Labor of Love, Labor of Sorrow: Black Women, Work, and the Family from Slavery to the Present* (New York: Basic Books, 1985), 275–321; Giddings, *When and Where I Enter*, 261–324; Karen Brodkin Sacks, "Computers, Ward Secretaries, and a Walkout in a Southern Hospital," in Karen Brodkin Sacks and Dorothy Remy, eds., *My Troubles Are Going to Have Trouble with Me: Everyday Trials and Triumphs of Women Workers* (New Brunswick, N.J.: Rutgers Univ. Press, 1984), 173–90.

86. Beverly Guy-Sheftall, "Feminism and the Writings of Nineteenth Century Black Women," University of Arizona, March 31, 1989; Rosalind Terborg-Penn, "Black Male Perspectives on the Nineteenth-Century Woman," in Sharon Harley and Rosalind Terborg-Penn, eds., *The Afro-American Woman: Struggles and Images* (Port Washington, N.Y.: Kennikat Press, 1978), 28–42. This does not mean that the black community was egalitarian. Since emancipation, black feminists have faced the conundrum of racism and sexism.

87. Sara Evans, *Personal Politics: The Roots of Women's Liberation in the Civil Rights Movement and the New Left* (New York: Vintage Books, 1979), 3–101.

88. Evans, *Personal Politics*, 69, 78–82, 88, 89; Mary Aickin Rothschild, "White Women Volunteers in the Freedom Summers: Their Life and Work in a Movement for Social Change," *Feminist Studies* 5 (Fall 1979): 466–94.

89. Rothschild, "White Women Volunteers," 466–94, quote on 482.

90. Ibid., 466–94.

91. Ibid., 486.

92. Ibid., 466–94; Evans, *Personal Politics*, 88–89.

93. Sara Evans, "Tomorrow's Yesterday: Feminist Consciousness and the Future of Women," in Carol Ruth Berkin and Mary Beth Norton, eds., *Women of America: A History* (Boston: Houghton Mifflin, 1979), 389–417.

94. Evans, "Tomorrow's Yesterday," 398.

95. Giddings, *When and Where I Enter*, 284.

96. Ibid., 277–97; Bernice Johnson Reagon, "African-American Women: A Continuing Tradition in American Radicalism," paper presented at the Berkshire Conference on the History of Women, Douglass College, June 8, 1990.

97. Ida Susser, "Political Activity Among Working-Class Women in a U.S. City," *American Ethnologist* 13 (Feb. 1986): 108–17; Guida West, *The National Welfare Rights Movement: The Social Protest of Poor Women* (New York: Praeger, 1981). It is interesting that welfare politics can be marginalized in scholarship on modern politics when welfare is so ideologically central to modern political discourse.

98. Cheryl Townsend Gilkes, "'Holding Back the Ocean with a Broom': Black Women and Community Work," in La Frances Rodgers-Rose, ed., *The Black Woman* (Beverly Hills, Calif.: Sage Publications, 1980), 217–31.

99. West, *The National Welfare Rights Movement*.

100. Ibid., 233–34.

101. Ibid., 235.

102. Elaine Brown, *A Taste of Power: A Black Woman's Story* (New York: Pantheon Books, 1992).

103. Giddings, *When and Where I Enter*, 317. As Elaine Brown notes, the Black Panther party was not ideologically nationalist, but advocated a campaign against race and class oppression. In practice, however, it represented the fullest expression of the black power movement in militant confrontation with the white power structure. Brown, *A Taste of Power.* Black Muslims also espoused these views. C. Eric Lincoln, *The Black Muslims in America* (Boston: Beacon Press, 1961), 31, 32, 55, 83. Giddings, *When and Where I Enter*, 317–18.

104. Giddings, *When and Where I Enter*, 314–24; Brown, *A Taste of Power.*

105. Dara Abubakari, "The Only thing You Can Aspire to Is Nationhood," in Gerder Lerner, ed., *Black Women in White America: A Documentary History* (New York: Vintage Books, 1972), 553.

106. Joseph and Lewis, *Common Differences*, 19–42.

107. Septima Poinsette Clark Oral History, July 25, 1976, SOHP, RG 4007, SHC, UNC.

108. Fannie Lou Hamer, "It's In Your Hands," in Gerda Lerner, ed., *Black Women in White America*, 612.

109. Gwaltney, *Drylongso*, 171.

110. Pauli Murray Oral History, Feb. 13, 1976, SOHP, SHC, UNC.

111. Patricia Hill Collins, *Black Feminist Thought: Knowledge, Consciousness, and the Politics of Empowerment* (New York: Routledge, 1990), 9.

112. Morrison, ed., *Race-ing Justice, En-gendering Power.*

113. Christine Stansell, "White Feminists and Black Realities: The Politics of Authenticity," in ibid., 264; Nell Irvin Painter, "Hill Thomas, and the Use of Racial Stereotype," in ibid., 204; Homi K. Bhabha, "A Good Judge of Character: Men, Metaphors, and the Common Culture," in ibid., 232–50.

114. As Michael Thelwell notes, the consensus regarding those meanings for African Americans is "dearly bought, compelled by the incontrovertible logic of America's racial history and the bitter evidence of our daily experience. It is not, as [conservatives] would glibly have it, the consequence of knee-jerk liberalism or our genetic predisposition to the herd mentality." Michael Thelwell, "False, Fleeting, Perjured Clarence: Yale's Brightest and Blackest Go to Washington," in Morrison, ed., *Race-ing Justice, En-gendering Power*, 95.

115. Lubiano, "Black Ladies, Welfare Queens, and State Minstrels," 334; Gayle Pemberton, "A Sentimental Journey: James Baldwin and the Thomas-Hill Hearings," in Morrison, ed., *Race-ing Justice, En-gendering Power*, 193; Kimberle Crenshaw, "Whose Story Is It Anyway? Feminist and Antiracist Appropriations of Anita Hill," in Morrison, ed., *Race-ing Justice, En-gendering Power*, 402–40.

116. Thelwell, "False, Fleeting, Perjured Clarence," 115.

117. Crenshaw, "Whose Story Is It Anyway?," 417.

118. Lubiano, "Black Ladies, Welfare Queens, and State Minstrels," 323–63; Bhabha, "A Good Judge of Character," 232–50. This does not deny the fact that many of Thomas's supporters exhibited a prurient (and racist) interest in the sexual charges leveled against him.

119. Pemberton, "A Sentimental Journey," 184.

120. Crenshaw, "Whose Story Is It Anyway?," 402–40.

121. Bhabha, "A Good Judge of Character," 232–50.

122. But see Giddings, *When and Where I Enter,* 252–53, 256; Roi Ottley, "What's Wrong with Negro Women?," *Negro Digest* 9 (Dec. 1950): 71–75; St. Clair Drake, "Why Men Leave Home," *Negro Digest* 8 (April 1950): 25–27; Gwendolyn Brooks, "Why Negro Women Leave Home," *Negro Digest* 9 (March 1951): 26–28.

123. Joseph and Lewis, *Common Differences,* 178–230, quote on 227; Lorde, *Sister/Outsider,* 60–65.

Index

AIM. *See* American Indian Movement
Alarcon, Norma, 140
Alarid, Kathy, 146
Albers, Patricia, 28, 57, 64
Alexian Brothers Order, 81–82
Allen, Paula Gunn, 9, 11, 19, 89–90
Allen, Ruth, 104, 111
All-Pueblo Council, 70, 84
American Indian Movement, 80, 82, 86
American Indian women, 3, 16, 17–91;
    and Aid to Families with Dependent
    Children, 74, 77–78; and allotment
    policies, 28, 42–43, 57; and arranged
    marriages, 22–23, 52–54; and arts
    and crafts production, 61–62, 71,
    73–74; and "conservatism," 38–39,
    51; and child custody, 86–87; and
    citizenship, 42–44; and cultural
    diversity, 17; and divorce, 22, 42–44,
    69, 74; and domestic labor, 39–40,
    58–65, 69, 72, 74, 82; and economic
    roles, 18–19, 21–26, 39–40, 50–51,
    56–65, 69, 71–80; and education,
    45–51, 72; and enforced
    acculturation, 37–51, 56–66; and
    families, 18, 22, 38, 42–65, 69,
    74–80, 83–88; and feminism, 89; and
    fetal alcohol syndrome, 87–88; and
    gender division of labor, 21–26, 28,
    39, 56–65, 71, 75–76, 90; and gender
    equality, 18–19; and Indian New
    Deal, 68–72; and involuntary
    sterilization, 85–86; and kinship, 18;
    and land, 18, 21, 43; and lesbianism,
    23; and male dominance, 19–20, 57,
    64–65, 67–70, 80–90; and marriage
    law, 44, 55–56; and maternal
    authority, 46–47, 50–51, 85–89; and
    meanings of sexual difference, 22; and
    political roles, 24, 68–72, 80–85; and
    poverty, 64, 69, 78, 80; and Public
    Law 280, 74, 77; and relocation
    policy, 74–77; and sexual harassment,
    48–49; and sexuality, 18, 23, 26, 38,
    45, 48–50, 52–56, 78; and
    termination policy, 74, 81–82; and
    violence, 23, 88; and World War II,
    73–74
American Indians, 4, 24–36, 85; and
    allotment policies, 28–30; and
    communalism, 41; and dispossession
    from lands, 20, 26–29, 56; and
    education by whites, 27, 29, 38,
    45–51, 75; and enforced
    acculturation, 24–33, 37–57; and
    New Deal, 32–33, 68–72; and
    poverty, 29–30, 34–35, 38, 56, 58,
    69, 75, 78; and relocation policy,
    34–35; and reservation system,
    26–27; and termination policy, 33–34,
    81–82; and Western medical practices,
    60; and World War II, 33
American Telephone and Telegraph, 194
Ames, Jessie Daniel, 185–86
Andelin, Helen, 90
Angelou, Maya, 189–90, 204
Anzaldua, Gloria, 15, 125, 145
Apaches, 23, 38, 45, 47; Jicarilla, 64
Aquash, Anna Mae, 82
Arrom, Silvia, 95, 98
As-ton-pia, 46–47
AT&T. *See* American Telephone and
    Telegraph
Aulette, Judy, 147

Baker, Ella, 211, 214
Balbo, Laura, 11, 14
Barrera, Mario, 113
Beloved Woman, 23
Bernard, Jesse, 204
Bernstein, Allison, 70
BIA. *See* Bureau of Indian Affairs
Biolsi, Thomas, 30
BIP. *See* Border Industrialization
    Program
Black Codes, 154
Black Power, 212–13
Blackfeet, 23, 55–56
Blackwelder, Julia Kirk, 107
Blackwell, Josephine, 190
Blevin, Audie, 126
Blood, Robert, 204
Board of Catholic Missions, 47
Board of Indian Commissioners, 38,
    53–54, 64
Bolden, Dorothy, 203
Bolt, Christine, 19
Bond, Jean Carey, 201
Border Industrialization Program, 128
Bozzoli, Belinda, 8
Bracero program, 112–13
Bronson, Ruth Muskrat, 70
Brophy, William, 33
Brown, Ebenezer, 157
Brown, Lizzie Fant, 156
Brown, Rina, 157–58

CPSIA information can be obtained at www.ICGtesting.com
Printed in the USA
BVOW02s0849221114

376305BV00002B/198/P